Character for Life

An American Heritage

Profiles of great men and women of Faith
who shaped Western civilization

DON HAWKINSON

Illustrated by Julie Bosacker

First printing: August 2005

ISBN: 0-89221-629-8
Library of Congress Control Number: 2005931544

Cover and interior design by Granite Design
Illustrations by Julie Bosacker
Edited by Frieda Nossaman

Printed in China

Please visit our website for other great titles:
www.newleafpress.net

For information regarding author interviews,
please contact the publicity department at (870) 438-5288.

New Leaf Press
A Division of New Leaf Publishing Group

Appreciation

Most of us have heroes whose character we admire. Often we don't have to look very far to find them. They may be our parents, grandparents, wives, sisters or brothers, cousins, aunts and uncles. They may be fellow travelers we meet on the road of life or even world leaders. We all need genuine examples or models of character. Allow me to introduce you to people whose lives incarnated the virtues presented in this book. I think you will discover that when people are abandoned to Jesus Christ, our Lord may express His character traits (virtues) in many ways in the lives of His followers. So, in reality, all the virtues could potentially be seen in the life of a Christian. Interestingly, some stand out more than others. For example, the virtue of integrity and George Washington seems to stand out. Another example would be Abraham Lincoln's example of suffering for righteousness.

I wish to thank Ruthie, my wife of 44 years, who has that rare sweetness and consideration that flows from a heart of love for our Lord Jesus. Without the encouragement of my wife and Mom over the last two years, this book would likely not have been written. I am blessed.

Ruthie and I wish to express our appreciation to some of our friends who have partnered with us for years, among them the chairman of the board of our ministry, John and Beth Genz, Ray and Coreen Bakke, Philip Rasmussen, Bob and Donna Leland, Jerry and Sharon Benson, Bob and Nancy Geyer, Brad and Michelle Scott, Vito and Olga Muilli, Nate and JoAnn Krupp, Charles and Donna Moren and Bob and Barb West. These are people who are exhorters. They define the word "friendship" for us and have been true partners in the mission God has given us.

I'd like to express my deep appreciation to Julie Bosacker, Frieda Nossaman, and Peter Schmidt for their part in the development of sketches, editing, and graphics. Whatever success this book may have is due, in large part, to their efforts.

Grandparents will tell you it's not the accumulation of "things" that brings happiness to our hearts and make us feel worthwhile, but growth and godly character in our kids and grandkids that really counts. Frankly, we had no idea the joy our grandchildren would bring into our lives, but more importantly, to God. Being involved in missions has meant personal sacrifices for us. Thank you, Mark, Pat-Marie, Luke, and Brooke.

Finally, I would like to thank those remarkable people who have spent their lives seeking to turn the hearts of Americans back to the original principles of freedom and righteousness. Christians are thankful for our national leaders who have stood for righteousness in our country: D. James Kennedy, Pat Robertson, Peter Marshall, David Manual, Ken Curtis, Chuck Colson, David Barton, Bill Gothard, John Eidsmoe, William Federer, James Dobson, and our friends at Oakbrook Christian Church. These are some of the people who have carried the torch of God's vision for America. May future generations be as faithful as they have been, to be custodians of God's purposes for our country. Hopefully, another generation will follow them to help "turn the hearts of the children to God." The purpose of this book is to help us discover "godly virtues" for our own lives as well as rediscover what God has done in our country in providing us with a "godly heritage." There have been times when our country has lost its moral compass, but Christians turned to God and God has graciously forgiven us as individuals and as a nation. It appears this healing came when we were desperate and hungry for God to heal our land. May the stories of the individuals in this book enrich your life as they have my own.

table of contents

about this book

The failure of the nineteenth century "materialistic" philosophies (built on atheism) to provide for us meaning in life and motivation for "goodness" has left America reeling. The American civilization was built on the premise that the Scriptures are the Words of God and Jesus Christ is God. This view was shared by almost all of the "Founders."

During my travels to the former Soviet Union, I began thinking about "universals" or virtues appropriate in any country or ethnic group. The book, "Life's Amazing Discoveries" resulted. This new book is an outgrowth of that first book. Are these "universal virtues" something we decide upon or are they built into the "nature of the universe?" I began to understand that "attitudes determine character." There is such a thing as "Eternal Law" which includes the "Ten Commandments" and the "Beatitudes."

As you come to know the lives of 37 people who "shaped the character of America," you will see that a "crisis revealed their character." Our "heroes" impacted millions of lives because they most often embraced the more difficult decision. They were "overcomers."

Attitudes plus actions determine our character. The premise is that all our character qualities must be rooted in God's character and His revealed truth. The presence of Jesus Christ in our lives makes the difference. When our ultimate choice is to live for God and embrace the Scriptures as our guide for life, we are on our way to living a life pleasing to God and of service to others. Christian virtues necessitate a "new birth" and "a new heart." The affections of an individual are transformed so knowing God becomes our most important relationship. In the Old Testament, virtue means "might, strength, power, valiant." In the New Testament virtue means "moral excellence."

When a person has experienced a new spiritual birth he or she wants to please God. Our gift to God is the development of these Christian virtues. The responsibility in the development of virtues lies with the Christian, however. For the Christian, attitudes and disciplines (abiding in Christ as John reminds us) produce "godly virtues," or "the fruit of the Spirit."

The shapers of America's virtues generally agreed with the fact that virtues originate with, and are sustained by God. In this book, I have chosen men and women who were committed to the Bible as the foundation of virtues and character. Just what were these essential "virtues"? How are these "virtues" exhibited in their lives? American political thought was shaped by European philosophers, theologians, and scientists. Among them are Marcus Tullius Cicero, Thomas Aquinas, Richard Hooker, Hugo Grotius, Charles de Montesquieu, Issac Newton, Emmerich de Vattel, Algernon Sidney, and William Blackstone, all of whom embraced a Biblical World View while others, such as René Descartes and John Locke, were characterized by a Materialistic World View. These two philosophies remain with American thought today.

To help us determine universal virtues, we need to develop standards to filter them through. Each virtue must be:

■ Universal—Virtues must be appropriate in any culture or ethnic group. They will be adaptable among the rich and poor alike.

■ Eternal—Virtues reflect what is happening in heaven where Jesus Christ is always honored and revered. Virtues must originate with God and not with man.

■ Transforming—Virtues must have a transforming effect on people to make them better.

■ Redemptive—Virtues must lead to man's redemption and wholeness rather than to man's disintegration.

■ Unifying—Virtues we embrace will bring us together for some universal goal or purpose.

■ Pro-Life—The virtues we embrace will have "cosmic backing" or will not run cross-purpose with the laws of the universe. They will bring health and preserve and restore relationships.

America is still a relatively young country and the "shapers of America's virtues" were influenced largely by Europeans who contributed to our thinking and way of life. The foundations were laid by people like Aristotle and Cicero. Evangelical historian Norman Geisler, notes Aquinas' influence on Christianity was "extraordinary."[1]

introduction

The Christian views "freedom" differently than does the Secular person. "Freedom," from a biblical perspective, opens the door to becoming what God intended us to be. It is freedom to allow Christ to express His life and character in us. This is true freedom. When we see how some Americans abuse this freedom and undermine the morality of other countries, we need to speak up. For example, if we are to truly live by the "golden rule," we have no right to export movies, magazines etc., which corrupt nations. We lose our "goodness" as a nation, when we allow this. Today, however, the idea of "freedom" is a word many hide behind to promote evil.

In 1972 I had my first experience of life "behind the Iron Curtain" as I traveled with friends to Romania. It was a transforming experience for me, so when the wall came down, I, like thousands of other Americans traveled to the former Soviet Union. At the time, I didn't realize I would meet people on the other side of that wall whom I would come to love so deeply. I started Mercy Institute and we became involved in helping some new friends begin an open-heart project in Perm, Russia. This led to other projects in Irkutsk, (Siberia). After 19 trips and several years of travel I can appreciate what happened to those living under Communism for so many years. Embracing an atheistic (materialistic) world view had led to heart-wrenching consequences for individuals and nations. The nations comprising the Soviet Union had been plundered in every way imaginable.

Both the Nazis and Marxist Communists fell into the "Kantian" and "Darwinian" view of life and trace their history to neo-Darwinian biology and their own "moral reasonings." The Nazis saw history as a competition of races, with the struggle for power. Nietzsche's philosophy taught that, "man has a will to power, whether over domesticated animals or nations." For Hitler, the "will to power" was man's most significant characteristic rather than reason or that human beings were made in the image of God. Nazis saw other nations as inferior to them, to be enslaved or exterminated.

The Communists saw everything in terms of "class struggle." Lenin and Stalin believed that anything "counter-revolutionary" was to be eliminated. For several years I have heard firsthand the stories of people who saw pastors, priests, parents, and grandparents executed or sent to Siberia because they did not go along with the Communists. No dissent was allowed. The absence of justice and human rights were evident everywhere it seemed. Threats and bribes had been the "norm." Many of us think that "the cold war is over" and America won! From my perspective, I am thrilled that America and Russia are drawing closer to each other and the doors are open for the "gospel" and commercial relationships. The real problem, however, is that the underlying philosophies which supported Communism are still present.

The Islamic nations look at America and tell us they prefer "virtue" over "freedom." Muslim philosopher, Sayyid Qutb, dismisses America as "immoral" and "contends, it is God, and not man, who rules. God is the source of all authority, including legitimate political authority. Virtue, not freedom, is the highest value. Therefore God's commands, not man's laws, should govern the society. The goal of the regime is to make people better, not to make them better off."[2]

In the final analysis, "virtue" is more important than freedom. America's "Founders" would say that we cannot survive as a nation without them. But they should be "virtues" based on a relationship with Jesus Christ. Virtues open the door to freedom and are necessary for maintaining freedom in a nation.

■ Dinesh D'Souza summarizes the urgency of the day for America with the following thoughts:

The West has been battling Islam for more than a thousand years. It is possible that this great battle has now been resumed, and that over time we will come to see the seventy-year battle against Communism as a short detour. But are we up to the challenge? There are some who think we are not. They believe that Americans are a divided people: not even a nation, but a collection of separate tribes. The multiculturalists actually proclaim this to be a good thing, and they strive to encourage people to affirm their differences. If, however, the multiculturalists are right in saying that 'all we have in common is our diversity,' then it follows that we have nothing in common. This does not bode well for the national unity that is a prerequisite to fighting against a determined foe. If the ethnic group is the primary unit of allegiance, why should we make sacrifices for people who come from ethnic groups other than our own? Doesn't a nation require a loyalty that transcends ethnic particularity? Of course it does. And fortunately America does command such a loyalty. The multiculturalists are simply wrong about America, and despite their best efforts to promote a politics of difference, Americans remain a united people with shared values and a common way of life.[3]

The Beginning of "isms" brought about the change from a "Newtonian" world view to a "Darwinian" one. Here are a few of these "isms":

■ The rise of "Empiricism." (All knowledge is derived from empiricism of the senses) beginning with Descartes, the rise of "Naturalism." All religious truth is derived from nature and natural causes and not from revelation) beginning with Kant and Hegel.

- The rise of "Darwinism," (species of living things originate, evolve, and survive through natural selection in response to environmental forces) beginning with Charles Darwin.

- The rise of "Reductionism," (oversimplification of something complex or the misguided belief that everything can be explained in simple terms) beginning with German philosophy.

- The rise of "Communism," (the political theory in which all property and wealth is owned by a classless society by all the members of a community) beginning with Karl Marx.

- The change in educational philosophies, beginning with William James and John Dewey.

- The change in American jurisprudence, beginning with Ralph Waldo Emerson.

To summarize, the shifts in the nineteenth century came to America primarily through our country's universities. None was so influential as Harvard. Emerson, Holms, and Dewey had set the stage for a radical new philosophy called "Pragmatism." This was distinctively American.

There are several models of "virtues" offered to Americans today. We present the "Christian model" based on the life of Jesus Christ and the Christian Bible.

Before we begin the study of those who shaped the "Virtues of Western Civilization," it is important we review competing philosophies shaping cultures and individuals over several centuries. We begin with Benjamin Franklin. While there were undoubtedly others whose lives were better expressions of "godly character," Benjamin Franklin went so far as to record his virtues.

FRANKLIN'S REPUBLICAN VIRTUES BASED ON EIGHTEENTH CENTURY PRAGMATISM

It may be that Franklin was the real "Father of Pragmatism" in America. If it worked, he was all for it.

BENJAMIN FRANKLIN'S LIST OF REPUBLICAN VIRTUES

"Republicanism" as a political system was based on the belief that the supreme power is in the hands of the electorate.

- Based in part on Greek thought and public consensus. To the ancient Greeks, the individual was of no value; the public was "everything."

- Based on self-interest of the group, yet lacked universal love for all people.

- Based on Natural Law, one's experience of life and to some extent, the Bible.

- Based on a combination of Greek, Roman, and Christian virtues.

FRANKLIN'S LIST OF VIRTUES

- Temperance - eat not to dullness, drink not in elevation.

- Silence - speak not but what may benefit others or yourself and avoid all trifling conversations.

- Order - let all your things have their places; let each part of your business have its time.
- Resolution - resolve to perform what you ought; perform without fail what you resolve.
- Frugality - make no expenses but to do good for others or yourself.
- Industry - lose no time; be always employed in something useful.
- Sincerity and no hurtful deceit - think innocently and justly, and you will speak accordingly.
- Justice - wrong no one by doing injuries or omitting the benefits that are your duties.
- Moderation - avoid extremes; forbear resenting injuries so much as you think they deserve.
- Cleanliness - tolerate no uncleanliness in body, clothes, or habitation.
- Chastity - rarely used but for health and offspring, never to dullness, weakness or the injury of your own or another's peace and reputation.
- Humility - imitate Jesus and Socrates.
- Tranquility - be not disturbed at trifles, or at accidents common and unavoidable.

ADDITIONAL "REPUBLICAN VIRTUES" FROM ANCIENT GREEKS

- Courage
- Frugality
- Independence
- Industry
- Morality
- Patriotism
- Against self-indulgence
- Self-denial
- Simplicity
- Unselfishness
- Vitality

Benjamin Franklin had his list of virtues then, but there came a time in his life when he realized he had fallen far short of his own expectations and could not live up to his own ideals. Franklin deeply admired George Whitefield and saw the good that came to the "city of brotherly love" from the efforts of the evangelist. Franklin noted that without morality the country could not survive but seemed to put off the importance of his own personal conversion, thinking that when he died, he would know for sure if what the Bible said was true.

"Rationalism" had a powerful impact on some of our "Founders," including Benjamin Franklin. It is "righteousness that exalts a nation" however, and Franklin believed this was true. He also strongly believed in man's reason to solve problems, yet was "reason" enough?

IMMANUEL KANT'S VIRTUES BASED ON REASON

Immanuel Kant was a seminal figure in the history of Western Civilization. Out of his philosophy came the "isms" of the nineteenth century. The problem with human reason is that it has limitations, since it requires a correct understanding of reality. It seems to me that "reason" requires that we are omniscient (have all knowledge) and only God is omniscient. "Reason" can also be a tool for manipulation of people since it appeals to the false notion of man's self-sufficiency and so-called greatness. It seems clear that there is a connection to the tragedy of two "World Wars" in the twentieth century and the nineteenth century philosophy of "reductionism." The Scriptures were devalued and man himself was conceived as a product of evolution, not made in the image of God.

The "Common Sense" philosophy is part of the culture and philosophy of America today. We live in two universes: the universe of common sense in which we come in contact with things by our senses, and the universe of revelation with which we come in contact by faith. Common sense, according to Oswald Chambers, "Is a gift which God gave to human nature, but it is not the gift of His Son; never enthrone common sense."[4]

Chamber continues "Every time you venture out in the life of faith you will find something in your common sense that flatly contradicts your faith. We hear it said that Jesus Christ taught nothing contrary to common sense; everything Jesus Christ taught was contrary to common sense. Not one thing in the Sermon on the Mount is common sense. The basis of Christianity is neither common sense nor rationalism, it springs from another center, in other words, a personal relationship with God through Jesus Christ in which everything is ventured on that which is not seen."[5]

Chambers reminded Christians that, "to have faith tests a man for all he is worth, he has to stand in the common-sense universe in the midst of things which conflict with his faith, and place his confidence in the God whose character is revealed in Jesus Christ."[6]

Immanuel Kant provided the basis for the nineteenth century philosophies with his "doctrine of empiricism" which:

- derived his principles from moral reasoning and not from divine commandments.

- taught that morality requires acts to be viewed from something other than self-interest, heaven, for example.

- says what we do is because of decisions we have made which are embodiments of values chosen.

- worked to develop a new human being who could grasp his own freedom and create his own destiny.

Kant's human being is autonomous. Marx and Nietzsche also embraced these concepts. Writes Kant, "He finds the strength within himself to unify his world with an act of self-will (faith). He is an individual who has looked profoundly into the world of men and seen that at the deepest level we are alone—in 'absolute isolation.'" Kant spoke of the "starry sky above and the moral law within"[7] but he lived in an age of "empiricism." There seems to be a dichotomy in the thinking of Kant but his followers maintained that the only reality was what you can see. He believed that the universe had always existed, a view Einstein was to refute a century later. It was Kant and Hegel then, who opened the door to the materialistic philosophies of the nineteenth century. Kant could have been considered a host for the PBS program, "Nature."

Kant believed, "Nature is all that ever has existed, all that does exist and all that will ever exist." The Creation event (or the "Big Bang") indicates that Creation required a Creator. Any mathematician using the "laws of probability" will say that the universe could not create itself, but required a Creator.

These nineteenth century philosophies resulted from embracing a "Materialistic world view." All that was needed was a creation story, which Darwin provided. New philosophies began to take hold first in Europe and then in the United States. Atheism built, often violently, its new world on the ruins of Christianity and most of Europe. The former Soviet Union and China abandoned the "faith of their fathers," whether it was Christianity or Buddhism. In most cases, however, evolution with its resulting atheism had to be imposed on people.

According to Ravi Zacharias, the concept of "Nazism" was conceived in German universities and the idea of a personal God to whom we were responsible was abandoned. Nieztsche's "death of God" had many terrible consequences in Germany and Russia and the result was that the twentieth century was the bloodiest in man's history. There was no God to be accountable to and the "will to power" became Germany's motto. When "reason" has its full expression, it can lead to disastrous consequences.

In 1919, President Woodrow Wilson noted the drift from a "Newtonian world view" to a "Darwinian world view." Both "world views" were prevalent in America. "Pragmatism" was also a powerful influence, especially in the universities, to push America to Kant's misguided view that the only reality is one you can see. The nation had become "Kantian" and the philosophical implications of acknowledging a Creator were quietly set aside. When Einstein's "Big Bang" was proven true, (the universe had a beginning) scientists and educators were embarrassed because of its philosophical implications. People did not want to be accountable to God. Man now thought himself to be "autonomous" and not responsible to God or God's eternal laws.

PROBLEM WITH RATIONALISM AND THE COMMON SENSE VIEW

The Common Sense View rules out the possibility that God would speak to mankind and offer a true view of eternal reality and a new understanding of the immense worth of a human being. We can "reason" our way to the wrong conclusions.

DESCARTES' VIRTUES BASED ON EXPERIENCE AND OBSERVATION

After "revelation knowledge" was excluded the natural outcome was "Empiricism." This view didn't deal with the necessity of a Creator and allowed man to define his own world in terms of his experience and observation.

KEY FOUNDERS: DAVID HUME, JOHN STUART MILL, JEREMY BENTHAM

David Hume was the first modern philosopher to be completely secular without any reference to God, God's will, or a divine plan for this life or the afterlife.

DAVID HUME'S NATURAL VIRTUES

- Benevolence
- Meekness
- Charity
- Generosity and justice
- Allegiance and keeping promises
- Chastity

HUME'S CATEGORY OF VIRTUES

- Qualities useful to others.
- Qualities useful to oneself.
- Qualities immediately agreeable to others.
- Qualities immediately agreeable to oneself.
- Believed human beings are motivated by unsatisfied needs and certain lower needs that need to be satisfied before higher needs can be satisfied.
- "When the deficiency needs are met: at once other (and higher) needs emerge, and these, rather than physiological hungers, dominate the organism. As one desire is satisfied, another pops up to take its place."
- Knowledge comes to a person exclusively through experience.
- What is true is what is experienced by the "senses."
- Hume questioned the process of the "inductive method." (Or reaching a conclusion based on observation or producing a universal claim on observed instances.)
- Introduced terms like "utilitarianism" into the moral vocabulary. (The greatest happiness of the greatest number should be the criterion of the virtue of action and practical use is more important than beauty.)
- Believed moral obligations cannot be deduced from statements of fact.
- Believed that moral judgments are based primarily on "feelings."
- Said, "Virtue is in proportion to the number of people to whom the happiness should extend." (The greatest happiness to the greatest numbers.)

PROBLEM: Experience can be manipulated and one's view of reality can be altered.

■ **David Hume's reflections in his declining years...**

I am appalled at the forlorn solitude in which I am placed by my philosophy; and I began to fancy myself in the most deplorable condition imaginable, environed in the deepest darkness." A writer, quoting his confession commented that "any man who, like Hume, regards himself as nothing but a bundle of natural forces and impressions which is to be unbound and scattered to the winds by death, who denies that there is any evidence for the existence of the soul after death, or the existence of God, must abide in a solitude which is indeed forlorn.

■ **John Stuart Mill in his declining years...**

I am not ashamed to confess that with the virtual negation of God, the universe to me has lost its soul of loveliness. Moreover, when I think, as at times I must, of the appalling contrast between the hallowed glory of that creed which once was mine, and the lonely mystery of existence as now I find it, at such times I shall ever feel it impossible to avoid the sharpest pang of which my nature is susceptible.

An observer writes, "The talent and success of John Stuart Mill make more distressing the periods of despondency in his early manhood, and the loneliness of his later years. His wife dies, and he tells his heart this is the end. He buries her, not her body only, but herself. She has ceased to be. He has no religion but his memory of her; no hope but of annihilation." John Stuart Mill proved one thing; life without God does not work.

DARWINIAN WORLD VIEW

People today generally see the world through Darwin's lens. It was not always so and many are now moving back to a "Theistic world view." (See Chapter Two.) There were many key people and events, which led to this shift, however. It is important to have an understanding about how this transition took place.

■ **TWENTIETH CENTURY PRAGMATISM BASED ON "WHAT WORKS."**

Pragmatic (American) virtues of John Dewey, Charles Peirce, William James, Oliver Wendell Holms, and Abraham Maslow. Dewey, Peirce, James, and Holms were all members of the "Meta-Physical Society" while students at Harvard. "Trancendentalism" was one such philosophy.

Darwin believed...

■ "If human beings are part of nature and nothing more, then the mind is simply an organ that has evolved from lower forms in the struggle for existence."

■ "There is no need for the 'transcendent.' There is no 'universal truth.' The only truth is 'Darwinism.' " "Darwinism" is, to them, "a fact of life and a world view."

Charles Peirce taught...

■ "Human beings are natural creatures who must change their beliefs, meanings, and sense of purpose throughout their lives" (Father of Philosophical Pragmatism).

William James introduced the view that...

■ "Truth is pluralism." He brought an emphasis on morals and psychological notions. He believed "truth" is short term and individual. "Truth" or meaning is dependent on the subjects "paradigm" or an idea based on his experience, making it ever changing. What is good or evil is dependent on its potential outcome.

Introducing the "fairness doctrine." Our culture seems to have a knee-jerk reaction when they see injustice yet most people seem oblivious to God's view of sin and unaware that their lives are offending God.

THE FAIRNESS PRINCIPLE IN ACTION

My friend, Ken Curtis, who currently has cancer, has been told many times, "It's not fair that you have cancer. This shouldn't happen to you. You don't deserve it." Ken's response is worth remembering. "Thanks, anyway, but as someone has said—the last thing I want is what I deserve. I shudder to think what would be coming to me if fairness was the ultimate criteria and I had to face the judgment and get what I deserved. What is unfair is that Christ should die for the sins of a fallen humanity, including mine, that I should be granted forgiveness, and a reserved seat at the heavenly festivities."

VALUES DEWEY AND MASLOW ROOTED IN EXPERIENCE

■ Competence/excellence
■ Community enhancement
■ Higher awareness
■ Discovery/exploration
■ Cross-curriculum
■ Global, national, local technological literacy
■ Life-long learning
■ Service
■ Creativity
■ Study well
■ Think well
■ Write well
■ Read well
■ Team skills

Dewey made two trips to the former Soviet Union. There are different opinions regarding his influence yet it appears to be substantial. One thing is certain, however, education was based on the notion of "Naturalism," the only reality is what you can see (Empiricism).

■ **THE DISCIPLES OF JOHN DEWEY**—The four major streams of humanistic education

1. Maslow's work with self-actualization and hierarchy of needs.
2. Rogers work with the non-directive classroom based on his model of psychotherapy.
3. Maslow and values clarification.
4. The works of Lawrence Kohber. (Six stages of moral reasoning.)

Non-directive therapy is known as values clarification, sensitivity training, mastery learning, and outcome-based education. It has wrecked disaster on our children and subverted their moral foundations. The results of "openness" and "acceptance" of everything– good or bad–results in the belief that permissiveness is now acceptable behavior. Esteem is a right. Once it was considered as a basic truth that self-esteem came from achievement... no longer.

As philosophers have pointed out, the results of a 'secular world view' would be diastrous and include: the loss of our God-given potential, the loss of a transcendent God, objective truth, the loss of a sense of wonder, true gratitude, the loss of reason, truth between people, integrity, decency, hope, the rise of pluralism, privatization of beliefs, shame, unresolved social injustice and the loss of sacred things. These are some of the fruits of "secularism." Unless America returns to the God of our Fathers, these will be common attitudes in future generations.

■ **WILLIAM COULSON**

Two years ago I was in Northern California and a friend told me an unusual story about a man who had been an associate of Carl Rogers and Abraham Maslow. He was William Coulson. Coulson lived long enough to see the great calamity he and his associates had brought about.* He was now able to see the "fruit of his labors" and the "fruit" broke his heart. An entire generation of young people had turned away from the faith of their parents and their lives were in shambles. William Coulson helps us understand Carl Rogers and Abraham Maslow. The following are "highlights" of his conversation with Maslow.

■ **PROBLEMS: FATAL FLAWS IN HUMANISTIC PSYCHOLOGY**

"We didn't have a doctrine of evil." Those were the words of Abraham Maslow. "We failed to understand the reality of evil in the human life, when we implied to people that they could trust their impulses, they also understood us to mean they could trust their evil impulses, that they were not really evil. But they were evil." Rogers believed in the innate goodness of man and believed every man is good. He created a miniature utopian society, the encounter group. Maslow said, "We didn't have a doctrine of evil we failed to understand the reality of evil in human life."[8]

The loss of guilt. Rogers sought to wipe out the consequences or penalty of immoral behavior. "Living in sin, committing adultery, lewd and lascivious conduct, fornication, homosexuality, ingesting illegal drugs...were all 'struggles for a better partnership.' "[9]

The ability to discern right and wrong.

Coulson on non-judgmentalism: "We're not going to call anything wrong, we're not

---

We are indebted to our friends at Probe.org for providing us a transcript between Dr. William Coulson and Probe's Don Closson. Closson spent considerable time with Coulson reflecting on his relationship with Carl Rogers and Abraham Maslow.

going to call drug use wrong, because we'll make some of the kids in this classroom feel bad because they are already using drugs. We've (Americans) trained (our children) to respect legitimate authority, and now the school is exercising authority to say, 'You've got to forget about what your church taught you or what your parents taught you; forget about that business about absolutes and right and wrong'…let us help you find what you really deeply inside want." [10]

The loss of fidelity.

The most important authority is within you; listen to yourself. They created the theory of "self-actualization," in which unstinting satisfaction of desires–bodily or otherwise–was implicit. This leads to infidelity. Said Rogers, "The most important authority source is within you, that you must listen to yourself. We created a miniature utopian society, the encounter group." [11]

The loss of social justice.

Justice demands that nobody be condemned for anything. One belief is as good as another. Everyone has the right to say his view is right. When a student proclaimed at a rally that, "There are no absolutes." The speaker asked him, "Are you absolutely sure?" Immediately, the student yelled back "yes" and so contradicted himself. [12]

The inherent destructiveness to a civilization.

"Psychology today is predominantly therapeutic psychology; and in that sense anti-thetical (to morals and values) because in therapy you don't ever want to tell a person how they should be, particularly in the moral dimension. I see therapy as being fundamentally opposed to the civilized life. The net outcome of sex education, styled as Rogerina encountering, is more sexual experience." [13]

The loss of God-given authority.

Rogers ultimately believed there should be no such thing as a therapist. He went from the "client-centered therapy" to "person-centered approach." With this approach the therapist disappeared, all authority disappeared, and all limits disappeared. Rogers corrupted a whole raft of religious orders on the West Coast in the 1960s by getting the nuns and priest to talk about their distress. After a year of Roger's approach, over 300 nuns submitted letters to Rome asking to be released from their vows. They no longer wished to be under religious authorities. Summary: Psychology has been called upon to substitute for all morality, and that is simply too much to ask. [14]

The secular man is to be both pitied and feared. In his attempt to become "autonomous" he cuts himself off from a true understanding of reality. He also cuts himself off from the only One who can help him meet his deepest longings. Rather than embracing self-evident truth, he determines truth based on the most primitive of notions; his own reason, experience, or consensus. Ephesians 2:12 says he is "without hope and without God in the world." This is where all his knowledge has brought him. The Father in heaven can only grieve over this lost child who has determined to "do it my way." Having spurned the salvation offered for his sins by the eternal Son of God, he faces an eternity of remorse. What a plight modern man, so full of himself, has chosen. He became the greatest loser but God, as a Father, became the greatest sufferer. He lost his child for whom he had such great hopes.

Acts 4:25b-26 exclaims," 'Why do the nations rage and the peoples plot in vain? The kings of the earth take their stand and the rulers gather together against the Lord and against his Anointed One.' " There is an element in America that has no room for God or the Scriptures in public life. We are willing to use deception and manipulation to continue the philosophy of "reductionism" of the Christian gospel.

In 1982, 180 years after the rise of Empiricism with Kant and Hegel, courts in the United States ruled that only the "materialistic world view" could be taught in the schools of America. We knew better but we lied about the fact of Creation as confirmed by Einstein. Values are now rooted in this materialistic world view. Francis Schaeffer maintains that the ultimate result is the cruel use of power over the lives of people and resulting injustice.

THE END OF THE ROAD FOR ROGERS, MASLOW, AND COULSON

■ **Rogers toward the end of his life, said:**

Well, I started this (expletive)…thing, and look where it's taking us; I don't even know where it's taking me. I don't have any idea what's going to happen next. And I woke up the next morning feeling so depressed, that I could hardly stand it. And I realized what was wrong. Where is it going to carry us? And did I start something that is fundamentally mistaken, and will lead us off into paths that we will regret.[15]

■ **Maslow toward the end of his life.**

Maslow expressed a lot of regrets at the end of his career. He began to think less about self-actualization and personal identity and more about self-forgetting. He condemned Carl Rogers' idea that we should follow our feelings whether they were right or wrong. Maslow taught that this idea of the human-potential movement was a civilization-destroying concept. It failed to understand the reality of evil in human life. "When we implied that they could trust their impulses, they also understood us to mean that they could trust their evil impulses."[16]

■ **Coulson in his latter years.**

Dr. William R. Coulson, long time associate of Rogers and his C.E.O., broke with Rogers and has spent years asking for forgiveness for the damage he and Rogers have done with humanistic education. Said Coulson, "Behavior that would have been confronted by the previous generation as shameful now became obligatory… One must be that self which one is." His students told him; you "set us free" and "thanks to you, I've discovered my gay nature."[17] He decided to cheat on his wife to be real.

Coulson confronted his grave deceptions. "I would raise a red flag…every time the word values is used. That's been a difficult word, because for a long time Christians were asking for value-oriented education. The problem is that values have become a relativistic world— it's subjective. In California, we taught people going through encounter groups to say… 'Well, you have your values, but who's to say your values should be my values?' We taught mothers and fathers to fear that they were selfish if they imposed their values on their children. Kids were told to tell their parents, 'We appreciate your value of church-going, it just doesn't happen to be mine. My experience is other than your experience. You grew up in a different era.'"[18]

"The truth is," continues Coulson, "that humanistic educators don't think their values are relativistic. They think that everybody ought to be doing this."[19]

Two "world views" are emerging in America.*

	CHRISTIAN CONTEXT	EUROPEAN CONTEXT
Respect	For what God calls good	For earth-centered values
Responsibility	To God first	To the collective community
Understanding	From God's perspective	From global perspective
Cooperation	According to God's plan	According to changing rules
Citizenship	Obey God's guidelines	Serve and conform to group
Altruism	God's love through us to others	Mandatory voluntary service
Empathy	Compassion for the needy	Oneness with all people world view
Justice	Fair trial, compensation for wrong	Socialist equality redistribution

According to Berit Kjos.

MULTICULTURALISM

Although there are different usages of the word "multiculturalism," the most alarming is the use in recent years to identify a movement that confronts certain perceived biases in Western society, particularly on college campuses. "Multicultural history" is now a part of the history courses offered to schools with the emphasis on how ethnic minorities affected American history. It down plays the importance of dead, white, European males. "The proponents of this believe that the Anglo-Saxon tradition is a racist, sexist plot designed to prefer white dominance."[20]

ARE ALL CULTURES EQUAL?

Perhaps the first question we need to ask ourselves is, "What is a culture?" Let's say a culture is "a people with shared beliefs and values/virtues, customs, practices and social behavior." Simply, a culture is "a way of life." If we accept this definition, is it not appropriate to ask what "ways of life" tend to produce stronger relationships, a sense of fulfillment, better health, an understanding of the immense eternal value of a human being? The common thought that all "cultures" are equally valuable is nonsense, since some lead to the degradation of women, and the perpetration of all kinds of evil and misinformation. For example, nineteenth century philosophy provided us with false pre-suppositions of what a human being really is.

- **Anthropologist Paul G. Hiebert maintains that embracing "cultural relativism" will mean...**
  - Withholding judgment and affirming the right of each culture.

- High respect for other people and their culture.
- Affirms the right for each culture to reach its own answers.[21]

- **The consequences of this will mean...**
    - The loss of righteousness and a "godly heritage" a country may have.
    - If all explanations of reality are equally valid, we can no longer speak of error. If all behavior is justified according to its culture context, we can no longer speak of sin. Then there is no need for the gospel.
    - The loss of "truth."
    - "Reality" is what I say it is. Again, man becomes the "measure of all things."
    - Government by "consensus" or what the "Founders" feared: "mobocracy."

Truth does not depend on what we think or say, but on reality itself. When we say the gospel is true, we are not claiming a superiority for ourselves; we are witnessing the truth of the gospel.

Every generation and every ethnic group brings something to America. When that group insists America must dismantle the foundations of the country to accommodate them because they are "offended," they will lose the essence of what America is all about and what it offers all those coming here to begin a new life. This is where we are at today. The "foundations" of righteous government, lasting relationships, and eternal truths have been marginalized and ridiculed. When Christians have been true to the Founder of their faith, it has brought forth the highest standard of living, and the greatest and most sustained efforts to relieve suffering and bring about justice in the history of the world. Christians brought about virtually every social reform in the history of America. These Christians humbled themselves before God, asking for forgiveness, justice, and mercy for those deprived of these God given rights.

VALUES OF GLOBAL SOCIALISM BASED ON "MULTICULTURISM"

- Transform the world by changing the children.
- Teach politically correct beliefs and values.
- Establish an outcome-based educational system.
- Implement master learning.
- Infuse new values through "real life" learning.
- Require community service.
- Revise history.
- Retrain teachers in the philosophy of "Global Socialism."

JULIAN HUXLEY'S VALUES (A DISCIPLE OF DEWEY)

Julian Huxley, the brother of Aldous Huxley, (author of "Brave New world") was the first Secretary-General of UNESCO (United Nations Educational, Scientific, and Cultural Organization). He promoted the same socialist and humanist values as John Dewey. Beret Kjos writes, "Vital to the implementation of this monstrous system are the deceptive marketing strategies needed to persuade the public to submit to its oppressive rules and laws."[22] Huxley's agenda would break down the moral fiber of a nation so it would be easily swayed.

- Children are raised collectively according to the needs of the global labor market.
- Group thinking has replaced individual views.
- Communal "feelies" or sensory experiences are encouraged.
- Casual sex is obligatory.
- Mandatory pills prevent pregnancy.
- People are too busy with work and trivia to think or complain.
- All must participate in mystical group rituals invoking a universal god.
- Peer pressure and constant surveillance ensure compliance.[23]

SHIFTS NECESSARY TO BRING ABOUT SOCIALISM IN AMERICA

- The cultural shift from a Christian to a global paradigm.
- The classroom shift from truth, fact, and logic to myth.
- The growing acceptance of an earth-centered spirituality without biblical truth.
- Media used to shape and promote this change.
- "Group thinking (or consensus decision-making) that would turn the young against the old and against absolutes."

UNICEF'S GLOBAL VALUES

If you could single out one person whose philosophies brought the most destruction to the world, it might be Fredrick Nietzsche. In 1895, Friedrich Nietzsche coined the word "values." "Values" replaced "virtues" and Western Civilization gave the common man the right to determine for himself what he wanted and ascribed worth to it, whether it was good or bad. These "values," of course, were subjective and relative. An individual did not need to look to a moral authority since "self" was the only authority. The notion of "values" is a logical outgrowth of the rising influence of Rene Descartes in Western Civilization. Nietzsche believed that with the death of virtues would come the death of truth and above all any morality. There would be no good or evil, no virtue or vice, but only values that were personal and subjective. Then, at last, Nietzsche believed humanity would be freed from the prison of virtues and morality.

The United Nations sought "to create a universal ethic and believed that the great need is consensus, not acrimony."[24] Of course, they forbid biblical absolutes, replacing God's unchanging truth with a compliant cultural consensus.

There is no "in the beginning God" at the U.N. Their list of "values" include: justice, altruism, diligence, and respect. These "values" may sound biblical, yet their intent fits the "NEA" vision of social control. To understand the prevailing philosophy behind the U.N., we turn to researcher Berit Kjos who writes:

"The driving vision of UNESCO's Culture of Peace is multicultural oneness. Never mind that such interfaith unity requires Christians to set aside biblical values. Biblical Christianity doesn't fit UNESCO'S Declaration on Tolerance or on Religion. But those who walk with God can't participate or approve of pagan practices and homosexual lifestyles. Unless we rewrite the Bible, God's Word and pagan lifestyles will clash."[25]

"The new tolerance" has the most effective proponent in the United Nations. Christians are the main targets in that we must accept the perverse values of all people since the values of all people are the same in terms of importance. If you don't accept them, you are an intolerant bigot. Christians must accept the lifestyle, belief system, and swing wide the doors of education for the 'evangelists' of these perverse ways of life.[26]

"This philosophy, initiated by a very few people, has permeated the universities, colleges, schools, and classrooms in the United States. Its ultimate persuasion will undoubtedly bring about oppressive government and a cruel use of power (tyranny) rooted in 'atheism.'"[27]

MY COUNTRY 'TIS OF THEE

Today, we still love America, yet many of us don't think we need to look to the "ancient ways." My travels with Mercy Institute have taken me all over the world. I come back more in love with my country than ever. I tell young people in Russia about the shapers of America's character and they long for those kinds of virtues to be true in their country.

Together, we can, we must, exhibit the character of those who laid down their lives for America. God still has a plan for America. Right now America is "hanging in the balance" yet God longs to be gracious to us when we put Him first in our lives

As a child growing up in the public schools in the state of Washington, my class sang "America" along with many other hymns about our country. Our breasts swelled with pride as we sang from the bottom of our hearts about "land where my fathers died" and "land of the pilgrim's pride." Our lungs were about to explode as we exclaimed "great God, our King!" Seeds of love for America were planted in young hearts which remained deeply rooted with love for this precious land.

America (My Country 'Tis of Thee)
Text: Samuel F. Smith, 1808-1895

1. My country, 'tis of thee,
    sweet land of liberty, of thee I sing;
    land where my fathers died,
    land of the pilgrim's pride,
    from every mountainside let freedom ring!

2. My native country, thee,
    land of the noble free, thy name I love;

I love thy rocks and rills,
thy woods and templed hills;
my heart with rapture thrills, like that above.

3. Let music swell the breeze,
   and ring from all the trees sweet freedom's song;
   let mortal tongues awake;
   let all that breathe partake;
   let rocks their silence break, the sound prolong.

4. Our fathers' God, to thee,
   author of liberty, to thee we sing;
   long may our land be bright
   with freedom's holy light;
   protect us by thy might, great God, our King.

BIBLICAL VIRTUES AND GODLY CHARACTER—DOES OUR CHARACTER AFFECT EVEN THE WAY WE APPEAR?

Novelist Oscar Wilde tells the story of a man, Dorian Gray, who thought he could live as he chose without it affecting his wholesome appearance. He tried, but sin and evil had twisted not only his thinking, but his appearance and his horrifying countenance was the result. Scotish writer Oswald Chambers reminds us that, "our features do speak of our moral character to those who can read them"[28] proving this is a moral universe. Chambers added that, "crisis reveals character."[29] Character then is the sum total of a person's actions. It is the whole trend of a man's life and not just isolated events.

Christian character comes through obedience to God. He gives us the life in His Son and we can either ignore Him and refuse to obey Him, or we can obey Him. Our goal is to bring every thought and imagination into captivity that the life of Jesus is manifested in our mortal flesh. The way I discern God is by my own character. God remains true to His character, and as I grow in integrity, I discern Him.

Chapters 1-3 will help you develop a Biblical World View. Chapters 4-15 cover the "Beattitudes" while Chapters 16-37 cover the "fruits of the Holy Spirit" in the life of a believer. Another way of describing the "fruits of the spirit" are "character traits."

The "Character of God" is presented in the lives of 37 individuals who have helped shape the character of America, as well as others I have known. Ultimately, God's character will require that it is seen as well through the revelation of God Himself. As we study the life of Jesus Christ, we see the image of God. To sum up all these different philosophies, one can notice they have a few things in common. The originators of these philosophies looked to reason, knowledge, experience etc., to determine what was right and wrong. The Christian realizes that our hearts can and do deceive us. The prophet Jeremiah describes our hearts as "desperately wicked." If we are wise, we will look to God's description of man's condition and not trust our own views.

Character is not something we are born with, but something that develops over a lifetime. Character is all about righteousness, the righteousness the Lord Jesus Christ gives to those who trust Him as their Lord and Savior. Followers of Jesus Christ will come to realize that God designed us to express Jesus' life. It was God's plan that from eternity past He would create people who reflect the character of His Son. Followers of Jesus know then that it's not about "our" character but the character of Jesus Christ in us that we were designed to express.

WHAT CAN BRING AMERICANS TOGETHER?

Currently, there is a battle going on to "define America." One group of people in America call themselves "Progressives" or "Liberals." This group believes that they are truly "reality based." The other group might be called "Traditional" or "Conservative. They are often referred to as "Faith based." These two groups have different visions for America and neither group seems willing to negotiate on deep commitments. In the years ahead, "character" may very well determine which group has the most influence in America.

The Westminster Shorter Catechism asks, "What is our chief end?" "The answer is, To glorify God and enjoy Him forever." Jesus interceded for His followers when He prayed, "All I have is yours, and all you have is mine. And glory has come to me through them." What did Jesus mean when He said that "glory has come to me through them?" May I suggest that God's glory is the revelation of His character and presence in our lives. It is the sum total of all His attributes. The very presence of Jesus Christ in the life of a Christian will reveal God's glory since Jesus is in our lives. Now, let's begin the great quest of understanding the "Character of God," through men and women whose lives bear witness to His presence, which then manifested itself in their character.

chapter 1

Truth—Thomas Aquinas

Purpose: Discovering the Natural Moral Laws of the Universe

character trait:
Truth

SUBJECT:
THOMAS AQUINAS
(1225-1274)

PURPOSE:
Discovering the Natural Moral Laws of the Universe

FAMOUS QUOTE:
"The theologian considers sin principally as an offense against God, whereas the moral philosopher considers it as being 'contrary to reason.' 'Moralists' then concerned themselves with man's happiness while 'theologians' were concerned with the joy God should receive from man who 'was created in the image of God.'"[1]

SCRIPTURE DOCUMENTATION:
"Do your best to present yourself to God as one approved, a workman who does not need to be ashamed and who correctly handles the word of truth" (2 Timothy 2:15).

"But whoever lives by the truth comes into the light, so that it may be seen plainly that what he has done has been done through God" (John 3:21).

"Now that you have purified yourselves by obeying the truth so that you have sincere love for your brothers, love one another deeply, from the heart" (1 Peter 1:22).

PERSONALITY PROFILE

Thomas Aquinas was born at his father's castle near Rome in 1225. At five years of age he entered the Montecassino where his studies began. Aquinas' commitment to the truth of Christ brought about rejection from his family. His father was Count Landulf. His mother was Countess Theodora of Theatre, a woman of noble descent. Aquinas' parents did not support his desire to follow Christ. In 1243, Aquinas chose to enter the Dominican Order. When he attempted to join the monastery, he was kidnapped by his brothers and held "captive" for two years. Efforts were made to "reprogram" him, but to no avail. Instead, he pursued God with all of his heart. Had Aquinas given up and not eventually entered the monastery, no one would likely have ever heard of him!

In the monastery Aquinas studied "scholasticism"—the medieval theological and philosophical system of learning (based on the authority of St. Augustine, the early Christian Church, and the works of Aristotle). Scholasticism sought to bridge the gap between religion and reason with leading scholars. Aquinas was mocked by other students and called "the dumb ox" because of his large size and slowness. In 1252 Thomas went to Paris to get his Master's degree. He stayed on and ended up teaching there for several years. At the invitation of the Pope, he took up his residence in Rome and founded a new "studium generale" in Naples. He wished to end his days at the monastery and later died at the monastery of Fossanova. For Aquinas, the virtue of "faith" was perfection of the human mind. He recalled the words of Hosea, "I will betroth you in faithfulness, and you will acknowledge the LORD" (Hosea 2:20).

Aquinas' greatest work was "the Summa" (his treatise on God). Aquinas worked on it from 1265 until the end of his life. From 1261-1265 he wrote commentaries on Job. Aquinas also was responsible for commentaries on the Psalms, the four gospels, and Jeremiah. Aquinas has provided fourteen philosophical works and also is known for his Fivefold Proof for the Existence of God. On December 6, 1273 he experienced a divine revelation, which so enraptured him that he abandoned "the Summa" saying it and his other writings were "so much straw in the wind compared to the reality of the divine glory." He died within a few months of this experience, as his health had deteriorated.

"When in the course of human Events, it becomes necessary for one People to dissolve the Political Bands which have connected them with another, and to assume among the Powers of the Earth, the separate and equal Station to which the Laws of Nature and of Nature's God entitle them...."

"We hold these Truths to be self-evident, that all Men are created equal, that they are endowed by their Creator with certain unalienable Rights, that among these are Life, Liberty and the Pursuit of Happiness," wrote Thomas Jefferson.

Sin can be defined as a violation of God's law. Sin not only affects our personalities and our bodies but it affects God as well. God is grieved in His heart over our sin since it brings about the destruction of individuals, families and nations.

Our "Founders" had a "Theistic World View" and embraced the views of Leibniz and later Emerich de Vattel. They were persuaded a Creator and Sustainer was necessary for the Universe to exist. Americans who embraced their understanding of reality came to view life as "sacred," dedicated to or set apart for the worship of a deity who is worthy of veneration. Rousseau and Descartes shaped American culture today, however. "Secularism" became a dominant "world view." Descartes and Rousseau's philosophy would lead to "Secularism" (worldly concerns which are earth-bound). Today, on college and university campuses, the battle for "truth" can be traced to the "Natural Law" philosophy.

NATURAL MORAL LAW

Thomas Aquinas introduced people to the Eternal Law of God, which is built into the universe and man's constitution (body). The written Law, known as the "Ten Commandments," are written down on the hearts or conscience of all. In the beginning God created man to live out of his "spirit," while the conscience served as a valid guide to right and wrong behavior. Man's conscience, however, became weak, defiled, and damaged, and man drifted from God's original design, becoming filled with envy, rebellion, and wickedness.

Aquinas preserved the "History of Natural Law" for America's founders, by influencing them concerning the truth of Scriptures and universal virtues. These men knew that the Eternal Law of God was higher than the American Constitution.

TRUTHFULNESS OF SCRIPTURE

Aquinas believed in the truthfulness of Scripture. He taught that there were four cardinal virtues: wisdom, courage,

> "we arrive at truth, not by reason only, but also by the heart."[2]
> francis bacon

> "The toppling of the Berlin Wall will seem small in comparison with the impending demolition of scientific naturalism. The collapse of the idea that nature is blind, purposeless and 'all there is' will not destroy the scientific study of nature but allow it to come into its own. There would be little point in speaking of a 'law written on the heart' if conscience were merely a meaningless byproduct of selfish genes."[3]

NATIONAL PURPOSE

temperance (moderation) and justice. The three Divine virtues were faith, hope and love while "the greatest of these is love," according to 1 Corinthians 13:13. There was nothing like this in ancient philosophy. Universal goodwill was a new concept. "Christian Virtues" are rooted in God's character or "theism" (the belief in God) and these eternal truths and principles have shaped Western Civilization, yet were first seen in the life of Jesus Christ.

Aquinas taught the "virtues" of Christ and His way. Aquinas used John 15:13 to express God's love. "Greater love has no one than this, that he lay down his life for his friends" (John 15:13).

Aquinas said, "Such a man was Christ on the cross. And if he gave his life for us, then it should not be difficult to bear whatever hardships arise for his sake. If you seek patience, you will find no better example than the cross. Christ endured much on the cross, and did so patiently, because when he suffered he did not threaten, he was led like a sheep to the slaughter and he did not open his mouth. If you seek the example of obedience, follow him who became obedient to the Father even unto death. By the obedience of one man, many were made righteous. If you seek an example of despising earthly things, follow him who is 'the King of Kings and the Lord of Lords' in whom are hidden all the treasures of wisdom and knowledge." [4]

MORAL LAW

Aquinas' "Five ways" by which God's existence can be demonstrated philosophically:

1. The "unmoved mover" argument. We know that there is motion in the world; whatever is in motion is moved by another thing; this other thing also must be moved by something; to avoid an infinite regression, we must posit a "first mover," which is God.

2. The "nothing is caused by itself" argument. For example, a table is brought into being by a carpenter, who is caused by his parents.

3. The cosmological argument. All physical things, even mountains, boulders, and rivers, come into being and go out of existence, no matter how long they last. Therefore, since time is infinite, there must be some time at which none of these things existed.

4. Objects in the world have differing degrees of qualities such as goodness, but speaking of more or less goodness makes sense only by comparison with what is the maximum goodness, which is God.

5. The teleological argument (argument from design). Things in the world move toward goals, just as the arrow does not move toward its goal except by the archer directing it. Thus, there must be an intelligent designer who directs all things to their goals, and this is God.

A man's conscience monitors his actions. When moral law is violated, an inner alarm goes off. Human beings know when they have violated their conscience. A person's conscience, however, may become ineffective and run down. The moral laws built into the foundation of the universe are God's Law in writing. Natural Law is part of the order of the universe and, unlike man's laws, no one may violate it without consequences. Breaking God's laws has consequences and a human being who does so will begin to break down internally. The summary of the law is undivided love for God and love for one's neighbor. Each of the commandments supports a particular virtue. Good laws can help in producing good character since standards are set for people to embrace.

The Lord Jesus never promised happiness, good luck, or favorable circumstances to His followers but "blessedness." People may be happy because something great has happened to them through salvation but being "blessed" means something deeper and lasting. This person has the "Kingdom of God" in him in the Person of Jesus Christ. Jesus Christ is God's standard for true righteousness. His life in us produces "righteous virtues." For Aquinas, his focus in life was not necessarily to be happy or healthy, but holy, and to live a life pleasing to God. Blessedness (or extreme happiness) should be considered a consequence of living a life pleasing to God and should not be a goal in itself.

We need to remember that we can reason ourselves to the wrong conclusions. The world knew God yet chose not to acknowledge God and their foolish hearts were darkened. This was the problem of Immanuel Kant. Philosopher Ravi Zacharias asserts that Kant led people to believe that "God is not necessary as a revealer of right and wrong since we can come to pure reason apart from God."[6]

Zacharias is convinced that the breakdown of morality in the East and West can be traced to a secular conviction that "morality can be deduced from reason alone!"[8]

"Grant me, O Lord my God, a mind to know you, a heart to seek you, wisdom to find you, conduct pleasing to you, faithful perseverance in waiting for you, and a hope of finally embracing you. Most loving Lord, grant me a steadfast heart which no unworthy desire may drag downwards; an unconquered heart which no hardship may wear out; an upright heart which no worthless purpose may ensnare. Impart to me also, O God, the understanding to know you, the diligence to seek you, a way of life to please you, and a faithfulness that may embrace you, through Jesus Christ, my Lord. Amen."[7]

Aquinas' prayer

Supreme Court Justices, such as James Wilson, rejected judicial activism. The 18th century English "Common Law Theory" as expressed through British jurist William Blackstone, influenced many of America's "Founders." The model of "Common Law" Blackstone had embraced from other European philosophers and theologians had two categories-"the law of nature and the law of revelation." The law of nature (which God placed within man's heart) originated with God's law, the "Ten Commandments" and since they came from God, provided a standard for society, families and individuals. Man's consciences affirm the moral law of God. He is bound to obey these "commandments" since he is made in the "image of God."

The role of government is to protect the unalienable rights God has given us. Subjective "rights" are of little consequence if they are objectively wrong. Keeping the laws of eternal justice and the "Ten Commandments" for life are essentials for true and lasting happiness.

Supreme Court Justices, such as James Wilson, rejected judicial activism. These twin arms of law, the "Law of Nature" and the "Law of Revelation,"(the Bible) provided early Americans with foundations of truth concerning the nature of reality for their personal lives and how government could exist to profit all it's citizens.

NATURAL LAW (The Law of Conscience) AND HOMOSEXUALITY

Professor Jaffe, of Claremont Mudd College poses the question, "Is homosexuality decidedly natural because it is the way someone was born or is it possible there are other reasons?[9] If you believe that homosexuality is unnatural, your view is rooted in a Natural Law ethic. This view is rooted in the fourth century BC philosopher Aristotle."[10]

It is abhorrent to think about these crimes against God. The reality of sin is that it breaks God's heart and brings about the destruction of families, and ultimately nations.[11] Nature itself awards chastity with health and punishes promiscuity with diseases. It is possible that if our main purpose for the discovery for a cure for AIDS is to allow unrestrained pursuit of 'safe sex' to continue, then it is probable that other diseases would occur. Antibiotics eliminated syphilis but it was not long before new diseases made an appearance.[12]

NATURAL LAW (The Law of Conscience) AND THE LAWS OF HEALTH

Virtues rooted in God's character as He has revealed Himself put us in harmony with Creation. Dr. William Sadler, a famous psychiatrist, has pronounced this judgment after looking for years into the minds, souls, and bodies of disrupted people: "If humanity lived in a truly Christian way, half of the diseases of humanity would drop off tomorrow and we would stand up a new healthy humanity."[13]

Dr. Karl Menninger tells us, "Love is the medicine for the sickness of the world."[14] Menninger believed many people who were in mental hospitals were there because they had not been loved. His experiences verified the desperate need for godly virtues like love to be extended to the entire world. The purpose of the Natural Law then is the development of "virtues" and a personal ethic.

Dr. E. Stanley Jones writes, "A woman's hospital reports that from 60 to 85 percent of all diseases of the body are rooted in the mental and spiritual. Every mental and moral and spiritual attitude that upsets the health and rhythm of the body is unchristian. Not one single authentic Christian attitude interferes with or upsets the body. Fear, resentment, guilt, self-preoccupation, a sense of inferiority, refusal to accept responsibility, dishonesty, quarrelsomeness, negativism, pessimism, hopelessness, retreat from life, refusal to cooperate, sexual impurity, anger, jealously, envy, pride, lust for money, criticism, backbiting, hate, and a lack of love are those attitudes defined as unchristian attitudes."[15]

No one was more influential in shaping jurisprudence in America than William Blackstone. He was not an original thinker but combined and preserved the thoughts of great people such as Aristotle, Cicero, Aquinas, and Hooker. Blackstone maintained that the "Law of Nature" (Conscience), and the "Law of Revelation" are of the same origin, the same obligation, and flow from the same source. The Laws are fixed and are for the purpose of man's happiness. The object of both is to discover the will of God. Both are necessary for the accomplishment to that end. One of the Roman philosophers whose influence profoundly affected the Founders was Cicero. He wrote, "Human laws are only copies of eternal laws. Those eternal laws are peculiar to man, for only man, on earth, is a rational being. The test of validity for the state's laws is their conformity to reason… learned men know that Law is the highest reason, implanted in Nature, which commands what ought to be done and forbids the opposite."[16] Notice the references to the Creator and His Law in the "Declaration of Independence."

"We hold these truths to be self-evident, that all men are created equal, that they are endowed by their Creator with certain unalienable Rights…"[18] "All law comes from God and human laws should conform to the revealed law of God as founded in nature and in the Scriptures"[19] (John Jay, First Chief Justice, U.S. Supreme Court).

Alabama's Chief Justice Roy Moore sought to restore Americans' historic conviction that the "Ten Commandments" are the foundation of law. Inscribed on the tablets were the words "The Laws of Nature and Nature's God." This was not a reference to "Pantheism" but to the Eternal Law of the Bible.

> "Aquinas taught that our natural knowledge of God is derived from his creation and since God made creation, it must resemble Him. Without God's sustaining power, no creature would continue to exist, much less act. The character, or tone of a society depends on what the society regards as most respectable or most worthy of admiration."[17]
> John Fielding

> "There is an 'oughtness' in the moral law. It is not the power of doing what we like but being able to do what we ought."[20]
> Lord Acton

NATIONAL PURPOSE

....
REVIEW
Q. Discuss Dr. Menninger's view that "love is the medicine for the sickness of the world."
Q. What does Dr. Sadler mean when he says we need to live in a Christian way?
Q. Dr. E. Stanley Jones defines unchristian attitudes and how they lead to sickness. What does this information tell us? (See Romans 2:14-15.)

Q. What would happen if a nation and its citizens embraced "natural law" including the Law of Christ (The Beatitudes)?

Q. Describe someone you know who continually exhibits "truth" in his or her character.

Character for Life

GOD'S PROMISE:

"I can do everything (including being a truthful person committed to truth) through him (Jesus) who gives me strength" (Philippines 4:13).

GOD'S GOAL:

Help you see that living truthfully is what God desires.

YOUR COMMITMENT:

Choose to live a life of truth.

YOUR DAILY RESPONSE:

1. Understanding that no one in the world is easier to get to than God. Only one thing prevents us from getting there—the refusal to tell ourselves the truth.

2. Realizing that every person is so constituted that at times his longing for truth is insatiable. It is not sufficient to long for the truth, because if we are honest, we know that we are driven to it. If for one moment we have discerned the truth, we can never be the same again.

3. Understanding that truth is not a system, not a constitution, even a creed. The truth is the Lord Jesus Christ Himself!

4. Believing that Jesus holds the truth about the Father just as He is the way to the Father. He is Truth, not just the one who proclaims it (Oswald Chambers).

FAILURE WILL MEAN:

Blind sightedness! Without Christ's truth, no person can please God. God has created each person with an innate longing for Him. Those who say they do not need to believe in God are only fooling themselves into a lost eternity.

BACKGROUND:

Living in truth doesn't mean living a perfect life. Professor Erik S. Jaffe described how a Christian should live in this way, "All normal people have within themselves, at one time or another, desires which they know they ought not to gratify. The difference, by-and-large between those who live moral and those who live immoral lives, is that the former refuse to indulge their passions merely because they have them. By habitually doing what is right, and by habitually abstaining from what is wrong, the bad passions gradually lose their power, and the good ones become increasingly pleasant."[21]

1. Remember Jesus and His sufferings for His righteous decisions. 2. Recognize His presence and approval will be yours as you stand alone for righteousness. 3. In the end, your commitment will bring honor to God and blessing to others. 4. Realize there is a price to pay and be willing to pay it.

FAILURE WILL MEAN:
You will constantly be defensive and blaming others for their attacks on you.

BACKGROUND
Behind the world "system" is the "prince of the world" or Satan himself. People who live in Satan's kingdom or do not have the love of God in their lives can mistreat believers. Most of the terrible persecution throughout church history has come from religious people. Often formal Christianity is a great enemy of faithful believers.

LIVING BY THE TRUTH MEANS . . .

- Knowing the truth about God.
- Preserving social harmony.
- Shunning ignorance.
- Doing good and avoiding evil.
- Remembering that all men are created equal.
- Doing unto others as you would have them do unto you.
- Condemning theft and adultery.
- Suffering rather than doing injustice.
- Remembering that families must be sustained.
- Being honest with the facts we know.
- Realizing that eternity has been put on our heart by our Creator.
- Insisting that children be protected from harm and be given a proper education.
- Pledging not to destroy life or commit suicide.
- Maintaining that homosexuality is contrary to scripture.
- Remember that "Moral Law", "the Beatitudes" and "godly virtues" are the foundations of a nation.

Chapter One: Learning more about Aquinas

Go to an Internet search engine.

Type in *Thomas Aquinas' Character.*

Find topics 1-7 below and open up the websites.

1. The Philosophy of Thomas Aquinas
2. Thomas Aquinas
3. Jacques Maritan Center of God and His Creatures
4. St. Thomas Aquinas' Five Ways
5. St. Thomas Aquinas
6. Aquinas and the Big Bang
7. St. Thomas Aquinas and Sola Scriptures Commentary on John

chapter 2
Wisdom—Isaac Newton

PURPOSE: Discovering the Right Use of Knowledge

character trait:
Wisdom

SUBJECT:
ISAAC NEWTON
(1642-1727)

PURPOSE:
Discovering the Right Use of Knowledge

FAMOUS QUOTE:
"This most beautiful system of the sun, planets and comets could only proceed from the counsel and dominion of an intelligent and powerful Being… This Being governs all things…as Lord over all."

SCRIPTURE DOCUMENTATION:
"All the angels were standing around the throne and around the elders and the four living creatures. They fell down on their faces before the throne and worshiped God, saying: 'Amen! Praise and glory and wisdom and thanks and honor and power and strength be to our God for ever and ever. Amen!'" (Revelation 7:11-12).

PERSONALITY PROFILE

Isaac Newton had a rough start. He was born prematurely and weighed about a pound. He never knew his father, as he died three months before Isaac was born. His widowed mother was to remarry and his stepfather was not interested in having a two-year-old boy around, so young Isaac was sent to live with his grandmother for the next ten years. There is no indication of bitterness on Isaac's part toward his stepfather. He was able to move on with his life. When he started school, he was not a good student. An accident, however, brought about a dramatic turn-around in his life.

Newton never published his biblical writings but he believed that Jesus Christ was the Savior of the world. He emphasized that the Bible did not mention the word "Trinity." Newton was thought by many to be an "Arian Christian."

Newton was a generous man and gave money so Bibles could be given to the poor. He helped friends who came to him in times of financial crisis. Those who expressed a frivolous attitude toward God in his presence were rebuked. He was a national hero in England.

Newton apparently gave little thought to his own personal comforts. He never married, and his niece cared for his home. He lived to be 84 years of age.

NEWTON'S SCIENTIFIC CONTRIBUTION

In the early part of the twentieth century, Karl Popper (1902-94), a scientist, pointed out the difference between true and false science. Popper spent the early part of his life in Vienna, Austria where Marxism and Freudian psychology dominated the intellectual life. At that time, those philosophies were widely accepted as branches of natural science. The world seemed full of verifications of their theories. A Marxist couldn't open a newspaper without finding confirming evidence for his interpretation of history. Popper contrasted the methods used by Marx or Freud with Einstein. Popper maintained that Einstein presented his findings and asked other scientists to disprove it. This was true science. The alternative group looked for confirming evidence, which ultimately did not hold up.

The entire meaning of virtue was lost during the nineteenth century and the word "virtue" itself became related to a women's purity. Frederick Nietzsche and Frederick Hegel, whose philosophies resulted in great suffering to millions, in the twentieth century were, according to historian Paul Johnson, also the men responsible for introducing the concept of "values" to our culture along with the loss of focus on "virtues."[1] The number of values is limitless; virtues, however, are universal.

"[Isaac] Newton single-handedly contributed more to the development of science than any other individual. He surpassed all the gains brought about by the great scientific minds of antiquity (history) producing a scheme of the universe which was more consistent, elegant, and intuitive than any proposed before."[2] Many think that Newton was the single most important contributor to modern science and should be the "Person of the Millennium." Einstein wrote about Newton, "[He] was placed by fate at the turning point of the world's intellectual development."[3]

Was the universe created? If not, how did it get here? Dallas Willard maintains, "The whole idea of the universe popping out or coming from nothing would violate the system of law built into the universe. Order first had to exist in a mind since nothing that is designed has come to be without first existing in a mind."[4] Nothing cannot create something and order has never come from disorder. "The laws that enabled the universe to come into being spontaneously seem themselves to be the product of exceedingly ingenious design."[5]

FURTHER SCRIPTURE DOCUMENTATION:

"Now, Stephen, a man full of God's grace and power, did great wonders and miraculous signs among the people. Opposition arose, however, from the members of the Synagogue of the freedmen (as it was called)—Jews of Cyrene and Alexandria as well as the provinces of Cilicia and Asia. These men began to argue with Stephen, but they could not stand up against his wisdom or the Spirit by whom he spoke. All who were sitting in the Sanhedrin looked intently at Stephen, and they saw that his face was like the face of an angel" (Acts 6:8-10, 15).

Despite Newton's views that God created the universe, most scientists believed that the universe always has existed. Now, virtually all scientists believe in some variation of the "Big Bang theory," which proves that the universe came into existence at a definite point of time in the past. None of the atheistic views of the universe can account for the universe as it is.

In many countries, information on the "Big Bang" or "creation event" was withheld from students for decades. During the nineteenth and twentieth century, Darwinism, Nazism, Marxism and Freudianism were gaining strongholds in country after country causing irreparable damage to people and their attitudes toward God. "Academics" were building their careers on deceptive lies, which resulted in destroying the very concept that man was made "in the image of God" and has eternal value. God was unnecessary to this generation who embraced the "materialistic world view."

A. Cressy Morrison, past president of the New York Academy of Sciences, wrote a remarkable book entitled *Man Does Not Stand Alone* challenging Julian Huxley's assertion in his book *Man Stands Alone*. "The speed of the earth's rotation, the heat of the sun and its distance from the earth, the tilting of the earth giving us our seasons, the distance from the moon affecting the tides and the earth's crust, the thickness of the earth's crust, the thickness of the atmosphere, the amount of carbon dioxide and nitrogen, the emergence of man and his survival all point order out of chaos. Thus when the Supreme Being formed the universe, and created matter out of nothing, he impressed certain principles on that matter from which it can never depart, and without which it would cease to be." [7] "Upon these two foundations, the law of nature and the law of revelation, depend all human laws; that is to say, no human laws could have suffered to contradict them." [8]

During the twentieth century attitudes toward "First Cause" began to change. J. Sidlow Baxter writes, "There has been a big battle between evolutionary scientists and theologians as to the existence of a personal 'First Cause.' Science has been defeated in that battle, not so much by the theologians but by its own further discoveries. So far as I know, most front-row scientists in the geology and biology classes today would gladly admit a 'First Cause,' even in the sense of a personal God. The battle today is rather in the realm of a second cause between a mechanical and a spiritual interpretation of the universe. In a mechanical interpretation of the universe, there is no place for prayer. But the mechanical theory is wrong, if for no other reason that the Lord Jesus is necessarily right. His is the voice not merely of science, but of conscience. And He has shown us that prayer is the greatest of all the second causes which operate in the running of the world."[9]

Astronomer Hugh Ross writes, "There was a beginning to our universe. Life started rapidly on earth and not through purely random reactions. The Bible tells us (correctly) not only the time of the origin of life (at the beginning of liquid water) but also proposes the mechanisms for the origin. 'The earth brought forth life.' Life appeared on earth immediately after water."[10]

"And God said, 'Let there be an expanse between the waters to separate water from water.' So God made the expanse and separated the water under the expanse from the water above it. And it was so. God called the expanse, 'sky.' And there was morning–the second day. And God said, 'Let the water under the sky be gathered to one place, and let dry ground appear.' And it was so. God called the dry ground 'land,' and the gathered waters he called 'seas.' And God saw that it was good. Then God said, 'Let the land produce vegetation:seed-bearing plants and trees on the land that bear fruit with seed in it, according to their various kinds.' And it was so" (Genesis 1:6-11).

Newton rejected the idea of a "Divine watchmaker." A cold mechanical universe with an impersonal being behind it was not the God Newton loved and worshiped or the image he imagined. He stressed the need for "revelation" and the "revelation" was Christ and His Word.

During his lifetime Newton developed the first reflecting telescope, the particle theory of light conservation, and laid the foundation for the great law of energy conservation. He defined three laws of motion (inertia, action, and reaction). Newton highlighted a Divine simplicity that permeated nature and Scripture as one would expect from a master Creator. Sir Isaac mathematized all the physical sciences and set forth the four rules for scientific reasoning called the "universal laws of nature."

NEWTON'S INTEREST IN PROPHECY

The amazing truth is that science occupied Isaac Newton's interest for a relativity short time. "At the age of 28, Newton had grown tired of science and was engrossed in interpreting the book of Daniel which had fascinated him much of his life. He believed that the book of Daniel was pre-written history of the world and to interpret it would unlock a treasure of understanding. The book had been sealed (Daniel 12:4), and Newton believed the appointed time had arrived to break the seal. He hoped that God had chosen him to interpret it. This remarkable fact surfaced from recently discovered manuscripts of his. Newton was haunted all his life by this calling." [12]

Newton's Christ was "the Christ of unadorned Scripture, the Christ whom God revealed to men, not the Christ of reason." Newton believed that Christ was the Messiah and the Son of God. "We account the Scriptures of God to be the most sublime philosophy. I find more sure marks of authenticity in the Bible than in any profane history whatsoever. Worshiping God and the Lamb in the temple: God, for His benefaction in Creating all things, and the Lamb, for His benefaction in redeeming us with His blood. I have a fundamental belief in the Bible as the Word of God, written by men who were inspired. I study the Bible daily." [13]

Newton believed, "Truth is ever to be found in simplicity, and not in the multiplicity and confusion of things. He is the God of order and not of confusion." [14] Newton taught that miracles exist for the purpose of creating astonishment in people. They would arouse in people a sense of wonder and conviction. Pichard noted, "He did not side with those who think science and religion to be incompatible. Newton had an active Christian faith, one that might influence everything he did." [15]

As one studies the prayers of Isaac Newton, it is easy to understand how he longed to be close to God. He desired that his affections might be upon God and pictured himself as a "boy playing on a seashore, diverting himself to finding a smoother pebble or a prettier shell than ordinary, while the great ocean lay all undiscovered all the time." [16]

Said Newton, "We must believe that there is one God or supreme Monarch that we may fear and obey Him and keep His laws and give Him honor and glory. We must believe that He is the father of all things, and that He loves His people as His children that they may mutually love Him and obey Him as their father." [17]

Newton was awestruck by the wonders of God's creation. His trust was in the Bible. "For us," he taught, "there is but one God, the Father, of whom are all things and one Lord Jesus Christ, by whom are all things, and we by Him. We are to worship the Father alone as God almighty, and Jesus alone as the Lord, the Messiah, the Great King, the Lamb of God who was slain, and hath redeemed us with His blood, and made us kings and priests."[18] He taught that science shows us "what is the first cause, what power He has over us, and what benefits we receive from Him…so that our duty towards Him, as well as that towards one another, will appear to us by the light of nature."[19]

THE NECESSITY OF A GOD

Newton believed in the "necessity of a God" and that He had a propensity to action within the world and had a providential role in nature. Newton observed that, "the most beautiful system of sun, planets and comets could only proceed from the counsel and dominion of an intelligent and powerful being."[20]

His scientific truth provided us with a concept of the universe that was "sustained by God Himself, which operates according to fixed, unchanging natural laws."[21] He was the single most important contributor to the development of modern science. Isaac Newton believed that Jesus Christ was the Messiah and the Son of God. He was the Christ of Scripture whom God revealed to men. Newton's motivation of studying nature was closely tied to his desire to bring to people the knowledge of God. He wanted to teach people about God and His eternal purposes and he used science to accomplish this goal.

Newton's views were diametrically opposed to with those of Darwin. Darwin wrote, "A man who has no assured and ever-present belief in the existence of a personal God or of a future existence with retribution or reward, can have for his rule of life, as far as I can see, only to follow those impulses and instincts which are the strongest or which seem to him the best ones."[22]

Darwin's doctrine denies that a supernatural being could, in any way, influence natural events or communicate with people. This doctrine tells us that the universe was not created—it evolved. So did the animals and plants that inhabit it, including our human selves, mind and soul, as well as brain and body—so did religion. Darwin provided a "creation story" for the materialistic worldview, something those who embraced the eternal view of the universe desperately needed.

NATIONAL PURPOSE

"God, in the beginning formed matter in solid; massy, hard, impenetrable, movable particles, of such sizes and figures, and with such other properties, and in such proportion to space, as most conduced to the end for which he formed them." [23]

Isaac Newton

Modern science is currently defined through a "Darwinian world view." This is an eternal tragedy for the human race and for individuals. For centuries mankind looked to creation and were in awe of the Creator. Today people stare at the miracles God has given us without the thought of God coming into their minds. Believers can really enjoy creation since it is a gift from God. Falling short of this response will lead us into "Pantheism" and idolatry.

Newton believed that the very orderliness and design of the universe spoke of God's awesome majesty and wisdom. The design of the eye required a perfect understanding of optics, and the design of the ear required a knowledge of sounds.

A LIST OF SINS

Newton would make lists of his sins. For example, "Not living to my beliefs; not loving Thee for Thy self; Not loving Thee for Thy goodness to Us; Not longing for Thee; Not fearing Thee so as to offend Thee; Fearing man above Thee." [24] His practice of the faith he embraced far exceeded those in the Anglican Church he attended. Without the "wisdom of God" which comes from the Bible, man is without understanding concerning the nature of reality. He is left to his own imagination, experience or resources to determine how to live. Newton believed what is found in Proverbs 1:7, "The fear (deep reverence) of the LORD is the beginning of knowledge."

BELIEVING GOD'S WORDS

Newton believed in miracles. He also believed in the prophecies of the Bible and wrote exhaustively on them. Against the advice of his peers, he was devoted to studying the Bible. It was after fifteen years of devotion to studying Scripture that most of his well-known scientific breakthroughs took place.

Newton accepted the Bible's account of Creation and spent his life studying the "Book of God" (the Bible) and the "Book of Nature" (God's Creation). He believed that whatever was revealed in the "Book of Nature" was harmonious with what was unfolded in the "Book of God." In later editions of his scientific works he expressed a strong sense of God's providential role in "nature."

HIS KINGDOM COME

Newton believed history was under the dominion of the Creator and prophecy showed how the Creator was to bring His Kingdom to earth. God not only created the world but remained in dominion over the universe and had a "propensity to action" within the world.

Roger Cotes, Newton's biographer, wrote that "Matter does not exist except by divine will. The whole world with all its diversity, could arise from nothing but the perfectly free will of God directing and presiding over all."[25]

Said Newton, "Having searched and by the grace of God obtained, after knowledge of the Prophetic Scriptures, I have thought myself bound to communicate it for the benefit of others, remembering the judgment of him who hid his talent in a napkin. For, I am persuaded that this will prove of great benefit (to Christians). For it was revealed to Daniel that the prophecies concerning the last times should be closed up and sealed until the time of the end, but then, the wise should understand, and knowledge should be increased" (Daniel 12:4, 9-10).

Many today see Newton as introducing the "Age of the Enlightenment." Newton exhorted people to study the prophecies. "If they (the biblical prophecies) are never to be understood, to what end did God reveal them? Certainly he did it for the edification of the church; and if so, then it is certain that the church shall at length attain to the understanding thereof. But search the Scriptures thyself and that by frequent reading and constant meditation upon what thou readest, and prayer to God to enlighten thine understanding if thou desirest to find the truth."[26]

On the subject of prophecies Newton writes, "Now considering that prophecies concerning our Savior's first coming were of more difficult interpretation, yet God rejected the Jews for not attending better to them. And whither they will believe or not, there are greater judgments at hand over Christians for their remissness then ever the Jews ever felt. But the world loves to be deceived, they will not understand, they never consider equally, but are wholly led by prejudice, interest, the praise of men, and the authority of the Church they live in: as it is plain because all parties keep close to the Religion they have been brought up in, and yet in all parties there are wise and learned as well as fools and ignorant."[27]

PREMISES FOR CHRISTIAN VIRTUES

Character and virtues must be rooted in a person who comes from outside our existence to show us the way to live. We must have a correct "worldview." The Scriptures tell us that God is "personable" and "knowable." With his "theory of relativity" and "general relativity," Einstein proved that a Creator was necessary to bring the universe into existence.

NATIONAL PURPOSE

Isaac Newton did not seek nor did he need the praises of man. "This is the guise of the world, therefore trust it not, nor value their censures and contempt. But rather consider it that it is the wisdom of God that His Church should appear despicable to the world to try the faithful. For this end He made it a curse under the Law to hang upon a tree that the scandal of the Cross might be a trial to the Jews; and for a like Trial of the Christians he hath suffered the Apostasy of the later times."[28]

"Wherefore then thou art convinced, be not ashamed to profess the truth but profess it openly and endeavor to convince thy Brother also that thou mayest inherit at the resurrection the promise made in Daniel."[29]

"Those who are wise will shine like the brightness of the heavens, and those who lead many to righteousness, like the stars for ever and ever" (Daniel 12:3).

"God who best knows the capacity of men does withhold His mysteries from the wise and prudent of this world and reveal them unto babes. They were not the Scribes and Pharisees but the inferior people that believed on Christ and apprehended the true meaning of His Parables and of the prophecies in the Old Testament concerning Him. The wise men of the world are often too much entangled in designs for this life. And God, who intended this Prophecy chiefly for their sake is able to fit their understanding to it. And it is the gift of God and not of human wisdom so to understand and to believe it."[30]

REVIEW
Q. How is "wisdom" important in your life right now?
Q. What evidence of design does Creation provide?
Q. Why do you think movements rooted in atheism did not accept new evidence for the probability of God as being the "first cause" in Creation?
Q. How did Darwinism change the world?
Q. What is the difference between wisdom and knowledge?
Q. What is needed to have a correct view of reality?
Q. How does Newton compare the Bible with other books?
Q. Discuss Newton's thoughts on the seashore as a boy. What is he trying to tell us?

Character for Life

GOD'S PROMISE:

"For I (Jesus) will give you words and wisdom that none of your adversaries will be able to resist or contradict" (Luke 21:15).

GOD'S GOAL:

To give you godly wisdom.

YOUR COMMITMENT:

Choose to live by God's wisdom.

YOUR DAILY RESPONSE:

1. A wise person makes his or her daily choices and applies God's true wisdom to life.

2. In order to be wise a person must approach life with deep awe and reverence for God.

3. A wise person must willingly submit to the Lordship of Jesus Christ.

4. A person who lives by God's wisdom is concerned with how his or her life is lived. Only when our lives are oriented to God and His revealed viewpoint can we be considered "wise."

FAILURE WILL MEAN:

Living life foolishly. Jesus said, "Therefore everyone who hears these words of mine and puts them into practice is like a wise man who built his house on the rock" (Matthew 7:24). The foolish man built his house on the sand and when the storms came, it fell down. Those who don't live by God's wisdom will see their lives crumble around them when life's storms approach.

BACKGROUND:

Jesus' presence in our lives produces true wisdom! The Bible promises, "If any of you lacks wisdom, he should ask God, who gives generously to all without finding fault, and it will be given to him" (James 1:5). Science is now in accord with the Scriptures that the universe required a first cause or a Creator. Modern man has thus far been unwilling to see the implications of this fact, having enshrined his own opinions of himself, and has decided to ignore evidence to the contrary. The Creator of the universe has revealed Himself in history as also being "a Redeemer" who has come to reconcile us to Himself.

LIVING WISELY MEANS . . .

■ Seeing the wisdom in the life of Jesus Christ as shown to us in the Bible.

■ Viewing everything as Jesus did—from the viewpoint of His Father.

■ Acting upon the Word of God.

■ Allowing God to speak through us to others.

■ Filling our minds with God's Word.

Chapter Two: Learning more about Newton

Go to an Internet search engine.
Type in *Isaac Newton's Wisdom*.
Find topics 1-3 below and open up the websites.
1. Isaac Newton by the Ocean of Truth
2. Wilson's Almanac Free Dailyezine Sir Isaac Newton
3. Sir Isaac Newton/Study Archived The Preterist Archive

Go to the Internet search engine again.
Type in *Isaac Newton and Jesus Christ*.
Find topics 1-2 below and open up the websites.
1. Sir Isaac Newton and the Rapture
2. Commentary, Observation on Daniel and the Apocalypse of St. John.

chapter 3
The Golden Rule

HUGO GROTIUS

PURPOSE: Discovering the Law of Love

character trait:

The Golden Rule

SUBJECT:
HUGO GROTIUS
(1583-1645)

PURPOSE:
Discovering the Law of Love

FAMOUS QUOTE:
"He knows not how to rule a kingdom, that cannot manage a Province, nor can he wield a Province, that cannot order a city, nor can he order a city, that knows not how to regulate a village, that cannot guide a family; nor can that man govern well a family that knows not how to govern himself."

SCRIPTURE DOCUMENTATION:
"For to us a child is born, to us a son is given, and the government will be on his shoulders. And he will be called Wonderful Counselor, Mighty God, Everlasting Father, Prince of Peace" (Isaiah 9:6).

"Make every effort to live in peace with all men and to be holy; without holiness no one will see the Lord" (Hebrews 12:14).

PERSONALITY PROFILE

Born April 10, 1583 to a family of educators, Hugo Grotius started composing Latin at age 8. His father was the Curator at the University of Leyden in Holland. Early in his life, it was clear to others that Grotius was a child prodigy. He began to study at the university at age 11. He received his doctorate at age 15 and was admitted to the bar in 1599 at the age of 16. The King of France referred to him as "the miracle of Holland." He was appointed attorney general in Holland at age 27.

Groitus struggled with the Calvinists in Holland all his life. He was arrested in a theological dispute and sentenced to life in prison. Grotius was willing to lay his life down for a cause he believed in. He suffered the consequences of going to prison and spent years running for his life. In prison he wrote a book (similar to Pilgrim's Progress) to encourage "believers." He was married to Marie van Reigersberch and they had four children. Wherever Grotius traveled, his family came with him. His persecution made it necessary to travel from country to country, just to stay alive. With the help of his wife, he escaped from prison in a chest that was supposed to have been filled with books. He fled to Belgium and eventually to France. As a result of his being sentenced to prison, he lost his property.

He lived with his family in Paris, but in poverty. In 1631, he left Paris to return to Holland and a bounty was put on him of 2,000 guilders. He then moved to Sweden and became the Swedish Ambassador to Paris after finding favor with the king. Apparently the king of Sweden had a copy of Grotius' book on the "Rights of War and Peace" under his pillow when he was a soldier during the war and knew of Grotius' writings. Upon the king's death, he commissioned Grotius as an Ambassador and sent him to help negotiate a treaty to end the Thirty Year War. Grotius died August 28, 1645 en route to visit his ill wife.

The real impact of the life of Hugo Groitus was felt a century after his death. His influence on America may have been greater than his efforts of lasting peace in Europe. Grotius paid a big price for his beliefs—his freedom was taken away from him; he lost his ability to support his family financially; and he fled from his country a hated man. Hugo Grotius was a man of undeniable piety and great learning. He was also a moralist and an advocate of religious idealism. His ideas of the unification of mankind, religious and otherwise, did not find acceptance in Holland. He was hated for his moral and religious views in his own country, but they did find acceptance in America. Politicians, such as Richelieu, supported the concept of the "right of the strongest" and were not at all interested in Grotius' conviction that no attack should be made on another country for the nation's own profit.

INTERNATIONAL LAW

The role of religion was to supply the moral sanction of legal obligations between states. The Bible was to be the basis for settling disputes among nations so that justice (peace, freedom and equity) could be maintained. Grotius argued "that the liberty of the sea is essential to the right of nations to communicate with each other and that no nation can monopolize ocean highways because of the immensity of the sea and its lack of stability and fixed limits."[1]

Prior to these arguments, however, Grotius became a member of counselors of the "Armenian Party" in Holland. Even today he is known as the "Father of International Law." Grotius conceived of international law as a set of rules governing people in communities and believed that the laws of war were based on the premise of "natural law principles." He produced his famous work, "On the Law of War and Peace" in which he divided his content between biblical quotes and the writings of classical authors and made references to about 120 different classical writers—Cicero being his favorite classical author. He also advocated the "Sovereignty of Provinces within a Nation." His greatest works were theological works and he later produced a book entitled, "A Defense of Christianity." He also wrote "The Truth of the Christian Religion." Grotius helped form the concept of an international society—a community joined together by the notion that states and rulers have rules that apply to all and that they must work together for peace.

Grotius' basic propositions remain the necessary requirements for international order. With his "laws of peace," he

FURTHER SCRIPTURE DOCUMENTATION:

"For, whoever would love life and see good days must keep his tongue from evil and his lips from deceitful speech. He must turn from evil and do good; he must seek peace and pursue it" (1 Peter 3:10-11).

"I have told you these things, so that in me you may have peace. In this world you will have trouble. But take heart! I have overcome the world" (John 16:33).

> "Jesus began his life in a borrowed stable in which he was born, and which was to include a borrowed boat from which he preached, the borrowed houses he lived in while on his travels, the borrowed donkey on which he entered Jerusalem, and the borrowed grave in which he was buried. The life that began in a borrowed womb ended in a borrowed tomb."[2]
>
> Derek Frank

presented to the world the ideal conception of a family of nations, united under the Sovereignty of God, in a commonwealth of mankind. Grotius must be regarded as one of the chief expounders of the basic ideas that are contained in documents like the League of Nations Covenant, the United Nations Charter, and the United Nations Declaration of Human Rights. Both Grotius and Woodrow Wilson (who was a disciple of Grotius) believed that "only a peace between equals shall last."[3]

GROTIUS' PASSION FOR PEACE BETWEEN NATIONS

■ The conviction that the nations of the world must find ways to care for each other

Grotius sought to be a peacemaker between nations and even tried to unite Christians in one church under a "holy reformation." His passion was justice based on the Revelation of God. Grotius writes, "I saw the whole Christian world a license of fighting at which even barbarous nations might blush. Wars were begun on trifling pretexts or none at all, and carried on without any reference of law, divine or human."[4]

Grotius prayed, "May God, who alone hath the power, inscribe these teachings on the hearts of those who hold sway over the Christian world. May He grant to them a mind possessing knowledge of divine and human law, and having ever before it the reflection that it had been chosen as a servant for the rule of man, the living thing most dear to God."[5]

Many Christians believe that since Christ has called us to be "peacemakers," the role Jesus had in mind should not be limited to families and churches or even local, state, or national governments. If Christians are not involved in "peace-building" between nations it is likely that secular principles will replace biblical principles. Grotius' faith in the orderliness of the world was basic to his worldview founded in theology and law.

Grotius decided to draw from both classical and biblical authority seeking to provide a construct (he put together several ideas in an orderly way) for modern statesmen. Grotius seemed called to discover how nations could get along with each other. "It may seem impossible for any state so long to subsist unless it were upheld by a constant particular care for the power of a divine hand. If authorities issue any order that is contrary to the law of nature, or to the commandments of God, the order should not be carried out."[6]

■ The conviction to associate "natural law" with other Old and New Testament Scriptures, the Ten Commandments, Beatitudes and the "Golden Rule" of Jesus

Both Montesquieu and Grotius linked "natural law" to Scripture. "The Ten Commandments and the Golden Rule are both expressions of the natural law commanded in the Scripture."[7] Grotius made an effort not only to associate natural law with both "Old and New Testament Scripture" but he also equated "Natural law with the Golden Rule of Jesus." He insisted, "The Ten Commandments (the moral Law) and the Law of Christ (the Beatitudes) would both provide common knowledge and serve the nations of the earth." Both knew that reason without revelation would ultimately turn to speculation.

Grotius saw that the function of the "Law of Christ" (the moral law) was to lead man to the second state—the Beatitudes. Grotius introduced a new way for nations to relate to each another—a way not based on "self-interest" or "might determines right," but on the Golden Rule to "Do unto others what you would have them do unto you" and "Love your neighbor as yourself" (Matthew 22:39) principles. Nations, he hoped, would function on the "law of love."

While most Christians are not "pacifists" and believe in the right of self-defense and the prevention of evil, Christians should stand behind the founders belief in the "law of the nations" based on the "golden rule."

My many trips to the former Soviet Union have brought both joy and sorrow to my life. A heart surgeon who had a "two pack a day" habit of smoking cigarettes was comforted by the fact that he was purchasing American cigarettes, since in his estimate, they were safer. As an American who believes in the "law of the nations," I feel angered toward American manufacturers who undermine the health of other countries through their global advertising. Further, I don't believe we as Americans have the right to undermine the "morals" of other countries through the distribution of pornography or immoral television programs. For years "Baywatch" has been the most popular television program in many countries of the world. Is this what the Founders had in mind?

"The Laws of Nature" (included in the Beatitudes) existed before civil government, thus the laws of God transcend the

James Madison, the fourth president of the United States called Grotius, "The father of the moral code of the nations."

NATIONAL PURPOSE

NATIONAL PURPOSE ▶

laws of states and nations. The view was that the "rights to life, liberty, and property were possessed in the state of nature (a basic harmony of interests that exist between human beings), not gifts of the state."[8]

■ The conviction that the nations needed secondary "Laws of Nature" or written agreements to exist between them

Groitus believed in a "primary law of nations" that was applicable to men and nations and in a "secondary law" which was defined in written pacts and agreements between states and in the established custom of those states. Primary laws of nature are laws that completely express the will of God. Secondary laws of nature are rules and laws that lie within reason. He believed that all rulers and states must submit to these laws.

Divine laws (which are eternal) are created directly by God; this law proceeds from God; it is approved by the common consent of all mankind. Some say that Grotius drew his universal rules from "right reason" rather than the fact that man was made in "the image of God." To bring unity among the nations, his intention for law was to write of it as "independent of religions opinions." He knew that "right reason" depends upon a clear, clean conscience and an accurate view of reality. This false dependence upon "reason" became its downfall.

Arthur F. Holms, professor of philosophy at Wheaton College writes that during the age of Grotius and Locke, "Man was standing on the brink of the most intensive, detailed observation of the creation yet undertaken by our race. The age of science was just around the corner and the intoxicating quality of the things man discovered during these three centuries of exploding knowledge is significant for man's restless fallen nature seeks a way of explaining himself and his circumstances while avoiding the Creator of that self and those circumstances."[10]

Grotius' famous book "The Law of War and Peace" was a breakthrough in relationships between nations. Wars in Europe had brought the nations into great peril. There were few enlightened leaders. "Although a Christian, Grotius relied far less on biblical arguments than was common for the time. Instead, he showed from Christian and heathen history how good men of all ages had been merciful and kept faith in international affairs."[11] Three years after his death the "Peace of Westphalia" which took place in 1648, embodied many of the principles set forth by Grotius.

■ The conviction that the Christian religion was the turning point in history

"Multiculturalism" prevails in the United Nations today so the ideas of Grotius have, for the most part, been rendered mute. Grotius believed that the Christian religion was the turning point in history. Its significance was in the fact that God finally revealed Himself to the individual, the nation, and the whole community of mankind. With his 'law of peace' Grotius presented to the world the ideal conception of a family of nations, united under a Sovereign God in a commonwealth of mankind. As a devout Christian, Grotius longed for the day when the majority of the people in the world would become Christians and follow the words of Micah. "Nation will not take up sword against nation, nor will they train for war anymore" (Micah 4:3b). He believed that one day the biblical prophecies would be fulfilled. He said that the "coming of Jesus Christ shattered the 'wall of separation' between Gentiles and the Jews because it offered all humankind a means of salvation."[12]

The convictions of Grotius had a powerful influence on 'America's founders' and future presidents, such as President Woodrow Wilson. Wilson was convinced that "friendship is the only cement that will ever hold the world together. Interest does not bind men together; interest separates men. There is only one thing that can bind men together, and that is common devotion to right."[14]

"It is not in the still calm of life, or there pose of the pacific station, that great characters are formed, great necessities call out great virtue."[13]
Abigal Adams

NATIONAL PURPOSE

REVIEW

Q. Is it possible to have peace between nations without some reference to a higher authority and truth?

Q. Are the ideas of Grotius familiar to you in the twenty-first century?

Q. Was Groitus a realist or an idealist?

Q. What impressed you about Grotius' life?

Q. What are some of the reasons the nations didn't wish to embrace his principles?

Q. What hindrances are there to these ideas being implemented today?

Q. How is "peacemaking" an extension of our relationship with God?

Q. Describe someone in whose life you see the heart of a peacemaker.

Character for Life

GOD'S PROMISE:

"I have told you these things, so that in me you may have peace. In this world you will have trouble. But take heart! I have overcome the world" (John 16:33).

GOD'S GOAL:

For you to live peacefully with others.

YOUR COMMITMENT:

Live a life of peace and strive to promote harmony as much as possible among those around you.

YOUR DAILY RESPONSE:

Living so as to gain the three blessings that come to those who have Jesus, the Prince of Peace, in their lives.

1. Realize that as Christians we have been given Jesus' peace and have been made righteous before God. "Therefore, since we have been justified through faith, we have peace with God through our Lord Jesus Christ" (Romans 5:1).

2. Understand that in addition to righteousness, we have been given peace and joy. "For the kingdom of God is not a matter of eating and drinking, but of righteousness, peace and joy in the Holy Spirit" (Romans 14:17).

3. Know that it is essential to get along with other believers, as well as to offer God's message of peace to others. "Make every effort to live in peace with all men and to be holy; without holiness no one will see the Lord" (Hebrews 12:14).

FAILURE WILL MEAN:

War! This war will be between ourselves and God, ourselves and others, and ultimately nations upon nations. Only with Jesus can we find lasting peace.

BACKGROUND:

Jesus demonstrated peace in His life and ministry by breaking down the wall that existed between people. "For he himself is our peace, who has made the two one, and has destroyed the barrier, the dividing wall of hostility (Ephesians 2:14). In Jesus Christ, God reconciled to Himself those who repented of their sin. "For God was pleased to have all his fullness dwell in him, and through him to reconcile to himself all things, whether things on earth or things in heaven, by making peace through his blood, shed on the cross" (Colossians 1:19-20). Because of Jesus, God's peace can now continually rule and control our hearts. "Let the peace of Christ rule in your hearts, since as members of one body you were called to peace. And be thankful" (Colossians 3:15).

LIVING THE GOLDEN RULE MEANS . . .

Following Life's Twelve Commitments:

■ Healthy are those who live their lives in dependence upon God.

■ Healthy are those who mourn over their own sin and the wrongs of the world.

■ Healthy are those of a gentle spirit, not lording it over others.

■ Healthy are those who hunger and thirst to see right prevail—those who care about the wrongs in the world and do something about it.

■ Healthy are those who show compassion, forgive, and are sensitive to others.

■ Healthy are the pure in heart, mind, and body who make God their most important relationship.

■ Healthy are the peacemakers—those who bring about peace between God and man.

■ Healthy are those who suffer insults and accept them without "self-pity."

■ Healthy are those who hear the Word of God and obey it.

■ Healthy are those who have confidence in God and His character.

■ Healthy are those who revere God and turn from sin.

■ Healthy are those who put the interests of God and others before their own.

E. Stanley Jones, 1–8 / Don Hawkinson, 9–12

Chapter Three: Learning more about Grotius

Go to an Internet search engine.
Type in *Hugo Grotius' Character*.
Find topics 1-6 below and open up the websites.
1. Hugo Grotius Study archive
2. Hugo Grotius
3. PDF Hugo Grotius
4. Hugo Grotius and the Natural Law Tradition
5. Virtue Theory (Internet Encyclopedia of Philosophy)
6. Moral Character

chapter 4

Dependence on God—fanny crosby

PURPOSE: Meeting the God Who Keeps on Giving

character Trait:
Dependence on God

SUBJECT:
FANNY CROSBY
(1820-1915)

PURPOSE:
Meeting the God Who Keeps on Giving

FAMOUS QUOTE:
"I never undertake a hymn without first asking the good Lord to be my inspiration."

SCRIPTURE DOCUMENTATION:

"Blessed are the poor in spirit, for theirs is the kingdom of heaven" (Matthew 5:3).

"You have made known to me the paths of life; (the Beatitudes) you will fill me with joy in your presence" (Acts 2:28).

"Listen to me, O house of Jacob, all you who remain of the house of Israel, you whom I have upheld since you were conceived, and have carried since your birth. Even to your old age and gray hairs I am he, I am he who will sustain you. I have made you and I will carry you; I will sustain you and I will rescue you" (Isaiah 46:3-4).

Crosby was born in New York into a family of strong Puritan ancestry on March 24, 1820. Crosby was to know more than her share of suffering. Sadly, her father died when Fanny was only an infant. While in the fields he caught cold and became chilled. He became gravely ill and died within a few days. Fanny's mother lived until the age of ninety-one and her grandmother was one-hundred-and-three. Fanny was able to take pride in the fact that her great-grandfather fought in the revolutionary war. Her grandmother was a woman of prayer and taught her to believe in the goodness of God in all things. "Our God in heaven will always give us what is for our own good." It was Fanny's grandmother who invested in her Christian training. Fanny learned to sing at her grandmother's rocking chair. It was her grandmother who taught her the importance of prayer.

As a baby, Fanny Crosby caught a slight cold in her eyes when the family physician was out of town. Another doctor, who proved not to be qualified to practice medicine, was called in to care for her. He prescribed hot mustard poultices to be applied in her eyes. It destroyed her eyesight and changed the entire direction of her life. The doctor fled town over the incident and eventually proved to be a fraud. God was able to use this tragedy, however, for His amazing purposes. Through her entire life Fanny was never known to express resentment toward this doctor. Praise and worship of God became a way of life; Fanny refused to sulk.

Eventually, due to her blindness, Fanny's family placed her in an orphanage. The children and staff of the orphanage became her family. At the age of 15, she moved to the New York Institution for the blind. At the institute, lessons were given to the blind students by reading and lectures. In her day, people viewed blind people as not capable of learning a great deal. It would be 15 years before the development of the Braille system was widespread. As a pupil and teacher, Fanny spent 35 years at the school. She insisted that a blind person could accomplish almost everything a sighted person could and set out to prove she was right. June Gothberg tells us, "She was a remarkable musician and learned to play the guitar, piano and eventually became an outstanding harpist." [1]

Christian hymns played a large part in shaping the virtues of America. Crosby was far more than a hymn writer and poet. Her life was given to others and she lived for her Savior.

CROSBY'S HYMNS

It appears Fanny "wrote over 8,500 hymns during her life and actually published more than 2,000 hymns."[2] She published her first poem at the age of 11. She was a pupil and then a teacher at the New York Institution for the Blind. As an adult, she met with presidents, generals, and other dignitaries. She dedicated her life to the poor and the needy in society. She charged $2.00 for a hymn, which was given to the work of the poor. Her goal was to serve others before herself. At the age of 92, she enjoyed her first visit to Harvard. Over 100 million copies of her songs were printed. Fanny was asked to sing and play at President Grant's funeral. She performed before Presidents and even addressed Congress on different occasions. Her mother came from earnest and devout people, noted for their longevity and she was able to do various jobs to provide for the family.

It may seem strange to propose that a blind song writer would be one of a select few who would help shape the virtues of America, but it is true. From the Civil War until the end of the twentieth century, America suffered not only wars, but also years of depression, deep suffering, and division. People of faith always had a song "to see them through the darkest night." Fanny Crosby was one of the great songwriters whose hymns turned the hearts of Americans to their source of strength.

Most of us would agree that sightless citizens would be more inclined to acknowledge their dependence upon God. Fanny Crosby was blind and knew experientially how dependent she was upon God. She became an amazing vessel God used to touch the hearts of generations.

FAITH AND SERVICE

Crosby realized that the enemy of the soul of all mankind (Satan) could use her blindness to drive her away from God. Instead of giving in to the suggestion that God had mistreated her and should not have allowed the terrible thing to happen, Fanny embraced her loss of sight and it resulted in blessing millions of people. "I have always believed from my

> "it seemed
> intended by the
> blessed providence
> of god that i
> should be blind all
> my life, and i
> thank him for the
> dispensation. if
> perfect earthly
> sight were offered
> me tomorrow i
> would not accept
> it. i might not have
> sung hymns to the
> praise of god if i
> had been
> distracted by the
> beautiful and
> interesting things
> about me."[6]
> crosby

NATIONAL PURPOSE ▶

youth…that the good Lord in his infinite mercy, by this means consecrated me to the work that I am still permitted to do."[3] She prayed that a million people would come to know her Savior through her hymns. Fanny knew there was no character development without suffering.

Affliction is the way God produces Agape love. Suffering, when embraced, revealed the character of Jesus in Fanny's life. At the age of 27, Fanny came to know God the way her grandmother had known Him. Her biographer Basil Miller records her words, "For the first time I realized that I had been trying to hold the world in one hand and the Lord in the other."[4] God became very real to her.

In 1858, Fanny married Alexander Van Alstine, a former pupil at the Institute. Alexander was a remarkable organist and their lives were blended together in ministry. Tragically, they lost their only child. Their marriage lasted 44 years until they were separated by death when Fanny died in 1915 of a massive brain hemorrhage.

Fanny would write as many as six or seven hymns each day with the goal of bringing the gospel to others. A biographer wrote, "There was probably no writer in her day who appealed more to the valid experience of the Christian life or who expressed more sympathetically the deep longings of the human heart than Fanny Crosby."[5]

Others went further, insisting she was the greatest song writer in the history of Christianity. Ira Sankey, who worked with Dwight L. Moody, said that the success of their evangelical campaigns was due largely to Fanny's hymns.

In the eighteenth century, Charles Wesley's hymns prepared the country for the hardships it was to go through. It was Fanny Crosby, however, who was the most well-known hymn writer of the nineteenth and twentieth century. God used them both in a mighty way to touch the hearts of Americans through hymns inspired by the Holy Spirit. A few of the songs Fanny wrote include:

"Tell Me the Story of Jesus,"
"To God Be the Glory,"
"Blessed Assurance,"
"Near the Cross,"
"Redeemed," and
"Saved By Grace."

FANNY CROSBY'S PASSIONS AND CONVICTIONS AND DEPENDENCE UPON GOD SHOWED...

■ A deep love for the Scriptures and desire to do God's will

"If I had a choice, I would still choose to remain blind…for when I die, the first face I will ever see will be the face of my blessed Savior." In her prayer life Fanny learned that she "must be careful not to ask Him for anything not consistent with His holy will."[7]

When asked about her longevity, her secret was that she guarded her taste, her temper, and her tongue. A famous saying through the years was, "Don't waste any sympathy on me. I am the happiest person alive."[8]

■ A commitment to memorize Scripture

Fanny recalls the kindness of a Mrs. Hawley who had no children of her own, "She became deeply interested in me, and under her supervision I acquired a thorough knowledge of the Bible."[10] Her tutor set Scripture memorization goals for Fanny of up to five chapters to memorize each week.

■ The conviction that God knew what was best for her life

In her day, Fanny observed that people were looking for a lighter, friendlier sound than the stern hymns of their parents and grandparents. She sought to write music for the masses. When writing a hymn, she would ask the Lord to give her the thoughts and feelings to help her write the hymn. Fanny realized that anything lasting would need to come from God and her intimacy with Jesus. Many of her hymns are characterized by this intimacy with Jesus as the hymns are sung to Him and were written in the first person.

Fanny gave herself to the urban poor of New York City. She lived her life selflessly and cared for people who had lost their way. Her missionary work continued almost until her death in 1915. She regularly visited the Bowery Mission where her music spread to widely touch millions of lives. One such person was a man who told her the following story: "Miss Crosby, I was the boy, who told you more than thirty-five years ago that I had wandered from my mother's God. The evening that you spoke at the mission I sought and found

"My love for the Holy Bible and its sacred truth is stronger and more precious to me at ninety than at nineteen."[9] Crosby

peace, and I have tried to live a consistent Christian life ever since."[11] It was hard for those who met Fanny to feel sorry for themselves. People saw the joy she experienced, even with her disability. Fanny sought out the wounded people and her songs spoke to their deep needs.

THE POOR IN SPIRIT

Today we tend to rely on government legislation to protect the moral decisions we make but it is important to realize that legislation cannot change hearts. Often we rely on medicine to prolong our lives but forget that God sustains our lives. We place our faith in financial security and forget to trust God for our needs. We act as though education and degrees guarantee our future without considering what God plans for our future. The opposite of being "poor in spirit" is being "self reliant" which is really an illusion and leads to pride, self-centeredness, or making oneself the center of the world.

Self-reliance comes out of pride and a sense of sufficiency. Prayerlessness brings us to a sense of living in the flesh and believing that, "I can do it myself!" A person who is "poor in spirit" does not rely on his or her natural or inherited gifts, but rather on God.

Jesus' teachings that seem to continually say, "Blessed are the dependent," seem as nonsense to our society. Most people spend their lives pursuing independence and think that this kind of dependence is for weak people. Jesus is saying that being dependent on Him is very appropriate. Since He is our Creator and Savior, we really are dependent upon Him for everything. The person who is "poor in spirit" is truly humble since he knows his true identity and recognizes God's authority in his life.

REVIEW

Q. Are human beings dependent or autonomous?

Q. In what ways are we dependent upon God?

Q. Describe how someone you know expresses continual dependence upon God. How does this person inspire you?

Q. If you were blind, would that make it more or less difficult to acknowledge your dependence on God?

Q. How did Crosby handle the temptation to be filled with self-pity?

Q. In what kinds of circumstances do you find yourself feeling self-pity?

Q. If a person is created by God, does that mean he or she is God's possession?

Q. What are some of the negative things we depend on to get through life?

Q. How do we develop dependencies to help us cope with pain in our lives?

Q. What do you think were some of the secrets to Crosby's remarkable life?

Q. How will being "poor in spirit" make a difference in your life?

Character for Life

GOD'S PROMISE:

People who know they have great spiritual needs are happy. "Blessed are the poor in spirit, for theirs is the kingdom of heaven" (Matthew 5:3).

GOD'S GOAL:

Acknowledge that Jesus is Lord of your life.

YOUR COMMITMENT:

Live your life in dependence upon God.

YOUR DAILY RESPONSE:

1. Acknowledge your trust and dependence upon Him.
2. Develop a grateful spirit.
3. Look to God for His solutions to problems you face.
4. Always abide in Christ.

FAILURE WILL MEAN:

You will continue to rely on yourself and not God.

BACKGROUND:

To be poor in Spirit is to be dependent on God. In reality, all you have is because of what Jesus has done for you. "For this is what the high and lofty One says—he who lives forever, whose name is holy: 'I live in a high and holy place, but also with him who is contrite and lowly in spirit, to revive the spirit of the lowly and to revive the heart of the contrite'" (Isaiah 57:15).

LIVING WITH DEPENDENCE ON GOD MEANS . . .

■ Realizing how spiritually bankrupt we are.

■ Knowing that everything we have has been given to us. We owe the fact of our origin, our temporal existence on this earth, and our future existence to the One who created and redeemed us. "'For in him we live and move and have our being.' As some of your own poets have said, 'We are his offspring'" (Acts 17:28).

■ Living without pride and self-righteousness.

■ Being submissive to God.

■ Having the spirit of a child—simple, unaffected, and teachable.

Chapter Four: Learning more about Crosby

Go to an Internet search engine.

Type in *Fanny Crosby's Life*.

Find topics 1-6 below and open up the websites.

1. Fanny Crosby's legacy of hymns is music evangelist's passion
2. Fanny Crosby
3. Postscript Fanny Crosby's music…
4. Rescue the perishing
5. Charles Wesley and Fanny Crosby Compared
6. Fanny Crosby Drama

chapter 5

Sorrow Over Sin

David Brainerd

PURPOSE: Sustaining Intimacy with God and Others

character trait:

Sorrow Over Sin

SUBJECT:
DAVID BRAINERD
(1718-1747)

PURPOSE:
Sustaining Intimacy with God and Others

FAMOUS QUOTE:
"Farewell friends and earthly comforts; farewell to the dearest, the very dearest of them all. I will spend my life to my latest moments in caves and dens of the earth, if the kingdom of Christ may thereby be advanced."

SCRIPTURE DOCUMENTATION:
"Blessed are those who mourn, for they will be comforted" (Matthew 5:4).

PERSONALITY PROFILE

Brainerd was the sixth of nine children. His father died when he was nine and his mother died when he was 14 years old, making him an orphan. At the age of 15, until he was 19, Brainerd lived with his pastor and was prepared for ministry. At the age of 22, he set aside prolonged periods of "fasting and prayer" to seek God.

In 1739, Brainerd enrolled at Yale. It was at Yale where he apparently contracted tuberculosis in his lungs. He never finished college and was expelled from school for criticizing a professor for the professor's coldness toward religion. Others sought to have him reinstated to no avail; he was unable to receive his diploma. This event could have caused Brainerd to abandon God, but instead God became his source of strength and wisdom.

After three years at Yale, Brainerd became a missionary to the Indians, under appointment of the Scottish Society for Promoting Christian Knowledge. He served as a missionary to the Stockbridge, Delaware, and Susquehana tribes of Indians. During his life he traveled 15,000 miles on horseback. His was a lonely life and he expressed this sentiment in his journal dated November 20, 1743: "I have no fellow Christian to whom I might un-bosom myself and lay open my spiritual sorrows, and with whom I might take sweet counsel in conversation about heavenly things, and join in social prayer." Brainerd struggled with incredible personal hardships and often felt cut off from other followers of Christ.

He was to be a missionary only four years. At 29 years of age, his life was drawing to a close. Jonathan Edwards took him into his house to be cared for by his daughter Jerusha, who loved Brainerd deeply. She was his nurse and constant companion. She apparently contracted tuberculosis during this time and died a few months later. His only joy was to do something for the glory of God and for the welfare of others.

THE PASSIONS AND CONVICTIONS OF DAVID BRAINERD

Brainerd's heart became captivated by the glory of Christ and His Kingdom. Many of his prayers were recorded in his journal. As his strength was diminishing, he prayed, "I was made for eternity, how I long to be with God and to bow in his presence…oh that the Redeemer may see the travail of this soul and be satisfied. Oh come, Lord Jesus! Come quickly!"[1] These were his last words on earth. His deep sorrow came from the longing that the Indians he loved were separated from the One who loved them. He grieved for God and the loss God must have felt.

Brainerd was abandoned to Jesus Christ. In his journal he wrote: "There appears to be nothing of any importance to me but holiness of heart and life and the conversion of the (Indians) to Jesus Christ. I was from my youth somewhat sober, and inclined rather to melancholy than the contrary extreme, but do not remember anything about conviction of sin…until I was about seven or eight years of age. Then I became concerned for my soul, and terrified at the thoughts of death."[2]

At 21 years of age Brainerd came to a deep awareness of his sin and his need for the Savior. He recalls, "As I was walking in a dark thick grove, unspeakable glory seemed to open to the view and apprehension of my soul. My soul was so captivated with the excellency, loveliness, greatness, and other perfections of God that I was even swallowed up in Him. Thirsting desires and longing possessed my soul after perfect holiness. God was so precious to my soul that the world with all its enjoyments appeared vile. I had no more value for the favor of men than for pebbles."[4]

BRAINERD'S JOURNAL ENTRIES

Salvation came to many Indians and resulted in them living godly lives. In his journal Brainerd wrote: "I have now baptized in all, forty-seven persons of the Indians. Twenty three adults and twenty four children…through rich grace, none of them as yet have been left to disgrace their profession of Christianity by any scandalous or unbelieving behavior."[5] Brainerd endured any hardship for the sake of bringing the Indians to Jesus. In his journal he wrote: "It is so sweet to be nothing and less than nothing."[6]

E. Myers Harrison wrote, "His [Brainerd's] love for the Indians required that he endure the lack of suitable foods, he was exposed to hunger and cold, lost in the forests, caught in

"Brainerd's life is a vivid, powerful testimony to the truth that God can and does use weak, sick, discouraged, beat-down, lonely, struggling saints, who cry to him day and night to accomplish amazing things for his glory."[3]

john piper

"The Indians thought of him as a 'prophet of God' and watched all his movements.... But when the braves drew closer to Brainerd's tent, they saw the paleface on his knees. And as he prayed, suddenly a rattlesnake slipped to his side, lifted up its ugly head to strike, flicked its forked tongue almost in his face, and then without any apparent reason, glided swiftly away into the brushwood. The Great Spirit is with the paleface!" [12]

F. W. Boreham

storms with no shelter available, obliged to forge raging streams and spend the night in the woods, in peril from wild beasts and wild savages." [7]

In Brainerd's journal, he wrote: "They all, as one, seemed in an agony of soul to obtain an interest in Christ. The more I discoursed the love and compassion of God in sending His Son to suffer for the sins of men, and the more I invited them to come and partake of His love, the more their distress was aggravated, because they felt themselves unable to come. It was surprising to see how their hearts seemed to be pierced with tender and melting invitations of the gospel, when there was not a word of terror spoken to them." [8]

An entry written in May of 1743 said: "I live poorly with regard to the comforts of life, most of my diet consists of boiled corn, hasty pudding, etc. I lodge on a bundle of straw, and my labor is hard and extremely difficult; and I have little experience of success to comfort me." [9] Brainerd suffered both physically and mentally in the wilderness. As a result of his tuberculosis, he coughed up blood and suffered physical deprivations. An entry written on July 6, 1744 said: "I long and love to be a pilgrim; and want grace to imitate the life, labors and sufferings of Paul among the heathen." [10]

Brainerd's lifelong desire was that he might be nothing, that Jesus would be everything.

In an entry dated January 2, 1744 he wrote: "We should always look upon ourselves as God's servants, placed in God's world to do His work; and accordingly labor faithful for Him. Let it then be your great concern, thus to devote yourself and your all to God. It is so sweet to be nothing and less than nothing that Christ may be my all in all." [11]

Brainerd gave himself fully to the Savior and His mission on earth. A journal entry dated November 22, 1745 said, "I have received my all from God. Oh that I could return my all to God." [13] Another entry dated June 14, 1742 said, "I set apart this day for secret fasting and prayer. Just at night the Lord visited me marvelously. I wrestled for an ingather of souls...I was in such an agony...that I was all over wet with sweat. Oh, my dear Savior did sweat blood for poor souls. I went to bed with my heart wholly set on God." [14] A separate entry dated July 21, 1744, said, "This morning about nine I withdrew to the woods for prayer. I was in such anguish that when I rose from my knees I felt extremely weak and overcome...I cared not where or how I lived, or what hardships I went through, so that I could but gain souls for Christ." [15]

"I have generally found that the more I do in secret prayer the more I have delighted to do. In seasonable, steady performance of secret duties in their proper hours, and a careful improvement of all time, filling up every hour with some profitable labor, either of head, or hands, are excellent means of spiritual peace and boldness before God."[16]

Brainerd desired to totally conform his life to that of the Lord Jesus. In his journal he wrote, "It is my fervent longing to be a flame of fire, continually glowing in the divine service, till my latest, my dying moment. Blessed Jesus, may I daily be more and more conformed to Thee. All I want is to be more holy, more like my dear Lord…that I may be fit for the blessed enjoyments and employments of the heavenly world."[17]

DAVID BRAINERD'S IMPACT ON WORLD MISSIONS

Prior to the death of David Brainerd, his friend and mentor Jonathan Edwards asked permission to make the thoughts of his journal available for the inspiration and encouragement of others.

J.M Sherwood writes, "No journal ever written has had such an impact. His story has done more to develop and mold the spirit of modern missions, and to fire the heart of the Christian Church, than that of any man since the apostolic age."[18] John Wesley admonished ministers by saying, "Let every preacher read carefully the life of David Brainerd."[20] Biographer Eugene Myers Harrison said, "It was chiefly the reading of the story of Brainerd's missionary labors that sent Henry Martyn to India and Persia and Robert McCheyne to become the Apostle to the Jews. God used Brainerd's life to open the eyes of William Carey to spread the Gospel, adding, "Brainerd was 'the pioneer of modern missionary work.'"[21]

REVIEW

Q. Do you think God gave Brainerd extraordinary revelation?

Q. Do you think one of Satan's strategies is to cut us off from other believers?

Q. Do you think he might have had a hard time getting a wife to go with him to minister to the Indians?

Q. What would motivate Brainerd to go through all these trials?

"Brainerd laid down his life for the dear Indians he sought to bring to the Lord Jesus. To him the material and physical world had little value. He was of the race of the early martyrs."[19]

E. Myers Harrison

NATIONAL PURPOSE

Q. Why do you think God used Brainerd in such a wonderful way?

Q. What do you most admire about Brainerd?

Q. When you find there is a blockage in your heart between you and God because of sin, how do you draw near to God for forgiveness and cleansing?

Q. Brainerd's mourning was often because of the sin of others. What is it that brings you the most pain in the world today?

Q. What did Brainerd find helpful to overcome the deep suffering he experienced?

Q. What did Brainerd really want to see accomplished?

Character for Life

GOD'S PROMISE:

"Blessed are those who mourn, for they will be comforted" (Matthew 5:4).

GOD'S GOAL:

For you to continually appropriate God's grace and forgiveness. A deepening love for Jesus comes through daily repentance.

YOUR COMMITMENT:

Repent daily of all known sin. Keep open to the convictions of the Holy Spirit. The Christian mourns not just over his own sin but the sin of others. He also mourns for God who is the greatest sufferer of all.

YOUR DAILY RESPONSE:

1. Ask God for a repentant heart to see sin and turn from it.

2. Make a list of those you have offended or hurt and determine to ask for appropriate forgiveness.

3. Pray that you might see sin as God sees it and turn from it.

4. Immediately confess your sin (of commission or omission to God). Don't let it control your life!

FAILURE WILL MEAN:

You will find ways to escape the conviction of the Holy Spirit.

BACKGROUND:

The world considers happy, not those who mourn, but the hedonistic and pleasure-seeking, who find "happiness" in transitory experiences. It is the one who is dissatisfied and pained by what this world has to offer who will find the comfort that is offered by a living relationship with God. When a man comes to the end of his own resources and thinking and knows only God can help him, he is in the right attitude to receive from God.

The teaching of Jesus contradicts everything in our world. Jesus is saying, "Happy are those who are sad." The world mourns because it doesn't have enough money, the right job, the right spouse, the right gift, etc. Jesus was talking about something else. If we fail to see how our sin grieves God's heart, we will start blaming others for our circumstances and acquire a hardened spirit.

LIVING A LIFE THAT SORROWS OVER SIN MEANS . . .

- Practicing daily self-examination. We see our sin as unworthy of a child of God and mourn over it.

- Receiving comfort from the Holy Spirit.

- Remembering that the Christian life is a cycle of sensing our "fallen-ness" and turning to our Father in heaven and starting over again. When we draw close to God we get upset over our sins. We mourn because we have failed Him. We just go to Him and experience His grace and comfort and forgiveness.

- We experience the blessing, joy, and peace Jesus promised.

- Living opposite of the philosophy of the world, which says "turn your back on your troubles, be as happy as you can, find ways to escape the problems you face."

- Grieving over the sins of the world.

- Knowing that our sorrow on earth will bring happiness since Jesus is coming back and sin will be banished forever.

Chapter Five: Learning more about Brainerd

Go to an Internet search engine.
Type in *David Brainerd's Character*.
Find topics 1-6 below and open up the websites.
1. Literature Character of David Brainerd
2. David Brainerd -Worldwide Mission
3. David Brainerd-Missionary Biographer Worldwide Mission
4. The Life and Diary of the Rev. David Brainerd and Notes
5. Spiritual Formation and Resources
6. The Character of a Missionary (7 qualifications)

chapter 6
Grateful & Submissive Spirit—blaise pascal

PURPOSE: Getting Above It All

character trait:
Grateful & Submissive Spirit

SUBJECT:
BLAISE PASCAL
(1623-1662)

PURPOSE:
Getting Above It All

FAMOUS QUOTE:
"The heart has its reasons which reason does not know."

SCRIPTURE DOCUMENTATION:
"Blessed are the meek, for they will inherit the earth" (Matthew 5:5).

Blaise Pascal is known as one of the great minds of Western intellectual history. He was born June 19, 1623 in Clemont, France. His mother died when he was three and his father, who was a respected mathematician, raised Blaise. His father took on the responsibility of educating Blaise and his sister. Blaise was a child prodigy and by the age of 10, was performing original experiments. At 11 years of age, young Blaise worked out on his own some of the basic propositions of Euclid, the Greek mathematician. Pascal was known for his work on the calculus of probabilities. Building later on his mathematical knowledge, he created the "theory of probability."

Between 1642 and 1644 Pascal developed a calculating machine for his father based on a series of rotating discs. The final model was finished in 1645 and some would say this was in reality the first computer. Pascal was known for other inventions as well, including the first syringe and the creation of the hydraulic press. In addition to being a mathematician, scientist, and an inventor, he became known as a Christian apologist or one who defends the faith. With his principle work, "Thoughts," Pascal confronted the skepticism of the new thinkers in Europe.

As a young man, Blaise Pascal's encounter with Jesus Christ changed the course of his life. He decided that he should abandon the idea of marriage and commit himself to the work of God. On November 23, 1654, Pascal's conversion to Jesus Christ included a miraculous vision. His friends found his words describing his encounter in the lining of his waistcoat and a piece of paper describing his experience of conversion on November 23, 1654. The paper mentioned the following statements and ideas: "From about half-past ten in the evening until about half-past twelve…fire…the God of Abraham, the God of Isaac, the God of Jacob, and not of the philosophers…certitude, feeling, joy peace."[1] Blaise subsequently joined a group of scholars who sought to present Christianity with the focus on "grace alone" for salvation. His life was to be a short one but few have invested their lives more fruitfully than Pascal. He died of cancer August 19, 1662, at the age of 39. His last words were "may God never abandon me."

PASCAL'S REASONING PROCESS

To understand how the virtues of America were shaped, we need to include several Europeans who influenced America. One of these was Blaise Pascal. Samuel Johnson, the President of King's College (now Columbia) had read Pascal and found some interesting parallels between Pascal and Jonathan Edwards. The spiritual experiences of Jonathan Edwards were similar to Pascal who was widely read by Benjamin Franklin, John Adams, James Madison and Benjamin Rush. They found his book "Provinciales" tremendously helpful and his views on social improvement remarkable. [2]

It is amazing when we see how someone who lived in the seventeenth-century could so accurately describe those of us who live in the twenty-first century. Pascal lived in a time like ours when people were trusting in their own "reason" and "feelings" while rejecting "revelation." These were the years leading up to the French revolution in the eighteenth century.

Pascal focused on the limitations of the reasoning process itself. He taught that through science man now knows how little he knows about the nature of reality. Pascal said, "Reason itself is limited and there are an infinite number of things beyond it." [3]

PASCAL'S FAITH IN JESUS

Pascal wasn't interested in defending the faith as a system of belief, rather, he just wanted people to believe in Jesus. He believed the most important question we can ask a person is, "What happens after death?" Pascal admitted he "did not feel competent to find natural arguments that will convince (stubborn and hard-hearted atheists) but because such knowledge, without Christ, is useless and empty." [4] Pascal would emphasize that life is a few short years and death is forever. Pascal did not enjoy good health, instead, he suffered from a variety of illnesses his entire life including: headaches, stomach pains, and partial paralysis of his legs.

The other person in France who was as popular as Blaise Pascal was Rene Descartes. They would seek to lead their country in two different directions. Descartes was the other great mind that wrestled with the new universe opening up in Europe.

It is interesting to note that Descartes played a major role in the "enlightenment" and the "age of reason" brought to

NATIONAL PURPOSE

Contrasting "The Enlightenment" with the "Kingdom of God"

"The Enlightment" taught that each person is an autonomous center of knowing, judging, and independence.

A Christian's dignity comes from the knowledge that he or she is made in the "image of God" and the realization that Christ suffered and died for his or her redemption.

Individuals find happiness through the acquisition of possessions, experiences, and recognition.

Divine blessings of life come from knowing the God who has revealed Himself to us.

People tend to see government as providing its citizens with rights, responsibilities, dignity, and the happiness they deserve.

Christians, however, believe inner satisfaction, respect, and mutual dependence come by embracing their God-given responsibilities.

Ultimate fulfillment and utopia come through the liberation of conscience from the shackles of dogma.

Christians, however, believe fulfillment comes through doing God's will, both in private and in public.

Modern science tells us how people can know what is truth.

Christians, however, believe truth comes from God's revelation of Himself in history, through the Scriptures, and ultimately through His Son, Jesus Christ.

America by Voltaire and others. Voltaire sought to destroy Pascal because of his Christian convictions. Voltaire's views on the authority of the state would be embraced by Marx and others, bringing ruin to many nations. I wonder if even Pascal could have imagined the spiritual darkness that would come to the earth a few hundred years later when both science and philosophy were propagating the notion that God was not personal. For example, Spinoza's God created the universe then walked away from it. Modern men of science tell us that the universe never required a creator.

The "Founders of America" wrote of the right to "life, liberty, and the pursuit of happiness." The "Creator," not government or mankind, provided us with these unalienable rights. Both theists and atheists were recipients of these (God-given) rights. This was common knowledge for America's first 300 years of existence.

Although secular people don't acknowledge that they are responsible to the "Creator" and "Redeemer" of mankind, they still benefit from this umbrella of protection the "Founders" provided. Both the Christian and the secular person enjoy a communal association resulting from the godly foundations early America embraced.

Leslie Newbegin, the beloved Archbishop of England, helps us understand the incredible growth of secularism and the demise of Christianity. Newbegin believed for more than 1,000 years, Europe was shaped by "the story" found in the Bible. Each person who embraced "the story of the revelation of Christ," helped shape the European continent. It was the story of God calling Israel and eventually sending His Son... and it came to be seen as "the Truth." It was not a religion but a unique interpretation of universal history that showed that the actions of human beings have eternal significance. What went wrong?

Europe began to look to the Greeks rather than the Bible. Newbegin maintains that the "Enlightenment" was really the crack that has grown into the rift between Christianity and society. "Knowing" whether something was true or not was suddenly possible apart from Divine revelation; by using one's mental powers. Newbegin insisted that the fundamental decision of the seventeenth century was to exclude religion and rely on the human powers of understanding.

How do people make important decisions? Much of the time decisions are made by "feelings" or "instincts." A high percentage of people go through life not making critical decisions on the basis of moral law, natural law, Holy Scripture, or "W.W.J.D."; their sole frame of reference is "self." How did our culture become so self-obsessed?

For example, no doubt you have heard people say, "A woman has a right to choose. It's her body." How did women come to this belief? How could anyone justify this killing of one's offspring? To find out how people can make these declarations, look back to the 1700s and to the French philosopher Rene Descartes, a man who changed twentieth century America.

Descartes repudiated that all true knowledge is based on Holy Scriptures. The work of Descartes led him to use mathematics to provide a kind of knowledge very appealing to the people of his day. He would say, "I think, therefore I am." On that basis he undertook a map of reality. Testing would be based on his philosophy. Words like "belief," were relegated and considered inferior to words like "knowledge." Knowledge was used in mathematical and scientific terms and elevated above religious knowledge. Descartes said that the only reality was in his head and he looked at the mind as if it were separate from everything. He became his own frame of reference. This was a seminal moment in history. The tests to determine what is truth were replaced by a subjective philosophy resulting in the loss of common truth and community.

THE LOSS OF TRUTH

In summary, there is no way of knowing about ultimate reality if you exclude Divine Revelation. "Values" have replaced "truth" and American culture now teaches that science deals with "facts," while the religious world deals with "values."

Now in the twenty-first century, however, the "state" has entered into an adversarial relationship with "people of faith." America has gone out of its way to accommodate its secular citizens. Yet, no one would wish to go back to earlier centuries when the power of the state was wielded together with religion and used to enforce the beliefs of the church. "God's victory," according to Newbegin, "would not come through coercion... the role of the state should be a limited one, that of protecting the space for grace in society."[6]

If the whole universe has any meaning, there is no way to know unless you include Divine Revelation. For America to survive as a nation, it must know which philosophies are healthy and which are deadly. A nation without a correct understanding of reality will disintegrate or eventually be taken over by another society with deep convictions.

"May God never abandon me."[5]
Pascal

Descartes would say, "I think, therefore I am." On that basis he undertook a map of reality. Testing would be based on his philosophy. Words like "belief," were relegated and considered inferior to words like "knowledge." Knowledge was used in mathematical and scientific terms and elevated above religious knowledge.

> "reason itself is limited and there are an infinite number of things beyond it." [7]
>
> Pascal

> "faith is different from proof. one is human and the other is a gift of god. That is the faith god puts into our hearts." [8]
>
> Pascal

PASCAL'S PRINCIPLES

Pascal lived by the following ten principles:

1. "Man was both noble and wretched. He is noble in that he is made in the image of God and wretched because he has rebelled against God and is alienated from him. What kind of freak is man! What a novelty he is, how absurd he is, how chaotic and a mass of contradictions, and yet what a prodigy! He is judge of all things, yet a feeble worm. He is a repository of truth, and yet sinks into such doubt and error. He is the glory and the scum of the universe. It is dangerous for man to know God without knowing his own wretchedness and to know his own wretchedness without knowing the Redeemer who can free him from it." [9]

2. "Man is limited by the fact that he is finite and cannot see clearly since he is in the darkness of sin. His will is turned away from God and his reasoning ability is profoundly affected." [10] Pascal pictured mankind as suspended between wretchedness and happiness. Helpless without God, people try to avoid the horror of their "lostness" by engaging in distractions.

3. "Since nature was corrupted, God left men to their blindness, from which they can escape only through Jesus Christ, without whom all communications with God are broken off. There is a God whom men can know, and there is a corruption in their nature which renders them unworthy of Him." [11]

4. "Salvation comes to a person when his will is changed. If man is to change, man's will must change from serving self to serving God and others. God wishes to move the will." [12] Man was both created and fallen. Man's need for God becomes evident when he recognizes his misery apart from God.

5. People are deceived when they rely exclusively on "reason and the senses." "The two so-called principles of truth 'reason and the senses' are not only genuine but are engaged in mutual deception. Through false appearances the senses deceive reason. The senses are influenced by the passions that produce false impressions." [13] Our emotions or passions are influenced by how we think about things, and our imagination, which Pascal says is our dominant faculty, often has precedence over our reason.

6. Pride and sensuality ultimately destroy people and any true understanding of God. "It is in vain, oh men, that you seek within yourself the cure for all your miseries. All your insight has led you to the knowledge that it is not in yourself that you discover the true and the good. The philosophers promised them to you, but they were not able to keep their promises. They do not know what your true good is or what your nature is. How should they have provided you with a cure for ills which they have not even understood? Your principle maladies are pride, which cuts you off from God, and sensuality, which binds you to the earth. And they have done nothing but foster at least one of these maladies. If they have given you God for your object, it has been to pander to your pride. They have made you think you were like him by your nature. And those who have grasped the vanity of such pretension have cast you down in the other abyss by making you believe that your nature is like that of the beast of the field and have led you to seek your good in lust which is the lot of animals." [14]

7. Mankind's restlessness prevents him from being able to ponder the realities of God and eternity. "I have discovered that all human evil comes from this, man's being unable to sit in a room." [15]

8. Man's heart, not his reason or experience, perceives true knowledge and wisdom.

One of the famous sayings Pascal is known for is, "The heart has its reasons which reason does not know." [16] He believed that the "heart is the intuitive mind" rather than the reasoning mind. God is to be known by faith but the evidences for validating Christianity are great, including the prophecies, the miracles, the witness of history. Pascal taught that it is the heart which perceives God and not the reason. He said, "Faith is different from proof. One is human and the other is a gift of God. That is the faith God puts into our hearts." [17] Since nonbelievers are in the darkness, they will find proofs hard to believe. Pascal taught, "God is to be known through Jesus Christ by an act of faith, itself given by God. Faith is not of reason; it is of the heart. If we do not know Christ, we cannot understand God as the judge and the redeemer of sinners."[18]

9. "Those with living faith in their hearts can certainly see at once that everything which exists is entirely the work of the God they worship. But for those whom this light has gone out and in whom we are trying to rekindle it, people deprived of faith and grace, to them, I say, that they have only to look at the least thing around them and they will see in it God plainly revealed; to give them their proof of this great and weighty matter than the course of the moon and the planets; to claim to have completed the proof with such an argument; this is giving them cause to think the proofs of our religion are indeed feeble…this is not how the Scripture speaks, with its better knowledge of the things of God."[19]

10. "The only 'One' we should fear is God. I fear God and therefore I have no other fear." Much of France was hostile to Pascal and he must have had to deal with the fear of man and even the church since it did not accept his views entirely. Pascal wrote of his "belief in God's providence and a constant reliance upon His power and goodness, which impart a composure and firmness to the mind which renders it incapable of being moved by all the real, or imaginary evils of life."[20] It is out of a deep fear (reverence) of God from which a sense of meekness comes.

REVIEW
Q. Discuss each of Pascal's ten principles.
Q. What do you agree with concerning Pascal's evaluation of mankind?
Q. What do you disagree with concerning his diagnosis of mankind?
Q. How do you think people would react to Pascal's message today?
Q. What do you think Pascal means when he says man's biggest problem is not being able to sit still in a room?
Q. Do you think we need to find proofs for the existence of God prior to sharing the "good news with people"?
Q. Is the word "enlightenment" an appropriate term to use in the light of prevailing philosophies today?
Q. How do you think this experience impacted the life of Pascal?
Q. What was it that kept people from coming to Christ?

Q. What are the hindrances to meekness in our lives? Write about someone you know who is yielded to God and how it affects his or her life and the lives of others.

Q. In light of the description of the meek person, how would this person function in the American culture?

Q. What are the hindrances to meekness in our lives?

Q. How does the phrase W.W.J.D. (What would Jesus do?) help us learn true meekness?

Character for Life

GOD'S PROMISE:

"Blessed are the meek, for they will inherit the earth" (Matthew 5:5).

GOD'S GOAL:

For you to identify yourself with the interests and viewpoint of Jesus Christ.

YOUR COMMITMENT:

Develop a grateful and submissive spirit.

YOUR DAILY RESPONSE:

1. Continually yield your rights to God.

2. Transfer the "ownership" of your possessions, reputation, and future to God.

3. Remember Jesus, the author and finisher of our faith, who did not cling to "His rights" but yielded them to the Father.

4. Be prepared to take any assignment God gives you, even though it may be humbling.

FAILURE WILL MEAN:

You will easily be offended when your personal rights are violated.

BACKGROUND:

Nietzsche, the German philosopher, when looking at the ethic of Jesus, believed it was the most seductive lie history had ever heard. His view was that man needed to assert himself; it was the arrogant, the aggressive, the Mafia, the military dictators who would take over the earth. Nietzsche correctly asserted, "When one gives up the Christian faith, one pulls the right to Christian morality out from under one's feet. This morality is by no means self-evident. Christianity is a system, a whole view of things thought out together. By breaking one main concept out of it, the faith in God, one breaks the whole. It stands or falls with faith in God."[21]

Hitler followed Napoleon and countless others in his quest for world domination, but God was not on the side of the country with the biggest cannons. Hitler ran into God in the form of a Russian winter and army, and the Germans never became masters of the world. The arrogant and the power hungry do not inherit the earth. When people don't get what they want, they often demand their rights and become hostile and manipulative.

■ Allowing the Spirit of God to shape one.

■ Not being confused with weakness but possessing inner strength.

■ Having a true view of oneself.

■ Not seeking glory and not being proud.

■ Not demanding anything or insisting on one's own rights.

■ Not being overly sensitive.

■ Realizing that nobody can harm one.

■ Being amazed that God and people think as much of one as they do.

■ Realizing that one's life is built on Jesus and not oneself.

■ Being submissive to God, knowing one's sinfulness, confessing and accepting the forgiveness of Jesus Christ.

■ Possessing a gentle spirit that is submissive to God and sensitive to the needs of others.

■ Relinquishing the circumstances of one's life to God.

■ Being controlled and balanced—getting angry at the right things at the right time.

■ Being upset about injustice in the world.

■ Voluntarily giving up one's rights since one knows he or she is owned by someone else—the Creator of heaven and earth.

■ Living in a way that is opposite of the person who hungers for power and believes he or she possesses the earth. In reality the earth possesses him or her.

Chapter Six: Learning more about Pascal

Go to an Internet search engine.
Type in *Blaise Pascals' Character*.
Find topics 1-7 below and open up the websites.
1. Blaise Pascal
2. Pascal before the computer age
3. World's Greatest Scientists from YIK to Y2K.
4. Blaise Pascal- (His character is decided)
5. Blaise Pascal (Afrouen Blaise Pascal)
6. Pensees Blaise Pascal part 8
7. Free Tips -New Life Ministries

chapter 7
Hunger After Righteousness—samuel adams

PURPOSE: Discovering How to Be Truly Satisfied

virtue:
Hunger After Righteousness

SUBJECT:
SAMUEL ADAMS
(1722-1803)

PURPOSE:
Discovering How to Be Truly Satisfied

FAMOUS QUOTE:
"Religion in a family is at once its brightest ornament and its best security."

SCRIPTURE DOCUMENTATION:
"Blessed are those who hunger and thirst for righteousness, for they will be filled" (Matthew 5:6).

"O God, you are my God, earnestly I seek you; my soul thirsts for you, my body longs for you, in a dry and weary land where there is no water" (Psalm 63:1).

PERSONALITY PROFILE

Samuel Adams was born September 27, 1722. He was one of twelve children and also was the second cousin to America's second president, John Adams. Adams attended Harvard and this experience shaped his life in many ways. A friend said, "He was a calm, serious-minded, deeply religious man, not given to jokes or gaiety." He developed a reputation for moderation in his habits, including his drinking and eating. The "First Great Awakening" impacted the lives of students at Harvard spiritually and one student who was profoundly touched was Samuel Adams.

Adams set aside days of fasting and prayer to 'seek the Lord' and by this means gave the American Revolution a moral religious Crusade. He had become a new creature in Christ and was one of many young men who were filled with a devotion to Christ and His Kingdom. He graduated from Harvard in 1740. (Harvard was founded in 1650.)

Samuel Adams was known to be the most "illustrious citizen Massachusetts ever produced." He was a leader in the "Sons of Liberty" and was called the "Man of the town meeting." From 1756 to 1764 he was one of the town's tax-collectors but was unsuccessful and apparently too compassionate. Adams was perhaps the first person to urge separation from the mother country based on the argument of "Natural Law" and "Natural Rights."

He urged opposition to the "Stamp Act" and managed the proceedings of the "Boston Tea Party." He strove for harmony among several colonies and brought about coordination of the colonies he called "committees of correspondence" which virtually created a revolutionary body. Samuel Adams was one who signed the Declaration of Independence and he also wrote the "rights of colonists as Christians." He helped draft the Massachusetts Constitution and in 1788 was a member of the Massachusetts convention to ratify the "Constitution of the United States." For nine years he worked in Congress until the war was near its end. He was rewarded for his efforts and became Governor of Massachusetts from 1794 to 1797. He died on October 2, 1803.

FATHER OF THE REVOLUTION

For a generation, Samuel Adams would give himself to the cause of the "American Revolution" and be known as the "Father of the Revolution." Most of his contemporaries would confess that he had done more than any other person to bring about "independence." To his last, Adams never lost sight of the cause of the common people. He retained his interest in the common school and counseled the legislature not to decrease the appropriations for grammar school so the poor and the rich could derive equal benefit.

He was simple and unaffected in his manner, unostentatious in his habits and mode of life; he was one of the plain people. He could speak in terms they understood, chat with them informally and unreservedly, and explain to them the issues of the day in words that they comprehended.

Adams was part of the third or fourth generation of Puritans to come to America and the devotion to "Christ and His Kingdom" had waned. Samuel Adams believed that Puritan manners and morals needed to be restored. He was convinced that the chief purpose of the American Revolution was to separate New England from the decadent mother country in order that Puritanism might again flourish as it had in the early seventeenth century.

Adams wife, daughter, and son shared a husband and a father with thousands who looked to him for leadership. We learn a great deal about his family life from the letters he wrote to his wife and daughter. On the passing of his wife, Mary, he wrote in the family Bible, "To her husband she was as sincere a friend as she was a faithful wife. She exacted economy in all her relative capacities, her kindred on his side as well as her own admire. She ran her Christian race with remarkable steadiness, and finished in triumph. She left two small children. God grant they may inherit her graces!"[1]

Upon the marriage of his daughter, he wrote the following, "I could say a thousand things to you if I had the leisure. I could dwell on the importance of piety and religion, of industry and frugality, of prudence, economy, regularity and even Government, all of which are essential to the well being of a family. But have not time. I cannot however help repeating piety, because I think it indispensable. Religion in a family is at once its brightest ornament and its best security."[3]

Thomas Jefferson spoke for most everyone when he said; "I always considered him [Samuel Adams] as more than any

"My soul I resign into the hands of my Almighty Creator, whose tender mercies are all over His works, who hateth nothing he hath made, and to the justice and wisdom of whose dispensations I willingly and cheerfully submit, humbly hoping from His unbounded mercy and benevolence, through the merits of my blessed Savior, a remission of my sins."[2]
Adams

NATIONAL PURPOSE ▶

other member in Congress, the fountain of our important measures. In mediating the matter of that address, I asked myself, is this exactly in the spirit of the patriarch of liberty, Samuel Adams? He was "The Father of the Revolution" [5] Jefferson wrote to Samuel Adams, "I have felt a great deal for our country in the times we have seen: but individually for no one so much as yourself. When I have been told that you were avoided, insulted, frowned on I could but ejaculate, 'Father forgive them, for they know not what they do.'" [6]

A friend told me once that, "Leadership is a price which anyone can pay." The price is often measured in terms of self-denial and self-control. It consists of loneliness, being misunderstood, self-denial, sickness, frustration, resolution, love of country, controlling your passions and the love of righteousness. This definition would characterize the life of Samuel Adams.

Prior to his death Adams spoke the following words, "My soul I resign into the hands of my Almighty Creator, whose tender mercies are all over His works, who hateth nothing He hath made, and to the justice and wisdom of whose dispensations I willingly and cheerfully submit, humbly hoping from His unbounded mercy and benevolence, through the merits of my blessed Savior, a remission of my sins." [7]

ADAM'S PASSIONS AND CONVICTIONS

This book is all about people who conquered life through Christ's victory! God's character is revealed through them. Samuel Adams was able to "master" his ambitions through his love for God and the righteousness that comes from Jesus Christ.

Samuel Adams was willing to "pay the price" to bring about the birth of America. Adams repeatedly failed in business, due to the fact that he was totally involved in the revolution and politics. He was poor while he lived, and had not the death of an only son relieved the latter day poverty, Samuel Adams, not withstanding his virtues, his patriotism, his unwearied zeal, and his acknowledged usefulness, while he lived, would have had to claim a burial at the hand of charity, or at the public expense. He had deep empathy for the struggles of people and knew how to win their confidence.

Adams sought the good of others he served and he exhibited the character of Jesus Christ in his life by seeking righteousness. He never abused the trust people had in him and cared nothing for personal glory. He worked behind the scenes and people loved him. His was leadership through love. "No one exhibited a more indefatigable zeal, or a firmer tone of character than Samuel Adams. He eats little, sleeps little, thinks much…is most indefatigable in the pursuit of his object. Adams countenance revealed a noble genius and he had a character of great sincerity and purpose. When others were discouraged, he was filled with hope and resolution. Mr. Adams was a Christian. His mind was early imbued with piety, as well as cultivated by science. He early approached the table of the Lord Jesus, and the purity of his life witnessed the sincerity of his profession. No man was more conscientious…his patriotism was a pure and lofty character. For his country he labored both night and day, with a zeal which was scarcely interrupted, and with an energy that knew no fatigue."[8]

President John Adams characterized his second cousin with these words: "Adams is zealous, ardent, and keen in the cause, is always for softness and delicacy and prudence where they will do, but is stanch and stiff and strict and rigid and inflexible in the cause…. He is a man of refined policy, steadfast integrity, exquisite humanity, genteel erudition, obliging, engaging manners, real as well as professed piety, and a universal good character, unless it should be admitted that he is too attentive to the public and not enough so to himself and his family."[9]

In his lifestyle, Samuel Adams chose to live with simplicity. He could have used his office to become rich but chose not to. His first revolt was against materialism…he avoided and condemned luxury, indolence and licentiousness throughout his life. "No personal considerations shall ever induce me to abandon the righteous cause of my country. Neither the wisest constitution nor the wisest laws will secure the liberty and happiness of a people whose manners are universally corrupt,"[10] Adam's said.

Adams believed all children in America needed a Christian education. He exhorted others to do the same with the words, "Let statesmen and patriots unite in their endeavors to renovate the age by educating their little boys and girls, leading them in the study and practice of the exalted virtues of the Christian system."[11]

Adams believed that character and virtue were a necessary preparation for leadership. "He who is void of virtuous attachments in private life is, or very soon will be, void of all regard

"Adams is zealous, ardent, and keen in the cause, is always for softness and delicacy and prudence where they will do, but is stanch and stiff and strict and rigid and inflexible in the cause…. He is a man of refined policy, steadfast integrity, exquisite humanity, genteel erudition, obliging, engaging manners, real as well as professed piety, and a universal good character, unless it should be admitted that he is too attentive to the public and not enough so to himself and his family." [12]

President John Adams—Samuel Adam's second cousin

NATIONAL PURPOSE ▶

of his country. There is seldom an instance of a man guilty of betraying his country who had not before lost of feeling of moral obligations in his private connections. Private and public vices are in reality connected...the public cannot be too curious concerning the character of public men. Those who have a share in making well as judging and executing the laws should be men of singular wisdom and integrity. While the people are virtuous they cannot be subdued, but when they lose their virtue they will be ready to surrender their liberties, to the first external or internal invader.... If virtue and knowledge are diffused among the people, they will never be enslaved. This will be their great security." [13]

"Let us contemplate our forefathers, and posterity, and resolve to maintain the rights bequeathed to us from the former, for the sake of the latter. The necessity of the times, more than ever, calls for our utmost circumspection, deliberation, fortitude and perseverance. Let us remember that, 'if we suffer timely lawless attack upon our liberty, we encourage it, and involve others in our doom.' It is a very serious consideration...that millions yet unborn may be the miserable sharers of the event." [14]

The goal of government was to produce a country where all would cherish mercy and justice, life, liberty and the ownership of property. Samuel Adams believed in the words of the Bible that man is to "do justice and mercy." He also believed that it was "evil and unnatural to allow those great fruits of liberty to spoil or rot through neglect or apathy." [15] He believed that "the grand end of government is for the support, protection, and defense of those very rights; the principle of which are life, liberty and property." [16]

Samuel Adams believed universal righteousness would come to the world with the appearance of Jesus Christ and His Kingdom.

Adams wrote, "It is our duty to extend our wishes to the happiness of the great family of man. I conceive that we cannot better express ourselves than by humbly supplicating the supreme ruler of the world that the rod of tyrants may be broken into pieces, and the oppressed made free, that ways may cease in all the earth, and that the confusions that are and have been among the nations may be overruled by promoting and speedily bringing on that holy and happy period when the kingdom of our Lord and Savior Jesus Christ may be everywhere established, and all people everywhere willingly bow to the scepter of righteousness." [18]

REVIEW

Q. Do you know people who had to practice self-denial and self-control to reach their goal?

Q. What was the one negative thing John Adams referred to regarding Samuel Adams?

Q. Do you think it is ever justified for a parent not to have quality time with his or her children?

Q. Is Samuel Adams right when he said there is a link between private and public vices and the betrayal of one's country?

Q. How important is character for public officials?

Q. If Samuel Adams were to run for president now, while expressing his beliefs about what America should be, do you think he would have much of a chance at being elected?

Q. What would need to happen for his views to become mainstream?

Q. How would America be different if the dream of Samuel Adams for virtues and knowledge was defused?

Character for Life

GOD'S PROMISE:

"Blessed are those who hunger and thirst for righteousness, for they will be filled" (Matthew 5:6).

"My flesh and my heart may fail, but God is the strength of my heart and my portion forever" (Psalm 73:26).

"My soul yearns for you in the night; in the morning my spirit longs for you. When your judgments come upon the earth, the people of the world learn righteousness" (Isaiah 26:9).

"Yet the LORD longs to be gracious to you; he rises to show you compassion. For the LORD is a God of justice. Blessed are all who wait for him!" (Isaiah 30:18).

GOD'S GOAL:

That you experience personal inner holiness in your life.

YOUR COMMITMENT:

Consecrate your thoughts and ambitions to God.

YOUR DAILY RESPONSE:

1. Ask God for a great longing for holiness and a deliverance from sin and selfishness.

2. Remember that Jesus experienced His suffering for the purpose of making a holy people for Himself.

3. Recognize God's holiness is at work in others.

4. Don't allow sin to take root in your life. Confess it and ask for Jesus to cleanse you.

FAILURE WILL MEAN:

You will seek fulfillment in experiences, material possessions, etc.

BACKGROUND:

Hunger is something that motivates all of us. Advertisers know how to get us to buy their products. Jesus wants to put us on a different diet, not for things or food but a hunger and thirst for righteousness. The great thing about this beatitude is that Jesus did not say, "Happy are those who are always righteous", but, "happy are those who hunger for righteousness." If we don't have an appetite for righteousness, we are in trouble spiritually. When we don't "hunger" for righteousness, we direct that intense desire into "hungering" for other things: experiences, material things, none of which satisfies.

To define "hunger" one might say it is a sign of being alive. If we do not have a desire for righteousness, something is wrong. The desire for righteousness means ultimately the desire to be right with God and a desire to get rid of sin because that keeps us from knowing God. Righteous conduct comes from a new heart.

LIVING A LIFE THAT HUNGERS & THIRSTS FOR RIGHTEOUSNESS MEANS . . .

■ Going in the opposite direction of the world, which says to pursue happiness and make it your supreme objective.

■ Not putting happiness before righteousness or you will never get it and be doomed to misery.

■ Being right with God and free from sin and its desire to express itself.

■ Getting rid of sin and whatever comes between you and God.

■ Being free from the desire of sin and the bondage it brings.

■ Being free from "self" and its terrible consequences.

- Being hungry and thirsty to be holy before God.

- Discovering true blessedness and happiness.

- Having a hunger to know God and His Word.

- Speaking and making decisions according to the Truth.

- Not deviating from the standard of fairness and impartiality.

- Believing Jesus Christ, "the author of life," who said when you put happiness before righteousness, you will be ultimately doomed to misery.

- Having a longing to be like Jesus. Our strongest motivations in life are to know God and make Him known.

Chapter Seven: Learning more about Adams

Go to an Internet search engine.
Type in *Samuel Adams' Character*.
Find topics 1-7 below and open up the websites.
1. The American Revolution
2. Mark Alexander: Samuel Adams, The Declaration Revisited
3. Samuel Adams
4. Colonial Hall: Biography of Samuel Adams Page 1
5. Quotes by Adams, Samuel
6. Douglas Samuel Adams "American Independence" 1 Aug. 1776
7. Samuel Adams (Thachor's Sermon)

chapter 8
Forgive & Extend Mercy—Alexander Hamilton

PURPOSE: Releasing Others and Finding Wholeness

character trait:
Forgive & Extend Mercy

SUBJECT:
ALEXANDER HAMILTON
(1755-1804)

PURPOSE:
Releasing Others and Finding Wholeness

FAMOUS QUOTE:
"Take a warning, and avoid my errors. Cultivate the virtues I have recommended. Choose the Savior I have chosen. Live disinterestedly and would you rescue anything from final dissolution, lay it up to God."

SCRIPTURE DOCUMENTATION:
"Blessed are the merciful, for they will be shown mercy" (Matthew 5:7).

PERSONALITY PROFILE

Rachel Levine, Alexander Hamilton's mother, was living with James Hamilton, a Scotsman seeking his fortune in the West Indies, at the time of Alexander's birth. James Hamilton died when Alexander was 7 years old and his mother died when Alexander was just 11. Young Hamilton received most of his early training, thought, theology, and academic training from his pastor who educated him at home. He was also taught by a Jewish schoolmistress and learned to recite the Ten Commandments in Hebrew.

At the age of 14 he was running an international business dealing with ship captains, planters, merchants, lawyers, slaves, and suppliers. At age 15 he knew some French and Hebrew, and had a basic knowledge of Latin, theology, and the classics.

He was zealous for God during his student years and eventually served as a Lieutenant Colonel under Washington. Captain of the artillery in the Continental Army (1776), Hamilton was a "Signer of the Constitution" and during the years 1782-83; 1787-88 he became a delegate to the Continental Congress. He provided leadership to enable the states to ratify the Constitution. Along with Madison and Jay, he authored 51 of the 85 Federalist Papers. He called for a more centralized government and succeeded in persuading the convention to ratify the Constitution by a 30-27 vote. He established a national mint and became the Inspector General of the United States. Hamilton established the "Christian Constitution Society," its twin goals being the support of the Christian religion and the support of the United States. Hamilton found little response to the "Christian Constitution Society," however.

As a boy, 15 years of age, on the isle of St. Croix, West Indies, Hamilton wrote the following. "Where now. Oh vile worm, is all thy boasted fortitude and resolution? What is become of thy arrogance and self-sufficiency? Why dost thou tremble and stand aghast? How humble, how helpless, how contemptible you now appear .... Oh, impotent presumptuous fool! How darest thou offend that omnipotence, whose God alone were sufficient to quell the destruction that hovers over thee, or crush thee to atoms? ... He who gave the winds to blow and the lightnings to rage—even him I have always loved and served—his commandments have I obeyed and his perfection have I adored. —He will snatch me from ruin—He will exalt me to the fellowship of Angels and Seraphs, and to the fullness of never ending joys."[1]

HAUNTED BY HIS BIRTH

Hamilton was continually reminded that he was "born out of wedlock." His pastor realized his genius and was determined to help him get a college education. He raised money from people on the island who admired Alexander and sent him to America. Having been abandoned by his father, Hamilton kept up the fiction of an endearing father-son relationship. He found this with his father-in-law and perhaps in General Washington. The feeling of being abandoned led to Hamilton's being an "overachiever," and he overcompensated at times. The stigma placed upon him as a child born out of wedlock made him enormously concerned about his reputation. In early America, "bloodlines" were very important and Hamilton was continually reminded of his humble beginnings. Extending forgiveness to those who brought painful reminders to him, was a life-long challenge.

"Hamilton's political principles were clearly formed by the time he was twenty-five... he did not believe 'in the people,' (that man's nature was bent toward doing good) but instead profoundly distrusted the political capacity of the common man, believing him to be too ignorant, selfish, and ill-controlled to be capable of wise self-government."[2]

Although they were both Federalists, Adams and Hamilton had separate visions for America and chose not to work through their disagreements. When Hamilton opposed John Adams' re-election in favor of Jefferson, Adams brought his birth up again and its ugly truth and the humiliating circumstances of his origins, childhood, and early poverty must have wounded him deeply. Offenses come to everyone, but this was more than Hamilton could bear. He went on the offensive opposing Adams re-election, which ultimately led to Thomas Jefferson being nominated as president.

SERVANT LEADERSHIP

Servant leadership characterized the life of Alexander Hamilton. He lived in extraordinary times and President Washington entrusted him with great responsibilities. Washington was a "father image" to Hamilton and he was clearly protective of Washington's reputation, even writing speeches for the beloved "Father of the Country."

Justice James Kent wrote, "When at work, and he worked almost incessantly, he had a marvelous faculty of concentration; many observers spoke of his ability to reach conclusions as by a lightning flash—to divine them. His character was of the highest stamp while his patriotism was unquestioned. His power as an orator was the greatest of his time,…his abilities as a political leader were surpassed by few, but again he chose to work upon and through small groups rather than the masses. His intellect was hard, incisive, and logical, but lacking in imagination and in subtlety."[3]

NATIONAL PURPOSE ▶

Alexander Hamilton, who ranks as one of the most influential men in our nation's history, truly had humble beginnings. In the end, he had done as much as any man to weld the states into a nation and thereby fulfill some of the noblest aspirations of that Revolution to whose success he had committed his life, his fortune, and above all, his sacred honor. Washington believed that "Hamilton's ambition was that of laudable kind which prompts a man to excel in whatever he takes in hand."[4]

Hamilton had his share of character faults and strengths, however. His beginnings did not prepare him for the great responsibilities he was to face in life and accounted for his poor choices. His aristocratic ideals, his love for clothes, glory, and admiration, impulsiveness, his need to be independent of others, and suicidal tendencies led to his downfall.

HAMILTON'S PASSIONS AND CONVICTIONS

According to his close friend Chief Justice James Kent, Hamilton developed the habit of getting on his knees before God in prayer on a regular basis. "Hamilton was attentive to public worship, and in the habit of praying upon his knees both night and morning. I have often been powerfully affected by the fervor and eloquence of his prayers. He was a zealous believer in the fundamental doctrines of Christianity." Kent added, "His strengths of character are also clearly seen; his decision-making, devotion to duty, empathy with his fellow-man, generosity, need to merge his identity with a cause, religious beliefs and tendency to ignore obstacles are also what made him a great man."[5]

Hamilton set out to destroy Aaron Burr who sought to be the President of the United States, yet whose character Hamilton thought was corrupted by greed. Alexander Hamilton was a flawed human being and those opposing him set him up for a "fall." He fell into pride and this brought about moral failure. He had not depended upon God and he found himself in an immoral relationship. He was a chastened man and begged forgiveness from God and his wife.

However, he had a fierce loyalty to George Washington and to the principles he believed in, and few people were as devoted to the country as Hamilton. There are many wonderful things to remember about Alexander Hamilton. There were times he knew the truth and had to stand alone. More than most men, he saw the direction which America should move toward.

He saw the death of his beloved son as divine providence. Upon the death of his oldest son Hamilton wrote, "My loss is indeed great. The brightest as well as the eldest hope of my family has been taken from me. You esteem him rightly. He was a fine youth. But why should I repine? It was the will of heaven and he is now out of reach of the seductions and calamities of the world, full of folly, full of vice, full of danger–of least value in proportion as it is best known. I firmly trust also, that he has safely reached the haven of repose and security."[6] With the loss of his son, there was no hint of bitterness in Hamilton's life, the only assurance he had was that his son was with God.

Following the death of his son, Hamilton's devotion to God became all important in his life. Alexander Hamilton explained in an 1802 letter to James Bayard how the rise of atheistic "Jacobinism" from France was beginning to divide the country. Hamilton wrote, saying: "I now offer you the outline of the plan they have suggested. Let an association be formed to be denominated 'The Christian Constitutional Society,' its object to be first: The support of the Christian religion. Second: The support of the United States."[7]

The first principle of the new society, even before supporting the Constitution, was "the support of the Christian religion." It would start out as a network of people dedicated to the support of candidates for elected office, pull information together for potential voters and ultimately start "academies" to educate urban populations. Hamilton saw his future clearly, but his days of service to his country were numbered.

A FUTILE DUEL

For the sake of his "reputation," and his concern over America's future, he was drawn into a duel that cost him his life. Aaron Burr, who was running for president, was unwilling to overlook the charge Hamilton brought against him (that

"What is Jacobinism? It is an attempt to eradicate prejudice out of the minds of men for the purpose of putting all power and authority into the hands of the persons capable of occasionally enlightening the minds of the people... they everywhere engage the poor by holding out to them as a bribe the spoils of the rich." [8]
Edmund Burke

Burr, "was unfit to run for office"). Hamilton openly exposed the character of Burr and Jefferson. He called Jefferson an "atheist" and a "fanatic" and had nothing but contempt for Aaron Burr.

In a letter to Gouverneur Morris on December 24, 1800 Hamilton wrote, "Jefferson or Burr? (for President) the former without doubt. The latter, in my judgment, has no principle, public or private; could be bound by no agreement; will listen to no monitor but his ambition, and for this purpose will use the worst part of the community as a ladder to climb to permanent power, and an instrument to crush the better part. He is bankrupt beyond redemption, except by the resources which grow out of war and disorder, or by a sale to a foreign power, or by great peculation. War with Great Britain would be an immediate instrument. He is sanguine enough to hope every thing, daring enough to attempt every thing, wicked enough to scruple nothing. From the elevation of such a man may heaven preserve the country." [9]

Since Hamilton refused to defend himself in a duel, his doom was sealed. Fortunately, prior to his death, he spent the last years of his life being restored to fellowship with his family, the Church, and the God he knew as a young man.

For those who wanted advice, he told them, "Take a warning, and avoid my errors. Cultivate the virtues I have recommended. Choose the Savior I have chosen. Live disinterestedly (with no personal gain) and would you rescue anything from final dissolution, lay it up to God." [10]

Having lost her husband in the duel, Hamilton's wife asked Chancellor (also Chief Justice of the New York Supreme Court) James Kent to provide her with a letter describing her husband's character which had been called into question. "I know General Hamilton's character well. His life and actions for the course of twenty-two years, had engaged and fixed my attention. They were passing under my eye and observation. For the last six years of his life he was arguing causes before me. I have been sensibly struck, in a thousand instances, with his habitual reverence for truth, his candor, his ardent attachment to civil liberty, his indignation at oppression of every kind, his abhorrence of every semblance of fraud, his reverence for justice, and his sound legal principles drawn by a clear and logical deduction from the purest Christian ethics, and from the very foundation of all rational practical jurisprudence." [11]

Alexander Hamilton believed the future of his country was more important than his own life. If anyone had to acquire a forgiving heart, it was he. He was not one of the "Founders" born with a supportive or wealthy family. He was born out of wedlock to a father who left him at seven years of age. He loved his country better than himself and wore himself out for love of America. He was ultimately truly popular after his death at the hands of Burr.

In the event of his death at the hands of Burr, Hamilton, now forgiven and free from bitterness, gave instructions to give the following revealing letter to his wife. "This letter, my dear Eliza, will not be delivered to you, unless I shall first have terminated my earthly career, to begin, as I humbly hope, from redeeming grace and divine mercy, a happy immortality. If it had been possible for me to have avoided the interview (with Burr) my love for you and my precious children would have been alone a decisive motive. But it was not possible, without sacrifice which would have rendered me unworthy of your esteem. I need not tell you of the pangs I feel from the idea of leaving you, and my exposing you to the anguish I know you would feel. Nor could I dwell on the topic, lest it should unman me. The consolations of religion, my beloved, can alone support you; and these you have a right to enjoy. Fly to the bosom of your God, and be comforted. With my last idea I shall cherish the sweet hope of meeting you in a better world. Embrace all my darling children for me." [13]

REVIEW

Q. Can you imagine what life must have been like for Eliza Hamilton after she lost her husband in what must have seemed a senseless duel?

Q. How did Hamilton's letter to his wife affect you?

Q. Discuss his comments on the death of his son.

Q. We can't all have the same start in life. We can have the opportunity of a good end in life. Hamilton was criticized his entire life because he was born out of wedlock. How do you think this impacted him?

Q. What does it mean to "live disinterestedly"?

Q. Were there other options open to Hamilton other than accepting Burr's invitation to a duel?

Character for Life

GOD'S PROMISE:

"Blessed are the merciful, for they will be shown mercy" (Matthew 5:7).

GOD'S GOAL:

That you experience forgiveness and mercy in your life.

YOUR COMMITMENT:

Choose daily to forgive others and show mercy.

YOUR DAILY RESPONSE:

1. Realize that God has forgiven you.

2. Remember that God's grace is sufficient.

3. Be aware of Satan's involvement in the lives of sinners and be willing to show them mercy and forgiveness.

4. Live a life of daily confession to God.

FAILURE WILL MEAN:

Being unmerciful and unforgiving and living in misery and self-pity.

BACKGROUND:

Alexander Hamilton was human. He lived a life where he made mistakes, had an affair that surely hurt his marriage, and entered into a duel that cost him his life. He also lost his son and had to constantly fight to defend his past. It wasn't an easy life. Hamilton, however, knew God and was a great defender of his faith. His impact on America was profound, and his life serves others as an example of God's faithfulness, even to those who fail.

LIVING A LIFE OF FORGIVENESS & MERCY MEANS . . .

- Looking at the consequences of sin. Being merciful means having a sense of pity and a desire to relieve suffering.

- Being repentant and seeing that the only claim one has on God is His grace and mercy to forgive.

- Forgiving those who sin against us, knowing God has forgiven them.

- Realizing that we cannot earn God's mercy since God deals with us in grace, we are the objects of God's mercy.

■ Understanding that since God has forgiven me, there should be no vindictiveness in my heart.

■ Not just being sympathetic, but moving out to heal the hurt of others since receiving mercy will make us more inclined to give mercy later on.

■ Seeing men and women as the dupes and victims and slaves of sin and seeing Satan as the one who brings pain and suffering into their lives.

Chapter Eight: Learning More about Hamilton

Go to an Internet search engine.
Type in *Alexander Hamilton*.
Find topics 1-8 below and open up the websites.
1. Introduction
2. Brookshire, Richard: Alexander Hamilton, American
3. The Bill of Rights Institute
4. Political Battles
5. Alexander Hamilton Quotes
6. A free Essay on Alexander Hamilton
7. Alexander Hamilton (One Nation Under God)
8. Alexander Hamilton: Was Hamilton a Christian?

chapter 9

Loving God with a Pure Heart—Jonathan Edwards

PURPOSE: Life's Amazing Discovery

character trait:

Loving God with a Pure Heart

SUBJECT:

JONATHAN EDWARDS
(1703-1758)

PURPOSE:

Life's Amazing Discovery

FAMOUS QUOTE:

"God is most glorified when we are most satisfied in Him."

SCRIPTURE DOCUMENTATION:

"Blessed are the pure in heart, for they will see God" (Matthew 5:8).

Born in 1703 in East Windsor, Connecticut, Jonathan Edwards was among the second generation of Puritans, and the only son among 11 children. At six years of age, he could conjugate Latin verbs. Before he was 13 he had a good knowledge of Latin, Greek, and Hebrew and was writing papers on philosophy. Often, he would spend up to 14 hours a day studying. He was fascinated with science and living creatures since it helped him understand the "mind of the Creator." During his time at Yale, he began to appreciate the redemption of Jesus Christ. He graduated first in his class.

Edwards married Sarah Pierrepont in 1727 and together they committed to raise their eleven children in the reverence of God. Between 1724-48, as pastor of the church in Northampton, Massachusetts, God used him to bring about the "Great Awakening." Their success as parents was revealed in a study in 1900 of their heritage over a period of 200 plus years. It showed that their descendants included 13 college presidents, 65 professors, 30 judges, 100 lawyers, a dean of a prestigious law school, 80 public office holders, nearly 100 missionaries, three mayors of large cities, three governors, three United States Senators, one comptroller of the United States Treasury, and one Vice President of the United States.[1]

In 1734, a spiritual fire was lit in Edward's church sparking a subsequent revival that fanned the flame along the entire East Coast until around 1743. Edwards writes; "The town seemed to be full of the presence of God: it was never so full of love, nor joy, and yet so full of distress as it was then…it was a time of joy in families on account of salvation being brought unto them; parents rejoicing over their children as new born, and husbands over their wives."[2]

"Over 50,000 people professed conversion, 150 new churches were organized and it impacted various evangelical denominations. The dominant Armenian cast of the New England Baptist became reshaped in the mode of evangelical Calvinism. Out of the revival, Harvard and Yale received spiritual blessings. Although they initially opposed it, new schools, such as Dartmouth College in New Hampshire and Brown University at Providence (the parent of all the Baptist colleges) were founded during the Great Awakening. Many colleges and seminaries of the present day owe their existence to the Great Awakening."[3]

THE GREAT AWAKENING

Edwards differed with church leadership over participation in the "Lord's Supper." He left his church in 1750 to pastor a church in Stockbridge and also went on a mission to the Housatonic Indians. With great reluctance, he accepted the position as President of Princeton in 1757. One month later, he died of the effects of a small pox injection. In the view of biographer Perry Miller, "Edwards was the greatest philosopher-theologian yet to grace the American scene. Edwards was a complete stranger to that separation of the 'heart and head' that has often plagued evangelical religion."[4] It appears there are some similarities in the theologies of Jonathan Edwards and those of Blaise Pascal. It was Pascal who first taught, "The heart (man's affections and will) must be deeply affected and changed." With Edwards began what is now known as evangelical churches. The result was the "Great Awakening" and the beginning of the evangelization of the world. Paul Helms writes, "There is probably no name more worthy of a place in the evangelical succession of truth than that of Jonathan Edwards."

Edwards was one of the great scholars in American history. He was extraordinary in his discipline and passionate in his love for the Savior. Edwards believed that sin was an inherent enmity against God; salvation meant a change of heart, calling for deep and earnest searching. He also saw repentance as a step toward salvation. He defined faith in terms of a "total response to Christ."[5]

Edwards' passions and convictions resulted in an understanding of the key to all other virtues. Edwards said, "Love, is the key to all the other 'virtues.' Love is that disposition or affection whereby one is dear to another."[6] The other "virtues" are "fruits" of the virtue of (Christian) love. The "heart" is the center of man's personality, and includes both his spirit and soul and is the seat of the "affections."

A longing for the glory of God for America motivated Edwards' leadership. Leadership without Christian love makes all virtues empty and vain. Edwards taught, "If there be no love in what men do, then there is no true respect to God or men in their conduct."[8]

"Without love, there can be no true submission to the will of God, and no real trust and confidence in Him."[9] Edwards said, "If a person does not truly love God that person will be

"Character cannot be developed in ease and quiet. Only through experience of trial and suffering can the soul be strengthened, vision cleared, ambition inspired and success achieved."[7]
Helen Keller

NATIONAL PURPOSE

unable to truly trust Him." Edwards taught that Christian love is from the Holy Spirit influencing the heart. "When God and man are loved with a truly Christian love, they are both loved from the same motives." [11]

WHY LOVE GOD?

"When God is loved, He is loved for His holiness, sacrificial love, and the beauty of His nature. Human beings are loved because they have the same spiritual image of God or are like God in some respect. The nature of love is that it will produce all virtues. Without it, there can be no sincere virtue. Christ teaches us that the sum of all our duty is to love God and love one another. All good works are produced by love." [12]

Faith works through love. All gracious and holy exercises and virtues of the spiritual life are by faith. Edwards resolved, "Never to do anything which I should be afraid to do if it were the last hour of my life." [13] "By examining our own affections we can judge whether they tend toward the true God. The character of Jesus Christ provides us with the inspiration to love and also motivates us to appropriate action. The glory of the sovereign God is compelling; it leads to obedience as well as delight. True Christians see God as worthy to be followed. Love seeks union with the beloved and acts on that desire. All finite (virtues), especially for other persons, are secure only when rooted in the love of God." [14]

EDWARDS' SECRET

Jonathan Edwards said, "God is most glorified when we are most satisfied in Him." [15] The sum of that eternal life which Christ purchased is holiness; it is a holy happiness. This leads us to obedience and to delight ourselves in Him. True Christians see God as worthy to be followed.

Edwards said, "It is not contrary to Christianity that a man should love himself or, which is the same thing, should love his own happiness. If Christianity did tend to destroy a man's love to himself and to his own happiness, it would therein intend to destroy the very spirit of humanity." [16]

NATIONAL PURPOSE ▶ Edwards' love and intimacy with God enabled him to understand God's purposes for Christ's Kingdom and for America.

Edwards said, "The histories of the past advancement of Christ's Kingdom have been sweet to me. When I have read histories of past ages, the pleasantest thing in all my reading has been, to read of the Kingdom of Christ being promoted...and my mind has been much entertained and delighted with the Scripture promises and prophecies, which relate to the future glorious advancement of Christ's Kingdom upon earth." [17]

THE PURPOSE OF CREATION

Edwards believed, "The end of God's creating the world, was to prepare a Kingdom for His Son...which should remain to all eternity...it is not unlikely that this work of God's Spirit (i.e., the religious revival) so extraordinary and wonderful, is the dawning, or at least a prelude of that glorious work of God, so often foretold in Scripture, which, in the progress and issue of it, shall renew the world of mankind...and there are many things that make it probable that this work will begin in America. It is significant that it shall begin in some very remote part of the world, with which other parts have no communication, but by navigation. Isaiah 61:9 states, 'Their descendants will be known among the nations and their offspring among the peoples. All who see them will acknowledge that they are a people the LORD has blessed.'" [19]

REVIEW

Q. What does Edwards mean by our "affections"?

Q. In referring to Christ, Jonathan Edwards said that love seeks union with the beloved and acts on (His) desires. How do we discover what Jesus desires His actions be for us?

Q. What needs to happen in our hearts before we can really trust God?

Q. What does Edwards mean when he says that both God and man must be loved with the same motives?

Q. What should bring us the greatest joy?

Q. What was God's ultimate purpose in creating the universe and earth?

Q. Read Isaiah 61:9. Do you agree that the Holy Spirit may have been referring to America in Isaiah's prophecy?

Q. How will this virtue (being pure in heart) make a difference in your life?

Q. What do you think Edwards meant when he said, "God is most glorified when we are satisfied in Him"?

Q. Why is a deep and earnest search of our hearts necessary as a step in repentance?

"There is probably no name more worthy of a place in the evangelical succession of truth than that of Jonathan Edwards." [18]
Paul Helms

"My heart has been much on the advancement of Christ's Kingdom in the world." [20]
Jonathan Edwards

Q. Why was Edwards concerned that both "heart and head be brought together in the service of God"?

Q. Is there a healthy way to love ourselves and pursue our own happiness?

Character for Life

GOD'S PROMISE:

"Blessed are the pure in heart, for they will see God" (Matthew 5:8).

GOD'S GOAL:

That you experience God's power to overcome the temptations of the world, the flesh, and the devil. "For everything in the world—the cravings of sinful man, the lust of his eyes and the boasting of what he has and does—comes not from the Father but from the world" (1 John 2:16).

YOUR COMMITMENT:

Continually affirm your love for God in various ways.

YOUR DAILY RESPONSE:

1. Love God with all your ability.

2. Pray as David did, for God to "give me an undivided heart" (Psalm 86:11).

3. Pray for a deep reverence for God and His holiness.

4. Ask God for His perspective.

FAILURE WILL MEAN:

Your heart will be filled with things that aren't of God.

BACKGROUND:

A pure heart is a heart without hypocrisy. The heart is no longer divided. David understood this when he said, "Teach me your way, O LORD, and I will walk in your truth; give me an undivided heart, that I may fear your name" (Psalm 86:11). The problem we have is a divided heart, which prefers its own way rather than God's way. Unless we long to have a pure heart, which is constantly being cleansed by the blood of Jesus, we will become careless and our hearts will be filled with selfish thoughts and desires. The weight of sin will bring terrible bondages in our lives.

LIVING WITH A PURE HEART MEANS . . .

■ Mourning over the impurity of our hearts and longing for a clean and pure heart.

- Realizing our problems are not within our environment but exist within the heart.

- Knowing that a pure heart is one without hypocrisy.

- Understanding that a pure heart is one that has been cleansed "by the blood of Jesus."

- Accepting that a pure heart is one that is undivided.

- Having a heart that meditates on "things above."

- Realizing that the closer a person comes to God the more he or she is aware of his or her sin. This comes from "walking in the light."

- Having a heart that says with David of the Bible, "Create in me a pure heart, O God, and renew a steadfast spirit within me" (Psalm 51:10).

Chapter Nine: Learning more about Edwards

Go to an Internet search engine.
Type in *Jonathan Edwards' Character.*
Find topics 1-6 below and open up the websites.
1. The works of Jonathan Edwards
2. Jonathan Edwards, A Life. Dr. Herbert Samworth
3. The Life and Character of the Late Reverend Mr. Jonathan Edwards
4. Biographical Sketch of Jonathan Edwards
5. Jonathan Edwards
6. Religious Attributes, Part 1. Jonathan Edwards

chapter 10

Blessed Are the Peacemakers—John Quincy Adams

PURPOSE: Finding What the World Longs For

character trait:

Blessed Are the Peacemakers

SUBJECT:
JOHN QUINCY ADAMS
(1767-1848)

PURPOSE:
Finding What the World Longs For

FAMOUS QUOTE:
"I pray heaven to bestow the best of blessings on this house and all that shall hereafter inhabit it. May none but honest and wise men ever rule under this roof."

SCRIPTURE DOCUMENTATION:
"Blessed are the peacemakers, for they will be called sons of God" (Matthew 5:9).

John Quincy Adams was the firstborn son of strong-willed parents, John and Abigail Adams. His uncle was Samuel Adams and he grew up very much aware of the injustice of the English toward the colonies. Since his father was one of the "Founders," he was exposed to people like Thomas Jefferson and spent entire afternoons with the third President talking about science, politics, and government. While his father was on a diplomatic mission to France, Adams served as his secretary (at the age of 11!). At 15, he was sent on a diplomatic apprenticeship to Russia.

Adams entered Harvard College in 1785 and had by then learned five or six foreign languages including Latin and Greek. Adams pursued formal education in the Netherlands, London, England, and Paris, France. On July 26, 1797, while in England on a diplomatic mission, he married Louisa Catherine, daughter of Joshua Johnson, who was of a Maryland family. He was thirty years old and his wife was 22. Louisa was delicate and had continual health problems throughout their 50 years of marriage. After a lot of hesitation, Adams began to take great delight in his marriage. He saw himself as fortunate and blessed since he was not, apparently, an easy person with whom to live. Louisa was similar to his mother, Abigal, in that she was intelligent, courageous, passionate, and deeply religious. Adams became depressed as he dealt with crisis in his family. After several miscarriages, however, a son, George Washington Adams, finally came into the world.

Adams was appointed Minister to Holland in 1794 and Prussia from 1797-1801. From 1803-1808 he served in the Massachusetts Senate. Adams was appointed Minister to Russia by James Madison, which resulted in a strengthened relationship with Russia. He then became the Secretary of State under President Monroe. Some say he was the most successful secretary of state in American history. In 1824, John Quincy Adams became president of the United States. He was known as an independent, but was defeated by Andrew Jackson in 1828. He was the only President to go back to the House of Representatives after having served. He reentered politics as a congressman in 1831. Adams wished to establish the United States as the foremost center for the studying of astronomy in the world. In the Smithsonian Institution, his efforts were justified.

As an independent, Adams sought to bring people together, but not at the expense of his principles. As Secretary of State he was involved in mediations between European nations. Like his father, John Quincy Adams, he was a scholar. His leadership was characterized by earnest preparation of both heart and head. He had a deep devotional life and was disciplined in his study of Scripture.

While in St. Petersburg, Russia, Adams was aware of Moscow surrendering to Napoleon and grieved with the Russian people as the city went up in flames. At the same time, he lost his son and said, "I mourned over the fallen city, and even its fallen conquerors, because I was a man and a Christian, but their fate would neither sharpen nor mitigate my private woe." [1]

The Last Puritan?

President Washington stated, "He (John Quincy Adams) is the most valuable public character we have abroad, and there remains no doubt in my mind he will prove himself to be the ablest of all our diplomatic corp." [2] Twentieth century biographers have had the advantage of looking at the whole life of John Quincy Adams. "Those who knew him only fleetingly might have been tempted to write him off as an irascible, anti-social Yankee, but the truth about John Quincy Adams ran much deeper; he was one of the most moral statesmen America ever produced. Historians hesitate to apply the word Puritan to him, as the Puritans had long since passed from the New England scene. Yet, in a profound sense, Adams properly deserves to be called 'the last Puritan.' "He owed his influence, not to his manner, presence or pleasing tones, but to the fact that what he said was worth hearing." [4]

Adams expressed the view that "America goes not abroad in search of monsters to destroy. She is the well-wisher to the freedom and independence of all." [5] As President, Adams was certainly not political but made appointments based on who he thought was the most qualified person and not an individual's political affiliations. There were other qualifications of course, and many believed that an atheist or a deist (someone who does not recognize the Deity of Christ) was not qualified to lead the nation. Adams stated, "A man, to be a Christian, must believe in God, in the Bible, in the Divinity of the Savior's mission, and in a future state of rewards and punishments." [6]

"The best index to a person's character is how he treats people who can't do him any good and how he treats people who can't fight back." [3]

Abigal Van Buren

Adams was convinced that, "The highest glory of the American Revolution was that it connected in one indissoluble bond the principles of civil government with the principles of Christianity. Human legislators can undertake only to prescribe the actions of men; they acknowledge their inability to govern and direct the sentiments of the heart."[7]

Adams believed that mediocrity was one of the worst sins. He put unbelievable pressure on his three sons, and they failed to excel at Harvard. His first son, George Washington Adams, was not up to the pressure. His father was horrified when George finished 13th in his class and his brother John finished 45th in a class of 85. Imagine naming your son after the first President and expecting him to perform up to the Adams' expectations! George was told that he must be in the top ten in his class to be able to visit his family in Washington, D.C. The pressure on young George, a hyperactive student, apparently, was too much to bear. He eventually was dismissed from Harvard and denied his degree. He lost his life in a swimming accident and it may have been suicidal. His father had been an absentee parent for many years and they drifted apart. Adams finally realized that he had pushed his son harder than young George could possibly sustain. Adams was grief stricken… "I have nothing left to rely on but the mercy of God,"[9] he concluded.

ADAMS VIEW OF THE BIBLE

At an oration delivered at Plymouth, December 22, 1802, at the Anniversary of America's ancestors at that place, Adams spoke of the history and future of America. "Among the sentiments of most powerful operation upon the human heart and most highly honorable to the human character, are those of veneration for our ancestors, and of love for our posterity,"[10] he said.

"It is of all books in the world, that which contributes to making men good, wise and happy."[11] From the Bible, Adams learned that God's justice was for all men. Each year, however, his efforts in the House of Representatives to bring an end to slavery were met with resistance.

"Man was not made for himself alone. No, he was made for his country, for his species, for all ages past and for all future times. He is not a puny insect shivering at a breeze, but the glory of creation."[12] Adams concluded the message with the words, "Think of your forefathers and of your posterity!" On leaving the presidency, he said, "I pray heaven to bestow the best of blessings on this house and all that shall hereafter inhabit it. May none but honest and wise men ever rule under this roof." [13]

In 1831 Adams returned to Washington to serve in the House of Representatives. In 1848 he was fatally stricken at the Capital as a result of a stroke. His last words were heard to be, "This is the last of earth. I am content." [14] "Although he was at times rigid, demanding and self-righteous, John Quincy Adams possessed persona integrity, devotion to principle, intellectual intensity and strong will." [16]

THE PASSIONS AND CONVICTIONS OF JOHN QUINCY ADAMS

The notion that all human beings are born free and not slaves can be traced to Adams' understanding of Scriptures and the "Law of Nature and Nature's God."

John Quincy Adams had probably seen more of the world than any of the "Founders." His experience and knowledge of Christian principles prepared him for some remarkable assignments. "Peacemaking" required taking unpopular positions but the eternal principles John Quincy believed in prepared him.

In the movie "Amistad," the role of John Quincy Adams is portrayed. In it he interceded for the Mendi people who are captive on the ship. In one scene, the captain has been overthrown and the crew is zigzagging around the Western Atlantic instead of taking the ship back to Africa. The ghost ship, as it was called then, is finally hauled into port in New London and the Africans are charged with piracy. Later Adams argues the case before the Supreme Court saying that according to the 'Law of Nature and Nature's God' "all people are born free and ought to be free, not slaves." Judge Joseph Story takes up the points Adams made and galvanizes the court in favor of the Africans. It is a powerful example of Adams' strong feelings against slavery. [17]

Adams could think of nothing more appalling than slavery and wrote a poem expressing his convictions:

> Who but shall learn that freedom is the prize
> man still is bound to rescue or maintain;
> That nature's God commands the slave to rise
> And on the oppressor's head to break the chain
> Roll, years of promise, rapidly roll round
> Till not a slave on earth be found. [18]

"America goes not abroad in search of monsters to destroy. she is the well-wisher to the freedom and independence of all." [15]

John Quincy Adams

> *"A man, to be a Christian, must believe in God, in the Bible, in the Divinity of the Savior's mission, and in a future state of rewards and punishments."* [20]
>
> *John Quincy Adams*

Those who knew John Quincy Adams knew that he possessed "an intense love of freedom for all men, and an invincible belief in the unalienable rights of man." [19] As his father had done before him, he went back to natural law (the Law of Nature and Nature's God) for the origin of rights.

Adams defended the Constitution and rested on the principles of natural rights. "Slavery and Democracy would need to be incompatible with each other and yet (at this time) the democracy of the country is supported chiefly, if not entirely by slavery," [21] said Adams. (At this time slavery was outlawed in seven of the states but laws were not enforced.)

ADAMS' IDEAS ON THE ROLE OF WOMEN

Upon the death of his mother, Adams said, "There is not a virtue that can abide in the female heart but it was the ornament of hers…never have I known another human being the perpetual object of whose life was so unremittingly to do good…her price indeed was far above rubies…life is no longer to me what it was; my home is no longer the abode of my mother. All the kindness and affection, at once silent and active as the movement of the orbs of heaven." [22]

John Quincy Adams embraced the notion that God desired to use both men and women in leadership. He used Scripture to back up this conviction. Adams was able to address many issues of his day and one was the role of women in daily life. "Are women to have no opinions or actions on subjects relating to the general welfare? Where did the gentlemen get this principle? Did he find it in the sacred history of the Bible…in the language of Miriam the prophetess, in one of the noblest and most sublime songs of triumph that ever met the human eye or ear? Did the gentlemen never hear of Deborah, to whom the children of Israel came up for judgment? Has he forgotten the deed of Jael, who slew the dreaded enemy of her country? Has he forgotten Esther, who by her petition saved her people and her country?" [23]

Adams believed in peace but it was not "peace at any price." For years his voice was the voice of "conscience" in the House of Representatives.

REVIEW

Q. Since Adams was a Christian and had a "Christian World View," do you think it was an advantage or disadvantage for him when it came time to negotiate treaties with other countries?

Q. Why do you think many people in this country have a hard time acknowledging the role Christianity has had in the formation of the American Republic?

Q. Do you ever feel your personal convictions have been "marginalized"?

Q. Why didn't the "Founders" deal with the problem of slavery at the Continental Convention?

Q. What are the unalienable rights we all enjoy?

Q. Adams effectively used the Scriptures to advance the natural rights of men, women, and those whose nations did not recognize their inalienable (God-given) rights. How do you think he became sensitized to the natural rights of women?

Q. What does Adams mean by nature's rights? Where does this concept come from? Is it still appropriate today?

Q. What do you think are the most important qualifications for a person running for public office?

Q. Why do you think veneration for one's ancestors was important to Adams?

Q. Do you think it would be easier to live for God now or during Adams' time?

Character for Life

GOD'S PROMISE:

"Blessed are the peacemakers, for they will be called sons of God" (Matthew 5:9).

GOD'S GOAL:

That you would become a witness to what Jesus has done in your life.

YOUR COMMITMENT:

Bring God's message of peace and salvation to others.

YOUR DAILY RESPONSE:

1. Let the peace of God be the umpire in your decisions.

2. When God's peace is missing in your heart, you will find God is anxious to show you why it has been withheld from you.

3. Look for ways to be an instrument of peace in others' lives.

FAILURE WILL MEAN:

You will focus on your own needs and not the concerns of Jesus.

BACKGROUND:

Six times in the New Testament, God refers to Himself as a "God of peace." Although we defamed His name and disobeyed His commands, He sent His Son to make peace through His death. God is a God of peace and His children are peacemakers. We can understand the word "peace" better when we understand the Hebrew word "shalom." When people in Israel say "shalom," they are wishing all the best for someone. This is especially true of God. People with pure motives want to be peacemakers, but people with mixed motives prefer "getting their own way" and this leads to strife and resentment.

LIVING AS A PEACEMAKER MEANS . . .

■ Knowing that there is no possibility of peace without coming to peace with God, our Maker.

■ Knowing that the real problem with nations and individuals is sin and the problems that follow are: lust, greed, selfishness, and self-centeredness.

■ Knowing that justice and righteousness will come when man's heart is changed.

■ Knowing that all people should be at peace with God.

■ Knowing that if we look at conflicts from the standpoint of our own self-interest: "How it this affecting me?" Or "What is this going to do to me?" we will fail.

■ Knowing that real and lasting peace will not exist between nations unless peace reigns in each country. This takes place only when people come to know and trust the "Prince of Peace."

■ Helping people find peace within themselves. If we can bring people to righteousness, they can know the "God of peace."

■ Loving our enemies and praying for our persecutors. A peacemaker destroys his enemies by making them his friends.

■ Being humble and dependent upon God.

■ Being a true disciple of Jesus Christ.

■ Being centrally concerned for God's glory to shine forth.

Chapter Ten: Learning more about Adams

Go to an Internet search engine.
Type in John *Quincy Adams' Character.*
Find topics 1-6 below and open up websites.
1. The Education of John Quincy Adams
2. John Quincy Adams
3. John Quincy Adams (Chaung Force)
4. John Quincy Adams Orations
5. MSN Encarta-Adams. John Quincy-(U.S. President)
6. John Quincy Adams "Washington's comment was that JQA was the most valuable public citizen now overseas."

chapter 11

Persecuted for Righteousness—Abraham Lincoln

PURPOSE: The Costs and Blessings of Suffering

character trait:

Persecuted for Righteousness

SUBJECT:
ABRAHAM LINCOLN
(1809-1865)

PURPOSE:
The Costs and Blessings of Suffering

FAMOUS QUOTE:
"Character is like a tree and reputation like its shadow. The shadow is what we think of it; the tree is the real thing."

SCRIPTURE DOCUMENTATION:

"Blessed are those who are persecuted for righteousness, for theirs is the kingdom of heaven" (Matthew 5:10).

"Not only so, but we also rejoice in our sufferings, because we know that suffering produces perseverance" (Romans 5:3).

PERSONALITY PROFILE

Before Abraham Lincoln was born, his family suffered greatly at the hands of the Indians and Lincoln's grandfather lost his life. After his death, Lincoln's father became "a wandering laborer who grew up without an education."

Abraham Lincoln and his family lived in a log cabin near Hodgenville, Kentucky. Few American presidents have had more humble beginnings than he. Lincoln's parents were devoted Christians and likely dedicated their son to the Lord. Lincoln's parent's marriage came to an end when his mother died of "milk sickness" when Abraham was only nine years old. Young "Abe" worked hard to help his father but eventually they were forced out of their home. Life in Kentucky was more than they could endure so father and son moved to Indiana to find work. Another reason for moving was simply that Lincoln's father abhorred slavery. The Baptists had taken a strong stand against slavery and Abraham Lincoln grew up being against slavery as well.

At 26, Lincoln was engaged but his sweetheart died. This broke Lincoln's heart. The second love of his life married someone else because she felt he didn't have the social skills needed to succeed in life. Lincoln had a nervous breakdown and spent the next six months in bed. Lincoln eventually met Mary Todd. Mary's mother had died when Mary was six years old and this left her with feelings of desolation. Mary had attended a prestigious women's academy in Lexington and could speak French fluently; she had a memory for poetry that impressed Lincoln. Mary was 26 when she met Lincoln and at that age in danger of becoming "an old maid."

Lincoln and Mary had much in common. Both were born in Kentucky, both were interested in politics, both were committed to the cause of the slaves and the temperance movements, and both had parents who were pioneer settlers of Kentucky. After three years of courtship Lincoln managed to overcome his lack of social skills and won her "hand in marriage." Lincoln was deeply in love with Mary and said, "My wife is as handsome as when she was a girl, and I...fell in love with her; and what is more, I have never fallen out." Lincoln and Mary had four sons: Robert Todd (1843-1926), Edward Baker (1846-50), William Wallace (1850-62), and Thomas "Tad" (1853-71). Three of the four died before entering adulthood.

THE FAILURES IN LINCOLN'S LIFE

In 1832, at the age of 23, Lincoln ran for the Illinois legislature and lost. He had lost his job and couldn't get into law school. Lincoln declared bankruptcy and spent the next 17 years of his life paying off the money he borrowed from friends to start his business. In 1838, Lincoln was defeated while running for speaker of the state legislature. He finally was elected to the state legislature and spent the next eight years in circuit courts. He eventually served a term in the U.S. House of Representatives. In 1846, 1848, 1854, and 1858, Lincoln was defeated again and again in an effort to win a seat to the U.S. Senate. In 1856, he lost in an effort to become the Vice President of the United States. Rusty Tugman writes, "In 1858 the Illinois legislature, using an obscure statute, sent Stephen A. Douglas to the United States Senate instead of Abraham Lincoln, even though Lincoln had won the popular vote. When a sympathetic friend asked Lincoln how he felt, he said 'Like the boy who stubbed his toe; I am too big to cry and too badly hurt to laugh.' "[1]

Lincoln's growing convictions grew and developed during the decade prior to his becoming president. In 1855 Lincoln wrote the following in a letter, "Our progress in degeneracy appears to me to be pretty rapid. As a nation we began by declaring, 'All men are created equal.' We now practically read it all men are created equal except Negroes. Blacks, slave or free, enjoyed neither citizenship nor rights under the Constitution, which declared them only three-fifths of a person." Lincoln went on to say, "When the No-nothings get control, it will read all men are created equal, except Negroes and foreigners and Catholics. When it comes to this, I shall prefer emigrating to some country where they make no pretense of loving liberty—in Russia, for instance, where despotism can be taken pure, and without the base alloy of hypocrisy."[3]

In 1861, Lincoln was finally elected President of the United States. On February 11, 1861, when leaving for Washington to assume the responsibilities of President, Lincoln said, "I now leave, not knowing when or whether ever I may return, with a task before me greater than that which was upon Washington. Without the assistance of that Divine Being who ever attended him, I cannot succeed. With that assistance I cannot fail. Trusting in Him who can go with me, and remain with you, and be everywhere for good, let us confidently hope that all yet will be well."[4]

"It is fit and becoming in all people, at all times, to acknowledge and revere the supreme government of God; to bow in humble submission to his chastisement; to confess and deplore their sins and transgressions to the full conviction that the fear of the Lord is the beginning of wisdom; and to pray, with all fervency and contrition, for the pardon of their past offenses, and for a blessing upon the prospective action."[2]

Lincoln

Perhaps there was no President so loved as Lincoln. Through his trials and tribulations, his soul was prepared to bring healing to a nation. Lincoln hated war and despised the pain and suffering the division in the country brought about. He believed, however, that "Slavery was a monstrous injustice…a cancer…one that is threatening to grow out of control in a nation originally dedicated to the unalienable rights of man." [6]

LINCOLN AS A FATHER

Lincoln's life was extraordinarily difficult and during his tenure as President he aged a great deal. His son, Willie died of typhoid while his wife suffered a nervous breakdown and Lincoln had to care for her. Lincoln and the "first lady" apparently had an emotionally volatile but warm and intimate relationship to the very end of their marriage. Lincoln was very tender toward his wife and she believed him to be "destined for greatness" and said, "His heart was as big as his arms were long." [7]

Lincoln's character brought personal integrity, intelligence, and humanity, all of which commanded deep respect. He had a warm sense of humor and was the most esteemed and maligned of the American Presidents. He guided the nation through its most perilous period. Count Leo Tolstoy thought of Lincoln as "A Christ in miniature." [8] President William McKinley wrote of Lincoln, "The purposes of God, working through the ages, were, perhaps, more clearly revealed to him than to any other…. He was the greatest man of his time, especially approved of God for the work He gave him to do." [9]

Lincoln brought freedom to millions of African-Americans. Some Americans don't realize that he gave the nation and the world a model of character and virtue. During his trials he developed a real serenity of soul and was able to speak to the deep of Americans. "Have been reading the Beatitudes," he tells a friend, "I can at least claim the blessing that is pronounced upon those who hunger and thirst after righteousness." [10] Lincoln was to hunger no longer. A few days before his death he told of the way in which the peace of heaven stole into his heart. "When I left Springfield not without a thought of the flag and its inscription, I asked the people to pray for me. I was not a Christian. When I buried my son—the severest trial of my life—I was not a Christian. But when I went to Gettysburg, and saw the graves of thousands of our soldiers, I then and there consecrated myself to Christ." [11] From that moment, Dr. Hill says, the habitual attitude of Lincoln's mind was expressed in the words: "God be merciful to me, a sinner!"

With tears in his eyes, he told his friends that he had found the faith that he longed for. He realized, he said, that his heart was changed, and that he loved the Savior. The President of the United States was at the Cross!

In 1864, Lincoln won re-election as the Union military triumphs brought an end to the war. Five days after he had freed millions of slaves, Lincoln was shot by the actor John Wilkes Booth while attending a performance at Ford's Theater in Washington. Lincoln, however, lived to see Peace and Union and Emancipation triumph. His last hours were spent amidst services of thanksgiving and festivals of rejoicing. Lincoln was in Ford's Theatre in Washington but his mind was not on the play. Indeed the play was almost over when he arrived. He leaned forward, talking, under his breath, to Mrs. Lincoln. He said he would like to take a tour of the East. They would visit Palestine—would see Gethsemane and Calvary—would walk together the streets of Jerusalem. A shot rang through the theatre…and Lincoln turned his pilgrimage toward the holiest heights of all. He was eventually killed for his love of righteousness.

Twenty-three-year-old surgeon Taft writes that "he spent most of the night supporting the President's head in order that he would not press on the pillow." [13] He died at 7:22 the following morning. He was taken home to Springfield, Illinois for burial.

The President's wife stayed weeping in the White House while the funeral cortege continued on to Springfield. She left the United States for six years, traveling with her son, Tad. When they returned to America, Tad unexpectedly died from a severe cold. Mary's fragile health resulted in her being institutionalized. She eventually died in Springfield at the home of her sister.

Lincoln realized that his country had strayed from the principles of the "Founding Fathers" and Lincoln sought to have his nation return to the principles they built the country upon. This was a bigger task than George Washington had in trying to unite the people, since he was leading a struggle to preserve the "last, best hope on earth."

God's purposes to bring righteousness to a nation will often include suffering. Lincoln said, "And whereas when our own beloved country, once, by the blessings of God, united, prosperous and happy, is now afflicted with faction and civil war, it is

"slavery was a monstrous injustice…a cancer…one that is threatening to grow out of control in a nation originally dedicated to the inalienable right of man." [12]

Lincoln

NATIONAL PURPOSE

peculiarly fit for us to recognize the hand of God in the terrible visitation, and in sorrowful remembrance of our own crimes as a nation and as individuals, to humble ourselves before Him and to pray for His mercy…that the inestimable boon of civil and religious liberty, earned under His guidance and blessing by the labors and sufferings of our fathers, may be restored." [14]

AMERICA GAVE HOPE TO THE WORLD

On February 22, 1861 at Independence Hall in Philadelphia, Lincoln said, "The Declaration of Independence which gave liberty not alone to the people… of this country, but hope to all the world, for all future time. It was that which gave promise in due time the weights would be lifted from the shoulders of all men, and that all should have an equal chance. This is the sentiment embodied in the Declaration of Independence…. I would rather be assassinated on this spot than surrender it." [15]

AN INSTRUMENT IN THE HANDS OF GOD

On September 11, 1858, Lincoln spoke at Edwardsville, Illinois on the nature of liberty, "What constitutes the bulwark of our own liberty and independence? It is not our growing battlements, our bristling seacoasts, our army and our navy. These are not our reliance against tyranny. All of those may be turned against us without making us weaker for the struggle. Our reliance is in the love of liberty, which God has planted in us. Our defense is in the spirit which prized liberty as the heritage of all men, in all lands everywhere. Destroy the spirit and you have planted the seeds of despotism at your own doors." [17] To Lincoln, disappointments were his lot in life.

THE FEAR OF GOD IS THE BEGINNING OF WISDOM

Lincoln said, "It is fit and becoming in all people, at all times, to acknowledge and revere the Supreme Government of God; to bow in humble submission to his chastisement; to confess and deplore their sins and transgressions to the full conviction that the fear of the Lord is the beginning of wisdom; and to pray, with all fervency and contrition, for the pardon of their past offenses, and for a blessing upon the prospective action." [18]

THE BIBLE—GOD'S GREAT GIFT

Lincoln earnestly studied the Bible as a youth and adult. He said, "In regard to this Great Book, I have but to say, I believe the Bible is the best gift 'God has given to man.' All the good the Savior gave to the world was communicated through this 'Book.' All things most desirable for man's welfare, here and hereafter, are to be found portrayed in it." [19]

Lincoln believed the Bible to be the totally reliable and said, "The character of the Bible is easily established, at least to my satisfaction. The Bible is the only history that claims to be God's book—to comprise His laws, His history. I decided long ago that it was less difficult to believe that the Bible was what it claimed to be than to disbelieve it." [20] Lincoln grew up to regard the Bible as a foundational tool for life. "This book is the best gift God has given to man...but for it we could not know right from wrong," [21] Lincoln concluded.

A MAN OF PRAYER

In July 1861, after the Union army was defeated at the Battle of Bull Run, President Abraham Lincoln declared a National Day of Fasting and Prayer.

Addressing the New Jersey State Senate, Lincoln poured out his concerns for the divided nation, "I am exceedingly anxious that this Union, the Constitution, and the liberties of the people shall be perpetuated in accordance with the original idea for which that struggle was made".... "[It may be that] I shall be a humble instrument in the hands of the Almighty... for perpetuating the object of that struggle." [26] Lincoln entered his second term of office in a forthright but still somber mood, in which the religious overtones in his voice had grown stronger. They echo through the mysterious way in which both sides in the struggle invoked their God, and God withheld his ultimate decision.

Said Lincoln, "I have been driven many times upon my knees by the overwhelming conviction that I had nowhere else to go. My own wisdom, and that of all about me, seemed insufficient for that day." [27]

It would be hard for some to believe that unbelief in God is a disqualifier for office but Lincoln said, "I do not think I could myself, be brought to support a man for office whom I knew to be an open enemy of, and scoffer of religion." [28]

At Gettysburg, Lincoln said, "I do not doubt that our country will finally come through safe and undivided. But do

"A house divided against itself cannot stand. I believe this government cannot endure permanently half slave and half free." [22]

Lincoln

Right at the foundation of America, Lincoln found a moral principle. The self-evident truth proclaimed in the Declaration of Independence—that all men are created equal—"is the father of all moral principles among us," [23] Lincoln said. He saw that the Founders had discovered the principle of equality in "the laws of nature and of nature's God" [24] and laid it down as America's cornerstone. In that way he approached even the most controversial political issues.

Finally, Lincoln was shot dead, but not before he told Americans what to preserve: the principle of equality, the Declaration, and the Constitution. He showed us how: "with malice toward none; with charity for all; and with firmness in the right, as God gives us to see the right." [25]

"I am conscious every moment that all I am and all I have is subject to the control of a Higher Power, and that Power can use me or not use me in any manner, and at any time, as in His wisdom and might may be pleasing to Him. The times are dark, the spirits of ruin are abroad in all their power, and the mercy of God alone can save us." [31]

Lincoln

not misunderstand me...I do not rely on the patriotism of our people, the bravery and devotion of the boys in blue...or the loyalty and skill of our generals...but the God of our fathers, who rose up the country to be a refuge and asylum of the oppressed and downtrodden of all nations, will not let it perish now. I may not live to see it, I do not expect to see it, but God will bring us safely through." [29]

Lincoln called the nation to prayer by saying, "And whereas when our own beloved country, once, by the blessings of God, united, prosperous and happy, is now afflicted with faction and civil war, it is peculiarly fit for us to recognize the hand of God in the terrible visitation, and in sorrowful remembrance of our own crimes as a nation and as individuals, to humble ourselves before Him and to pray for His mercy...that the inestimable boon of civil and religious liberty, earned under this guidance and the blessing by the labors and sufferings of our fathers, may be restored." [30]

A HOUSE DIVIDED CANNOT STAND

During his trials Lincoln developed a serenity of soul and was able to speak to the deep pain of the people. "A house divided against itself cannot stand. I believe this government cannot endure permanently half slave and half free." [32] "With malice toward none; with charity for all," Lincoln looked forward to binding up the nations wounds and hoped to "achieve a cherished, just and lasting peace." [33]

SUFFERING FOR RIGHTEOUSNESS

Humility and repentance before God are required for healing to come to the nation. National repentance was a theme of Lincoln's administration. Lincoln said, "It is fit and becoming in all people, at all times, to acknowledge and revere 'The Supreme Government of God'; to bow in humble submission to his chastisement; to confess and deplore their sins and transgressions to the full conviction that the fear of the Lord is the beginning of wisdom; and to pray, with all fervency and contrition, for the pardon of their past offenses, and for a blessing upon the prospective action." [34]

Lincoln's goal was that justice would be extended to every American. Lincoln said, "Fondly do we hope, fervently do we pray, that this mighty scourge may speedily pass away. Yet, if God wills that it continue until all the wealth pied by the bondsman's two hundred and fifty years of unrequited toil shall be sunk, and until every drop of blood drawn with the lash shall be paid by another drawn with the sword, as was said three thousand years ago, so still it must be said 'the judgments of the Lord are true and righteous altogether.' I know there is a God…. If He has a place and a work for me, and I think He has, I believe I am ready. I am nothing, but truth is everything. I know I am right, because I know that liberty is right, for Christ teaches it, and Christ is God."[35]

Lincoln believed that forgiveness and mercy would bring about reconciliation. Lincoln said, "With malice toward none, with charity for all, with firmness in the right as God gives us to see the right, let us strive on to finish the work we are in, to bind up the nations wounds, to care for him who shall have borne the battle and for his widow and his orphan, to do all which may achieve and cherish a just and lasting peace among ourselves and with all nations."[37]

Lincoln was able to take the wounds of those who have suffered great loses and point them to the Heavenly Father. To a mother who had lost five sons in battle, Lincoln wrote, "I feel how weak and fruitless must be any words of mine which should attempt to beguile you from the grief of a loss so overwhelming. But I cannot refrain from tendering to you the consolation that may be found in the thanks of the Republic they died to save. I pray that our Heavenly Father may assuage the anguish of your bereavement, and leave you only the cherished memory of the loved and lost, and the solemn pride that must be yours to have laid so costly a sacrifice upon the altar of freedom."[38]

Lincoln believed that each citizen had the responsibility to pray to Almighty God for his or her country. He observed, "Both (the North and the South) read the same Bible, and pray to the same God: and each invokes His aid against the other. It may seem strange that any men should dare to ask just God's assistance in wringing their bread from the sweat of other men's faces; but let us judge not that we be not judged. The prayers of both could not be answered: that of neither has been answered fully. The Almighty has His own purposes."[39]

THE EMANCIPATION PROCLAMATION

Lincoln issued the Emancipation Proclamation on January 1, 1863. In 1864 he won re-election, as Union military triumphs brought an end to the war. In 1865, at his Second Inaugural, Lincoln called on the whole nation to embrace peace and reconciliation asking the nation to lay aside revenge

"I do not think I could myself, be brought to support a man for office whom I knew to be an open enemy of, and scoffer of religion."[36]
Lincoln

and embrace reunification. Lincoln commented, "If we shall suppose that American slavery is one of those offenses which, in the providence of God, must need come, but which, having continued through His appointed time, He now wills to remove, and that He gives both North and South this terrible war as the woe due to those by whom the offense came, shall we discern therein any departure from those divine attributes which the believers in a living God always ascribe to Him?" [40]

REVIEW

Q. Lincoln believed that his running for President could very well cost him his life but he was prepared to give it for the healing of the union. What does that tell you about him?

Q. In Lincoln's mind, what was the disqualifier for running for office?

Q. How do you think Lincoln came to the viewpoint that God had allowed the terrible war between the states?

Q. List some of the reasons Lincoln is endeared so much even today.

Q. Would it not be appropriate for us today to acknowledge and revere the Supreme Government of God and humble ourselves before Him?

Q. Lincoln's character was known throughout the world. Why do you think the world was amazed over his character and "Christ-like" spirit?

Q. Lincoln was not ashamed to point people to the Bible and to the Savior. What kind of response would the President get if he chose to make these kinds of statements today?

Q. How could national repentance come about?

Q. Writing to a mother who lost five sons in battle, Lincoln poured out his heart to her pain. How did his letter to the mother affect you?

Q. Discuss Lincoln's view that America would be an asylum for the oppressed.

Q. It had only been 80 years, but Lincoln believed the nation had lost the vision of Washington and the "Founders" of America. What does this tell us about the fragility of the "government of the people"?

Q. Lincoln called the nation to prayer and repentance. Compare 2 Chronicles 16:9 with the situation facing the divided America.

Q. What was Lincoln's greatest fear?

This is the sentiment embodied in the Declaration of Independence.... I would rather be assassinated on this spot than surrender it." [41]

Lincoln

Character for Life

GOD'S PROMISE:

"Blessed are those who are persecuted for righteousness, for theirs is the kingdom of heaven" (Matthew 5:10).

GOD'S GOAL:

Help you to see that persecution for righteousness brings eternal benefits.

YOUR COMMITMENT:

Relinquish the injustice you experience to God.

YOUR DAILY RESPONSE:

1. Remember Jesus and His sufferings for His righteous decisions.

2. Recognize His presence and approval will be yours as you stand alone for righteousness.

3. In the end, your commitment will bring honor to God and blessing to others.

4. Realize there is a price to pay and be willing to pay it.

FAILURE WILL MEAN:

You will constantly be defensive and blaming others for their attacks on you.

BACKGROUND:

Behind the world "system" is the "prince of the world" or Satan himself. People who live in Satan's kingdom or do not have the love of God in their lives can mistreat believers. Most of the terrible persecution throughout church history has come from religious people. Often formal Christianity is a great enemy of faithful believers.

LIVING AS A PEACEMAKER MEANS . . .

■ Knowing that Jesus calls those blessed who have a great inner hunger and thirst for righteousness. Jesus promised they would be satisfied. In dependence upon Him, our needs will be met.

■ "Marching to the beat of a different drummer." Christians are different in how they see things because their motives are different.

■ Not conforming to this world. The world prizes conformity and difference is often looked upon as dangerous.

■ Being a kind of "conscience to the community." It bothers those with no integrity to live and work with people who live according to God's standards.

■ Your reward in heaven is great. If you are persecuted for righteousness, you will have a great reward. You are in a great company of people.

■ You have the reward of a relationship with Jesus. If you go through the fires, you will not be wiped out. In the middle of persecution, God will never forsake you.

■ Believing that in Jesus you have an endless supply of the Bread of Life (John 6:25-58), and the living waters (John 7:37-39) bubbling up to eternal life.

■ Being righteous, practicing righteousness, and being like the Lord Jesus Christ.

Chapter Eleven: Learning more about Lincoln

Go to an Internet search engine.
Type in *Abraham Lincoln's Character.*
Find topics 1-5 below and open up the websites.
1. Abraham Lincoln. "Have faith that right makes might."
2. Abraham Lincoln Quotes and Quotations Brainy Quotes
3. Abraham Lincoln Quotes
4. Quote by Abraham Lincoln?
5. AbfiMagazine-Abraham Lincoln

chapter 12

Walking in God's Truth—patrick henry

PURPOSE: Making God's Truth the Foundation of My Life

character trait:
Walking in God's Truth

SUBJECT:
PATRICK HENRY
(1736-1799)

PURPOSE:
Making God's Truth the
Foundation of My Life

FAMOUS QUOTE:
"Give me liberty or give me
death."

**SCRIPTURE
DOCUMENTATION:**

"He replied, 'Blessed rather are
those who hear the word of God
and obey it'" (Luke 11:28).

"Therefore everyone who hears
these words of mine and puts
them into practice is like a wise
man who built his house on the
rock. The rain came down, the
streams rose, and the winds blew
and beat against that house; yet it
did not fall, because it had its
foundations on the rock"
(Matthew 7:24-25).

"Now the Bereans were of more
noble character than the
Thessalonians, for they received
the message with great eagerness
and examined the Scriptures every
day to see if what Paul said was
true" (Acts 17:11).

PERSONALITY PROFILE

Patrick Henry was famous for the
words, "Give me liberty or give me
death." He was, by all standards, a
remarkable man. Young Henry was
raised in a Christian family. His mother
was the daughter of a Presbyterian
immigrant to Virginia and a woman with
great abilities, warmth, and charm. His
father, John Henry, realized young
Patrick's love for learning as a child and nurtured it.

Henry's ability to quickly comprehend Latin and the Scriptures
provided a strong foundation for his adult life. Henry was educated by his father and at the age of 15 became a clerk at a
small store. At 16, Henry opened a store along with his brother
and at 18, he met and married Sarah Shelton.

John Henry was a family man with 17 children. When his first
wife, Sarah Shelton died in 1777, John Henry married Dorthea
Dangridge. In John Henry's last will and testament he wrote,
"This is all the inheritance I can give to my dear family. The religion of Christ can give them one which will make them rich
indeed."

One of the greatest influences on Henry's life was the Rev.
Samuel Davies who later became the President of Princeton. He
was known as the finest preacher in the South and his sermons
were filled with deep emotion and love for the Savior.

Patrick Henry was known as the "Oracle of Liberty." "His main
goal was to establish true Christianity in our country" (Patrick
Henry Fontaine). Henry was a member of the "House of
Burgesses," and a member of the Continental Congress from
1774 to 1775. Henry served three terms as Govenor of Virginia
in 1776, 1778 and 1784.

He gave what was to be his last speech on the steps of the
courthouse in Richmond. Mary Harland, in her autobiography,
described the scene as told to her: Patrick Henry delivered his last
speech to his adoring constituents. He was tottering upon the
verge of the grave, into which he sank gently a few weeks later.
A crisis of national and state importance had called him from his
home at Red Hill, a dozen miles away. Keyed up by a sense of
the imminence of the peril to the country he had saved, his magnificent will-power responded to the call; the dying fire leaped
high. He had never reasoned more cogently, never pleaded with
more power than on that day. But as the last word fell from his
lips, he sank fainting into the arms of his attendants.

Eventually, Henry determined to prepare for a career in law. At age 27, he put forth the case against England of taxation without representation and he was instrumental in writing the "Constitution of Virginia." Henry eventually became as popular in Virginia as Samuel Adams was in Massachusetts. He served five terms as governor of Virginia and this cost him his health and the loss of his financial fortune. After the passing of the Constitution, Washington offered him the option of becoming Secretary of State or Chief Justice of the Supreme Court. Even though he admired Washington, Henry declined these offers. Henry considered what was right in the eyes of God more important than the changing opinions of man. In 1774, knowing what was before his beloved Virginia, Henry, as Virginia's governor, called for a "day of fasting, humiliation and prayer."

HENRY'S CONVICTIONS AND PASSIONS

The truth of the Scriptures set Patrick Henry on a path of righteousness. Henry's uncle, Patrick Henry, was a rector at St. Paul's Parish for 40 years. He taught his nephew that it was his desire, "To be true, and just in all my dealings. To bear no malice nor hatred in my heart. To keep my hands from stealing. Not to covet another man's goods; but to learn and labor unto which it shall please God to call me."[2]

Henry was a man with deep convictions about the Bible and the Christian religion. Henry believed, "The Bible is worth all the other books that have ever been written."[3] Henry also said, "I think of religion of infinitely higher importance than politics."[4]

Henry was the "Oracle of the Revolution." Founder George Mason said, "He (Henry) is the most powerful speaker I have ever heard. Every word he says not only engages, but commands the attention, and your passions when he addresses them. But his eloquence is the smallest part of his merit. He is, in my opinion, the first man upon this continent, as well as in abilities in public virtues."[5]

Henry sought to establish true Christianity throughout the country. The ancestors of Henry sought to preserve his legacy. William Wirt Henry writes, "He looked to the restraining and elevating principles of Christianity as the hope of his country's institutions."[6] Patrick Henry Fontaine spoke of Henry's attitude towards Christianity saying, "He had committed himself to the earnest efforts to establish true Christianity in our country. Patrick Henry was not less admirable as a man than as an

"unto ourselves, our own life is necessary, unto others, our character."[1]

st. Augustine

orator, for his religious convictions were even more profound than his political, and he was irreproachably faithful, besides, to every obligation of civic, social and domestic life." [8]

HENRY'S PROMOTION OF THE BIBLE

Patrick Henry did not seek national offices and declined them all. He was a symbol of the American struggle for liberty and self-government. He was a man of the Bible and sought to live according to its precepts. His last will and testament, penned in his own hand, told about his affirmation of faith.

As governor of Virginia, Patrick Henry supported a bill establishing a provision for teachers of the Christian Religion. Henry looked to the restraining and elevating principles of Christianity as the hope of his country's institutions. The following are a few of the things Henry said:

> Whether this will prove a blessing or a curse, will depend upon the use our people make of the blessing, which gracious God hath bestowed upon us. If they are wise, they will be great and happy but if they are of a contrary character, they will be miserable.
>
> Reader! Whoever thou art, remember this, and in thy sphere practice virtue thyself, and encourage it to others.
>
> The great pillars of all government and of social life are…"virtue, morality and religion." This is the armor, my friend, and this alone renders us invincible. Righteousness alone can exalt America. Whoever thou art, remember this; and in thy sphere practice virtue thyself, and encourage it to others. [9]

Henry's convictions in the truth of the Scriptures led him to believe that God's purposes for mankind are eternal and bring unity in the family of Christ. Upon the death of his sister's husband, he wrote the following to his sister:

> Would to God I could say something to give you relief to the dearest of women and sister…perhaps I may never see you in this world. O may we meet in heaven, to which the merits of Jesus will carry those who love and serve Him. Heaven will, I trust, give you its choicest comfort and preserve your family. Such is the prayer of him who thinks it is an honor and pride to be,
> Your affectionate brother,
> Patrick Henry [11]

GIVE ME LIBERTY OR GIVE ME DEATH

Said Henry, "My earnest wish is that Christian charity, forbearance and love may unite all different persuasions as brethren who must perish or triumph together, and I trust that the time is not far distant when we shall greet each other as peaceable possessors of that just and equal system of liberty." [13]

The final comments of Henry's famous speech deserve close evaluation:

> Sir, we are not weak, if we make a proper use of those means which the God of nature hath placed in our power. Three million of people armed in the holy cause of liberty and in such a country as that which we possess are invincible by any force which our enemy can send against us.
>
> Besides sir, we shall not fight our battles alone. There is a just God who presides over the destinies of nations and who will raise up friends to fight our battles for us. The battle, sir, is not to the strong alone; it is to the vigilant, the active, the brave… Besides, sir, we have no election. If we were based enough to desire it, it is now too late to retire from the contest. There is no retreat but in submission and slavery! Our chains are forged! Their clanking may be heard on the plains of Boston! The war is inevitable—and let it come! I repeat! I repeat, sir, let it come!
>
> It is in vain, sir, to extenuate the matter. Gentlemen may cry peace, peace—but there is not peace! The war is actually begun! The next gale that sweeps from the north will bring to our ears the clash of resounding arms! Our brethren are already in the field! Why stand we here idle! What is it that gentlemen wish! What would they have? Is life so dear, or peace so sweet as to be purchased at the price of chains and slavery? Forbid it, Almighty God! I know not what course others may take; but as for me, *give me liberty or give me death!!!* [14]

On his deathbed Henry spoke to his physician saying, "Doctor, I wish you to observe how real and beneficial the religion of Christ is to a man about to die… I am, however, much consoled by reflecting that the religion of Christ has, from its first appearances in the world, been attacked in vain by all the wits, philosophers and wise ones, aided by every power of man, and its triumphs have, been complete." [16]

"what we have in us of the image of god is the love of truth and justice." [12]

Demosthenes

"*Seize upon truth, whenever it is found, amongst your friends, amongst your foes, on Christian or on heathen ground, the flower's divine where'er it grows.*" [15]

Issac Watts

REVIEW

Q. Pilate asked the question of Jesus, "What is truth?" Jesus gave no reply. What is your definition of "truth"?

Q. What do you think Henry's reasons were for making the statement that "religion" is more important than politics?

Q. What do you think Henry meant by the, "restraining principles of Christianity"?

Q. How do you think Henry could conclude that there was a judge, God, who oversees the nations? Who would be the victors of the battle?

Q. What do you think Henry meant when he said, "Righteousness can exalt a nation"?

Q. As Henry reflects on eternity awaiting him, he is mindful of the victory of Christ over evil. What does that tell you about the man who was the "Oracle of the Revolution"?

Q. Based on the quote "Give me liberty or give me death," is there something more important than just staying alive?

> "The Bible is worth all the other books that have ever been written." [17]
>
> Henry

Character for Life

GOD'S PROMISE:

"He replied, 'Blessed rather are those who hear the word of God and obey it'" (Luke 11:28).

GOD'S GOAL:

That you not only hear the Word of God but obey it.

YOUR COMMITMENT:

To walk in the light of God's Word and be open to the conviction of the Holy Spirit.

YOUR DAILY RESPONSE:

1. Daily meditate on, renew, and obey God's Word.

2. Revere God's Word above all else.

3. Seek God's perspective by bringing your mind under the control of the Scriptures.

4. Rejoice in the great honor you have been given of having the Word of God available to you!

FAILURE WILL MEAN:

We try to hide what we really are and become a hypocrite.

BACKGROUND:

The Greeks associated darkness with ignorance, sinful doings, and particularly being afraid of death. Light symbolized light and happiness and even ethical goodness. There is only one hope for those in the grip of darkness; the light provided by Jesus.

If a person follows Jesus, he will never walk in darkness since Jesus is the light that shines in darkness bringing light. In Isaiah the Bible predicts that God will one day live among men and "the LORD will be your everlasting light" (Isaiah 60:19-20).

LIVING AS ONE WHO WALKS IN GOD'S TRUTH MEANS . . .

■ Living in the light and truth of God (1 John 1:5).

■ Knowing that only through the Lord Jesus Christ can light shine out of darkness (2 Corinthians 4:6).

■ Understanding that Satan has blinded people so they can't recognize Jesus (2 Corinthians 4:4; 1 Thessalonians 5:5-6).

■ Realizing that those who have come out of the kingdom of darkness are expected to live as children of light (Matthew 5:16).

■ Understanding that walking in the light means accepting God's verdict on our actions and attitudes and asking for His forgiveness and cleansing when we sin (John 12:46).

■ Learning that blessing comes to our lives as we begin to meditate on and obey God's Word (Romans 6:16-17).

Chapter Twelve: Learning more about Henry

Go to an Internet search engine.
Type in *Patrick Henry's Character, Bible.*
Find topics 1-6 below and open up the websites.
1. Patrick Henry "If they are of a contrary character..."
2. Patrick Henry On Religious Freedom
3. Forsaken Roots
4. James M. Elson "What Patrick Henry Accomplished"...
5. Computer Cops
6. WorldNetDaily "We need a Patrick Henry to lead us again"

chapter 13

Trusting God's Character—william penn

PURPOSE: Finding the Heart of the Universe

character trait:
Trusting God's Character

SUBJECT:
WILLIAM PENN
(1644-1718)

PURPOSE:
Finding the Heart of the Universe

FAMOUS QUOTE:
"Be sure you speak evil of none, not of the meanest, much less of your superiors as magistrates, guardians, teachers, and elders in Christ."

SCRIPTURE DOCUMENTATION:
"And without faith it is impossible to please God, because anyone who comes to him must believe that he exists and that he rewards those who earnestly seek him" (Hebrews 11:6).

"Now that you know these things, you will be blessed if you do them" (John 13:17).

William Penn was the founder of Pennsylvania. His father was a famous British Navy Admiral and a friend of King Charles II. William was a student at Oxford and after studying law and graduating, he encountered true Christians. His heart was changed and he determined to give of his life to spread the truth of Christianity.

Penn was an incredible leader but it was leadership learned through suffering. On three occasions he was imprisoned for his faith and one time it was for eight months in the Tower of London. God used this time of suffering in his life and he wrote a classic called, "No Cross, No Crown." Having everything in terms of wealth and opportunity, he embraced the cross of Jesus and admonished others to do so as well. In this book he said, "Make your conversation with the most eminent for wisdom and piety, and shun all wicked men as you hope for the blessing of God and the comfort of your father's living and dying prayers. Be sure you speak evil of none, not of the meanest, much less of your superiors as magistrates, guardians, teachers, and elders of Christ."[1]

At the death of Penn's father, King Charles owed William Penn a great amount of money, which he apparently did not have. Penn was awarded a land grant in America since he was the heir. This land consisted of all the land between Maryland and New York. It became known as "the Quaker State," and soon became a haven for people from all religious backgrounds.

Upon his death, a friend said the following about William Penn: "He was a Man of great Abilities, of an Excellent sweetness of Disposition, quick of thought, and ready utterance; full of the 'Qualifications of true Discipleship,' even Love without dissimulation. His character may be ranked among the learned good and great."[2]

To many, William Penn was the first great hero of American liberty. He was born and spent most of his life in England where he was a writer and religious nonconformist. Penn married Guilielma Springett on April 4, 1672. They had seven children yet only three lived to adulthood. He became the leading defender of religious toleration in England and this activity resulted in him becoming a fugitive for four years, where he had to hide in London's slums. He traveled much and was able to see his wife just before she died at the age of 48. Penn and John Locke were close friends. Locke believed in Penn's character and restored his reputation. Penn desired to establish a refuge in the new world for the persecuted sect called "Quakers." Coming to America, he designed Philadelphia and other towns with a grid pattern of streets, buildings, and public squares to promote health and fire safety.

Churches from throughout Europe found a haven in America. Penn was well-trained in his Christian faith and knew of the suffering of other denominations: Quakers, Mennonites, Lutherans, Church of the Brethren, and Moravians. Penn went beyond the natural rights theory of his friend John Locke and showed how a free society would actually work. He demontrated how people from many different races and religions can live together in peace.

On a plaque in the Philadelphia City Hall, a prayer for the City of Philadelphia is inscribed, "And thou, Philadelphia, the virgin settlement of this province named before thou wert born, what love, what care, what service and what travail have to bring thee forth and preserve thee from such as would abuse and defile thee. O that thou mayest be kept from the evil that would overwhelm thee. That faithful to the God of thy mercies, in the Life of Righteousness, thou, mayest be preserved to the end. My soul prays to God for thee, that thou mayest stand in the day of trial, that thy children may be blest of the Lord and thy people saved by His Power."[3]

PENN'S FAITH IN GOD AND SCRIPTURE

Penn's commitment to his faith and the Scriptures taught him to love his neighbor (the native Indians) as he loved himself. Penn had to deal with the Indians, of course, and as a man of principle, he dealt fairly by paying them full price for their land. As a result of his relationship with the Indians, there

FURTHER SCRIPTURE DOCUMENTATION:
"If that is how God clothes the grass of the field, which is here today and tomorrow is thrown into the fire, will he not much more clothe you, O you of little faith? So do not worry, saying, 'What shall we eat? or 'What shall we drink? or 'What shall we wear?' For the pagans run after all these things, and your heavenly Father knows that you need them" (Matthew 6:30-32).

"If you think about what you ought to do for other people, your character will take care of itself. Character is a by-product (of a relationship with God) and any man who devotes himself to its (character) cultivation in his own case will become a selfish prig." [Someone who considers himself morally superior to others and takes pride in behaving in a very proper and correct way.] [5]

Woodrow Wilson

never was war between them. To the Indians, he wrote, "I desire to gain your love and friendship by a kind and peaceable life." [4]

Penn taught the truth of Jesus; he preached love and taught that Christians should work together. Philadelphia became known as the "City of Brotherly Love" as a result. The acclamations of others who would come to this country and praise William Penn were many. He believed in the "Divine right of government" and sought to form the government of Pennsylvania as a "holy experiment" in governing. If he is known for anything, it was that everything should be done with Christian love. He believed that love would sway the mind and provide "even scales of justice."

Penn's faith was rooted in the admonition of Scripture that both women and men are equal in the sight of God. Penn gave Pennsylvania a written constitution, which guaranteed many fundamental liberties. He even insisted that women deserved equal rights with men.

Penn said the following related to his faith:

> For in Jesus Christ, the light of the world are hid all the treasures of wisdom and knowledge, redemption and glory; they are hid from the worldly Christian, from all that are captivated by the spirit and lusts of the world: and whoever would see them must come to Christ Jesus and the true light in their consciences, bring their deeds to Him, love Him and obey Him; whom God hath ordained a light to lighten the Gentiles, and for His salvation to the ends of the earth.
>
> I do declare to the whole world that we believe in the Scriptures to contain a declaration of the mind and will of God in and to those ages in which they were written; being given forth by the Holy Ghost moving in the hearts of holy men of God; that they ought also to be read, believed, and fulfilled in our day; being used for reproof and instruction, that the man of God may be perfect. They are a declaration and testimony of heavenly things themselves, and, as such, we carry a high respect for them. We accept them as the words of God Himself. [6]

William Penn wrote, "When it is tried, Christian faith will stand the test of trials and is part of "embracing the cross." William Penn went further to define faith as a "faith that overcomes." Penn admonished his fellow believers saying, "While we are following Christ in patience, humility and self denial, and bearing his cross, for [if there is] no cross there is no crown." [7]

He also said, "We are travelers here in this vale of tears, in this earthly pilgrimage, into the land of rest, the heavenly Canaan."[8]

For Penn the "cross" (the consequences of obedience to Christ) became a reality when he encountered people who were hostile to righteousness. Penn testified, "I related the bitter mockings and scorings that fell upon me, the displeasure of my parents, the cruelty and invective of the priests, the strangeness of all my companions, and what a sign and wonder they made of me; but, above all, that great cross of resisting and watching against my own vain affections and thoughts."[9]

"That which is pleasing to God is walking by faith; what is this faith? A pure resolution of living to God, in a holy dependence on him, and committing ourselves entirely to him, so we may know, and enjoy the purifying virtue of his Word, that we may not offend God, for without faith, saith the apostle, it is impossible to please him. By what means, saith the royal psalmist, shall a young man cleanse his way? By taking heed thereto according to thy Word; this is the blessed word, that hath a root of life in all ages, let us abide to this Word all our days, and we shall then be blessed with that life which shall never end, but shall remain when time shall be no more,"[11] Penn wrote.

PENN'S FAMILY SITUATION

Penn had to trust God with his family's future. Separated by an ocean, he never was sure what was going to happen to him or to his family who were going through great persecution in England. His was a faith and confidence in the ability of God to care for his children and wife.

William Penn, if anything, was a man of faith and love. His love for God, his fellow believers, and his family is extraordinary. The following letter to his wife was his last. It expressed the depth and breath of his great heart:

> My dear Wife and Children,
> My love, which neither sea nor land nor death itself can extinguish or lessen toward you, most endearly visits you with eternal embraces, and will abide with you forever; and may the God of my life watch over you and bless you, and do good in this world and forever!
> Some things are upon my spirit to leave with you in your respective capacities, as I am to the one a husband and to the rest a father, if I should never see you more in this world. My

"I desire to gain your love and friendship by a kind and peaceable life."[10]

Penn, addressing the Indians

dear wife, remember thou wast the love of my youth and much the joy of my life; the most beloved as well as the most worthy of all the earthly comfort; and the reason of that love was more thy inward than thy outward excellencies; which yet were many.

God knows, and thou knowest it, I can say it was a match of Providence's making and God's image in us both was the first thing, and the most amiable and engaging ornament in our eyes. Now I am to leave thee, and that without knowing whether I shall ever see thee more in this world; take my counsel into thy bosom and let it dwell with thee in my stead while thou livest.

First, let the fear of the Lord and a zeal and love to his glory dwell richly in thy heart, and thou wilt watch for good over thyself and thy dear children, and family, that no rude, light, or bad thing be committed, else God will be offended, and He repent Himself of the good He intends thee and thine. They that love beyond the world cannot be separated by it. Death is but crossing the world as friends so the seas; they live in one another still.

And now, my dearest, let me recommend to thy care my dear children; abundantly beloved of me as the Lord's blessings, and the sweet pledges of our mutual and endeared affection. Above all things endeavor to breed them up in the love and virtue, and that holy plain way of it which we have lived in, that the world in no part of it get into my family. I had rather they were homely than finely bred as to outward behavior; yet I love sweetness mixed with gravity and cheerfully tempered with sobriety. Religion in the heart leads into this true civility, teaching men and women to be mild and courteous in their behavior, an accomplishment worthy indeed of praise. [13]

REVIEW

Q. What do you think it must have been like for Penn, who was the son of a famous British military hero, to identify himself with a despised group of people called the Quakers?

Q. What was the "holy experiment" that Penn proposed to begin in Pennsylvania?

Q. What did he mean by the "divine right of government"?

Q. "Now faith is being sure of what we hope for and certain of what we do not see..." William Penn began to envision a different kind of society based on love and Christian principles. As the custodian of this vision, how do you think his faith sustained him until the vision became a reality?

Q. What is your definition of "overcoming faith"?

Q. What other group of people in church history had "overcoming faith"?

Q. Should "overcoming faith" be the norm or an exception for Christians?

Q. Can you trust God's character when you are surrounded by confusion? (See Job 23:10-12; 2 Corinthians 7:5-6)?

Q. If Christian love plants love deeper in the heart, the years of separation between Penn and his wife must have been painful. How do you think they sustained their love while being apart?

Q. What were his goals for his children?

Q. What were his fears for his wife and his children?

Q. What does the word "Philadelphia" mean, and what city was it named for?

Q. What do you think Penn meant by referring to a "day of trial" ahead for Philadelphia?

> "while we are following christ in patience, humility and self denial, and bearing his cross, for [if there is] no cross there is no crown." [14]
>
> Penn

Character for Life

GOD'S PROMISE:

"And without faith it is impossible to please God, because anyone who comes to him must believe that he exists and that he rewards those who earnestly seek him" (Hebrews 11:6).

GOD'S GOAL:

That you abandon all trust in your own resources and rely on the finished work of Christ for salvation and daily strength.

YOUR COMMITMENT:

To believe that God will do for you what He has promised in His Word.

YOUR DAILY RESPONSE:

1. Our response is faithfulness to God and His Word

2. Our faith rests on the integrity of Jesus Christ whose faithfulness endures forever.

3. Our responsibility is to allow Jesus Christ to live His life in us. Jesus Himself is the very foundation of our faith.

FAILURE WILL MEAN:

Depending on our own common sense rather than the Holy Spirit. This leads to infidelity and unfaithfulness.

BACKGROUND:

Faith means abandoning all trust in one's own resources and casting oneself on the mercy of God for salvation. It is the trial of our faith that is precious to God.

TRUSTING GOD'S CHARACTER MEANS . . .

■ Believing that what He has said in the Bible is true.

■ Living one's life by what the Bible says.

■ Having faith that one's future is in God's hands.

■ Living by faith each day.

■ Being a witness for God in everything one does.

■ Resting assured in eternal life if one is a Believer.

DEFINITION OF FAITH

◆ Faith is confidence in a person (Jesus Christ) who is not deceived in anything He says or the way He looks at things. It is confidence in the character of God.

◆ Faith is the inborn capacity to see God behind everything, the wonder that keeps you an eternal child.

◆ Faith is not a bargain, (I will trust you if you provide money, health, etc.) but trust in a God you cannot trace, but whose character you know, and remaining true to that character no matter what happens.

◆ Faith is centering your entire life on God and the giving over of your life to Jesus.

◆ Faith is having confidence in God and whether you are visibly delivered or not, you will stick to your belief that God is love and a God of honor.[15]

—Oswald J. Chambers

Chapter Thirteen: Learning more about William Penn

Go to an Internet search engine.
Type in *William Penn's Character*.
Find topics 1-5 below and open up the websites.
1. George Fox to the Princess Elizabeth1
2. William Penn founder of Pennsylvania
3. Primitive Christianity Revived, By Wm. Penn, 1696
4. Cached William Penn
5. On the character of Generation X

chapter 14

Reverence for God—john witherspoon

PURPOSE: God's Most Important Attribute

character trait:
Reverence for God

SUBJECT:
JOHN WITHERSPOON
(1723-1794)

PURPOSE:
God's Most Important Attribute

FAMOUS QUOTE:
"It is only the fear of God that can deliver us from the fear of men."

SCRIPTURE DOCUMENTATION:
"Then those who feared the LORD talked with each other, and the LORD listened and heard. A scroll of remembrance was written in his presence concerning those who feared the LORD and honored his name" (Malachi 3:16).

PERSONALITY PROFILE

John Witherspoon was an American revolutionary patriot of Scottish birth and a descendant of John Knox, whose prayers made Mary Queen of Scots, more afraid than "an army of ten thousand men."[1]

At the age of 14 he attended the University of Edinburgh where he made rapid advances in his training. He graduated from Edinburgh after studying the Arts and Theology. Theology was his major focus during the next seven years and by the age of 21 he assumed a position as an associate with his father, who was a pastor.

After working with his father a few years, he assumed a position in Paisley in a large congregation. He was to be at this church until he came to America in 1768 to become the president of Princeton College.

He ministered in parishes from 1745-57. He was known as a leader of the evangelical or "popular party" in the Church of Scotland. After disciplining parishioners, Witherspoon was hauled into court and sentenced to prison in the castle of Dounne (Scotland) for his strong Christian convictions. Witherspoon and his wife finally gave in to requests from his friends to move to America and become the president of Princeton college. This brought to Princeton a new emphasis for a well-trained clergyman and the need for the church to have converted ministers.

During his lifetime, Witherspoon trained a president, vice-president, nine cabinet officers, twenty-one senators, thirty-nine congressmen, three justices of the Supreme Court, and twelve state governors. Five of the 55 members of the Constitutional Convention of 1787 were students of Witherspoon! Five months after he cast his vote for independence, the British burned his personal library.

John Witherspoon, by all accounts, was an extraordinary man who had a profound influence on America. His life could be characterized as "leadership through preparation." Witherspoon was blessed with godly parents who provided him with a wonderful education and the security of being loved. John Adams said of Witherspoon that he was, "A true son of liberty. But first he was a son of the cross. Few appeared to be enriched with greater political wisdom; few enjoyed a greater share of public confidence."[2]

THE MOVE TO AMERICA

The influence of Dr. Benjamin Rush, who was in Scotland for medical training, and Richard Stockton, a signer of the "Declaration of Independence" helped the Witherspoons make their decision to come to America. Leaving behind the respect and comfort of their native land and moving to America was a family decision, and the Witherspoon family finally arrived in America in 1768.

The fame of Witherspoon's education brought many new students to Princeton, and the college began to thrive. Witherspoon was an outstanding administrator. He brought 300 books from his personal library across the Atlantic with him and served as president of Princeton for the next 25 years. Witherspoon effected a revolution at Princeton by introducing a wide range of subjects into the curriculum with his Scottish system of lecturing on eloquence, moral philosophy, divinity, history, French, principles of taste, and handwriting, as well as a mastery of the English language. It was his conviction that education should fit a man for public usefulness. Witherspoon had been influenced by the "Scottish Enlightenment" and offended Orthodox Presbyterianism. He sought to point out the dangers of the new philosophies coming from Europe.

In 1774, Witherspoon wrote an essay that laid out the course of action that was identical with the one followed by Congress, "To profess loyalty to the King and our backwardness, to break connection with Great Britain unless forced thereto; to declare the firm resolve never to submit to the claims of Great Britain, but deliberately to prefer war with all its horrors, and even extermination, to slavery. To resolve union and to pursue the same measures until American liberty is settled on a solid basis."[3]

Witherspoon was known as an affectionate husband, a tender parent, and a kind friend. Witherspoon had lost two sons in

"character is
what you do
in the dark." [4]

The American
scholar

the Revolutionary War. He was a true patriot and loved his country. Witherspoon gave everything he had to the cause of liberty in America. He was a strategist and his school was a school for the leadership of the country. Only five of the Witherspoon's ten children, born in Scotland, survived. After the war, he traveled to Great Britain to raise money for Princeton but was deeply rejected by his former countrymen when visiting England, his mother country, as they had not forgiven him. Witherspoon's first wife died in 1789 and after she died, Witherspoon decided to go back into politics. At 68, he was married again, to a woman who was only 24 years old. They had two daughters.

RELIGIOUS VIEWS IN AMERICA

Deism (the view that God was not personally involved in relating to mankind) was advancing in America and seemed to be set forth in terms difficult to understand. From Scotland came the "common sense philosophy" (knowledge derived from experience rather than study) with its positive view of man. Witherspoon knew as well as anyone that the real nature of man was bent toward evil and selfishness, yet he allowed that "reason" could be used as an aid to revelation. His view was, "If the Scripture is true the discoveries of reason cannot be contrary to it, and therefore, it has nothing to fear from that quarter." [5] "Rationalism" had its foot in the door in Princeton, however, and ultimately Scripture was dethroned.

Witherspoon was elected representative to the general congress by the people of New Jersey and was the only clergyman to sign the Declaration of Independence. He served on over 100 congressional committees and his patriotism and judgment won the respect of his colleagues. Witherspoon took an active part in the debates on the Articles of Confederation and assisted in organizing the executive department. His strong emphasis on biblical principles impacted the government of the United States. In 1782 he was elected to congress. Witherspoon yearned for revival in the college but his responsibilities with the new government made his personal involvement impossible. Two years before death he became legally blind yet he continued on with his pastoral responsibilities. During the closing years of his life Witherspoon could boast that a decided majority of the members of the General Assembly had been his own students.

NATIONAL PURPOSE ▶

Witherspoon sought to unify the Presbyterian Church in America during his latter years. Even in old age, Witherspoon was assisted to the pulpit and delivered his message with great clarity and conviction. He was always patient and cheerful but at age 73 the pleasures of life were over. He was a man of piety and virtue, universally venerated and loved. When Witherspoon died, America experienced a great loss.

A DEEP REVERENCE FOR GOD

Witherspoon took steps that would have been considered dangerous and foolhardy by most people. "It is only the fear of God that can deliver us from the fear of men,"[6] he said. His speeches came together in his closet; he could memorize them after reading them about three times.

"There is a tide in the affairs of men, a nick of time. We perceive it now before us. To hesitate is to consent to our own slavery. That noble instrument upon your table should be subscribed this very morning by every pen in this house…. For my own part, of property I have some, of reputation more. That reputation is staked, that property is pledged on the issue of this contest, and although these gray hairs must soon descend into the sepulcher, I would infinitely rather that they descend thither by the hand of the executioner than desert the sacred cause of my country,"[7] Witherspoon stated.

WITHERSPOON'S VIEW ON AMERICAN LIBERTY

Witherspoon proclaimed, "If your cause is just, if your principles are pure, and if your conduct is prudent, you need not fear the multitude of opposing souls."[8] He also said, "The friend of American liberty would be one 'who is most sincere and active in promoting true and undefiled religion, and who sets himself with the greatest firmness to bear down on profanity and immorality of every kind.'"[9]

Witherspoon laid everything on the line for the sake of liberty. He said that piety was indispensable to republican government. Along with 56 other signers, they pledged "our lives, our Fortunes, and our sacred honor." In the fall Witherspoon and his family would need to flee as the British troops arrived and took over the college. The battle of Princeton was to follow.

"Shall we establish nothing good because we know it cannot be eternal? Shall we live without government because every

"Witherspoon was a profound theologian, simple in manner, a universal scholar, acquainted with human nature, a grave, dignified solemn speaker. Few of the founders appeared to be enriched with greater political wisdom, few enjoyed a greater share of public confidence, few accomplished more for the country than he did in the sphere he was called to action." [10]

NATIONAL PURPOSE

constitution has its old age and its period? Because we know that we shall die, shall we take no pains to preserve or lengthen our life? Far from it sir, it only requires the more watchful attention to settle government on the best principles and in the wisest manner so that it may last as the nature of things will admit," Witherspoon taught. [11]

Witherspoon had to first experience a "death to self" before he could overcome the fear of man and what others might seek to do to him. "Witherspoon was a profound theologian, simple in manner, a universal scholar, acquainted with human nature, a grave, dignified solemn speaker. Few of the founders appeared to be enriched with greater political wisdom, few enjoy a greater share of public confidence, few accomplished more for the country than he did in the sphere he was called to action." [12]

The convictions of Witherspoon led him to mistrust himself and trust only God. "While we give praise to God, the supreme disposer of all events, for His interposition on our behalf, let us guard against the dangerous error of trusting in, or boasting of, an arm of the flesh. If your cause is just, if your principles are pure, and if your conduct is prudent, you need not fear the multitude of opposing hosts," [14] Witherspoon concluded.

On the charge that Christianity is harmful to a society, Witherspoon replied, "Let us try it by its fruits. Let us compare the temper and character of real Christians with those of infidels and see which of them best merits the approbation of an honest and impractical judge. In which of the two is to be found the greatest integrity and uprightness in their conduct between man and man? The most unfeigned goodwill? And the most active beneficence to others? Is it the unbeliever or the Christian who clothes the naked and deals his bread to the hungry?" [15]

Witherspoon was to be an example to others of true patriotism. "It is the man of piety and inward principle, that we may expect to find the uncorrupted patriot, the useful citizen, and the invincible soldier—God grant that in America true religion and civil liberty may be inseparable and that the unjust attempts to destroy the one, may in the issue tend to the support and establishment of both. He is the best friend of American liberty, who is most sincere and active in promoting true and undefiled religion, and who sets himself with the

"If your cause is just, if your principles are pure, and if your conduct is prudent, you need not fear the multitude of opposing souls." [13]

witherspoon

greatest firmness to bear down profanity and immorality of every kind. Whoever is an avowed enemy of God, I scruple not to call him an enemy to his country"[16] he stated.

As president of Princeton, Witherspoon provided historic wisdom for generations to follow concerning the dangers to liberty when a nation loses the "fear of God" (reverence for God and his Word). "If your cause is just, you may look with confidence to the Lord, and entreat him to plead it as his own. I am satisfied that the confederacy of the colonies has not been the effect of pride, resentment, or sedition, but of a deep and general conviction that our civil and religious liberties, and consequently in a great measure the temporal and eternal happiness of us and our posterity, depended on the issue. The knowledge of God and his truths have from the beginning of the world been chiefly, if not entirely confined to those parts of the earth where some degree of liberty and political justice were to be seen. There is not a single instance in history, in which civil liberty was lost, and religious liberty preserved entire. If therefore we yield up our temporal property, we at the same time deliver the conscience into bondage,"[18] Witherspoon stated.

"Whatever state among us shall continue to make piety (respect for God) and virtue (character strengths) the standard of public honor will enjoy the greatest inward peace, the greatest national happiness, and in every outward conflict will discover the greatest constitutional strength. True religion always enlarges the heart and strengthens the social tie."[19]

True religion always enlarges the heart and strengthens the social tie."[17]
Witherspoon

"There is a tide in the affairs of men, which taken at the flood, leads on to fortune. omitted, all the voyage of their life is bound in shallows and in miseries. on such a full sea we now afloat. And we must take the current when it serves, or lose our ventures."[20]
william shakespeare

REVIEW

Q. What do you think is the secret of going to the closet for a sermon?

Q. What do you think the phrase, "There is a tide in the affairs of men" means?

Q. What was the danger coming from "Common Sense" philosophy?

Q. If Christians are "the salt of the earth" in a society, how should they shape a nation?

Q. According to Witherspoon, who were the truest friends of America?

Character for Life

GOD'S PROMISE:

"Then those who feared the LORD talked with each other, and the LORD listened and heard. A scroll of remembrance was written in his presence concerning those who feared the LORD and honored his name" (Malachi 3:16).

GOD'S GOAL:

That you love and practice righteousness while hating evil.

YOUR COMMITMENT:

Pray for a continual awareness of God's great holiness.

YOUR DAILY RESPONSE:

1. Live in reverent obedience of God.

2. Remember that walking in the "fear of God" is a continual commitment.

3. Reverence for God will mean we revere His name and honor others who lead us in this direction.

FAILURE WILL MEAN:

We will eventually bring destruction and ruin to our lives.

BACKGROUND:

How may we obtain a deep reverence for the Lord? When a Christian begins to take the view that it doesn't matter whether God is holy or not, it is the beginning of being a traitor to Jesus Christ. God is holy and we must learn reverent obedience to Him and honor Him as God. To learn from the Lord we must first have a great reverence of Him. The thought that He continually sees us, hears everything we say, and knows our thoughts would both comfort us and fill us with a sense of awe. We must also fear sin because of its terrible consequences.

Two kinds of fear are mentioned in the Bible. There is a godly fear, which helps our spiritual life. God could not love righteousness if He did not hate evil. For example, a child learns to fear certain things if he is to keep from hurting himself. Who would argue that if would be wrong to teach a child about the dangers of electricity, stairs, running out in the street? Only a foolish parent would fail to teach a child about these things and let him, "learn for himself."

When it comes to this "fear of the Lord" we fail to understand that there are areas of life where to yield is loss. As a Father, God tells us to run from certain things, not to spoil our happiness but because He loves us and wants what is good for us. If we refuse to understand and embrace the "fear of the Lord" we will eventually bring ruin to our lives and the lives of others.

There is a "spirit of fear" which harms our spiritual life. This kind of fear is something that we would experience if we were to meet something alien or someone out of control. Jesus is not like that. During His earthly ministry, people flocked to Jesus, especially children. God made creation beautiful as an expression of His heart.

We need to have a sober attitude toward Satan and the "powers of darkness" but confidence of the authority of Jesus Christ over the evil powers.

"My son, if you accept my words and store up my commands within you, turning your ear to wisdom and applying your heart to understanding, and if you call out for insight and cry aloud for understanding, and if you look for it as for silver and search for it as for hidden treasure, then you will understand the fear of the LORD and find the knowledge of God" (Proverbs 2:1-5).

"But they have no regard for the deeds of the LORD, no respect for the work of his hands. So man will be brought low and mankind humbled, the eyes of the arrogant humbled" (Isaiah 5:12b, 15).

LIVING WITH REVERENCE FOR GOD MEANS . . .

- Understanding God's wisdom (how God intends for us to live) (Psalm 111:10; Proverbs 15:33, 19:8, 24:3).

- Finding God's blessing (the favor of the Lord) (Proverbs 10:27, 19:23).

- Understanding God's holiness. Those who revere God will have a hatred of evil and sin because of how it affects God and others (Proverbs 8:13).

- Having strong confidence based on what God can do (Proverbs 14:2).

- Trusting in God's provision (Proverbs 8:11, 22:4; Psalm 34:9).

- Having faith in God's protection (Psalm 23:4, 34:7, 115:11).

- Trusting in God's great mercy (Psalm 103:11, 17).

- Believing in God's grace (Proverbs 8:13, 14:27; Hebrews 1:9).

Chapter Fourteen: Learning more about Witherspoon

Go to an Internet search engine.
Type in *John Witherspoon, Fear of God*.
Find topics 1-7 below and open up the websites.
1. John Witherspoon
2. Famous quotes
3. New page 18
4. John Witherspoon, Disciple of Freedom
5. Christian Quotations
6. Government should promote religion
7. The Works of the Rev. John Witherspoon (the Dominion of Providence over the Passions of Men)

chapter 15
*Seeking God's Kingdom First—*Benjamin Rush

PURPOSE: Establishing Eternal Objectives and Goals

character trait:

Seeking God's Kingdom First

SUBJECT:
BENJAMIN RUSH
(1745-1813)

PURPOSE:
Establishing Eternal Objectives and Goals

FAMOUS QUOTE:
"I have alternatively been called an Aristocrat and a Democrat. I am neither. I am a Christocrat."

SCRIPTURE DOCUMENTATION:
"But seek first his kingdom and his righteousness, and all these things will be given to you as well" (Matthew 6:33).

The "Kingdom of God" is advanced as God is honored and His presence and programs are inaugurated throughout a nation and in individual lives. Benjamin Rush's efforts to bring God's program into existence have not been matched by any individual in American history to date.

John Adams said of Rush, "He [Rush] saw the whole of a subject at a single glance. A man of science, letters, philosophy, patriotism, religion, morality, merit, usefulness, taken together, Rush has not left his equal in America, nor that I know in the world."[1]

Benjamin Rush was raised by his mother, as his father died when he was six years old. Rush prepared himself for leadership through a life of discipline. He spent five years acquiring knowledge of the Greek and Latin languages and developed steady habits of discipline, reverence for religion, biblical principles, and conduct. Rush's character was developed early in life; at age 16 he began the study of medicine in Philadelphia and continued to study in Edinburgh where he received his M.D. in 1768. Rush was greatly influenced by his pastor Jonathan Witherspoon. Witherspoon, encouraged by Dr. Rush, became the president of Princeton. Rush married Julia Stockton, daughter of Richard Stockton, (who also signed the Declaration of Independence). Together, Julia and Benjamin brought 13 children into the world. Sadly, four died in their first year of life.

Rush's compassion for his patients was amazing. The more they suffered as a result of life's "batterings," the more Rush was ready to sacrifice his own comfort, safety, and life on their behalf. He was worn down by caring for the thousands of people who came to him and eventually, he too, came close to death.

"Rush was a one-man crusade to remake America. He wrote dozens of public letters, broadsides and pamphlets attacking strong drink, slavery, war, capital punishment, public punishments, test law, tobacco, oaths, and even country fairs; and, on the other hand, advocating beer and cider, free schools, education for women, a college for Pennsylvania, Germans, a national university, the study of science rather than Greek and Latin, free postage for newspapers, churches for Negroes, and cultivation of the sugar-maple tree."[2]

RUSH'S INFLUENCE ON ADAMS AND FRANKLIN

Over his lifetime, Rush's closest friends were John Adams and Benjamin Franklin. Adams had lost to Jefferson in a run for the Presidency and a rift developed between them over the years. Dr. Rush set about to bring them together. Dr. Rush was known for many things but making "peace" between John Adams and Thomas Jefferson may be one of his enduring legacies. Rush wrote to Jefferson and Adams and appealed to their patriotism. When Adams would say something good about Jefferson and as Jefferson spoke kindly toward Adams, Rush would tell Adams of Jefferson's fond thoughts of him.

Below is a letter from Dr. Rush to Thomas Jefferson, appealing reconciliation with John Adams:

> When I consider your early attachment to Mr. Adams, and his to you; when I consider how much the liberties and independence of the United States owes to the concert of your principles and labors; and when I reflect upon the sameness of your opinions at present upon most of the subjects of government and all the subjects of legislation, I have ardently wished a friendly and epistolary intercourse might be revived between you before you take a final leave of the common object of your affections. Such an intercourse will be honorable to your talents and patriotism and highly useful to the course of "republicanism," not only in the United States but all over the world. Posterity will revere the friendship of two ex-Presidents that were once opposed to each other. Human nature will be a gainer by it. I am sure an advance on your side will be cordial to the heart of Mr. Adams. Tottering over the grave, he now leans wholly upon the shoulders of his old Revolutionary friends…. Adieu! My dear friend, and believe me to yours truly and affectionately,
> Benjamin Rush[4]

Few people in American history have undertaken and accomplished as much as Benjamin Rush. His academic career began at the College of New Jersey (Princeton) and was followed by medical school in Scotland. His services as a Surgeon-General of the Continental Army came to the attention of General Washington and ultimately brought him a distinguished reputation. This was followed by service as a member of the Continental Congress. He was one of the original signers of

"He was renowned for his faithful attention to the sick as he was for his sympathy and kindness and gentleness of manner. Rush was tender and sensitive by nature but lacked the humor to temper the hostility from others."[3]

Mark Van Doren

NATIONAL PURPOSE

"In his vision for America there must be social and political institutions that provided spiritual healing and reconciliation to the transcendent God. Without this there could be no therapy of order. Man is dependent upon ultimate Reality. We the people are not autonomous but under God and His law. The great work of bringing the principles, morals, and manners of our citizens into conformity with republican institutions remains to be done." [5]

Donald J. Elia

the Declaration of Independence and a member of the Pennsylvania Convention that ratified the U.S. Constitution. He was a person who didn't feel totally comfortable with either party since he said, "I have alternatively been called an Aristocrat and a Democrat. I am neither. I am a Christocrat." [6]

ACQUIRING KNOWLEDGE

In describing his regimen in his autobiography, Rush said that he by no means depended "exclusively upon books" in acquiring knowledge. "I made, as far as was in my power, every person I conversed with contribute to my improvement." [7]

Rush expressed his ecumenical leanings by attending Presbyterian, Episcopalian, and Baptist Churches and he simply enjoyed them all.

President John Adams appointed him to take on the duties as Treasure of the U.S. Mint and Rush did so until he died (1797-1813). Few people have lived such a full life and contributed so much. Said his friend John Adams, "From him we learned to be good, as well as great. The sneers of infidels and the fascinations of pleasure, had no power to divert him from the correct principles and virtuous habits which had been engrafted on his mind in early youth." [8]

"My only hope of salvation is in the infinite transcendent love of God manifested to the world through the death of His Son upon the cross. Nothing but His blood will wash away my sins. I rely exclusively upon it. Come Lord Jesus. Come quickly!" [9] Rush said. During his final illness, Rush wrote to his wife, "My excellent wife, I must leave you but God will take care of you." [10]

RUSH'S PASSIONS AND CONVICTIONS

Fraternity (brotherly love and feelings of good will) was the end to which liberty and equality were means. True fraternity could only be attained in world-transcending Christian religious faith. "Rush sought to find a way out of man's moral, social and political chaos and believed that teaching virtue was the answer." [11]

"In his vision for America there must be social and political institutions that provided spiritual healing and reconciliation to the transcendent God. Without this there could be no therapy of order. Man is dependent upon ultimate Reality. We the people are not autonomous but under God and His law. The great work of bringing the principles, morals, and manners of our citizens into conformity with republican institutions remains to be done." [12]

"I know there is an objection among many people to teaching children doctrines of any kind, because they are more likely to be converted. But let us not be wiser than our Maker. If moral precepts alone could have reformed mankind, the mission of the Son of God into all the world would have been unnecessary." [13] Rush reminded people that, "This country was founded, not by religionists, but by Christians, not on religions but on the Gospel of Jesus Christ. For this very reason peoples of the faiths have been afforded asylum, prosperity and worship here." [14]

ON A MISSION TO HELP THE MENTALLY ILL

America has its roots with man made "in the image of God." Rush believed that man is disoriented and is not entirely capable of reasoning. He felt there was a need for a "therapy of order" to produce good mental health.

Rush was considered the "Father of American psychiatry." He was a remarkable man and all knew his compassion. It was Rush who wrote America's first textbook on chemistry as well as the first American psychiatric textbook to treat mental patients. He started the "Philadelphia Dispensary to the Poor" and began the "Society for alleviating the miseries of Public Mental Health." The injustice of slavery and seeking to free people from the bondages of both slavery and destructive habits dominated his life. In a letter from Rush to John Seward, a clergyman and physician, Rush wrote that Christianity "contains the greatest scope for genius of any science in the world." [16]

A WORLD-TRANSCENDING FAITH

Rush was known for his deep convictions concerning the future of America. He chose to link America's future with the future of the Christian religion. Rush said, "Let the children be carefully instructed in the principles and obligations of the Christian religion. This is the most essential part of education. The great enemy of the salvation of man, in my opinion, never invented a more effective means of (removing) Christianity

"education has for its objection the formation of character." [15]
spencer

NATIONAL PURPOSE

"This country was founded, not by religionists, but by Christians, not on religions but on the Gospel of Jesus Christ. For this very reason peoples of the faiths have been afforded asylum, prosperity and worship here." [17]
Rush

from the world than by persuading mankind that it was improper to read the Bible at schools." [18]

A VISION FOR HEALTH CARE

In terms of his medical contributions to the country, Dr. Benjamin Rush was a Professor who taught Practices of Medicine at the University of Pennsylvania. During his lifetime he trained 3,000 medical students. During the later part of his life he began mental health hospitals in Philadelphia, urging reforms in all asylums. Rush became known as "the American Hippocrates."

FOUNDER OF SUNDAY SCHOOL AND THE AMERICAN BIBLE SOCIETY

Rush was the founder of the American Sunday School movement as well as of the American Bible Society. "The only foundation for a useful education in a republic is to be laid in religion. Without this there can be no virtue, and without virtue there can be no liberty, and liberty is the object of life of all republican governments," [20] he said.

THE AMERICAN ABOLITION SOCIETY

Rush had a passion to establish true justice in America and started the "American Abolition Society" to dismantle slavery. "The people who are to exist a hundred years hence are as much our fellow creatures as those who are our contemporaries. It only requires more grace to love them than the persons who we see and converse with every day; but in proportion as we attain to this sublime act of love, we approach nearer the Source of all Love—for he loves and serves all the generation of his creature with an equal affection," [21] Rush stated.

FIRST WOMEN'S COLLEGE AND BIBLE-HONORING PUBLIC SCHOOLS

Rush participated in starting five colleges and universities, including the first women's college in America and was considered by many "the Father of public education."

Rush believed, "America would fulfill its destiny and become the theatre on which human nature will reach its greatest civil, literary and religious honors. One day, ignorance would be overcome by knowledge and virtue would overcome vice."[22]

"By renouncing the Bible, philosophers swing from their moorings upon all moral subjects. It is the only correct map of the human heart that ever has been published. All systems of religion, morals, and government not founded upon it must perish."[23]

REVIEW

Q. What Christian principles do you think Rush could have built his hospital for the mental health upon?

Q. What are some of the qualities you think a Christian physician should possess?

Q. As he treated the mentally ill, what did Rush say was required?

Q. Why do you think religion is the foundation for liberty and virtue?

Q. What happened when philosophy abandoned the Bible and how is the Bible unique?

Q. What is the difference between morality and Jesus' righteousness?

Q. Since Rush was the "Father of public education" in America, what would he have to say to judges who passed laws prohibiting teaching religion in schools or even the mention of God in schools?

Q. Do you agree with Dr. Rush's hopes for America's destiny?

Character for Life

GOD'S PROMISE:
"But seek first his kingdom and his righteousness, and all these things will be given to you as well" (Matthew 6:33).

GOD'S GOAL:
That your greatest motivations would be to know God and make Jesus Christ known throughout the world.

YOUR COMMITMENT:
Seek God first each day!

YOUR DAILY RESPONSE:
1. Seek first the Kingdom of God
2. Understand that often seeking His Kingdom means self-denial.

3. Realize that eternity will reveal to us the total impact of seeking God's Kingdom first.

4. Only then will our joy be fully complete!

FAILURE WILL MEAN:

God's purposes in the world and in your life will not be fulfilled.

BACKGROUND:

At the center of the universe, where God dwells, we discover our real character. As we live close to Jesus and allow Him to manifest His life in us, we fulfill the purpose for which we were created. God's virtues have always existed in heaven but through Jesus' life and ministry on earth, He brought mankind a revelation of God's character.

Occasionally, the Bible provides us with glimpses into heaven. Jesus said, "Your kingdom come, your will be done on earth as it is in heaven" (Matt. 6:10). We can actually trace our virtues into the throne room of God where Jesus is always honored and worshiped. It was God's plan then, that the virtues of heaven would become the virtues here on earth. The "Kingdom of God" came to earth then, when Jesus Christ, the Co-Creator of the universe, lived among humans. God's virtues are seen in our lives as Christ, the eternal Son of God, manifests them to us.

The "Beatitudes" are part of God's Eternal Law, which includes the "Ten Commandments." They should be viewed as "the law of (man's) nature." In other words, these are the attitudes God desires we maintain throughout our lives. They bring about the "fruit of the Spirit." Christians always need to be reminded that the key to God's character in our life is to "abide in Christ" (John 15). An unbeliever can muster up "courage" or "compassion" from time to time but a Christian has the "Holy Spirit" within him to empower and sustain him. The "character qualities" that we strive to imitate are qualities seen in the "life of Jesus Christ" as he walked among us. They are also seen in those who claimed to be his followers.

Natural virtues fall far short of what Jesus Christ offers. The truth is that every virtue we possess is "His" alone. It is written in Psalm 87:7, "As they make music they will sing, 'All my fountains are in you.'" Oswald Chambers wrote, "The sign that God is at work in us is that He corrupts confidence in the natural virtues, because they are not promises of what we are going to be, but remnants of what God created man to be. We will cling to the natural virtues, while all the time God is trying to get us into contact with the life of Jesus Christ which can never be described in terms of the natural virtues. It is the saddest thing to see people in the service of God depending on that which the grace of God never gave them, depending on what they have by the accident of heredity. God does not build up our natural virtues and transfigure them, because our natural virtues can never come anywhere near what Jesus Christ wants. No natural love, no natural patience, no natural purity can ever come up to His demands. But as we bring every bit of our bodily life into harmony with the new life which God has put in us, He will exhibit in us the virtues that were characteristic of the Lord Jesus."[24] Virtue is acquired through an inner struggle and overcoming "the world, the flesh" and the enemy of our soul, Satan himself.

When Christians have been faithful to the "author and finisher" of our faith, God has been glorified. When we have acted independently of Him and have lived as if he didn't exist, we have failed.

All of us have heroes through which we have seen God's character revealed. I would like to introduce you to some of my heroes. In addition to previous stories, here are the additional stories of 22 followers of Jesus who made a difference in America. These are Christians I have learned from and who have shaped my life. We remember them for their commitments to the Savior and Lord of the world!

SEEKING FIRST GOD'S KINGDOM MEANS . . .

■ Understanding the need for self-surrender. This concept applied to Jesus since He knew if He went to Jerusalem He would be crucified and die for man's sins. So the law of self-surrender applies both to God and man. Do we save our lives or lay them down that others may live (John 12:23-24)?

■ Becoming a disciple of the Kingdom of God. When Jesus Christ becomes the Lord and Savior of our life we inherit a "Kingdom" made from the foundation of the world. We find our true identity, and since we are made for the Kingdom, discover how life is to be lived. Also, the resources of the Kingdom become ours.

■ Having and developing God's attitudes in our lives. This is our gift to God! These result in godly character or the "fruit of the spirit" which are the attributes of God.

■ Taking on as best we can the character of Jesus Christ. The Bible tells us that God places more value on a single individual than the entire world. He has made us in His image and we have the ability to respond to Him and love Him.

Chapter Fifteen: Learning more about Rush

Go to an Internet search engine.
Type in *Benjamin Rush, Kingdom of God*.
Find topics 1-7 below and open up the websites.
1. Rev. Elhanan Winchester Testimony Dr. Rush
2. Trumpet America
3. The Real Bicentennial
4. Why use the Bible as Primary Reader
5. National Alliance against Christian Discrimination
6. Hope in a hopeless world
7. Separation of Church-state letter

chapter 16

Compassion—

william wilberforce

PURPOSE: Discovering the World's Greatest Need

character trait:

Compassion

SUBJECT:

WILLIAM WILBERFORCE
(1759-1833)

PURPOSE:

Discovering the World's Greatest
Need

FAMOUS QUOTE:

"The best way of dealing with that
general spirit of licentiousness
which is present in every species of
vice was to change the hearts of
men."

SCRIPTURE DOCUMENTATION:

"Yet he [God] was merciful; he
forgave their iniquities and did not
destroy them. Time after time he
restrained his anger and did not
stir up his full wrath. He remembered that they were but flesh, a
passing breeze that does not
return" (Psalm 78:38-39).

"Therefore, as God's chosen
people, holy and dearly loved,
clothe yourselves with compassion,
kindness, humility, gentleness and
patience" (Colossians 3:12).

PERSONALITY PROFILE

William Wilberforce was born in Hull,
England. He came under the influence
of Joseph Milner, the headmaster of his
school. After two years at the school,
William's father died. Soon after, he
went to live with an aunt who was a
staunch Methodist. As a result, his conscience and concern over the plight of
slavery was tender even as a youth. At
the age of 14, he wrote a letter to a York paper about the evils
of slave trading. He eventually attended St. Johns College, in
Cambridge.

Wilberforce was frail and sick most of his life. He was deeply
grieved over the War with the Colonies and the War with France.
In his own family, he lost both his oldest and youngest daughter.
He also felt the pain of indifference to slavery in his country.

His transparent kindliness and simplicity made him lovable, even
to his antagonists. He had freedom from the coarser indul-
gences…he escaped contamination at the cost of standing aside
from the world of corruption and devoted himself to purely phil-
anthropic measures. The charm of his character enabled him to
take the part of moral censor without being morose.

In 1784, like the "rich young ruler," Wilberforce came to see
John Newton, the former slave trader, at night. He had not seen
Newton since he was a boy of eight years of age. Wilberforce
had become a Christian while in Europe with a friend. He came
in secret and poured out his heart to Newton. Wilberforce didn't
know whether God was calling him to remain in Parliament or to
resign and join the clergy. John Newton prayed with him and
encouraged him to stay in Parliament, thinking that perhaps God
had raised him up to serve in that position. Wilberforce accepted
Newton's counsel, and became the voice against slavery until his
death in 1833. As a result, slave trade in England was abolished.
It has been estimated that up to eleven million Africans had been
taken from their homeland to the "New World." Wilberforce was
the foremost Christian Reformer in Christian History.

The general influence of Wilberforce and his fellow evangelicals
on the climate of England can scarcely be over-estimated.
Wilberforce was called to endure great opposition but gradually
came to lead a great crusade and capture the affections of the
nation.

Rather than seeing Wilberforce's frailties, people saw his strength of character. Wilberforce eventually became a politician who reversed the course of his country. His leadership was based on a deep and genuine love for God and others—especially people whose lives had been maimed and deprived of justice.

WILBERFORCE'S FAITH AND INFLUENCE

Wilberforce became a follower of Jesus Christ through the friendship of Isaac Milner as they studied the New Testament together while traveling in Europe. In 1780, he was elected as a Member of Parliament for Hull. One of the strongest influences in his life was John Newton, the former slave trader. He had come to Christ and out of his experience wrote "Amazing Grace," a hymn that later transformed the lives of thousands throughout the world. During his lifetime, Wilberforce put most of his energies into the abolition of the slave trade. After decades of persuading his fellow legislators and speaking to the conscience of Britain, Wilberforce finally saw slave trade abolished in 1833. Wilberforce knew that the heart of man needed to be transformed by God in order to see true justice. With this in mind, he sought to evangelize the upper classes in England and encouraged them to use their wealth and influence in many good causes. Wilberforce was able to reshape the social conscience of his own generation. He commanded the respect of Parliament for 50 years.

The following was said about Wilberforce: "His was a name, with which there is probably associated more love and veneration than ever fell to the lot of any civilized individual throughout the civilized globe. His warfare is accomplished. He kept the faith. Those who regard him merely as a philanthropist, in the worldly sense of that abused term know but little of his character."[2]

He was not quite 74 but he was very frail and very infirm at his death in 1833. Wilberforce's achievements were amazing. After his death, England lost its primary voice for the freedom of slaves. Wilberforce decided that he would speak in love to the conscience of his countrymen. It took a lifetime, but he was finally successful. England's loss was great, however, and a friend best described it with the following words: "Wilberforce, Sir, is a little creature, he is an ugly creature; but look into his face, hear him speak, and you forget it all, he is the incarnation of love."[3]

"Character is that which reveals moral purposes, exposing the class of things man chooses or avoids."[1]

Aristotle

THE STATE OF ENGLAND

The corruption of the culture had taken its toll on the manners of England. As a Christian, Wilberforce saw the depravity of eighteenth century society. London's teenagers were involved in prostitution, and drunkenness was an accepted part of their lives. Wilberforce felt most keenly that "the best way of dealing with that general spirit of licentiousness which is present in every species of vice was to change the hearts of men."[5] There was widespread concern over rampant social evils of such things as child prostitution. The culture in England had become coarse and Wilberforce was passionate about its restoration.

Wilberforce also became deeply grieved over the social conditions of children in England. His motivation was a sense of duty he had for those who were defenseless and needed protection. His passion was not only to provide better housing and living conditions for the poor, but to do whatever he could to provide an opportunity for children to hear the gospel. He was outraged that children would not have an opportunity to live for Jesus. The plight of the chimneysweepers was particularly appalling since they were often beaten, or starved and frequently died agonizing deaths. He wanted them to know of the love of Jesus. Wilberforce also had a heart for the factory children who had no time to learn to read and write and study the Bible for themselves. He was involved in various movements including the Sunday School movement, relief of prisoners, prison reform, working conditions, the mentally ill, "the reform of manners," and others.

According to Archbishop of Canterbury MacIntosh, "No one touched life at so many points, and still had all the charm of his youth."[6] Archbishop MacIntosh spoke highly of Wilberforce, "Wilberforce believed there is a principle above everything political and that is the Divine will expressed through the Christian faith and the Christian gospel. Man's inhumanity to man—so exemplified in the slave trade was, like evil itself, to be conquered rather than merely condemned."[7]

Wilberforce set about to bring slave trading to an end throughout the British Empire. Wilberforce and his fellow workers knew that if they were to be successful, they needed to free themselves from distractions of personal ambitions. This would allow them to seek the "glory of Christ." There were powerful forces against their causes, however. The public thought that both slave trading and child labor were economic necessities for the nation. It would take Wilberforce his entire life to see the changes God had put in his heart to accomplish.

On his deathbed, John Wesley wrote to Wilberforce, "Unless God has raised you up for this undertaking, you will be worn out by the opposition of men and devils, but if God be for you who can be against you? Are all of them stronger than God? Oh, be not weary of well-doing. Go on in the name of God, and in the power of His might."[8]

Wilberforce was committed to the view that all of life is precious to God. As a Christian, his heart was filled with God's love, even for those who opposed him. He literally wore his enemies down with his love and compassion. It was the task of Wilberforce and the abolitionists to expose the horrors of slavery and reveal how it was affecting the lives of all concerned. Over a fifth of the crews of some 350 Liverpool and Bristol slave ships perished from 1784 to 1790.

The dreadful conditions in which slaves were kept, manacled side by side with wrists and legs joined to each other began to speak to England. Wilberforce had become "the conscience of England." It wasn't until 1833 that Parliament voted to set slaves free throughout the British Empire. It was just in time to tell Wilberforce, gravely ill on his deathbed, "That the cause had now been won!"

Wilberforce loved almost every particular human being. His extraordinary breath and sympathy led to his taking part in a vast variety of undertakings. His relationship with his family seems to have been perfect and no one had warmer or more lasting friendships.

Wilberforce saw through the eyes of compassion the plight of slaves, children who were abused, and the lost people of England. Inspired by his concept of the "Brotherhood of Man," he disciplined himself, learning great passages from the Bible and ordered his life according to God's Word. He would spend nine or ten hours a day, walking without company, preparing his mind and heart for the battles in Parliament.

"Wilberforce believed there is a principle above everything political and that is the Divine will expressed through the Christian faith and the Christian gospel. Man's inhumanity to man—so exemplified in the slave trade was, like evil itself, to be conquered rather than merely condemned."[9]

Archbishop of Canterbury

MODERN-DAY EXAMPLE OF COMPASSION: Mark Buntain

Mark Buntain was a missionary who spent much of his adult life in Calcutta, India. I first met Mark in 1977 on a short missions trip. He had so much to share with our team and was so proud of what God was doing in India! We were able to see the wonderful hospital they were able to build, one of the finest in Calcutta at that time. His heart throbbed with excitement when he spoke of his plans to reach the outcasts of Calcutta through the Mercy Hospital.

He had a full agenda for us during our time in Calcutta. Teams had been working all night to prepare the milk and flat bread (chi pa'ti) for the hundreds of children we would meet. For many, this was the only meal they would have that day. Kids came running to the flatbed truck with their arms extended and tin cups in hand waiting for their milk. I was deeply humbled through this experience. Anyone who ever prayed with Mark Buntain would never forget it; he was a weeping prophet whose heart must have been continually hurt with the pain of India. He could see India coming to faith in Jesus and would exclaim, "This is God's day for India!"

Millions have come to the Savior in the past few decades. Dr. Mark Buntain's health was severely affected by the adverse environmental situation in Calcutta as well as the heavy load he carried. His heart failed him and a few years ago he left us to go to be with the Savior he adored. Thousands lined the streets of Calcutta to honor him as his casket was carried through the streets. He has passed on his love to thousands of young people but more importantly, thousands in Calcutta knew God loved them because of Dr. Mark.

REVIEW

Q. Discuss how this statement is true. Each time you show compassion your character is strengthened.

Q. How will the character trait of compassion make a difference in your life?

Q. What are the elements that have produced a coarsening of American culture?

Q. If you were charged to change the manners of your country, what would you do?

Q. When God calls us to change an injustice, opposition can be expected. How does God want us to win over our adversaries?

Q. What are some of the evils in your world that you think ought to be changed?

Q. What distractions in your life keep you from doing the will of God?

Q. If you knew your efforts would not be successful until you were on your deathbed, would this deter you from following God's assignment?

Q. When God calls us to an undertaking, he sustains us. How do you know if something is what God has called you to do?

Q. Describe someone you know who exhibits compassion in his or her life. What are his or her motivations?

Q. When we demonstrate compassion to others, how does it affect us?

Q. What moves you to express compassion toward others?

Character for Life

GOD'S PROMISE:

"Yet he [God] was merciful; he forgave their iniquities and did not destroy them. Time after time he restrained his anger and did not stir up his full wrath. He remembered that they were but flesh, a passing breeze that does not return" (Psalm 78:38-39).

GOD'S GOAL:

For us to live compassionately.

YOUR COMMITMENT:

To see others through the eyes of Jesus.

YOUR DAILY RESPONSE:

1. Be aware of the needs all around you.

2. Be willing to stop and help others.

3. Look outwardly, not inwardly when living your life.

4. Trust God with the outcome after you have stopped to help.

FAILURE WILL MEAN:

Being focused only on your own needs and missing out on the opportunity to influence others in your world.

BACKGROUND:

Jesus lived compassionately. Notice Jesus' reaction to human pain and suffering in the following verses:

"When he saw the crowds, he had compassion on them, because they were harassed and helpless, like sheep without a shepherd" (Matthew 9:36).

"Filled with compassion, Jesus reached out his hand and touched the man. 'I am willing,' he said. 'Be clean!' " (Mark 1:41).

"When the Lord saw her, his heart went out to her and he said, 'Don't cry.' Then he went up and touched the coffin, and those carrying it stood still. He said, 'Young man, I say to you, get up!' The dead man sat up and began to talk, and Jesus gave him back to his mother" (Luke 7:13-15).

LIVING A LIFE OF COMPASSION MEANS . . .

- Looking to the needs of others before looking at your own needs.

- Living your life through the eyes of Jesus.

■ Genuinely caring about those around you who have needs.

■ Being willing to trust God with the outcome of your human works.

■ Giving of your time and money to help others.

■ Looking at the "big picture" of your life and living each day with meaning.

Chapter Sixteen: Learning more about Wilberforce

Go to an Internet search engine.
Type in *William Wilberforce, Character, Compassion.*
Find topics 1-8 below and open up the websites.
1. Fighting Violence with Virtue
2. Renewing one nation
3. Christian politicians in English history
4. Peculiar doctrine, public morals and political welfare
5. A mother's influence
6. Evangelicalism
7. Moral leadership newsletter
8. Jesus in the end of ethnocentrism

chapter 17

Courage—john winthrop

PURPOSE: Learning to Overcome Fear

character trait:

Courage

SUBJECT:

JOHN WINTHROP
(1588-1649)

PURPOSE:

Learning to Overcome Fear

FAMOUS QUOTE:

"When there is no other means whereby our Christian brother may be relieved in his distress, we must help him beyond our ability."

SCRIPTURE DOCUMENTATION:

"So do not fear, for I am with you; do not be dismayed, for I am your God. I will strengthen you and help you; I will uphold you with my righteous right hand" (Isaiah 41:10).

PERSONALITY PROFILE

John Winthrop's grandfather, Adam Winthrop, was part of the English reformation and passed down both his economic and religious positions to his son and grandson. John Winthrop was born in Suffolk, England, and given the fact that he was raised in wealth, first indulged himself in vices during his youth, but later had encounters with God.

At age 14, Winthrop became a student at Trinity College in Cambridge. There, God used a lingering fever to drive Winthrop to the Savior. Four years later, after some spiritual ups and downs, Winthrop abandoned himself into the hand of God and sought to live a godly life. He developed a deep love for the Word of God and this longing for God continued the rest of his life.

In 1629, John Winthrop was troubled by the sinfulness of London's society and began to think it might cost him his children. The Puritans believed England was to encounter dark afflictions from God because of their sins against God and one another. The king was hostile to the Puritans and people in general shared this view of the monarch.

At the age of 42, John Winthrop recruited 700 "colonists" for Massachusetts Bay Colony and decided to go to the Americas. Winthrop sought religious freedom and led the migrating Puritans to Massachusetts in 1630. He arrived in Massachusetts Bay with 700 people in 11 ships. This migration lasted 16 years and saw more than 20,000 Puritans leave for New England.

CHRISTIAN LEADERSHIP

Crossing the Atlantic Ocean in the 1600's was no small feat and it cost the lives of many in John Winthrop's company. During the crossing on the Arabella, Winthrop wrote "A Model of Christian Charity," a sermon he delivered to the little flock gathered with him. This was to lay the foundations for the new community of Jesus. Here is a part of his sermon:

> Now the only way to provide for our posterity, is to follow the counsel of Micah 6:8, 'To act justly and to love mercy and to walk humbly with your God.' For this end, we must be knit together, in this work, as one man. We must entertain each other in brotherly affection. We must be willing to abridge ourselves of our superfluities, for the supply of others' necessities. We must uphold a family commerce together in all meekness, gentleness, patience and liberality. We must delight in each other; make others' conditions our own; rejoice together, mourn together, labor and suffer together, always have our eyes on our commission and community in the work, as members of the same body. So shall we keep the unity of the spirit in the bond of peace.[1]

John Winthrop and the Puritans believed that a person's relationship with God was the most important part of his life. "This love among Christians is a real thing. Not imaginary…as absolutely necessary to the well-being of the Body of Christ, as the sinews and ligaments of a natural body are to the well-being of that body."[3]

REASONS FOR LEAVING ENGLAND

Winthrop's main reasons for leaving England were "to erect a bulwark against the kingdom of the anti-Christ and to provide a refuge for the deteriorating European church."[4] His was a life of leadership through courage and personal sacrifice.

The corrupt ministers and teachers in England had been a terrible influence on Puritan children. Along with other Puritans, Winthrop had been committed to reforming English society. Their goal was to lay aside any ritual or ceremony that did not have the authority of the Bible behind it. Ultimately, they felt this goal impossible and believed England to be under God's judgment. Winthrop became a Puritan and caught the fever of Puritanism, which caused him to leave his motherland.

"sure, it takes a lot of courage to put things in god's hands…to give ourselves completely, our lives, our hopes, our plans, to follow where He leads us and make His will our own."[2]

betsy kline

"No one was more cognizant of the need for personal sacrifice than John Winthrop—nor was anyone ready to give as generously and cheerfully. Winthrop understood clearly that to belong to Christ was to belong to one another. The fall and winter of 1630 would test their covenant commitment to the utmost. Shipload after shipload of impoverished would-be settlers landed on the shore with no suppliers whatever, so that what might have started off to be ample food stocks soon dwindled away to the point where only emergency rations were left." [5]

Winthrop was elected governor of the Bay Colony 12 consecutive times. He also wrote "A Model of Christian Charity," which was based on the principles of the "Law of Love." (As seen in Old Testament Israel, as the major condition whether God would bless a nation or enterprise.)

During this time in Winthrop's life, Cotton Mather described him as "a discreet and sober man, wearing plain apparel, assisting in any ordinary labor, and ruling with much mildness and justice." [6] The Colonial state papers stated, "Governor Winthrop was a gentleman of that wisdom and virtue, and those manifold accomplishments, that after-generations must reckon him no less a glory, than he was a patriot of the country." [7]

A PURITAN LIFE

There are many today who look down at Puritans with their lives of separation to God. Yet, all can appreciate and marvel at the courage of the Puritan leader John Winthrop.

Winthrop taught his followers, "We must consider that we shall be as a 'City upon a Hill,' the eyes of all the people are upon us; so that if we shall deal falsely with our God in the work we have undertaken…we shall be made a stony and a by-word (throughout) the world. Whereas we all came to these parts of America with the same end and aim, namely, to advance the kingdom of our Lord Jesus Christ, and to enjoy the liberties of the gospel thereof with purities and peace, and for preserving and propagating the truth and liberties of the gospel." [9]

The Puritans intention from the beginning was to be a God-honoring state. They were theocratic in one respect in that Winthrop was convinced that God ordained the magistrates. Winthrop taught that they should listen to the ministers although they were not under the control of ministers. Their goal was to establish a godly community that would be honored by God in the eyes of the world.

Winthrop taught that justice and mercy would characterize the community of believers. "If the Lord shall please to hear us, and bring us in peace to the place we desire, then hath He ratified this Covenant and sealed our Commission (and) will expect a strict performance of the Articles." [10]

THE HIGH COST OF LEADERSHIP

"It would cost John Winthrop everything he had to undertake and sustain this endeavor. His first step was to organize 11 ships with sailors and officers and recruited skilled craftsman who could build the colony. The very courage and compassion of John Winthrop was a model of true Christianity and even today he is known as one of the princes of our civilization. His privileged life was behind him. He was to follow God's leading the remainder of his days on earth." [11]

"His justice was impartial...his wisdom did exquisitely temper things according to the art of governing...his courage made him dare to do right, and fitted him to stand among the lions that have sometimes been supporters of the throne: all which virtues he rendered the more illustrious, by emblazing them with the constant liberality and hospitality of a gentleman. A great lover of the saints...especially ministers of the gospel, he was the wisest champion the clergy could have had. Man of great judgment, calm disposition...purity of his moral character. His mind, more than any other, arranged the social state of Massachusetts; mass molded the society of New England." [12]

THE ESTABLISHING OF A CHRISTIAN COMMONWEALTH

John Fiske writes, "Of Winthrop it is enough to say that under his skillful guidance Massachusetts had been able to pursue the daring policy which had characterized the first twenty years of her history, and which in weaker hands would almost surely have ended in disaster." [13]

Winthrop's goals were clear. "To better carry on economic pursuits; to order a state where God's laws would be obeyed." [14] NATIONAL PURPOSE It was Winthrop's hope that a "Christian Commonwealth" would eventually change Europe. He thought it was God's sovereign plan to redeem Europe from its spiritually deteriorating conditions. Tragically, within 200 years the influence of European philosophies would change America.

WINTHROP'S COMFORT IN CHRIST

Courage is necessary for other character traits to become real in our lives. Because of his great courage, Winthrop took huge risks and experienced great losses in his life. Winthrop's wife Mary, with whom he had five children, died upon arrival in the New World. Ultimately Winthrop's second and third wives died from the harshness of life in America. The loss of his children caused Winthrop to deeply examine his beliefs, yet he was called to a higher plane. He did not bury himself in sorrow, but used it overcome other adversities. He shared his inner longings with his first wife, Mary, who was living in England:

> Oh! The riches of Christ! Oh! The sweetness of the word of grace! It ravisheth my soul in the through hereof…let us trust in him, and cleave to him with denial of ourselves, and all things besides, and account our portion the best in the world…so, with my inmost affectionate desires of they welfare, and my blessing to all our children, I kiss my sweet wife, and commend thee and all ours to the gracious protection of our heavenly Father. Be of good comfort, the hardest that can come shall be a means to mortify this body of corruption, which is a thousand times more dangerous to us than any outward tribulation, and to bring us into nearer communion with our Lord Jesus Christ, and more assurance of His Kingdom. [16]

Winthrop revealed his thoughts about his third wife after her death in 1647. "She was a woman of singular prudence, modesty and virtue, and specially beloved and honored of all the country." [17]

A COLONY IN NEW ENGLAND TO DO GOD'S WILL

The Puritans and Pilgrims didn't come to America to establish a colony where toleration and religious freedom would be practiced, but they came to do God's will. As they saw it, there was no reason for everyone to come. "Winthrop was a great lover of the saints…especially ministers of the gospel. He was the wisest champion the clergy could have had. He was a man of great judgment, calm judgment, not vindictive, [and possessed] purity of his moral character. His mind, more than any other, arranged the social state and shaped the society of New England. Another historian, of the early nineteenth century, ranks him second only to Washington in terms of stature among the founding fathers."[18]

"Winthrop was graced by God with an unusual gift of wisdom. As far back as September, he had foreseen that their supplies would give out long before spring. He had sent the Lyon home to Bristol, with a long list of supplies…. Winthrop believed that one committed everything to the cause, even the last of one's personal funds."[19]

Winthrop spoke of the depths of community that must be experienced among Christians. Relationships were to be built on 'Covenants' made in the presence of God:

> We must hold a familiar commerce together in each other in all meekness, gentleness, patience and liberality. We must delight in each other, make one another's condition our own, rejoice together, mourn together, labor and suffer together. The Covenant between you and us is the oath you have taken of us, which is to this purpose, that we shall govern you and judge your causes by the rules of God's law.[20]

Winthrop spoke of the need for sacrifice and unity among believers:

> There was a time when a Christian must sell all and give to the poor, as they did in the Apostles times…. Likewise community of perils calls for extraordinary liberality, and so doth community in some special service for the church. Lastly, when there is no other means whereby our Christian brother may be relieved in his distress, we must help him beyond our ability.[21]

MODERN-DAY EXAMPLE OF A COURAGEOUS LIFE
wilfred Noiyaks

In 1971, Wilfred Noiyaks, a missionary from Germany, came to our church in West Stephentown, New York, where I served as pastor and worked with students at Albany State (University of New York). Wilfred was one of those people you never forget. He had found the key to real joy and celebrated life. No one enjoyed a "Big Mac" more than Wilfred, but his real excitement was in spreading the "gospel" behind the "Iron Curtain." Brother Andrew had recently been in Albany with Loren Cunningham of "Youth with A Mission" and they too were urging Christians to pray for believers in Eastern Europe and do everything possible to get Bibles to these believers. Spending time with these men and hearing their stories...I felt I was with the Apostles Peter and Paul. I decided to accept Wilfred's invitation to travel with him on his next trip to Eastern Europe and Romania.

There were many in those days who had similar ministries as Brother Andrew. Wilfred risked his life on many occasions for the "gospel." I'm glad I didn't know about what was ahead of me or I really would have had "second thoughts." The travel to Siegen (West Germany) was uneventful and I quickly re-established my friendship with Wilfred and my two other travel companions. One hundred sixty seven Bibles were carefully inserted into the panels of a Volkswagen Bus. One suitcase, mine, had room for the much needed pharmaceuticals. A former member of the secret service, Hans, traveled with us. He had become a Christian and his face radiated the love of Jesus.

It took a few hours to get our visas in Belgrade and we headed toward the border of Yugoslavia and Romania arriving about 9:00 pm. By this time I had heard about a number of believers whose mission to take Bibles into Romania had been interrupted by a visit to a Romanian jail. As we approached the crossing and the inspection booths it appeared as if we were going into a prison-like situation with wire fencing and viewing stations stretched out as far as the eye could see. As I recall, these were placed about every 500 feet to catch anyone who wanted to smuggle into the "workers paradise" or so we were told!

Wilfred had a homemade sign in the windshield passing on New Years greetings to the border guards with the hope this (and a bunch of candy bars) would distract them from our real mission. "Take out all the suitcases," we were told. We dutifully pulled them out and the guards took their flashlights and checked out hidden places under the van where contraband could be stashed. They instructed us to open up all the suitcases...Wilfred and Hans opened up three of them but left mine (the one with the pharmaceuticals) unopened. "Okay...Get out of here." We jumped into the van and within a couple hundred yards began shouting, "Praise the Lord." Then Wilfred turned the radio on and we were listening to "Radio Belgrade" a communist station. Mahalia Jackson was singing "How Great Thou Art." Never was any song more meaningful. We wept with tears rolling down our cheeks and continued exclaiming, "How great God really is!" He got us through the border and we were moving deeper into Romania with hearts of joy and thanksgiving to God.

I asked Wilfred why Radio Belgrade would allow this song to be on their station. He thought the man who played it probably didn't understand English but those in the "V.W." believed the song was meant just for us.

Our first encounter was with a Christian physician. He had been translating a book called "The Calvary Road" from English into Romanian. He had also completed the translation of the "Four Spirit Laws" into Romanian. We took these precious translations with us to have them when we left for the West.

We arrived in central Romania the evening of the 31st of December. We were to attend a New Year's Eve service. A Christian family had built a worship center in the back of their house that seated several hundred people. It resembled a large warehouse. I was amazed at the warmth of the Romanian people and their love and concern. The singing was something I'll never forget and the testimonies of love for the Savior were powerful. The service lasted about five hours and then there was another meeting with the young people. They shared aloud how they felt. "Living in Romania is like living in a prison..." said one teenager. The kids all agreed. They wanted desperately to be able to travel to the West. "YWAM" (Youth with a Mission) had big plans for the Munich Olympics and we were able to share some of our hope for getting the "good news" into the hands of those who came to the games.

After the meeting two brothers arrived at the church. They had traveled 150 kilometers and told us the Holy Spirit had told us that there would be people with Bibles coming from the West. "Could they help us?" I thought to myself how incredible it was to be able to "hear the voice of God" and move at His direction. I felt like I had just stepped into a first-century church. They stuffed 35 Bibles into their jackets and quickly left.

My third day in Romania I knew I was in trouble! I was sick and had some kind of food poisoning. Years later my friend Wilfred told me they thought I was going to die. I had a temperature of 107 and was really out of it. I do remember the love of the believers, however. I remember a grandma coming over with a "special tea" every day. Another godly saint came to rub my feet with "a special lotion" while I was sick. The doctor came to visit me each day and I shall never forget the love and concern all had for me. The compassion of the saints in Romania was something to experience. Their intense love for the Savior shaped my thinking about Christianity in the East. I could see why Wilfred was willing to risk his life for the Romanian people. They were hungry to know God.

As I was feeling better after three or four days, Wilfred took our small team of four to a village where we found a bed-ridden Christian in a small house. She had been bed ridden for 23 years, since 1948. Here is her story:

In 1948 Wilfred's friend and her husband were owners of a large vineyard. When the Communists took over Romania they decided to take over the vineyard. They accused them both of being spies for the "C.I.A." and put them in prison. The husband of Wilfred's friend was executed and she was told she too was to die. Day after day she was told she would be executed for her alleged crimes against Romania. The allegations were trumped up of course. Many times she was lined up for a firing squad and blanks were fired. Finally something in her mind snapped and she took a piece of glass and cut her throat. Amazingly, she survived but she had lost her voice box and could not speak. We found her in bed feeling that perhaps God had forsaken her. Wilfred read the wonderful passage from Romans 8. "Who shall separate us from the love us Christ..." ending with the passage, "For I am convinced that neither death nor life, neither angels nor demons, neither the present nor the future, nor any powers, neither height nor depth, nor anything else in all creation, will be able to separate us from the love of God that is in Christ Jesus our Lord." Tears ran down our cheeks as we realized how true these words are. I was in the presence of a man of courage who came to strengthen and a sister who was in great need of encouragement.

REVIEW

Q. How will the character trait of courage make a difference in your life?

Q. It appears that the Puritans thought they were living in the last days prior to the return of Christ. If you knew when Jesus was coming, would you be willing to take more risks for the Kingdom of God?

Q. How can the church foster the concept that "we belong to each other."

Q. Why do you think it wasn't until Winthrop was on the ship "Arabella" that God gave him the sermons and principles he would need to build a Christian community?

Q. Do you think a "sense of community" is more real during times of distress?

Q. Where do you think Winthrop got the idea of a "city set on a hill"?

Q. What is a "theocratic state" and how is our government today different from the Puritans?

Q. What did Winthrop think would happen if the Puritans didn't honor God?

Q. Do the "covenants" the Puritans made with God affect us today?

Q. What happened to Winthrop's idea of a Christian Commonwealth?

Q. Do you agree with President Roosevelt's view that it is better to do something and fail than do nothing?

Q. In spite of his many losses, why do you think Winthrop was able to live a life without apparent bitterness?

Q. Describe the most courageous person or event you know about. What makes people courageous?

Q. Describe something you personally did that required courage.

Q. What would motivate you to take a personal risk?

Character for Life

GOD'S PROMISE:

"So do not fear, for I am with you; do not be dismayed, for I am your God. I will strengthen you and help you; I will uphold you with my righteous right hand" (Isaiah 41:10).

GOD'S GOAL:

For Christians to live courageously.

YOUR COMMITMENT:

To put aside your own fear to do the will of God.

YOUR DAILY RESPONSE:

1. Pray daily for courage.

2. Be willing to obey God even in difficult circumstances.

3. Trust God's control in the outcome of your life.

4. Live each moment for Christ without fear of what man may do to you.

FAILURE WILL MEAN:

Living a life that is cowardly and selfish.

BACKGROUND:

Courage is associated with strength. A person who lacks or loses courage feels himself to be weak, unequal to the task. The courageous person vigorously attacks the challenges before him. In Christ, we can abandon our negative attitudes and face life's problems with a confident attitude that allows us to act with faith and certainty. We can be willing to take risks when our objective is worthwhile.

LIVING A LIFE OF COURAGE MEANS . . .

■ Taking risks for the gospel.

■ Getting rid of fears that can keep you from doing God's will.

■ Trusting God with the outcome of your life.

■ Being strong for Christ.

■ Living by faith.

Chapter Seventeen: Learning more about Winthrop

Go to an Internet search engine.

Type in *John Winthrop, Character, Courage.*

Find topics 1-6 below and open up the websites.

1. John Winthrop

2. John Winthrop. "The courage, faith and sacrifice of their governor"....

3. John Winthrop's Christian Experience

4. John Winthrop's "experiencia"

5. (PDF) Biography of John Winthrop

6. General Court of Commonwealth of Massachusetts

chapter 18

Faithfulness—noah webster

PURPOSE: Learning What God Prizes Most

character trait:
Faithfulness

SUBJECT:
NOAH WEBSTER
(1758-1843)

PURPOSE:
Learning What God Prizes Most

FAMOUS QUOTE:
"I am ready to go; my work is all done. I know whom I have believed. I am entirely submissive to the will of God."

SCRIPTURE DOCUMENTATION:
"Know, therefore, that the LORD your God is God; He is the faithful God, keeping his covenant of love to a thousand generations of those who love him and keep his commands" (Deuteronomy 7:9).

"Now it is required that those who have been given a trust must prove faithful" (1 Corinthians 4:2).

"His master replied, 'Well done, good and faithful servant! You have been faithful with a few things; I will put you in charge of many things. Come and share your master's happiness!'" (Matthew 25:21).

PERSONALITY PROFILE

Webster was born on October 16, 1758 in West Hartford, Connecticut. He was reared in a home where there were no frivolities from sundown on Saturday and of course, all day on Sunday. There were seven in the Webster family and they all lived in a small house with four rooms. His father saw that Noah was a bright child and sought to provide an education for him since he was the eldest son. As a child, Webster learned discipline. He was able to subordinate his natural desires and see his role as a citizen of the community very clearly. When he was 14, his father sent him to study with Rev. Nathan Perkins, a local pastor. "The religious instruction at school, the Sunday services lasting two to three hours, grace at every meal, daily Bible readings, and frequent visits from the parish minister all formed so much a part of his early life that he [Webster] couldn't possibly have lost their impressions, and probably carried them with him throughout his life."[1]

Webster enrolled at Yale in 1774 and at the age of 16 had a life-changing experience. Timothy Dwight, his tutor and the future president of Yale, poured his vision for America into his students. This was part of the "Second Great Awakening," and the future of America was about to change! Students at Yale were taught to redeem every hour of the day. Each day was broken down into segments for classes, studying, prayers and meditation, exercises, and interaction with other students. Great use of time was practiced. These words spoken by Timothy Dwight stuck with Webster his entire life:

> You should by no means consider yourself as members of a small neighborhood, town or colony only, but as beings concerned in laying the foundations of 'American greatness.' Your wishes, your designs, your labors, are not to be confined by the narrow bound of the present age, but are to comprehend succeeding generations, and be pointed to immortality. You are to act, not like inhabitants of a village, nor like beings of an hour, but like citizens of the world. And like candidates for a name that shall survive the conflagration. These views will enlarge your minds, expand the grasp of your benevolences, ennoble all your conduct, and crown you with wreaths which cannot fade...remember that you act for the empire of America, and for a long succession of ages.[2]

President Theodore Roosevelt put things into perspective when he said, "It is better to be faithful than famous."[3] A phrase often stated related to faithfulness goes, "It is not success that God rewards but faithfulness in doing his will."[4] Related to faithfulness, President Abraham Lincoln said, "Many free countries have lost their liberty, and ours may lose ours; but if she shall, be it my proudest plume, not that I was the last to desert, but that I never deserted her."[5] By any standard of measurement, Noah Webster was faithful to the country he loved, to God's calling on his life, and to Scripture.

WEBSTER'S FAITH IN GOD

It was during his days at Yale that Webster encountered the "Living God." Webster also was unable to marry the love of his life because she had fallen in love with another. Webster recounted that during this time, "my mind became more and more agitated, I was suddenly seized with impressions, which called my mind irresistibly to religious concerns. The impressions however grew stronger till at length I could not pursue my studies...books yielded to the influence which could not be resisted and I was led to a spontaneous impulse to repentance, prayer and entire submission and surrender of myself to my Maker and Redeemer. My submission appeared to be cheerful and was soon followed by the peace of mind which the world can neither give nor take away."[6]

Noah Webster was an Active Federalist who believed in centralized government. Webster was successful as a result of being faithful to the mission he was given. Through his books and writings, Webster helped shape the character of the children of America. Webster believed a "sense of nationality is vital to the preservation of unity" and lived accordingly.

Webster was faithful in building up the lives of the children in America and provided an education for them. As a result, Webster was called, the "schoolmaster of America." He constantly sought to instruct youth on cleanliness, deportment, and the proper role of young people in society. Webster taught that the "ruling passions of a young person's life must be the 'Love of Virtue' (righteousness)." Webster spent ten months with Benjamin Franklin in Philadelphia and helped develop the Americanization of spelling. His dictionaries sold between 24 and 100 million copies. After 1843, his dictionaries were based on the Bible and Christian virtues. At the same time, he rescued the English language from corrupting political and social influences in Europe. Webster also learned 26 languages. One of his greatest tasks was to start Amherst College. Noah Webster also considered the translation of the Bible his crowning achievement.

One virtue that characterized the life of Noah Webster was "faithfulness." Yale President Timothy Dwight had passed on "the big picture" of where America was heading and influenced Webster to use his life to instill Christian "virtues" to his generation and generations to follow. Webster's inspiration came from God. Webster's education was for the express purpose of "the moral and religious elevation of character, and the glory of my country."[7]

Webster charted the course for nineteenth-century America based on the eternal truth found in Scripture. Few people have accomplished so much in one life. He viewed himself as a man of destiny and was able to lay foundations for generations who came after him. On his deathbed Webster said, "I am ready to go; my work is all done. I know whom I have believed. I am entirely submissive to the will of God."[8]

Webster was the first to insist upon an American language, and an American style in manners and education. He was the first to prepare books to teach children such principles and was the first to write and teach American history and civics. He established the need for—and did something about securing copyright laws. Webster also was the first to publish selections from new and promising American writers. Webster undertook what many would say was an impossible undertaking. It required amazing faithfulness to the calling on his life. His efforts also impacted future generations. His was not so much a public life, but a life of research. Only God and his family knew many of his efforts.

THE LOSS Of AMERICA'S PURPOSE

Webster wrote, "Education comprehends all that series of instruction and discipline which is intended to enlighten the understanding, correct the temper, and form the manners and habits of youth, and fit them for usefulness in their future station. To give children a good education in manners, arts and sciences is important, to give them a religious education is

NATIONAL PURPOSE

Henry Dunant was the founder of the Red Cross. Dunant devoted himself to the Red Cross and paid a price in his personal life since he ultimately wound up living in poverty. In 1901, he received the Nobel Prize for Peace. To this day, the Red Cross continues helping people wherever there is suffering because of war or disasters, with the consent of the signatories of the Geneva Convention. If there are wars or disasters, you will find the Red Cross there caring for people in need. Dunant embraced many other causes, such as the abolition of slavery, the creation of a homeland for Jews and the treatment of prisoners of war. He was also the founder of the Young Men's Christian Association (YMCA). He was often heard to say, "If Jesus Christ is God and died for me, there is no sacrifice too great that I can make for Him."

indispensable, an immense responsibility rests on parents and guardians who neglect these duties."[9]

The young Noah Webster believed in a rosy future for America. "Her people were bound for utopianism, to build a temple of freedom on a divinely favored continent, moral reformation, complete religious toleration, equal distribution of property, and the abolition of slavery."[11] These were ideas he espoused, yet his positive belief in the perfectability of mankind had been shattered. Webster's life covered 84 years, yet it must have been heartbreaking for him and others who had known the "Founders" personally–and seen the terrible price paid for the birthing of the country–as they watched their cherished principles slowly dismantled over time. Webster symbolized a modern-day Jeremiah as he grieved over the plight of America.

"His final years were full of despair and disillusionment. His rejection of democracy was total."[12]

WEBSTER'S VIEW OF THE BIBLE

Christian virtues must be taught in the schools or America would cease to exist with strong character. This, in essence, was Webster's firm conviction. Webster used his books to encourage families and children to be faithful to the Bible. Webster writes, "Education is useless without the Bible. The Bible was America's basic textbook in all fields. Virtue is the foundation of the Republic and 'virtue' will maintain a free government since people obtained freedom when they were 'virtuous or willing to sacrifice their private interests for the public good.'"[13]

"We do not know God by examining His works or by any other means except the Bible, a book in which God has graciously revealed His character to man. It is from this same book that we learn what God wants from us. His first command is to 'love the Lord, your God with all the heart and soul and mind and strength' God sent to earth a Redeemer, Jesus Christ. Faith in Christ and a sincere attempt to follow His footsteps are the sure keys to immortality,"[14] stated Webster.

"Real religion, [is that] which implies a habitual sense of the divine presence, and a fear of offending the Supreme Being."[16] Webster believed that this attitude "subdues and controls all the turbulent passions; in the Christian is seen 'meekness, forbearance, and kindness, accompanied by a serenity of mind and a desire to please, as uniform as they are cheering to families and friends.'"[17]

Webster also stated, "The religion which has introduced civil liberty is the religion of Christ and His Apostles, which enjoins

"Success is going from failure to failure without losing your enthusiasm."[10] *Churchill*

"Happiness is not the end of life; character is."[15]

Henry Ward Beecher

humility, piety, and benevolence…this is genuine Christianity, and to this we owe our free Constitution of government. The Christian religion is the most important and one of the first things in which all children, under a free government, ought to be instructed." [19]

Webster believed, "The Christian loves his Bible. In short, we love whatever gives us pleasure and delight…and if our hearts are right, we love God above all things, as the sum of all excellence and all the attributes which can communicate happiness to intelligent beings." [20]

"We must be careful to distinguish the real religion taught by Christ and the Apostles, from those systems which interested men have established. We find the true religion of Christ in the Bible only…supreme love to God…is the foundation for the whole system of Christianity; from this principle in the heart flow all the benevolent (good will)…the persons who love God supremely will reverence His character and laws, and will extend his benevolent affections and charities to all his creatures. From this source will proceed love to man and the careful performance of social duties." [21]

Webster testified, "The Christian religion is the most important and one of the first things in which all children, under a free government, ought to be instructed. No truth is more evident to my mind than that the Christian religion must be the basis of any government intended to secure the rights and privileges of a free people. It is the business of Americans to select the wisdom of all nations, as the basis of her constitutions, to avoid their errors to prevent the introduction of foreign vices and corruptions and to check the careers of her own, to promote virtue and patriotism, to embellish and improve the sciences, to diffuse the uniformity and purity of language, to add superior dignity to this infant Empire and to human nature." [22]

SEPARATION OF CHURCH AND STATE

Webster was faithful to the vision of the "Founding Fathers." He was persuaded that "separation of church and state was necessary." However his concept of "separation" was nothing like that being advocated by the A.C.L.U. (American Civil Liberties Union). Webster said of the church and state that they were "two different forms of government; one dealt with the temporal happiness of man, the other with his spiritual redemption. The messengers of salvation should not be allowed to sit in judgment of commercial and political affairs, nor should those involved in politics have any voice in church matters, let alone actively support one specific sect. The two different types of government could not be reconciled, and to attempt to do so, he believed, was to attempt 'to mix oil with water, or to make the most discordant sounds in nature harmonize.'" [24]

"As surely as there is a God in Heaven who exercises moral government over the affairs of this world, so certainly will the neglect of the Divine command be followed by bad laws, crimes etc.," [25] Webster wrote as he worried aloud about America's future.

Webster advocated that the virtuous life be taught to students, "For this reason society requires that the education of youth should be watched with the most scrupulous attention. Education, in a great measure, forms the moral characters of (mankind) and morals are the basis of government," [26] he stated.

Webster believed that the "virtues" of men are of more consequence to society than their abilities. He was persuaded that the heart should be cultivated more than the head. Webster opposed those who only saw religion as a system of "morals." "Webster believed that all the miseries and evils which men suffer proceed from their despising or neglecting the precepts contained in the Bible." [27] Webster was faithful in cultivating Christian virtues within his generation.

REPUTATION VERSUS CHARACTER

God prizes "faithfulness" in His children. Oswald Chambers wrote: "What God looks at is what we are in the dark; the imaginations of the mind, the thoughts of our heart, the habits of our body, these are most important in God's sight. Reputation is what other people think of you and character is what you are in the dark when no one sees you but yourself. What we stand up for proves what our character is like. If we stand up for our reputation, it is a sign it needs standing up for. The devil tells lies about people but no slander on earth can harm a person's character." [28]

"Many free countries have lost their liberty, and ours may lose ours; but if she shall, be it my proudest plume, not that I was the last to desert, but that I never deserted her." [23]

President Abraham Lincoln

A MODERN-DAY EXAMPLE OF FAITHFULNESS
PAT ROBERTSON

Pat Robertson, the "founder" of the Christian Broadcasting Network was a man who also exercised faithfulness to the calling of God on his life. When I first joined the staff at the Christian Broadcasting Network, I learned the source of all their faith; it was confidence in God and a dedication to a life of prayer. Each day the staff would gather together to pray for America and the cities across the country. Regular fasting and prayer were part of the prayer meeting. Pat was truly humble before God and led the staff in asking for God to exalt Himself in our lives and in the country. I learned so much from Pat about faithfulness to the mission God gives you.

Looking back on those years, I don't think I could adequately appreciate what God was doing right before my eyes. Now, it all seems rather astonishing that I had a small part in this mission. Pat Robertson was abandoned to the mission of seeing God glorified in America and around the world. If he was to ask others to join him in this mission, he had to first give up everything for the sake of the "gospel." This meant possessions and reputation and other ambitions would need to go. In reality, he knew that there is no real sacrifice when there is love. Pat is a brilliant man who can speak to just about any subject but the thing I'm most thankful to God for concerning Pat is his faithfulness. Many, many times God used him to lift the entire staff to believe God for what seemed to be impossible.

In the early years of the Christian Broadcasting Network there were few people who believed that CBN would survive, let alone touch the nations of the earth. If Pat wavered over the possible demise of his company, he sure didn't show it. So many miracles of provision and many thousands of answers to prayer were evidence of God's hand on the ministry. The 1970's were exciting days to be a follower of Jesus. Thousands of people were coming to Jesus Christ in America and throughout the world. Each night we were thrilled with the testimonies of some of God's choice servants throughout the world. The pressure of being the president of CBN and the host of the "700 Club" was enormous! Of course most of us are followers but we want to follow someone who knows where he or she is going. On one occasion Pat took me to Virginia Beach and showed me the land where CBN would build its future. He saw it as if it already existed. That is what God appears to be looking for in his followers. Pat Robertson, who seemed to be a modern-day Joshua, didn't waver, but obeyed God.

Now, the Christian Broadcasting Network and Regent University (founded by Robertson) are touching the nations for Christ. It was a privilege to work with this ministry to help develop the "follow-up" and "counseling ministry" and later to be a part of the "700 Club." Pat's life has been a model of "faithfulness" to the calling of God.

A MODERN-DAY EXAMPLE OF FAITHFULNESS
RUSSELL YOUNGSTROM

At the age of seven, my wife Ruthie had confessed Jesus Christ as her Lord as the result of Russell Youngstrom's testimony in her church. God had called Russell to work with the homeless in Chicago. He had headed up the Chicago Gospel Mission for over 50 years. Russell and his family lived in Wheaton but his heart was in Chicago. He supported himself as a meat cutter and combined with his ministry at the mission, Russell worked 15-hour days. The men loved him as he cared for their physical needs as well as their spiritual needs. Each evening an opportunity for men and women to find their way home to God was given. My wife's father came to Jesus through this ministry.

In 1982 Russell invited me to join him on the board of Chicago Gospel Mission. He had started a youth center to reach families in the Henry Horner Projects. It was a wonderful program and provided a haven for kids whose lives were surrounded by dangers. Hundreds of kids were introduced to Jesus and were memorizing the Scriptures.

What God required of this dear man and his wife, Florence, was "faithfulness." This included overcoming the harsh driving conditions through the winter months. Russell has already gone to be with the Lord, but he taught many of us about faithfulness. His faithfulness to God and the assignment God gave him is rare these days but he carried it out to the end of his journey. He combined those rare qualities of faithfulness and kindness, speaking only words of encouragement to others.

REVIEW

Q. How will the character trait of faithfulness make a difference in my life?

Q. Is our love for God measured by our love for the Bible?

Q. If Webster's conviction is true in that "we love that which gives us pleasure and delight," how can we be sure we love the right things?

Q. What are the blessings coming to the world when people love God?

Q. In what way does the Christian religion secure the rights of individuals?

Q. Do you agree that education is useless without the Bible? Explain.

Q. At the time of the writing of the Constitution, Webster subscribed to conviction that evil would be overcome by righteousness. Why do you think he believed this?

Q. Why did Webster think that Jefferson's principles were responsible for the disintegration of public virtue and morality?

Q. Discuss Webster's understanding of the two different forms of government.

Q. How do you think it was possible for Webster to sustain his mission during his entire lifetime? How can you do the same?

Q. What did Webster mean when he said both our hearts and heads should be educated?

Q. According to Webster, what did the education of a young person involve?

Q. Do you think one can build a society on dishonesty and have it sustain itself?

Q. Describe someone you know whose life is characterized by faithfulness.

Q. Why is faithfulness critical in relationships?

Q. What are the motivations for faithfulness in our lives?

Q. Why do you think God prizes faithfulness in our character?

Character for Life

GOD'S PROMISE:

"Know, therefore, that the LORD your God is God; He is the faithful God, keeping his covenant of love to a thousand generations of those who love him and keep his commands" (Deuteronomy 7:9).

GOD'S GOAL:

For Christians to live lives of faithfulness.

YOUR COMMITMENT:

To be willing to live according to what God has called you to do.

YOUR DAILY RESPONSE:

1. To live by faith each day.

2. To trust that God will always remain faithful to you, no matter what the circumstance.

3. To be willing to stand by your convictions, no matter how unpopular.

4. To live life according to God's purpose and trust Him to bring all things together for good.

FAILURE WILL MEAN:

Being afraid to live for God and instead living for yourself.

BACKGROUND:

Disloyalty and unfaithfulness weaken nations and families and eventually cause the breakdown of societies. Since graft and corruption ruin the possibility of trust and honesty, do you think one can build a society on dishonesty and have it sustain itself?

"We come to this conclusion. Every dishonest man is a parasite on the honesty of some other man or woman. Every selfish man is a parasite on some unselfish man. Evil is an attempt to live life against itself—it cannot be done. So, evil is not only bad—it is stupid. It is trying the impossible—namely, to live life against itself and get away with it. If a society is built on absolute dishonesty, no one would trust anyone else; on absolute impurity, it would rot; on absolute selfishness, no one would think in terms other than himself; on absolute hate, it would be so divisive it wouldn't hold together over night." [29]

Faith is confidence in the character of God and His Son Jesus Christ, and whether I am delivered or not, I will stick to my belief that God is a God of honor! To be faithful in every circumstance means that we have only one supreme loyalty, and that is to our Lord. This is the greatest test in the life of a disciple.

Jesus was faithful to His Father and the task He was given: "Therefore, holy brothers, who share in the heavenly calling, fix your thoughts on Jesus, the apostle and high priest whom we confess" (Hebrews 3:1).

Jesus also was loyal to His disciples: "Jesus knew that the time had come for him to leave this world and go to the Father. Having loved his own who were in the world, he now showed them the full extent of his love" (John 13:1).

Jesus also was faithful to His task of taking care of His mother who was a widow: "When Jesus saw his mother there, and the disciple whom he loved standing nearby, he said to his mother, 'Dear woman, here is your son,' and to the disciple, 'Here is your mother.' From that time on, this disciple took her into his home" (John 19:26-27).

LIVING A LIFE OF FAITHFULNESS MEANS . . .

■ Choosing faithfulness to God above all other things.

■ Living in such a way that you are always ready to die and meet your Maker.

■ Entering heaven and being commended by God for how you lived your life.

■ Making life's decisions based on what would please God.

■ Trusting God with the outcome of all circumstances.

■ Being willing to make sacrifices in order to further the gospel and God's will.

Chapter Eighteen: Learning more about Webster

Go to an Internet search engine.

Type in *Noah Webster's Character*.

Find topics 1-6 below and open up the websites.

1. Noah Webster's letter to President Clinton
2. Noah Webster's speech on the Anniversary of the Declaration
3. When Noah Webster missed the boat
4. The character of inflation
5. Character and political leadership
6. Definitions courtesy of Noah Webster's 1828 Dictionary

chapter 19
Goodness—Joseph story

PURPOSE: Learning How Jesus Walked on Earth

19

character trait:
Goodness

SUBJECT:
JOSEPH STORY
(1779-1845)

PURPOSE:
Learning How Jesus Walked on Earth

FAMOUS QUOTE:
"Republics are created by the virtue, public spirit, and intelligence of the citizens. They fall, when the wise are banished from the public councils, because they dare to be honest, and the profligate are rewarded, because they flatter the people in order to betray them."

SCRIPTURE DOCUMENTATION:
"And the LORD said, 'I will cause all my goodness to pass in front of you, and I will proclaim my name, the LORD, in your presence. I will have mercy, and I will have compassion on whom I will have compassion'" (Exodus 33:19).

"Surely goodness and love will follow me all the days of my life, and I will dwell in the house of the LORD forever" (Psalm 23:6).

"I myself am convinced, my brothers, that you yourselves are full of goodness, complete in knowledge and competent to instruct one another" (Romans 15:14).

PERSONALITY PROFILE

Joseph Story was known as a kind person who cared deeply for people. Warm, talkative, and immensely industrious, Story labored prodigiously in the formative years of American law to provide firm constitutional doctrines for the new nation and a reliable heritage of private law principles for its inhabitants.

Joseph Story was born in Marblehead, Massachusetts. Story was the oldest of eleven children of Elisha and Mehitable Story. His ancestors arrived in America around 1700 and his father was a friend of the Indians at the Boston Tea Party. Story's father was a prominent physician and surgeon and was one of the famous, "Sons of Liberty" under Samuel Adams. Even as a child, Joseph was known for his powers of concentration. Without a great deal of help, he prepared himself for his college training. Story graduated from Harvard in 1798.

He married May Lynde Oliver on December 9, 1804. She died the next year, however. Story was crushed over the death of his wife and threw himself into his work to somehow ease his pain. Four years later he married Sarah Waldo Wetmore. Of the seven children of this marriage, only two survived. Sarah Story became an invalid after the death of her third surviving child. Through these trials in his family, Story learned unconditional love. From 1805-07, Story served on the Massachusetts circuit court and eventually became its speaker. Story was admitted to the bar in 1801 and was appointed by Madison as an "associate justice" to the Supreme Court in 1811 and served until 1845.

Story was one of the towering figures in U.S. legal history and lived over a period of time where he knew firsthand the intentions of the "Founders." He even was known to have delivered a eulogy at the death of Washington. Story was 32 years old and the youngest person ever to sit on the Supreme Court. He held circuit court in New Hampshire, Rhode Island, Massachusetts, and Rhode Island.

Story was the founder and president of Harvard Law School from 1829-45. While on the Supreme Court he authored 286 opinions with 269 being in the majority. Because of his commitment to scholarship and law, his legacy is simply profound. His was a leadership based on commitment to excellence and scholarship.

In the field of constitutional law, Joseph Story must be placed next to John Marshall and James Kent. His three-volume work on the "Commentaries of the Constitution" (1833) was his most important contribution. They dominated constitutional interpretation for over 100 years until the Supreme Court was filled with justices appointed by President Roosevelt. Story, almost single-handedly, established Harvard Law School. It began with only one student registered for class in 1828. The following year 28 students registered for the university law program. By 1844, the school had 156 students from 21 states. Story's impact on America was enormous.

Alfred Konesfsky writes, "Story seized the opportunity of influencing not only his generation but the generations to follow. He was a guiding influence in the Americanization of the legal process in the young republic."[1]

CHRISTIANITY'S ROLE

Story wrote, "The Bible, is of common inheritance, not merely of Christendom, but of the world. Where can the purest principles of morality be learned so clearly or so perfectly as from the New Testament? Where are benevolence, the love of truth, sobriety, and industry, so powerfully and irresistibly inculcated as in the sacred volume."[2]

Story ruled that, "any plan to build a non-Christian school which would not teach the Bible and would instead propagate 'Deism, or any other form of infidelity' would be impermissible. Such a case is not to be presumed to exist in a Christian country."[3]

"The Promulgation of the great doctrines of religion, the being, and attributes and providences of one Almighty God; the responsibility to Him for all our actions, founded upon moral accountability. A future state of rewards and punishments, the cultivation of all the personal, social and benevolent virtues—these can never be a matter of indifference in any well-ordered community. It is, indeed, difficult to conceive how any civilized society can well exist without them."[4]

Story understood, and was committed not to favor, establishing one denomination over another. Story maintained that, "The federal government should not have any authority in the field of settling questions on religion; in some of the states, Episcopalian, constituted the predominant sect, in others, Presbyterians, in others, Congregationalists; in others, Quakers, and in others gain, there was a close numerical rival among

Story had a clear understanding of what was good for a nation and the commitment to stand behind what he believed. The idea of all religions being equally respected (multiculturalism) and supported was not a view the "Founders" embraced at all. Story, considered the "Father of American jurisprudence," states in the Commentaries on the Constitution, "The real object of the First Amendment was not to countenance, much less advance Mohammedanism, Judaism or infidelity by prostrating Christianity, but to exclude all rivals among Christian sects and prevent any national ecclesiastical establishment which should give a hierarchy. Any attempt to level all religions, and to make it a matter of state policy to hold all in utter indifference, would have created universal disapprobation, if not universal indignation." Story believed that the Christian religion provided the 'First Principles' to build the nation.

contending sects. It was impossible that there should not arise perpetual strife and perpetual jealously on the subject of ecclesiastical ascendancy, if the national government were left free to establish a religious establishment."[5]

STORY'S COMMITMENT TO OTHERS

Story was committed to self-sacrifice and self-discipline for the sake of others. Story had tremendous industry and power of concentration with which he was later to amaze the legal world by producing volume after volume of commentaries in rapid succession. He wrote, "I was most thoroughly devoted to all the college studies, and scarcely wasted a single moment in idleness. I traced this back to this cause, a serious injury to my health. When I entered college I was robust and muscular, but before I left I had become pale and feeble and was inclined to dyspepsia."[7] For months at a time Story frequently devoted fourteen hours a day to study. As a result, he graduated second in his class.

The pattern of selfless work followed Story throughout his life. Story wrote his friend Daniel Webster, whose wife had also died, and provided some counsel to the famous orator. "Having been a like sufferer (having lost his wife and children in times prior) I can say, that the great secret of comfort must be sought, so far as human aid can go, in employment. It requires effort and sacrifices, but it is the only specific remedy against unavailing and wasting sorrow; that canker which eats into the heart and destroys its vitality."[8]

Story demonstrated a commitment to bring about justice for all people. Story also had a deep animosity for slave trading. He spoke out against extending slavery to Missouri and drafted resolutions "condemning slavery as a moral and political evil." In the Amistad case he wrote the following: "The Africans were not pirates and were justified in seizing the Amistad for they had exercised the ultimate right of all human beings in extreme cases to resist oppression."[9] The eternal principles had to prevail. Story's decision had far-reaching implications. Story "ignored differences of color in affirming the black rights to a fair trial in American courts; ruled that the Africans were free blacks, though of foreign nationality; recognized their status as persons having the right to participate in the nation's legal process."[10] Alexis de Tocqueville, the French author of Democracy in America, a classic analysis of U.S. society and government, used Story's commentaries in writing his work.

Story demonstrated a commitment to build the country on just laws resulting in his three-volume work, "Commentaries of the Constitution." He wrote of them, "If these Commentaries shall but inspire in the rising generation a more ardent love of their country, an unquenchable thirst for liberty, and a profound reverence for the constitution and the union, then they will have accomplished all that their author ought to desire."[11]

CHARACTER DEVELOPMENT AND VIRTUES

Story showed a commitment to character development and virtues.

Let the American youth never forget that they possess a noble inheritance, bought by the toils and sufferings, and blood of their ancestors; and capable, if wisely improved, and faithfully guarded, of transmitting to their latest posterity all the substantial blessings of life, the peaceful enjoyment of liberty, property, religion, and independence.[13]

"The structure (of America)," wrote Story, "has been erected by architects of consummate skill and fidelity; its foundations are solid; its defenses are impregnable from without. It has been reared for immortality, if the world of man may justly aspire to such a title. It may, nevertheless, perish in an hour by the folly, or corruption, or negligence of its only keepers. Republics are created by the virtue, public spirit, and intelligence of the citizens. They fall, when the wise are banished from the public councils, because they dare to be honest, and the profligate are rewarded, because they flatter the people in order to betray them."[14]

STORY'S PASSION

Story was concerned with the whole fabric of American education for both boys and girls. He asked, "Why may not the Bible, and especially the New Testament, without note or comment, be read and taught as a Divine Revelation in the school, its general precepts expounded, its evidences explained and its glorious principles of morality inculcated? What is there to prevent a work, not sectarian, from being read and taught in the college by our lay teachers? It may well be asked, what's there in all this, which is positively enjoined, inconsistent with the spirit or truths of the religion of Christ? Where can the purest

"Goodness is love in action, love with its hand to the plow, love with the burden on its back, love following his footsteps who went about continually doing good. A Christian should always remember that the value of his good works is not based on their number and excellence, but on the love of God which prompts him to do these things."[12]

San Juan de La Cruz

NATIONAL PURPOSE

principles of morality be learned so clearly and so perfectly as from the New Testament?" [15] Story believed that the works of religion might be carried on without a special priesthood but a priesthood of all believers.

"One of the beautiful boasts of our municipal jurisprudence is that Christianity is part of the Common Law…. There never has been a period in which the Common Law did not recognize Christianity as lying at its foundation. I verily believed Christianity necessary to the support of civil society." [16]

Story knew something that most of us don't know, "Government cannot long exist without an alliance with Religion to some extent, and that Christianity is indispensable to the true interests and solid foundation of all governments." [17]

In a letter to Jasper Adams, Story writes, "I know not, indeed, how any deep sense of moral obligation or accountableness can be expected to prevail in the community without a firm foundation of the great Christian truths. It yet remains a problem to be solved in human affairs whether any free government can be permanent where the public worship of God, and the support of religion, constitute no part of the policy or duty of the state in any assignable shape." [18]

Judge Story believed in "the divine mission of Christ, the credibility and authenticity of the Bible, the miracles wrought by our Savior and his apostles and the efficacy of his precepts to lead men to salvation." [19] Story believed that Christ was the Son of God and that he was a special messenger of God who came to teach God's Word.

Even though the Storys lost their children, Story maintained confidence in God's character and admitted the pain was eased by the confidence that his trust was in the ways of providence and his belief that he would join his children in heaven. Knowing his death was near, Story bade a serene farewell to his family. His last words praised God. Newmyer writes, "With his death in 1843 went a vision of a Republican community rooted in virtue, dedicated to the tradition of public service. Story was only 49 when he died." [20]

Judges John Marshall, James Story, and James Kent were the three most influential judges during nineteenth-century America for laying down the foundations for years to come. (For more information on Marshall, see Chapter 23 and "Humility.") Judge Kent was convinced that whatever good would come to

America would be because of the influence of Christianity. Kent was the author of the "Commentaries on American Law" published in 1833.

Kent's views are notable as a contemporary of Story. He wrote, "Probably at the time of the adoption of the Constitution, and of the amendment to it now under consideration, the general, if not the universal sentiment was, that Christianity ought to receive encouragement from the state, so far as was not incompatible with the private right of conscience and the freedom of religious worship. And, at all events, it is impossible for those who believe in the truth of Christianity as a Divine revelation, to doubt that it is the special duty of government to foster and encourage it among all the citizens and subjects."[23]

"Christianity in its enlarged sense, as a religion revealed and taught in the Bible, is part and parcel of the law of the land."[24] In "The People vs. Ruggles," Kent rendered the opinion of the court saying: "The defendant (Ruggles) was indicted since he wickedly, maliciously and blasphemously, uttered and with a loud voice, published in the presence and hearing of diverse good and Christian people...the false, scandalous malicious, wicked and blasphemous words: Jesus Christ was [illegitimate] ..."[25] Ruggles was tried, found guilty, sentenced to three months in prison, and fined $500.

Judge Kent was persuaded that, "whatever strikes at the root of christianity tends manifestly to the dissolution of civil government. Blasphemy against God and profane ridicule of christ or the holy scriptures are offenses punishable by common law...because it tends to corrupt the morals of the people and destroy good order."[26]

MODERN-DAY EXAMPLE OF GOODNESS
ROSS TOOLEY

The event most people remember about the Olympics of 1972 was the Arab terrorist attack on the Israeli athletes at the Olympic Village. As one of the coordinators on the Olympic grounds that day, I saw firsthand the terror that shook everyone to the core of their beings. In response to this horror, the leadership of "Youth with a Mission" decided to print up thousands of newspapers depicting a picture of a Jew and an Arab showing love—their arms wrapped around each other. The caption read "Eine Jude und Ein Araber" (A Jew and an Arab). The newspaper story explained that these individuals enjoyed a friendship because of Christ. Our group handed out tens of thousands of these newspapers to somber visitors of the 1972 Olympics.

None of us could imagine the significance of that event. In front of the entire world, any hope that the Olympics could bring nations permanently together were dashed. This was the beginning of terrorist attacks that has stirred fear among people throughout the world. In recent years, we have continued to see similar kinds of attacks. As a result, a radical shift in the priorities of our nation has occurred. The wisest among us struggles with how to respond to such terror.

At times it may seem that people portraying goodness are hard to find. I, however, have met one and would like to tell you about him.

Ross Tooley was originally from New Zealand, but he and his wife, Margaret, had spent about 35 years as missionaries with "Youth with a Mission" working in the Pacific and Asia. Ross wrote an amazing book entitled, "We Cannot But Tell." Ross is a man abandoned to Jesus Christ and is a wonderful speaker.

After the Munich Olympic Games were over, I started the long journey back to the U.S. Checking with the airline and I discovered that the charter flight I had come over on had gone bankrupt and I had no way to get home. All of us were learning how to trust God for our finances and knowing my plight, Ross gave me $70, which I believe was all the money he had for his travels. He insisted I take it and use it to get home. I was to learn about a "life of faith" through Ross. I had no way of knowing how I would get back to the United States with only $70, however. I called other countries to see if there were flights to New York for $70. Nothing. I sat in the phone booth at the Frankfurt Airport and a man I had never seen before walked up to me and told me to travel to London and go to a travel agency called "Underground Travel Service" in Piccadilly Circus. I had no other option, so I used the $70 to get a one-way ticket to London, which took about $60 as I recall.

I shared my story with an Indian agent who listened patiently and decided to help me with a ticket on Japan Airlines to New York. He said I could pay them when I got back to America. I was amazed and realized God's hand in this. God put me together with one of his choice servants from Hungary en route to the United States. Evangelist Don Odon was a man God wanted me to meet and help in the years ahead. This could only have happened if my friend Ross had been willing to give his few "loaves and fishes" to a new friend who was really in a fix and needed a miracle.

REVIEW

Q. What is our motivation for "goodness" toward others?

Q. Story paid a big price in terms of his health to write "The Commentaries." What were his hopes and dreams in writing them?

Q. Describe someone you know whose life was directed toward doing good for others.

Q. What would the "Founders" have thought about court rulings against Christianity today?

Q. When Ruggles blasphemed Christ, it was treated as a crime. What does this say about our current culture's loss of "the fear of God"?

Q. To what extent do you think government encourages or discourages Christianity?

Q. What was Story's view regarding teaching the Bible in public schools?

Q. What do you think motivated Story to abuse his body in his studies and throughout his life?

Q. Was Story's effort in vain for modern Americans?

Q. If possible, view the movie "Amistad" and discuss the rulings of Joseph Story.

Character for Life

GOD'S PROMISE:

"And the LORD said, "I will cause all my goodness to pass in front of you, and I will proclaim my name, the LORD, in your presence. I will have mercy, and I will have compassion on whom I will have compassion" (Exodus 33:19).

GOD'S GOAL:

For Christians to live lives of goodness.

YOUR COMMITMENT:

Choose goodness over other means of living each day.

YOUR DAILY RESPONSE:

1. Live your life as Jesus did, full of goodness toward all.

2. Be willing to do the right thing, no matter what the consequence.

3. Trust that God will reward you for your goodness, even if it isn't until heaven.

4. Know that no matter how "good" we are, it isn't enough. Everyone needs Jesus Christ's redemption to enter heaven.

FAILURE WILL MEAN:

Living a life bent on doing evil and selfish deeds.

BACKGROUND:

Goodness was seen in the life of Jesus. "How he [Jesus] went around doing good and healing all who were under the power of the devil, because God was with him" (Acts 10:38b). Jesus said about Himself, "I am the good shepherd. The good shepherd lays down his life for the sheep" (John 10:11). Jesus also told us, "In the same way, let your light shine before men, that they may see your good deeds and praise your Father in heaven" (Matthew 5:16).

LIVING A LIFE OF GOODNESS MEANS . . .

■ Understanding that experiencing the loss of my own interests is the only way to enter into communion with God.

■ Not being aware every time you do a good thing, because you ruin it by noticing it.

■ Not sparing a gentle rebuke but allowing it so that good can come to others.

■ Being like Jesus and making the test of goodness the actual carrying out of God's will.

■ Understanding that it is the goodness of God that leads us to repentance.

Chapter Nineteen: Learning more about Story

Go to an Internet search engine.
Type in *Joseph Story's Character*.
Find topics 1-5 below and open up the websites.
1. Amendment (Religion) Joseph Story's Commentaries on the...
2. Joseph Story's ongoing war with Thomas Jefferson
3. Joseph Story's Republican Protestantism
4. Story, Joseph
5. Stories Commentaries on the Constitution

chapter 20

Grace— george whitefield

PURPOSE: Discovering a New Way of Living

character trait:

Grace

SUBJECT:
GEORGE WHITEFIELD
(1714-1770)

PURPOSE:
Discovering a New Way of Living

FAMOUS QUOTE:
"O thought divine! I shall soon be in a world where time, age, pain, and sorrow are unknown. My body fails, my spirit expands. How willingly I would ever live to preach Christ! But I die to be with Him."

SCRIPTURE DOCUMENTATION:
"Let us then approach the throne of grace with confidence, so that we may receive mercy and find grace to help us in our time of need" (Hebrews 4:16).

PERSONALITY PROFILE

Whitefield's parents were proprietors of the well-known "Bell Inn" in Gloucester. This inn was used for stage plays and other performances. At two years of age George's father died and his grandfather raised him. When George was eight years old, his mother remarried and the marriage almost cost the family their business. Eventually, his stepfather left the family.

Whitefield started school at the age of 12 and became proficient in Latin and New Testament Greek, as he had a wonderful ability to memorize. His early life, however, was spent away from God. George and his mother, with the help of her oldest son, ran the family business. George waited tables and learned a great deal about many types of people, which likely helped him later in life to communicate with people's deep needs.

There was, however, no money to send George to college. His mother saw George was gifted in the ability to communicate and she was determined to get him an education. Eventually, Whitefield was able to get a scholarship to Oxford as a servitor or butler. His experience was hard on his pride, however, since as a servitor, students of a high rank were not able to talk with him due to the "class system" in England. He married Elizabeth James, an older widow, and this union brought about the birth of a son who died at the age of one. His many travels likely caused pain to his already unhappy marriage.

John Wesley referred to Whitefield as "a giant of a preacher as well as poet. It seem as if he never preached in vain."[1] The former slave trader, John Newton said, "His [Whitefield's] messages were fresh and full of spiritual joy. It was like lightning shock to the heart. He was declaring not his message but God's."[2]

THE "HOLY CLUB"

During Whitefield's time at Oxford, he desperately wanted to earn God's approval and with Charles Wesley and others, started the "Holy Club" for those earnest about seeking God. As Whitefield studied for his Master's degree, he presided over the "Holy Club." The "Holy Club" members got up early in the morning, had lengthy devotions, strove for self-discipline, and determined that no time during the day was to be wasted. At night there was time to review the day and deal with the sin in their lives. They kept journals of their progress and fasted on Wednesdays and Fridays. They cared for the younger students and helped them develop character in their lives. Being part of the "Holy Club" meant visiting prisoners, poorhouses, shining shoes for people, washing clothes of those in need, attending the Eucharist, visiting prisons, and contributing to a relief fund. The "Holy Club," however, had missed the one thing that was all-important; their efforts at obtaining righteousness were based on "works."

Fellow students ridiculed members of the "Holy Club" and Whitefield, despite his disciplines, became sick, emaciated, and weak and was confined to bed for seven weeks. During this time of recuperation he experienced a spiritual awakening. He dropped all of his own ideas and efforts to please God and began instead to listen to God. He cried out to God in utter helplessness and, for the first time in over a year, was filled with incredible joy.

Through his sickness, the discovery of the love of God came into his life. "Joy, joy, unspeakable joy that's full of glory."[4] Now he had one desire, to share the Good News that Jesus had come to save sinners. All a person needed to do was repent of their sins and trust Jesus' atoning death, while giving their life to God. This encounter with the living God changed Whitefield's life with an intense sense of calling to preach the "gospel." A new thought came to his mind, "George, you have what you asked! You ceased to struggle and simply believed and you are born again! I now receive you who are the price of my soul's redemption, I receive you who are the food for my final journey, and for love of whom I studied, kept vigil, and struggled: indeed, it was you, Jesus, that I preached and you I taught. Never rest until you can say, 'the Lord our righteousness.'"[5]

England had never seen anything like the revival in the fields as Whitefield spoke about how much Jesus loved them and how in cruel crucifixion He died for them, to save them

"Happy for us if the grace of God enables us to live so that we retain innocently and freshness of character down to old age."[3]

Mary Ann Wendell

"Have we read or
heard of any person
who called so many
thousands, so many
myriads of sinners to
repentance? Above all,
have we read or heard
of anyone who has
been God's blessed
instrument to bring so
many sinners from
darkness to light and
from the power of
Satan to God as
Whitefield?" [7]

Benjamin Franklin

from their sins. On one occasion he preached to 10,000 miners who shed tears of joy on hearing that the "good news" was for them. "The character of this truly pious person must be deeply impressed on the heart of every friend to vital religion. In spite of a tender constitution (weakness of body), Whitefield continued to the last day of his life, preaching with a frequency and fervor that seemed to exceed that natural strength of the most robust." [6]

GOD'S MESSAGE OF GRACE TO THE WORLD

It is said of Whitefield that during this time of his life he stopped eating certain foods and gave the money to the poor, wore only a patched gown and dirty shoes and would often spend all night in fervent prayer while avoiding conversations with other people. Whitefield made seven trips to America, (spending two-and-a-half years on water) lasting from half a year to four years. He spent 24 years of ministry to the British Isles and nine more years in America speaking to 10 million souls. He preached more than 18,000 sermons between 1736 and 1770, an average of 500 a year. What a life!

After hearing Whitefield preach time after time, poverty-stricken miners collected money to build a school for their children. Whitefield believed that the impoverished were not to be exploited by the socially privileged. Whitefield preached in England, Scotland, Wales, Gilbraltar, Bermuda and the American colonies. He was the foremost figure in the "Great Awakening." Whitefield's voice was like a trumpet and he had a tremendous voice of praise. He preached throughout the land and was sustained for 50 years. It was said of Whitefield that he "spoke as a lion." Benjamin Franklin said his voice was like "a powerful organ."

WHITEFIELD HELPED THE "POOREST OF THE POOR"

Whitefield's heart was moved to compassion by the suffering of children. The insensitivity of the rich to the poor characterized England in those days, and street children and those with mental problems were treated cruelly. The censure of Anglican ministers toward his ministry and the lack of true spirituality in the clergy must also have brought great pain to Whitefield. During his trips to America Whitefield spent considerable time in Georgia. He brought many provisions of medicine and food with him having raised $4,000 for his orphanage. He rented a large house for a temporary home and soon built the first main building, which he named Bethany, "house of mercy."

As a result of the "awakening" a new social philosophy was born with prison and education reform being affected. Education now became available to everyone. Whitefield was asked by John Wesley to come to Georgia and minister to the needs of people. His efforts to bring provisions, medicines, and food to the poor of Georgia made a lasting impression. Whitefield's heart was to help the orphaned children and the many Georgians who were being released from debtor prison but had no education, poor health, and no knowledge of farming. Whitefield brought two educators with him to establish a school.

Whitefield also started the first orphanage in the Colonies in Philadelphia. Whitefield had a powerful impact in the Colonies and begged them not to live as 13 Colonies but as one nation under God. Whitefield helped Christians in America overcome their "denominationalism." He preached in all the churches and believers discovered their common joy in the gospel of Jesus.

Whitefield had experienced great difficulties in life that no doubt prepared him for his time in the Colonies. In all probability, no one in the eighteenth century impacted America as did George Whitefield. Whitefield's spiritual leadership brought Americans into a new understanding of the "gospel of God's grace."

LOVE, REGARDLESS OF DENOMINATION

America had been founded by many different denominations from Europe and Whitefield spread the common joy of faith in the Savior. The sectarian spirit was being transformed to a common experience of faith. Whitefield was the first person to preach the "gospel" to all the denominations. He encouraged ministers to warm themselves with the love of God and preached that unless they were warmed with the love of God themselves, they could not be instruments that diffused love. It didn't seem to matter to Whitefield what denominations they belonged to since he enjoyed them all.

"Tragically, the attitudes toward God of many in America were characterized by 'duty' rather than 'grace,' 'law and

"In his public labors he has, for many years, astonished the world with the eloquence and devotion. It was the love of God shed abroad in his heart...filling his soul with tender, selfless love to every child or man."[9]

John Wesley

morals,' rather than 'the imparted righteousness Jesus Christ provides.'"[8]

Whitefield's preaching in America changed this and enraptured even Benjamin Franklin who wrote, "It was wonderful to see the change made by his [Whitefield's] preaching in the manners of the inhabitants of Philadelphia."[10] The entire city was growing religious and a crowd of 78,000 had packed the streets of Philadelphia. John Wesley questioned his readers saying, "Have we read or heard of any person who called so many thousands, so many myriads of sinners to repentance? Above all, have we read or heard of anyone who has been God's blessed instrument to bring so many sinners from darkness to light and from the power of Satan to God as Whitefield?"[11]

The message of God's grace for all people was preparing the country for what was just ahead of them. George Whitefield died in 1770, just before the "Revolutionary War." The crowds coming to see Whitefield were larger than ever, but his health was failing. His last message was preached in New Hampshire on the "incomparable excellencies of Christ." During his preaching he seemed all the while to look straight into heaven. Dr. Rimas J. Orentas writes, "Finally, he cried out, 'I go! I go to rest prepared. My sun has arisen and by the aid of heaven has given light to many. It is now about to set. It is about to rise to the zenith of immortal glory.... O thought divine! I shall soon be in a world where time, age, pain, and sorrow are unknown. My body fails, my spirit expands. How willingly I would ever live to preach Christ! But I die to be with Him.'"[12]

On the day of Whitefield's departure, "He rose at four in the morning...and went into the closet; and his companion observed he was unusually long in private. He left his closet, returned to his companion, threw himself on the bed, and lay about ten minutes. Then he fell upon his knees, and prayed most fervently to God that if it was consistent with His will, he might that day finish his Master's work. He then desired his man to call Mr. Parsons, the clergyman, at whose house he was; but, in a minute, before Mr. Parsons could reach him, died, without a sigh or groan."[13]

Upon his death, Whitefield had asked his life-long friend, John Wesley, to speak at his funeral. About Whitefield, John Wesley later wrote, "In his public labors he has, for many years, astonished the world with his eloquence and devotion. It was the love of God shed abroad in his heart ... filling his soul with tender, selfless love to every child or man."[14] Wesley remembered, "his indefatigable activity, his tender-heartedness to the afflicted, [his charity] toward the poor. With steadiness wherewith he pursued whatever he undertook for his Master's sake, witness one instance for all—the Orphan-house in Georgia; which he began and perfected, in spite of all discouragements."[15]

"His [Whitefield's] message was no other than a faith in a bleeding Lord...filling his soul with tenderness...his head as waters, and his eyes a fountain of tears. The most hardened person could not resist his message. With what divine pathos did he persuade the impenitent sinner to embraced the practice of piety and virtue! Filled with the spirit of grace, he spoke from the heart, and, with a fervency of zeal perhaps unequalled since the day of the Apostles, adored the truths he delivered with the most graceful charms of rhetoric and oratory."[16]

MODERN-DAY EXAMPLE OF A LIFE OF GRACE
ESTHER LEE JAMES

In 1975, I met George McLean, a well-known Southern California architect, and we became close friends. The McLeans wanted Ruthie, my wife, and I to meet their friend, Esther Lee. George and his wife, Jeannie, tried to prepare us for this meeting by talking about this remarkable person. When Esther Lee contracted lupus, her husband abandoned her and the children. She was overcome with grief and wanted only to die. They were living in Las Vegas at the time. She took her two children and walked to the cemetery and just sat down on the grass waiting for something to happen. From her perspective, her life was over, she had given up. She didn't realize, however, that the Lord "sustains the fatherless and the widow" (Psalm 146:9). Through some remarkable events, Esther Lee had an encounter with Jesus. She met a Christian man who felt God had brought them together and they eventually married. He married Esther Lee, not knowing what was ahead for both of them.

Ruthie and I grew close to Esther Lee and her family. Lupus is a terribly disabling disease and over a period of nine years Esther Lee's bones disintegrated. On one occasion someone squeezed her hand and the bones in her hand simply broke. She was totally confined to bed and when we met her she could only move one finger.

The amazing thing about all this, was the presence of Jesus in her life. She was blind, but her face was radiant. Her friends wired up an earphone for her and she began a counseling ministry on the phone. She spoke with people who called from all over the country and continued this until her "home going." With the one finger still useable she could push a button to answer the many calls. Through the night hours people in crisis would call Esther Lee. On a few occasions her spirit left her body and she was taken to celestial dwellings. Esther Lee could see her husband stretched over her lifeless body pleading with God to allow her to live longer. Her spirit and her life came back to her body and she continued to minister to people of God's grace and love as long as she was able.

Esther Lee knew God's grace experientially from moment to moment. She was filled with joy. After the Vietnam War she learned of thousands of men who were in veteran hospitals throughout the country. Esther Lee decided to travel on her bed in an R.V. to these hospitals. It is hard to imagine the pain she had to bear traveling to the East Coast and back, but what a testimony she gave to men and women whose bodies had been broken through their war experiences! Our vets saw her broken body but also a spirit of joy. She was thankful they were inspired in spite of their own personal suffering. God's grace was sufficient, she said. They had seen a living example!

REVIEW

Q. How will the character trait of grace make a difference in your life?

Q. According to Whitefield, "the light had become darkness" at Oxford, yet there were still students who were pursuing God with all their hearts. If you are attending school where there is great hostility to the "gospel," how can this turn out for God's good in your life?

Q. What does it mean to know our salvation is based upon "grace"?

Q. What does "cheap grace" mean?

Q. Tell, if you can, of an experience where you learned something from being sick.

Q. What did Whitefield mean when he exclaimed with joy "the Lord our righteousness"?

Q. The disciplines of the Holy Club were amazing, but God's grace and mutual accountability made the difference. If you belong to a club, what could you learn from Whitefield's Holy Club?

Q. The suffering of children on the other side of the Atlantic brought great suffering to the heart of Whitefield. Can young people in this country make a difference in the lives of suffering children in other countries?

Q. Tell of experiences you or your friends have had in reaching out to suffering children.

Q. What could we learn today from Whitefield about emphasizing what we have in common instead of focusing on our differences?

Q. How did Benjamin Franklin describe the effects of Whitefield's preaching in Philadelphia?

Q. How do you think Whitefield could preach to 78,000 without loudspeakers?

Q. Why do you think Whitefield could pray as he did, asking God to take him home that day?

Q. What can we learn from the life of George Whitefield?

Q. Before he died, a missionary once said, "If I had loved Him more I could have served Him better." What comes before service to Jesus?

Character for Life

GOD'S PROMISE:

"Let us then approach the throne of grace with confidence, so that we may receive mercy and find grace to help us in our time of need" (Hebrews 4:16).

GOD'S GOAL:

For those who love him to live a life filled with grace.

YOUR COMMITMENT:

To be willing to deal gracefully with all situations that may arise in life.

YOUR DAILY RESPONSE:

1. Look up to God and around you to others when you feel sorry for yourself.
2. Keep in mind that God's grace is enough.

3. Be willing to suffer for the sake of the gospel.

4. Trust God to perfect His will in your life.

FAILURE WILL MEAN:

Focusing only oneself and feeling sorry for oneself when difficulties arise.

BACKGROUND:

Grace teaches us that God's attitude toward us is one of acceptance and love. Knowing God's heart, we can "approach the throne of grace with confidence" (Hebrews 4:16).

Relying totally on Jesus to work within us, we can experience God's unlimited power, enabling us to live lives pleasing to God. Jesus shows us that God stoops to help the undeserving and pardons the sinner.

God has brought us, in Jesus, a righteousness which comes from trusting in His sufferings for our sins. Relying totally on Jesus to work within us, we experience God's own unlimited power, enabling us to live lives pleasing to God.

LIVING A LIFE OF GRACE MEANS . . .

- Doing a favor without any expectation of anything in return.

- Finding the only motive in the bounty and heart of the giver.

- Finding unearned and unmerited favor in God's eyes.

- Living in direct contrast to works.

- Forgiving the repentant sinner and bringing joy and thankfulness to him.

- Knowing that, "God's grace not only forgives the repentant sinner, but brings joy and thankfulness to him. The grace of Christ without which neither infants or adults can be saved, is not rendered for any merits, but is given gratis, on account of which it is also called grace."[17]

Chapter Twenty: Learning more about Whitefield

Go to an Internet search engine.
Type in *George Whitefield's Character, Grace.*
Find topics 1-6 below and open up the websites.
1. George Whitefield and His Ministry/Grace Online Library
2. George Whitefield and His Ministry/Grace Online Library
3. George Whitefield
4. George Whitefield, Life, Times and Influences
5. George Whitefield's Farewell Sermon
6. 19-7inc

chapter 21

Holiness—john wesley

PURPOSE: Consecrating Yourself to God

character trait:
Holiness

SUBJECT:
JOHN WESLEY
(1703-1791)

PURPOSE:
Consecrating Yourself to God

FAMOUS QUOTE:
"The serene silent beauty of a holy life, is the most powerful influence in the world, next to the might of the Spirit of God."

SCRIPTURE DOCUMENTATION:
"For this is what the high and loft One says—he who lives forever, whose name is holy: 'I live in a high and holy place, but also with him who is contrite and lowly in spirit, to revive the spirit of the lowly and to revive the heart of the contrite'" (Isaiah 57:15).

"But now that you have been set free from sin and have become slaves to God, the benefit you reap leads to holiness, and the result is eternal life" (Romans 6:22).

PERSONALITY PROFILE

Dr. Benjamin Rush said of John Wesley, "I admire and honor that great man above any man that has lived since the time of the Apostles."[1] Said C.T. Winchester, "John Wesley was the most candid of men. Seldom has a great religious reformer been so little of a dogmatist, or shown so little stubborn persistence in his own views, simply because they were his own. And this openness to persuasion was joined with a will as inflexible as iron."[2]

Wesley was born in Epworth, Lincolnshire where his father was Rector. He was one of 19 children and was educated at home by his mother Susannah. Wesley participated in the "Holy Club" as a student at Oxford and was ordained a priest in 1725. He left Oxford in 1735 to become a chaplain to an English community in Savanna, Georgia. At the time he probably was not a true Christian.

On the ship to America, he met the Moravians and this is his account: "On shipboard, I was again active in outward works; where it pleased God, of his free mercy, to give me twenty-six of the Moravian brethren for companions, who endeavored to shew me a more excellent way. But I understood it not at first. I was too learned and too wise, so that it seemed foolishness unto me. And I continued…trusting in that righteousness whereby no flesh can be justified. At the time I was in Savannah, I was thus beating the air. Being ignorant of the righteousness of Christ, which, by a living faith in him bringeth salvation to every one that believeth. I sought to establish my own righteousness, and so labored in the fire all my days."[3]

Wesley tells about his encounter when the ship was almost lost: "At seven I went to the Germans. I had long before observed the great seriousness of their behavior. Of their humility they had given continual proof, by performing those servile offices for the other passengers, which none of the English would undertake; for which they desired, and would receive no pay, saying, 'it was good for their proud hearts,' and 'their loving Saviour had done more for them.' Every day had given them occasion of showing a meekness which no injury could move. If they were pushed, struck, or thrown down, they rose again and went away; but no complaint was in their mouth. There was now an opportunity (to determine) whether they were delivered from the spirit of fear, as well as from that of pride, anger, and revenge. In the midst of the psalm wherewith their service began, the sea broke over, split the mainsail in pieces, covered the ship, and poured in between the decks, as if the deep had already swallowed us up. A terrible screaming began among the English. The Germans calmly sang on. I asked one of them afterwards, 'Was you not afraid?' He answered, 'I thank God, no.' I asked, 'But were not your women and children afraid?' He replied mildly, 'No; our women and children are not afraid to die.'"[4]

Soon after his return to England, Wesley had an encounter with God. He writes of his experience: "In the evening, I went very unwillingly to a Society on 'Aldersgate Street,' where one was reading Luther's preface to the Epistle to the Romans. About a quarter before nine, while he was describing the change which God works in the heart through faith in Christ I felt my heart 'strangely warmed.' I felt I did trust in Christ; Christ alone, for my salvation; and an assurance was given me, that he had taken away my sins, even mine, and saved me from the law of sin and death."[5]

Aldersgate Street marked the change in the life of John Wesley when his heart was changed forever. John Wesley birthed the Methodist movement as well as trained other avid students of the Bible. His goal was to return the church to its apostolic moorings. Wesley stressed personal faith and holiness of life. Said Wesley, "The goal of a devout person is to make God's character and Jesus' life real to others. Whether this took the believer to a pulpit or the 'marketplace' it made little difference."[6] All of life was to be a sacred service to the Lord Jesus.

> "He that sees the beauty of holiness, or true moral good, sees the greatest and most important thing in the world...unless this is seen nothing is seen that is worth seeing; for there is no other true excellence or beauty. He who would truly and feelingly understand the word of Christ, must study to make his whole life conformable to that of Christ." [7]
>
> Thomas à Kempis

A LIFE CONSECRATED TO GOD

The ministry of John Wesley was carried out largely on horseback. He thought of "the world as his parish." He organized his followers into small groups of "societies" using the newfound gifts of people in teaching, administration, and preaching. In 1784, the new Methodists were separated from the Anglican Church. Wesley rode over 250,000 miles on horseback and preached 40,000 sermons to bring spiritual renewal to the English-speaking world. His break with the Anglican Church his father had served led him to be excluded from many churches. Wesley taught, "The serene silent beauty of a holy life, is the most powerful influence in the world, next to the might of the Spirit of God."[8] True goodness is woven through the lifestyle of the believer and expressed in everyday activity and every relationship.

A NEW UNDERSTANDING OF GOD'S GRACE

Wesley also taught that "the grace of love of God, whence cometh our salvation, is free in all, and free for all…. It is freeing all to whom it is given. It does not depend on any power or merit in man, no, not in any degree, neither in whole, nor in part. It does not in anywise depend either on the good works or righteousness of the receiver; nor on anything he has done, or anything he is. It does not depend on his endeavors. It does not depend on his good tempers (disposition) or good desires, or good purposes and intentions; for all these flow from the free grace of God; they are the streams only, not the fountain. They are the fruits of free grace, and not the root. They are not the cause, they are the effects of it."[10]

Through their lives and actions, Wesleyans have taught us about the beauty of holiness as well as the aesthetics. Holiness is a reflection of God's beauty. They seek to know God in a beautiful way that transforms lives and leads to purity of heart and mind. Their goal is not to just know the truth, but the God behind the truth.

Wesley believed that there were three marks of the Spirit's activity in a believer's life: "The witness of the Holy Spirit with love, peace and joy to all mankind."[11]

Wesley wanted to return the (Anglican) church to the power of worship seen in the early church. He failed to return the Anglican Church to the convictions of the Apostolic Fathers, yet his influence in evangelicalism was worldwide, especially in America. The very basis for the Pentecostal movement came out of the teachings of John Wesley and Charles Finney.

ACTS OF MERCY AND THE GOSPEL

With regard to works of mercy, Wesley wrote, "Take heed, saith he, that ye do not your alms before men, to be seen of them; otherwise ye have no reward of your Father which is in heaven. Every work of charity included, every thing which we give, or speak, or do, whereby our neighbor may be profited; whereby another many may receive any advantage, either in his body or soul. The feeding the hungry, the clothing the naked, the entertaining or assisting the stranger, the visiting those that are sick or in prison, the comforting the afflicted, the instructing the ignorant, the reproving the wicked, the exhorting and encouraging the well-doer; and if there be any other work of mercy, it is equally included in this direction."[12]

A DEEPER UNDERSTANDING OF DISCIPLESHIP

Wesley was separated unto the gospel as few people ever were. He suffered from various ailments, including hereditary gout (from which his mother died) and became a diabetic in 1789. He said he had not felt lowliness of spirits for one quarter of an hour since he was born. At age 85 he had not lost one night's sleep. He recommended getting up at 4:00 a.m. to avoid sleeplessness and fasting on Fridays.

"Wesley's disciplines for those who chose to become participants in the churches he began would need to embrace the following habits: To meet once a week, at least; To come together at the hour appointed, without some extraordinary reason; To begin exactly at the hour, with singing and praise; To speak, each of us in order, freely and plainly, the true state of our souls, with the faults we have committed in thought or deed and the temptations we have felt since our last meeting; To end every meeting with prayer suited to the state of each person. These small groups functioned as the church. They did what the church was supposed to do. The 'classes' were the 'real church' to Wesley and were therefore his primary focus. Wesley protected his small groups because he correctly identified them as the very heart of the movement. He simply would not waste his time with people if they would not meet together."[13]

"John Wesley was the most candid of men. Seldom has a great religious reformer been so little of a dogmatist, or shown so little stubborn persistence in his own views, simply because they were his own. And this openness to persuasion was joined with a will as inflexible as iron." [14]

C.T. Winchester

MODERN-DAY EXAMPLE OF A LIFE OF HOLINESS
GEORGE KEHOU

Have you ever met anyone whose heart was so tender and so in love with Jesus that they wept for joy? I have. Not just in my family, but in the life of a special teacher. I was a student at Multonomah School of the Bible in 1960 and took a class from George Kehou. He was a man in his late 60's at the time, but his heart was so tender before God it made a lasting impact on his students

When he spoke of the love of God, his eyes began to fill with tears and, as with George Whitefield, it seemed as if his "whole head was filled with tears." As students, we felt we were in the presence of God. We could only bow our heads toward our desks as we heard of the excellencies of God from this tender heart. The class I took studied I John. We began to understand through this teacher that it was not just what you said but how you said it. Brother Kehou was simply overcome by the revelation of God's holiness and beauty. We may forget his words but we will never forget him. He taught us about a wonderful Redeemer and Friend.

MODERN-DAY EXAMPLE OF A LIFE OF HOLINESS
BRUCE THOMPSON

Dr. Bruce Thompson, a medical doctor from New Zealand, had a wonderful impact on my wife, Ruthie, and I. Ruthie worked for "Dr. Bruce" in the clinic at the University of the Nations and we both had the privilege of being in a small group with Bruce and his wife Barbara. If you met Dr. Bruce you would notice a radiance about him coming from deep within his soul. Without any self-consciousness, he reflected the beauty and holiness of Jesus Christ. He was a man who was "set apart" for the gospel. His book on the "Walls of the Heart" has helped thousands of people. Dr. Bruce was involved in our lives during a time when Ruthie and I attended a "Discipleship Training School" in Kona, Hawaii. It proved to be one of the most important times of our lives.

Bruce helped Ruthie and I develop better communication skills. It made a huge difference in our marriage. I think I had fallen into the false notion that what I did determined my value. I'll never forget the question Dr. Bruce asked, "Don," he said, "Suppose we had a tidal wave and everyone on this island was lost at sea. You are hanging onto a log. Now the big question, 'Would Jesus be enough for you?'" That's a profound question for any person to answer because it gets to the root of what it is that we need to satisfy us and make us happy. In other words, "Do I need the recognition of other people, money, etc., to be fulfilled?" Dr. Bruce reminded us that when we have Jesus in our lives and are set apart to please him, we have everything! Dr. Bruce had learned firsthand that Jesus really was enough. Walking with Jesus had brought him deep satisfaction in his soul.

REVIEW

Q. How would the character trait of holiness make a difference in your life?

Q. What would it mean if the church was to return to the convictions of the Apostolic Fathers?

Q. Discuss how you think Wesley overcame "depression" (lowliness of spirits).

Q. What did Wesley mean when he said that the small groups were "the heart of the movement"?

Q. How could these kinds of "works of mercy" begin to happen in our lives?

Q. What do you think Wesley meant when he said he was "too learned and too wise to receive their message"?

Q. At one point in Wesley's life he was filled with self-righteousness. How did God humble him?

Character for Life

GOD'S PROMISE:

"For this is what the high and loft One says—he who lives forever, whose name is holy: 'I live in a high and holy place, but also with him who is contrite and lowly in spirit, to revive the spirit of the lowly and to revive the heart of the contrite'" (Isaiah 57:15).

GOD'S GOAL:

For Christians to live holy lives.

YOUR COMMITMENT:

To strive for holiness in all you do.

YOUR DAILY RESPONSE:

1. Allow Jesus to live through me to make me "holy."

2. Understand that without God's intervention and Jesus' work on the cross there would be no way to come to God.

3. Jesus has made it possible for Christians to live in holiness.

4. Realize that only in heaven will we truly understand God's holiness.

FAILURE WILL MEAN:

Living a life that blatantly goes against God's laws.

BACKGROUND:

The holy life is one involving an inner separation from those passions that bubble up from our sinful desires. God's holy chosen people are known by their commitment to compassion, kindness, humility, gentleness, and patience. It is these things, with mutual forgiveness and deepening love, that express the reality of holiness. What Jesus Christ does in the new birth is to put in us a disposition that transforms morality into holiness. He came to put into the man who knows he needs it His own heredity of holiness. There is only one kind of holiness, and that is the holiness of the Lord Jesus.

It is quite true to say, "I can't live a holy life, but you can let Jesus make you holy. Jesus never expected men to be holy; He knew that they could not be. When the holiness of God is understood, men are convicted of sin. We are partakers of His holiness."

LIVING A LIFE OF HOLINESS MEANS . . .

■ Partaking in Jesus' holiness.

■ Understanding your own sinfulness and being repentant of it.

■ Striving to do the right thing.

■ Being open to what God wants to do in your life.

■ Daily living out the moral holiness and active love that is revealed so beautifully in God's own character.

■ Knowing that holiness is always rooted in a relationship with Jesus and with the Spirit, whom Jesus sends to be with every believer. The key to understanding holiness is found in the character of God.

■ Believers are to separate themselves from evil while living among people who remain uncommitted to the divine standards. The New Testament presents a dynamic concept of holiness as moral purity.

THE CHARACTER OF A METHODIST

◆ "All Scripture is inspired by God." He does not attach his religion to peculiar modes of speaking or any quaint or uncommon expressions nor deviate from the usual way of speaking.

◆ His religion does not lie in doing what God has not enjoined. His salvation is by faith alone.

◆ He, who is a Methodist, has "the love of God shed abroad in his heart."

◆ He is therefore happy in "God, yea, always happy, as having him a well of water spring up unto everlasting life."

◆ He who has this hope, thus "full of immortality, in everything giveth thanks."

◆ "For indeed, he prays without ceasing."

◆ "He rejoices evermore and does good to them that hate him." For he is "pure in heart."

◆ His one design in life is "not to do his own will, but the will of Him that sent Him."

◆ "All the commandments of God he accordingly keeps, and that withal his might." By consequence, whatever he doeth, it is all to the glory of God.

◆ "Nor do the customs of the world at all hinder his running the race that is set before him. He cannot, therefore, follow even a multitude to do evil or make provision for the flesh to fulfill the lusts thereof." [15]

Chapter Twenty-One: Learning more about Wesley

Go to an Internet search engine.
Type in *John Wesley's Character, Holiness.*
Find topics 1-7 below and open up websites.
1. The Character of a Methodist by John Wesley
2. John Wesley Site Map
3. The Life
4. The Tyndale Series
5. The Journal of John Wesley (toc)
6. John Wesley-the Methodist Revival
7. John Wesley's "On a Catholic Spirit" in modern English

chapter 22

Hospitality—

florence nightingale

PURPOSE: The Key to Knowing Others

character trait:
Hospitality

SUBJECT:
FLORENCE NIGHTINGALE
(1820-1910)

PURPOSE:
The Key to Knowing Others

FAMOUS QUOTE:
"Nursing is an art; and if it is to be made an art, it requires an exclusive devotion as hard a preparation as any painter's or sculptor's work; for what is the having to do with dead canvas or dead marble, compared with having to do with the living body, the temple of God's spirit? It is one of the Fine Arts: I had almost said, the finest of Fine Arts."

SCRIPTURE DOCUMENTATION:
"God sets the lonely in families" (Psalm 68:6a).

"Then the King will say to those on his right, 'Come, you who are blessed by my Father; take your inheritance, the kingdom prepared for you since the creation of the world. For I was hungry and you gave me something to eat, I was thirsty and you gave me something to drink, I was a stranger and you invited me in, I needed clothes and you clothed me, I was sick and you looked after me, I was in prison and you came to visit me'" (Matthew 25:34-36).

PERSONALITY PROFILE

Florence Nightingale was born in Florence, Italy in 1820 but was raised in Derbyshire, England. Nightingale received a thorough classical education from her father in which she learned Italian, Latin, Greek, philosophy, history, and mathematics. At the age of 17, at Embley, she believed God spoke to her and called her to His service. She was unsure, however, how she was to serve Him. When she began to visit the local hospital in her community, her parents were horrified, as the conditions were deplorable. When she asked her parents if she could work at the hospital, she was told, "A cultured lady did not enter hospital work."

Nightingale gave up an opportunity of wealth and companionship to work as a nurse. She had to overcome the objections of her family to pursue her heart's calling. The disapproval of her parents' choice of her career, however, brought her great pain.

Nightingale's views on the family were anything but traditional. "The family?" she said, "It is too narrow a field for the development of an immortal spirit, be that spirit male or female. The family uses people, not for what they are, not for what they are intended to be, but for what it wants for…its own uses. It thinks of them not as what God has made them, but as the something which it has arranged that they shall be. This system dooms some minds to incurable infancy, others to silent misery."[1] Florence turned down an invitation to be married and chose to serve in her chosen profession instead. She concluded that marriage would destroy her chance of serving God's call. In 1849, she began traveling to Europe to study the European hospital system. She actually began nursing in 1850 at Saint Vincent de Paul in Egypt when she was 30 years old. In 1853 God spoke to Nightingale again and "asked me would I do good for Him alone without reputation." She decided to serve Him by serving the "sick poor," and became a supervisor of a hospital for invalids in London. At the age of 31, she went to Germany to study to become a nurse at the Institute of Protestant Deaconesses. In 1854 the Crimean War broke out in Turkey. The reports of the conditions of the British soldiers were terrible and the fact that war wounds were only accounting for one out of six deaths was appalling. Diseases such as typhus, cholera, and dysentery were the main reasons why the death rate was so high among wounded soldiers. Nightingale volunteered and assumed the nursing responsibilities at the war front accompanied by 38 nurses. It was the first time the government had allowed women to do this.

Nightingale taught her students; "Nursing is most truly said to be a high calling, an honorable calling. But what does the honor lie in? In working hard during your training to learn and to do all things perfectly. The honor does not lie in putting on Nursing like your uniform. Honor lies in loving perfection, consistency, and in working hard for it; in being ready to work patiently; ready to say not 'How clever I am!' but 'I am not yet worthy; and I will live to deserve to be called a trained nurse.'"[2]

The founder of the Red Cross, Henri Durant, a Christian, said, "It was her [Nightingale's] work in the Crimea that inspired me…to relieve the helplessness of the unfortunate victims of the great struggle."[4] In 1855, the mortality rate at the hospital was 42.7 percent of all cases treated. She reduced it drastically.

In a letter to the *London Times*, a reader wrote, "Wherever there is disease in its most dangerous form, and the hand of the spoiler distressingly nigh, there is that incomparable woman sure to be seen; her benignant presence is an influence for good comfort even amidst the struggles of expiring nature. She is a ministering angel without any exaggeration in these hospitals, and her slender form glides quietly along each corridor, every fellow's face softens with gratitude at the sight of her."[5]

The invalid saw only the aged and beautiful face, the unfaded keen eyes, the cheerful smile, the eager listener. One noted most the surprisingly strong full voice of Nightingale. "She was one of those souls whose sudden visitation daze the world, vanish like lightning, but they leave behind a voice in the distance far away, wakens the slumbering ages."[6]

Nightingale reminded herself that if failure were God's will, then to rebel was the worst failure of all. She forced herself to believe that her present sufferings were not useless but part of God's scheme for the world. "I must remember that God is not my private secretary,"[7] said Nightingale.

Nightingale referred to herself as an "empiricist" (the only reality is what you can see) and her concept of God was not orthodox. She only believed in what she saw, but somehow she hung on to a belief in a Heavenly Father. Nightingale seemed to be doing a lot for people, but in her own energy and strength. She needed to learn to operate in God's strength. She also had a pride problem and it caused her to make some serious mistakes.

On one occasion she (mistakenly) said, "There was no such thing as 'infection' since she had never seen it so it must not

"The biggest disease today is not leprosy or tuberculosis but the feeling of being unwanted."[3]

Mother Teresa

"O Father, I submit, I resign myself, I accept with all my heart this stretching out of Thy hand to save me…. O how vain it is, the vanity of vanities, to live in men's thoughts instead of God's!"[8]
Nightingale

Florence Nightengale's voice was heard around the world. In the United States, the Seventh Day Adventist's vision to bring the love and compassion of Christ would eventually affect millions throughout the world. In 1866, the Adventist's established the first health reform institute in Battle Creek, Michigan. The hospital was one of the largest in the world, with 3,200 beds. Out of this grew a missionary society which was to touch the world with the healing compassion of Jesus Christ. Dr. Lotie Blake became the first African American doctor. She established a school of nursing at Oakwood College, Alabama, and ultimately she and her husband became missionaries in the Caribbean and Central America. Adventists in America number about one million, but their membership worldwide is about 14 million. In terms of compassion for the sick and afflicted, their reach is unmatched, with over 165 hospitals and 370 clinics. More than 5,800 schools and training colleges have been established around the world.

exist."[9] She had seen the effects of good fresh air; therefore there could be no doubt about it. Ventilation was the key to good health, she thought. This theory, however, didn't work when she was in India where the humidity required windows to be closed. Her views on healthcare sometimes became a fetish with her.

"Before Florence Nightingale, nurses were untrained and nursing was considered a menial chore, but after her, nursing became a responsible and respected profession. The accomplishments of Nightingale were legendary; almost all modern nursing systems and techniques we know about can be traced back to Nightingale and 'there is no great hospital today which does not bear upon it the impress of her mind.'"[10]

NIGHTINGALE OPENS HER HEART TO GOD

Nightingale went through years of great depression and had a new encounter with the living God. She prayed; "O Father, I submit, I resign myself, I accept with all my heart this stretching out of Thy hand to save me.... O how vain it is, the vanity of vanities, to live in men's thoughts instead of God's! Thou knowest that through all these horrible twenty years, I have been supported by the belief that I was working with Thee who will be bringing everyone, even our poor nurses to perfection, and yet, after all, what was the result? Had not even she been an unprofitable servant?"[11]

Nightingale's early childhood had twisted her ideas about family life. Although she may have been right, she struggled her entire life with the broken relationships between family members. From 1857, when she suffered her first major attack, until 1880 when she was an invalid, she spent much of her waking hours on the couch. She remained bedridden, unable to walk for six years. Her symptoms were weakness, headache, nausea, breathlessness, tachycardia, palpitations, and precordial (heart) pain. It was during these years that she developed a neurotic disposition. However, Nightingale published many works, even during this time. She published "Notes on Nursing" in 1860 and 1861 with a special section on caring for babies. In 1867 she worked on rural hygiene deaths in childbirth and Indian sanitary questions. Despite her failing health, in 1887 she organized the British Nurses Association.

Fortunately most people do not know about the struggles she faced in the declining years of her life. What she accomplished during the years she had the strength was nothing short of phenomenal, however.

A LIFE OF HOSPITALITY AND NURSING CARE

Nightingale's vision for training nurses eventually touched the nations of the world. Cecil Woodham-Smith said this of Nightingale, "She should perform the dual function which was her conception of education; it must not only teach the mind, but it must form the character. It must be a place of training of character, habits and intelligence, as well as of acquiring knowledge."[12]

She remembered those who, in years past, had worked side by side with her in unseen places. Said Nightingale, "I am no longer even a memory, just a name, I hope my voice may perpetuate the great work of my life. God bless my dear old comrades of Balaclava and bring thee safe to shore."[13]

NURSING—A NOBLE PROFESSION

Nightingale began to understand the consequences of keeping Divine Laws which lead to good health. She taught that good health is not something we can take for granted. It requires constant attention as one uses all his faculties to understand his/her health condition. She believed these laws of health require a "Lawgiver."[15]

As a result of her efforts, she suffered from "post traumatic stress disorder" for the rest of her life and her health continued to deteriorate. At the age of 60, Nightingale's depression lifted and she was able to have normal relationships again. A friend of Nightingale wrote the following, "During the ten years I have known you...you have repeated to me the expression the 'Character of God,' about 1,000 times, but I cannot say I have any clear idea of what you mean."[16]

Nightingale believed that nurses must reflect the "character of God" and described nurses as the "handmaidens of the Lord." In her older years, her character blossomed into benevolence. The thin, emaciated, mature woman became a dignified stout old lady with a large good-humored face.

In 1884 her sight began to fail, and in 1901 she became totally blind. In 1902, Nightingale could no longer read and was cared for until her death in 1910.

Nightingale's amazing character and leadership introduced healthcare hospitality and spread it to the ends of the earth.

"Before Florence Nightingale, nurses were untrained and nursing was considered a menial chore, but after her, nursing became a responsible and respected profession. The accomplishments of Nightingale were legendary; almost all modern nursing systems and techniques we know about can be traced back to Nightingale and 'there is no great hospital today which does not bear upon it the impress of her mind.'" [14]

Lytton Strachey

Because of her life, millions of people throughout the world experienced genuine hospitality in a hospital during their time of need. Nightingale lived to be 90 years old. What a difference she made in the world.

MODERN-DAY EXAMPLE OF HOSPITALITY
FRANK & SHIRLEY BEACH

Frank and Shirley Beach lived in West Stephentown, New York. My wife, Ruthie, and I met Frank and Shirley when we were involved with students at the State University of New York at Albany. We served as interim pastor at the West Stephentown Baptist Church for a few years and came to know this couple. We saw firsthand their gift of hospitality. They had five kids, but it seemed like "the more the merrier."

Some of the students from Albany State were "hippy-types," but to Frank and Shirley and most of the congregation, it really didn't matter what the kids wore to church. We became known in the community as "the hippy church" and our doors and heart swung open to young people who were working through their struggles with the establishment and, of course, the church. Would we accept them just the way they were? The students at SUNY experienced real agape love from these "straight types" and Frank and Shirley led the congregation in making everyone feel welcome.

To be honest, we lost a few folks who thought this was definitely not the way to go, but the struggles of these young people became our struggles and they endeared themselves to all of us. After church each Sunday, we had a feast and Shirley would pull things together as usual. There was always enough food and love to go around. Those were incredible days when God did some wonderful things. Hearts were open to Jesus and many young people found their way.

Shirley is gone from us now, but I'll never forget her. She had a "can do" attitude and decided to "go with the flow." Whether it was a camp outing or youth activity, the Beach family taught us about hospitality. They had "an open home." You just showed up and they would put the coffee on for you. What an example they were of people who gave of themselves to serve others!

REVIEW

Q. How can the character trait of hospitality make a difference in your life?

Q. Do you think Nightingale was a "perfectionist"? Explain.

Q. What are the pros and cons regarding perfectionism?

Q. Much of her life Nightingale failed to recognize how God had used her. Do you think this is true with many Christians? Why?

Q. For a Christian, what is "the high calling" meant to be?

Q. Discuss how our work (careers, jobs, etc.) shapes our character.

Q. What did Nightingale believe about suffering?

Q. What do Nightingale's views on "family" tell us about her relationship with her own family?

Q. Give examples of people you know who have struggled as a result of damaged family relationships.

Q. Do you think there are reasons why people are often unaware of their accomplishments?

Q. Share your views concerning the passage on hospitality found in Hebrews 13:2.

"she [Nightingale] should perform the dual function which was her conception of education; it must not only teach the mind, but it must form the character. It must be a place of training of character, habits and intelligence, as well as of acquiring knowledge." [18]

cecil woodham-smith

SIX PURPOSES OF HOSPITALITY

1. To bring God's peace to your guest.
2. To help a person meet their needs at your expense
3. Often it may mean providing lodging and even protection for your guest.
4. To bring healing to those who are broken, bruised, and battered by fellow human beings.
5. To introduce your guest to Jesus Christ and to fellow believers
6. To demonstrate love for your guest in a very practical way.

HOW IS CHRISTIAN HOSPITALITY UNIQUE?

1. It requires mature, stable Christian families to be emissaries of God's love.
2. It requires family members who are consciously working on their relationship with God and each other.
3. It is done out of love for Jesus.

Character for Life

GOD'S PROMISE:

"God sets the lonely in families" (Psalm 68:6a).

GOD'S GOAL:

For Christians to be hospitable to others.

YOUR COMMITMENT:

To treat people with dignity and respect and be hospitable at all times.

YOUR DAILY RESPONSE:

1. Ask for Jesus' help in humbling yourself.

2. Understand that we can't be hospitable on our own; we need God's help to show true hospitality

3. How we treat people reflects Jesus' love for them.

4. Realize that we may one day be in need of hospitality.

FAILURE WILL MEAN:

Living a life without regard for others.

BACKGROUND:

Jesus expressed hospitality! In His conversation with Mary and Martha, Jesus showed us what was really important. "'Martha, Martha,' the Lord answered, 'you are worried and upset about many things, but only one thing is needed, Mary has chosen what is better, and it will not be taken away from her'" (Luke 10:41-42).

Jesus was also able to receive hospitality from anyone. "When a woman who had lived a sinful life in that town learned that Jesus was eating at the Pharisee's house, she bought an alabaster jar of perfume, and as she stood behind him at his feet weeping, she began to wet his feet with her tears. Then she wiped them with her hair, kissed them and poured perfume on them" (Luke 7:37-38).

In relation to hospitality, consider these words: "Suppose a brother or sister is without clothes and daily food. If one of you says to him, 'Go, I wish you well; keep warm and well fed,' but does nothing about his physical needs, what good is it? In the same way, faith by itself, if it is not accompanied by action, is dead" (James 2:15-17).

"If anyone has material possessions and sees his brother in need but has no pity on him, how can the love of God be in him?" (1 John 3:17).

LIVING A LIFE FULL OF HOSPITALITY MEANS . . .

■ Sharing with someone what you have.

■ Obeying the Golden Rule or doing to others what we would like to have done to us.

■ Emphasizing not the host or hostess, but the guest; not what I have, but what you share.

Chapter Twenty-Two: Learning more about Nightingale

Go to and Internet search engine.
Type in *Florence Nightingale's Character.*
Find topics 1-5 below and open up the websites.
1. Florence Nightingale Adelaide's Introduction
2. Florence Nightingale, "over recent years"....
3. Florence Nightingale, "Lea Hurst...Derbyshire"....
4. Florence Nightingale's "reactionary character actually had two facets"
5. Rescind

chapter 23

Humility—John Marshall

PURPOSE: Learning to Live Like Jesus

character trait:
Humility

JOHN MARSHALL
(1755-1835)

PURPOSE:
Learning to Live Like Jesus

FAMOUS QUOTE:
"The American population is entirely Christian, and with us Christianity and Religion are identified. It would be strange indeed, if with such a people, our institutions did not presuppose Christianity, and did not often refer to it, and exhibit relations with it."

SCRIPTURE DOCUMENTATION:
"For the Lamb [Jesus] at the center of the throne will be their shepherd; he will lead them to springs of living water. And God will wipe away every tear from their eyes" (Revelation 7:17).

"Before his downfall a man's heart is proud, but humility comes before honor" (Proverbs 18:12).

"Young men, in the same way be submissive to those who are older. All of you, clothe yourselves with humility toward one another, because 'God opposes the proud but gives grace to the humble'" (1 Peter 5:5).

PERSONALITY PROFILE

John Marshall's maternal grandparents came from distinguished Scottish nobility and settled a large Virginia plantation. Besides John, there were eight girls and six boys in his family. All of them had some education, although they were poor and possessed scarcely any fortune. Marshall's mother was the daughter of a pastor and for a year, Marshall was sent to be tutored by a pastor (a clergyman of great respectability) and then was taught by the local pastor who lived with the Marshall family.

John Marshall maintained, "His father was his only intelligent companion and was both a watchful parent and an affectionate friend."[1] He referred to his father's superior intellect and his strength of character. He told Joseph Story (who sat on the Supreme Court with him) that his father was "more abler than any of his sons. To him I owe the solid foundation of all my success in life."[2] His mother "found time to impart to her children a remarkable love of learning."[3] Marshall's heritage was similar to Jefferson's in that they both descended from Welch stock and inherited small farms. Both became surveyors and then married Randolphs.

Marshall fought in the "Revolution" and survived the harsh "Winter at Valley Forge" in 1777-78. He was a soldier, attorney, diplomat, jurist, officer in the minuteman, studied law at William and Mary, and was admitted to the bar in 1780. He was a member of the "House of Burgesses" from 1782-88. Marshall became "Secretary of State" in 1800 under John Adams and eventually Adams appointed him the "Chief Justice of the Supreme Court" where he held office for 34 years. When Marshall and the team he led refused the demands of the French, he returned home in 1797 and became a national hero. Marshall had sought to be a "peacemaker" without compromising his principles.

During the Revolutionary War, John Marshall joined the "Culpepper Minute Men" and was chosen as Lieutenant and eventually became Captain. His military service for General Washington was described as "gallant" and he went on to endear himself to the first President. He was not at all an admirer of Thomas Jefferson, however. Adams referred to Marshall as "a plain man, very sensible, cautious, and learned in the law of nations."[4]

EXACT LEARNING, PROFOUND REASONING, SOLID PRINCIPLES

In dedicating his "Three Volumes on the Constitution," Joseph Story wrote of Marshall, "Sir, I ask the favor of dedicating this work to you. I know not, to whom it could with so much propriety be dedicated, as to one, whose youth was engaged in the arduous enterprises of the Revolution; whose manhood assisted in framing and supporting the national Constitution; and whose maturer years have been devoted to the task of unfolding its powers, and illustrating its principles. When, indeed, I look back upon your judicial labors during a period of thirty-two years, it is difficult to suppress astonishment at their extent and variety, and at the exact learning, the profound reasoning, and the solid principles, which they everywhere display. Your expositions of constitutional law enjoy a rare and extraordinary authority. They constitute a monument of fame far beyond the ordinary memorials of political and military glory. They are destined to enlighten, instruct and convince future generations; and can scarcely perish but with the memory of the Constitution itself." [5]

After John Adams left office, it was Marshall who became the leader of the "Federalist Party." Just prior to his leaving office, President Adams appointed Marshall Chief Justice of the Supreme Court. He was to serve the country in that capacity for 34 years. Under Marshall, the Supreme Court assumed a supervisory role over state courts.

In addition to his duties as Chief Justice of the Supreme Court, he set about to put together a five-volume set of books on America's President. Such was his devotion to Washington.

Marshall summarized his view on the "Constitution," as follows, "A constitution, from its nature, deals in generals, not in details, the framers cannot perceived minute distinctions which arise in the progress of the nation, and therefore confine it to the establishment of broad and general principles. A constitution is framed for ages to come, and is designed to approach immortality as nearly as human institutions can approach it. Its course cannot always be tranquil. It is exposed to storms and tempests, and its framers must be unwise statesmen indeed, if they have not provided it, as far as its nature will permit, with the means of self-preservation from the perils it maybe destined to encounter." [7]

FURTHER SCRIPTURE DOCUMENTATION:
"For you know the grace of our Lord Jesus Christ, that thought he was rich, yet for your sakes he became poor, so that you through his poverty might become rich" (2 Corinthians 8:9).

NATIONAL PURPOSE

"The measure of a man's real character is what he would do if he knew he would never be found out." [6]

Lord Maccaulay

Marshall warned that "Powerful and ingenious minds [could]…explain away the Constitution of our country, and leave it to a magnificent structure indeed to look at, but totally unfit for use."[8]

OTHERS' VIEWS OF MARSHALL

During a time in the nation's history when people were very much aware of their legacy and the fact that their roles would be judged by future generations, it is wonderful to find a person like Marshall. He seemed secure in himself and proved right the words of G.K. Chesterton who said, "It is always the secure who are humble."[10]

Oliver Wendall Holms believed, "If American law were to be represented by a single figure, skeptic and worshipper alike would agree that the figure could be one alone, and that one, John Marshall."[11]

Historian David McCullough suggests, "Marshall was an impressive man, tall, solidly handsome, unmistakably intelligent, and without airs. It was not his physical appearance however that marks Marshall but his character."[12]

"He [Marshall] was deeply committed to a principled jurisprudence that was based on a steadfast devotion to a 'science of law' richly stepped in the common law tradition."[13]

HUMILITY AS A CALLING

Marshall knew his source of strength and realized, "Humility is the acceptance of the place appointed by God, whether it be in the front or in the rear."[14] Had Marshall been a man absent of humility, his accomplishments would have been marginal. Years before Marshall was born, William Penn observed, "Sense shines with a double luster when it is set in humility. An able and yet humble man is a jewel worth a kingdom."[15] Marshall was such a jewel. He said, "The events of my life are too unimportant and have too little interest for any person not of my immediate family, to render them worth communication or preserving."[16] His self-appraisal was anything but true. The absence of self-importance in his life disarmed people and taught about the true nature of humility. Humility "is not anxious to impress."[17]

Humility and the "reverence of God" were prerequisites for the wisdom needed for a Constitution that would last for generations. Members of the Supreme Court worked together in unity and laid foundations of justice for the United

States. An engaging intellectual humility enabled Marshall to defer, when necessary, to the superior learning of others. The key to his success was his willingness to subordinate his own view, when necessary, to obtain a single opinion on the court.

Associate Justice Joseph Story served under Chief Justice Marshall for over two decades and knew him intimately. In a letter he requested the honor of dedicating his three volumes on the "Commentaries on the Constitution" to Chief Justice Marshall.

Story described Marshall's character and virtues as "patient, moderate candid, urban, quickness of perception, dignity of deportment, gentleness of manners, genius which command respect, and learning which justifies confidence." [18] Said Story of Marshall, "He was a man of the most unaffected modesty. He was far more anxious to know others, than to be known by them." [19]

John Marshall was a humble man. According to Story, "Marshall developed the habit of mind and heart corresponding to our comparative unworthiness and vileness before God. He was sensible of the small extent of his knowledge, sensible of his weakness, of his dependence upon God and that he needs God's wisdom." [20]

AN EXAMPLE TO THE NATION OF TRUE AND LASTING LOVE

"He was tall and gaunt and most girls lost interest in him," [22] said Mary Ambler, his future wife to be. Mary (called Polly by Marshall) claimed, however, that she fell in love with him immediately. Mary became an invalid shortly after they were married, but in spite of her handicap, their marriage lasted almost 49 years and theirs became one of the great love stories of American history.

His invalid wife needed to be cared for constantly and this cut Marshall off from society. Of their 10 children, four died early in life. A frequent sight in Richmond was the Chief Justice, basket in hand, doing the family marketing. After his wife died in 1831, he was never the same. Such was the nature of their relationship. Bereavement over the loss of their children had drawn them together. Upon the death of his wife, Marshall told his lifelong friend Joseph Story that he rarely passed a night without crying for "Polly." Story wrote, "She must have been a very extraordinary woman and I think he is the most extraordinary man I ever saw, for the depth and tenderness of his feelings." [23]

"if american law were to be represented by a single figure, skeptic and worshipper alike would agree that the figure could be one alone, and that one, john marshall." [21]

oliver wendall holms

A LEADER WHO DIDN'T NEED TO IMPRESS OTHERS

"The first impression of a stranger, upon introduction to him [Marshall], was generally that of disappointment. It seemed hardly credible that such simplicity should be the accompaniment of such acknowledged greatness. Meet him on a stagecoach, as a stranger, and travel with him a whole day and you would only be struck by his readiness to administer to the accommodations of others and his anxiety to appropriate the least to himself. Be with him, the unknown guest at an inn, and he seemed adjusted to the very scene, partaking of the warm welcome of its comforts, whenever found; and if not found, resigning himself without complaint to the meanest arrangements. You would never suspect, in either case, that he was a great man; far less that he was the Chief Justice of the United States." [24]

John Edwards described Marshall as one who "excluded warmth and good humor in his personal and social relations. In his unaffected modesty, polite but informal manner of plain attire, and easy familiarity with social inferiors, he lived up to the idea of republican gentleman. More so than Jefferson, he possessed the common touch." [26]

MARSHALL'S HUMBLE FAITH

Allen B. McGruder, in the American Statesmen Series, writes that a group of young men were debating whether Jesus Christ was truly Divine. After five hours had passed they tuned to an old man (Marshall) and asked his opinion. Marshall responded eloquently. "He talked for an hour answering every argument urged against the teachings of Jesus. There was so much simplicity and energy, pathos and sublimity, that not another word was uttered." [27] Later, the young men, to their surprise, learned he was the Chief Justice of the United States.

Says McGruder, "Without making ostentatious professors of religion, he was a sincere believer in the Christian faith, and a truly devout man. So great was his winning charm and so absolute his integrity that he gained the admiration of his enemies and the unbounded affection of his friends." [28]

In a letter to Jasper Adams, Marshall wrote, "The American population is entirely Christian, and with us Christianity and Religion are identical. It would be strange indeed, if with such a people, our institutions did not presuppose Christianity, and did not often refer to it, and exhibit relations with it."[29]

Jasper Adams concluded, "He was content with that situation amongst men as God is pleased to allot to him."[30]

A MAN WHO HONORED WOMEN

"Marshall maintained through life and carried to his grave a reverence for women, as rare in its kind as in its degree. He brought not only the love and piety…which they excite in the minds of the pure, but the steady conviction of their intellectual equality with men, and with this a deep sense of their social injuries. Throughout life he so invariably sustained their cause that no indulgent libertine dared to flatter and humor, no skeptic…dared to scoff at the claims of women in the presence of Marshall."[31]

MODERN-DAY EXAMPLE OF HUMILITY
JUAN CARLOS ORTIZ

One person who impacted my life was Juan Carlos Ortiz of Argentina. I had read his books, but it never occurred to me that I would meet him, since he lived thousands of miles away. While on the road I met a friend who had heard of my interest in Juan Carlos. He loaned me some audio cassettes of his teachings. I remember driving from Buffalo to Virginia Beach and listening to the stories of this humble servant of Jesus.

Later in my life I was privileged to travel with Juan Carlos to the Philippines. It was a memorable experience! I noticed how he deferred to others; stood when women entered the room; didn't call attention to himself and I began to see a man who preferred the interests of others before his own. Once we were at a Bible school in a northern province and the students lined the road by waving palms and a path between the two lines was there to receive Juan Carlos. He pushed me ahead of himself. Somehow they thought I was the teacher but I could only feel humbled. Who was I? I was honored to be the "audio technician." Juan Carlos knew about being humbled, so many people came to his church he suggested they go to other churches in the city where they would be fed spiritually. His denomination was outraged and tried to take his church away from him. He let God fight his battles and his church was restored. He sought to restore ministers who had fallen. Juan Carlos Ortiz is a remarkable person and it was an honor to see Jesus living through him.

Marshall spoke of the impact of mothers on their children saying, "If the agency of the mother in forming the character of her children, is, in truth, so considerable as I think it–if she does so much toward making her son what she would wish him to be–how essential it is that she should be fitted for the beneficial performance of these important duties."[32]

Marshall said, "I have always believed that national character, depends more on the female part of society than is generally imagined. Precepts from the lips of a beloved mother…sink deep in the heart, and make an impression which is seldom entirely effaced. These impressions have an influence on character which may contribute greatly to the happiness or misery, the eminence of insignificancy of the individual."[33]

REVIEW

Q. How does the character trait of humility make a difference in your life?

Q. Discuss Marshall's view that "humility is acceptance of the place appointed by God."

Q. With all he accomplished, how do you think Marshall remained humble?

Q. Discuss Marshall's conviction on the role of mothers in America and the necessity of training for this role.

Q. How did Associate Justice Joseph Story characterize Marshall's character?

Q. Discuss Marshall's comment concerning women's intellectual equality with him and their social injuries. Is this still true today?

Q. Do you believe that national character depends more on the female part of society than is generally imagined? Explain.

Q. What was the deepest concern of Chief Justice Marshall in respect to the Constitution?

Q. Marshall didn't "put on airs" nor did he draw attention to himself. Why do you think people see this as one of his great strengths?

Q. Marshall's wisdom concerning Christ was not debated. Can you think of a similar situation from the gospels?

Q. What did Marshall mean when he said, "It would be strange indeed if with such a people, our institutions did not presuppose Christianity"?

Q. What did Edwards mean when he said Marshall possessed the "common touch"?

Q. Explain the following definition of humility: "Humility is the willingness to be known for what you really are."

Character for Life

GOD'S PROMISE:

"For the Lamb [Jesus] at the center of the throne will be their shepherd; he will lead them to springs of living water. And God will wipe away every tear from their eyes" (Revelation 7:17).

GOD'S GOAL:

For us to live lives of humility.

YOUR COMMITMENT:

To live life humbly and in obedience to how God would have you live.

YOUR DAILY RESPONSE:

1. To live a peaceful life that honors God.

2. To not think more highly of yourself than you should.

3. To put others first.

4. To be willing to sacrifice your own comfort for the comfort of others.

FAILURE WILL MEAN:

Living a life where you only look out for yourself.

BACKGROUND:

In the Greek culture, humility was a word for contempt. To be low on the social scale, to know poverty, to be socially powerless, was seen as shameful. God, however, sees the universe quite differently. It is the humble, Jesus said, whom God will exalt in good time. (See Luke 14:11, 18:14.) Jesus presented humility as a description of what we shall be when we have become rightly focused in Him. "Who is like the LORD our God, the One who sits enthroned on high, who stoops down to look on the heavens and the earth?" (Psalm 113:5-6).

The Son of God, the Co-Creator of the universe, provided us the example of true humility as He lowered Himself and was born into a homeless family. His family members were refugees and had to flee for their lives. People in the town He grew up in thought He was illegitimate and questioned His birth. What an example He is to us of humility!

"Your attitude should be the same as that of Christ Jesus: Who, being in very nature God, did not consider equality with God something to be grasped, but made himself nothing, taking the very nature of a servant, being made in human likeness. And being found in appearance as a man, he humbled himself and became obedient to death—even death on a cross!" (Philippians 2:5-8).

Jesus embodied true humility expressed in His willingness to be confined in the womb of a woman. His life of simplicity and identification with the poor and His willingness to become a servant of all by enduring the humiliation of the cross helps us to see the true humility that God values most!

LIVING A LIFE FULL OF HUMILITY MEANS . . .

■ Living as Jesus did, with His focus on others, not Himself.

■ Being willing to be thought of as lowly, yet remain full of purity of character.

■ Understanding that there will be a time when God will lift up the humble.

■ Committing to serving Jesus, no matter where it takes you in life.

Chapter Twenty-Three: Learn more about Marshall

Go to an Internet search engine.
Type in *Chief Justice John Marshall's Character, Humility.*
Find topics 1-4 below and open up the websites.
1. Contacts and links
2. Conversation with our benefactors
2. "Why he carried the turkey"
3. Remarks of the Chief Justices
4. Brothers Judd

chapter 24

Impartiality—

richard hooker

PURPOSE: Learning to Love Like Jesus

character trait:
Impartiality

SUBJECT:
RICHARD HOOKER
(1554-1600)

PURPOSE:
Learning to Love Like Jesus

FAMOUS QUOTE:
"Oh, that men would more give themselves to meditate with silence what we have by the sacrament and less to dispute of the manner how."

SCRIPTURE DOCUMENTATION:
"Now let the fear of the LORD be upon you. Judge carefully, for with the LORD our God there is no injustice or partiality or bribery" (2 Chronicles 19:7).

"I charge you, in the sight of God and Christ Jesus and the elect angels, to keep these instructions without partiality, and to do nothing out of favoritism" (1 Timothy 5:21).

PERSONALITY PROFILE

Hooker was born in 1554 into a prominent Devon family in a village near Exeter, England. His associates described him as "an obscure harmless man, in poor clothes, his loins usually girt in a course gown...of small stature and stooping."[1]

Hooker suffered the loss of his father when he was young and lived in poverty much of his early life. Hooker's sister died young, at the age of 21. His uncle, John Hooker, a renowned historian, educated him. His uncle was England's premier theologian of the Anglican/Episcopal religious tradition. This opportunity provided Hooker with something he greatly desired, an education.

Hooker was educated at Corpus Christi College in Oxford. While there, he eventually became the Assistant Professor of Hebrews. Later he took holy orders and became a clergyman. In 1585 Richard Hooker was appointed by Queen Elizabeth to be rector of the most influential church in England. Hooker married Joan Churchman in 1588 and they were blessed with four daughters. His wife, Joan, apparently had concerns other than spiritual and no real understanding of the greatness of the man she was married to or his remarkable writings. (Most of Hooker's writings weren't published until after his death.) In a fit of anger one day, she destroyed several of his writings.

From 1585-1591, Hooker became the Dean of the Anglican Law School. Hooker was a great defender of the Christian faith and was the premier theologian of the Anglican/Episcopal religious tradition. Hooker was the closest counterpart for Anglicans and Episcopalians to Luther for Lutherans, Calvin for Presbyterians, and Wesley for Methodists. Hooker died on November 3, 1600.

Hooker's influence on American Jurisprudence was profound. One of the most brilliant justices of the Supreme Court, Chief Justice James Wilson, acknowledged Hooker as his intellectual superior when it came to Law and theology. In 1592, Hooker published the "Laws of Church Policy" and continued working on the book for several years. He was the key person in the development of modern constitutional law and became the founder of Anglican Theology, writing eight volumes on church organization.

Bishop Andrews wrote extensively, recalling Hooker and the quality of his character:

> What admirable height of learning and depth of judgment dwell in the lowly mind of this true humble man, great and wise in all men's eyes, except his own; with what gravity and majesty of speech his tongue and pen uttered heavenly mysteries, whose eyes in the humility of his hear were always cast down to the ground; how all things that preceded from him were breathed, as from the spirit of love. For out of these, even those who otherwise agree not with him in opinion, do afford him the testimony of a mild and a loving spirit; and of his learning, what greater proof can we have than this; that his writings are most admired by those whom themselves do most excel in judicious learning, and by them the more often they are read, the more highly they are extolled and desired. He was a man who thought little of himself. He wore himself not with age but study and holy mortification. He lived a sedentary life. He would not look people in the face...this may be due to the fact that he was nearsighted. God and nature had blessed him with a bashfulness ... His works and worth were such as behind him he hath not left anyone near him.[2]

REASON, REVELATION, AND HISTORY

Hooker was known to be an active and exemplar parish priest who practiced much fasting and prayer. During his lifetime Richard Hooker became skillful in combining reason and revelation and history. Hooker forged a body of knowledge on human reason and the historic affirmations of the church. He sought to bring about a church that was inclusive and tolerant of one another where a wide variety of opinions were allowed to be shared just as long as a public affirmation of Christ was embraced.

"simplicity of character is no hindrance to subtlety of intellect."[3]

gladstone

Based on his biography, his friends described his humility as his chief virtue and also that of having a "dove-like simplicity."[4] "I observe there is in Mr. Hooker no affected language; but a grave, comprehensive, clear manifestation of reason, and that backed with the authority of Scriptures, the fathers and schoolmen, and with all both sacred and civil."[5]

Cicero, Aquinas, Grotius, and Hooker would be looked to as key founders of "Natural law." Chief Justice James Wilson summarized Hooker's doctrines as "The Law of Nature and the Law of Revelation. They are of the same origin and of the same obligation and flow from the same adorable source. The laws are fixed for the purpose of man's happiness."[6] "The Law of Revelation" tells us that "we are to love our neighbor as we love ourselves" and the "Law of Nature" (conscience) tells us that people are to preserve themselves. For example, don't commit suicide, take care of oneself, transmit life to the next generation, rear our offspring, etc.

TWO VIEWS OF FAIRNESS— INCLUSIVENESS AND MULTI-CULTURALISM

The secular world view of God emphasizes "fairness." "There is a law of fairness or justice that is higher and more absolute than God. It is binding even for God. God must act in response to that law to be fair."[7]

The biblical view emphasizes how God uses His power according to His own moral perfections. Whatever God does is fair, even if we don't understand it. Our response is to appeal directly to Him. "Of law there can be no less acknowledged than that her seat is the bosom of God, her voice the harmony of the world. All in heaven and earth do her [the Law] homage—the very least as feeling her care, and the greatest as not exempted from her power."[8]

"Hooker shows that nature itself points men toward virtue and the Christian religion. He develops and rectifies the promising parts in accord with a nature ruled by God's eternal law."[10] Hooker said, "God is no captious sophister [Someone using clever talk to deceive] eager to trip us up whenever we say amiss, but a courteous tutor, ready to amend what, in our weakness or our ignorance, we say ill, and to make the most of what we say aright."[11]

Hooker taught that the universe was governed by Natural Law. Natural Law embodies God's supreme reason, and is

"An obscure harmless man, in poor clothes, his loins usually girt in a course gown…of small stature and stooping."[9]

Hooker's associates in describing him

appointed to the whole field of natural, moral as well as physical. The insufficiency of the light of nature for understanding the Creator's purposes requires "The Law of Revelation."

GOD'S IMPARTIALITY

The God of the Bible insists, "I am God, and there is no other; I am God, and there is none like me" (Isaiah 46:9). To modern ears this may sound intolerant, or even arrogant. It certainly conflicts with certain fashionable beliefs today, which claim that more or less everyone and everything is "God." Hooker defined reason as the "ultimate principle."

Hooker also demonstrated the impartiality taught in Scripture. "All law comes from God and human laws should conform to the revealed law of God as founded in nature and in the Scriptures." [13]

God wills that all should be saved (impartiality) and come to the knowledge of the truth in Jesus Christ. Hooker preached "a tolerant and inclusive church in which a wide variety of opinions were allowed and a public affirmation of Christ was maintained." [14] It must be pointed out, however, that the essentials, such as the virgin birth, the sinless life of Christ, His death for the sinner, redemption for those who repent, and the Resurrection were essentials for all believers. The Moral law (the Ten Commandments) applied to all followers of Christ. All who turned to Christ for salvation were also to love righteousness.

The inclusiveness or impartiality is revealed in the teachings and atonement of Jesus Christ. In the New Testament we read, "I now realize how true it is that God does not show favoritism" (Acts 10:34). In the parable of the 99, Christ demonstrates how the good shepherd risked His life to save one lost sheep. Jesus is not willing that any should perish but that all should come to repentance. When Jesus invited people to receive the salvation He offered, the word "whosoever" is used, indicating that salvation is extended to all. The fact that Jesus tasted death for every man is proof that God desires everyone to be brought into His family through faith in His Son.

Stanley Archer believed the legacy of Hooker was to "bring all Christians to agreement about essentials and tolerance in non-essentials. For Hooker, the most important element in Christianity is love of God and the Savior. This would bind Christians together. His tone is that of a Christian doctor binding the founded faith, urging clemency and caution in place of zeal and rigor."

"His works and worth were such as behind him he hath not left anyone near him." [12]

Bishop Andrewes

The Declaration of Independence reflects the truth of impartiality taught by Hooker.

"Since man is created in the image of God, unalienable rights are the rights all men are born with. Natural rights, such as life and liberty, are rights that God has established since man is made in the image of God. Our Savior's great rule 'that we should love our neighbor as ourselves' is a fundamental truth for regulating society." [16]

Hooker taught that God "causes his sun to rise on the evil and the good, and sends rain on the righteous and the unrighteous" (Matthew 5:45). The blessings of life and eternal salvation would be offered to all.

Hooker determined to empathize the unity of Christendom before its division by pointing out first the things in which all Christians agreed and then to show our disagreements. Hooker sought to carve out a Christian core of truth upon which the various schools must agree. Some beliefs are necessary for salvation, he taught, while others may vary without jeopardizing salvation. Hooker believed that what distinguishes Christianity from other religions is the belief that Christ is the Savior. Besides that, everything else is secondary. He sought to restore devotion to the Savior while reducing contention over how He saves. He prayed, "Oh, that men would more give themselves to meditate with silence what we have by the sacrament [Sacrifice of Jesus] and less to dispute of the manner how." [17]

21ST CENTURY PARADIGM

	OLD PARADIGM	NEW PARADIGM
Beliefs	Based on the Bible	New age, earth-centered blend
View of self	Individual	Part of a greater whole
Values	Based on the Bible	Human idealism based on consensus
Morals	Biblical boundaries	Sensual freedom
Rights	Personal freedom	Social controls
Economy	Free enterprise	Socialist/collective
Government	By the people	By those who control the masses through consensus

Berit Kjos

MODERN-DAY EXAMPLE OF IMPARTIALITY
LEWIS & LEAH HAWKINSON

My grandfather died when my father was a small child, so I never had the opportunity of knowing him. His legacy and love came to me through my Dad, however, who provided me with an understanding of what it means to "lay down your life" for others. During times of great poverty in Norway, Grandpa John spent years away from his family and came to America seeking to make a new life for his family and those of us in succeeding generations.

I have a great heritage. When I was trying to think about someone I knew first-hand who was impartial, Ruthie, my wife, suggested, "How about your Mom and Dad?" Good choice. My Dad was in a head-on collision as a result of someone who had been drinking too much and this turned our entire lives upside down. He was in and out of hospitals for nine years and lost his life due to tumors developing as a result of the accident. Despite his weakened condition, he steadfastly refused to give in to pity or blaming others.

I'd love to tell you about him and how I saw this impartiality in action. He held a position as treasurer of an airline in Seattle and had a reputation for "fairness" among the employees.

Dad (Lewis Hawkinson) along with his brother Nels, came to Christ in 1929 as Pentecostal prayer meetings flourished in northern Washington. We found ourselves in the Evangelical Free church much of our lives but "denominationalism" was not that important to Dad. Prayer meetings on Wednesday night were important along with church both Sunday morning and evening. "What is done for Christ will last" he said.

After his home-going, Joanie, my youngest sister boasted that Dad had told her "of all the kids, she was his favorite." Of course the rest of us chimed in that he had given the same message to all of us. The truth is that he didn't need to say this; he treated us all the same. We were equally precious to him.

Mom and Dad took real joy in what their kids were doing. Linda, my oldest sister, traveled to Africa and spent several years working to establish clinics. Dad and Mom could not have been more excited. Dad was a businessman and was involved in establishing Trinity Western College and was on the Board of Trinity Evangelical Seminary. There was not only time for us, but also time for his 60 plus nieces and nephews. At his funeral, one cousin said "Uncle Louie brought hugs into our family."

Mom (Leah) is one of the most sought out people I have ever met. At 88, her mind is still sharp and engaging. She has always had "an open home" and people knew they didn't even have to call her in advance to stop by. Her inclusiveness is real. Whoever shows up is made welcome. It didn't matter who you were or what you did…you felt she was delighted with your visit and you were the only person with whom she was talking. Ruthie, my wife, often mentions how my Mom mentored her. She forgets at times she's not one of the biological children. I don't know if anyone ever felt excluded or snubbed when visiting Mom.

REVIEW

Q. How would understanding "impartiality" make a difference in my life?

Q. In the final analysis, can we know what God is like if He never reveals Himself except through Creation?

Q. Why are both the "Law of Nature" and the "Law of Revelation" necessary to bring us an accurate understanding of God?

Q. When the Scriptures remind us that, "God is no respecter of persons," what does that imply?

Q. Do you agree with Hooker that love for God and love for Jesus Christ is really what binds us together or are there other doctrinal views critical for fellowship?

Q. Provide some experience in your life where you felt discriminated against.

Q. What are some of the consequences of exclusiveness in a group?

Q. Describe someone you know who is a good example of "inclusiveness" and who practices impartiality.

Q. How is Jesus inclusive in His life and death?

Character for Life

GOD'S PROMISE:

"Now let the fear of the LORD be upon you. Judge carefully, for with the LORD our God there is no injustice or partiality or bribery" (2 Chronicles 19:7).

GOD'S GOAL:

For Christians to understand God's impartiality when it comes to all people coming to faith in Him.

YOUR COMMITMENT:

To treat people as Jesus would.

YOUR DAILY RESPONSE:

1. Understand that Jesus died for everyone.

2. Treat people as if you truly believe God sent Jesus for them too.

3. Live a life where you strive to include all types of people.

4. Be willing to step outside of your comfort zone.

FAILURE WILL MEAN:

Being exclusive and believing that God didn't send Jesus to die for everyone.

BACKGROUND:

Until Jesus Christ comes into our lives, we only see along the lines of our prejudices; God's Spirit will blow away the lines of our prejudices with His dynamic power. God is no respecter of persons. Christianity cuts out a man's personal prejudices. Whenever you find prejudices in yourself, take it to Jesus Christ. Our Lord is the only standard for prejudice.

One way Jesus showed us He did not consider the rank or position of a person as important was the choice of His disciples. He chose mainly fishermen from Galilee. He did not seek out men of power to establish His Kingdom, but those who had a heart to find truth. The Bible says, "Do not show partiality to the poor or favoritism to the great, but judge your neighbor fairly" (Leviticus 19:15b).

"I now realize how true it is that God does not show favoritism but accepts men from every nation who fear him and do what is right" (Acts 10:34b-35).

"As for those who seemed to be important—whatever they were makes no difference to me; God does not judge by external appearance—those men added nothing to my message" (Galatians 2:6).

LIVING A LIFE FULL OF IMPARTIALITY MEANS . . .

- Treating people fairly and without bias.

- Realizing that God sent Jesus to die for every person in every nation.

- Being humble before God and appreciating who He created you to be.

- Understanding that all people are worth "saving" and all people need Jesus.

Chapter Twenty-Four: Learn more about Hooker

Go to an Internet search engine.
Type in *Bishop Richard Hooker's Character.*
Find topics 1-4 below and open up the websites.
1. Izaak Walton's Life of Hooker
2. English Historical Review: Richard Hooker's Reputation
3. The Creation of Richard Hooker's Public Authority
4. Hooker's Policy (1)

chapter 25

Integrity—

george washington

PURPOSE: Living a Life Without Regrets

character trait:
Integrity

SUBJECT:
GEORGE WASHINGTON
(1732-1799)

PURPOSE:
Living a Life Without Regrets

FAMOUS QUOTE:
"Few men have virtue to withstand the highest bidder. I hope I shall always possess firmness and virtue enough to maintain what I consider the most enviable of all titles, the character of an honest man."

SCRIPTURE DOCUMENTATION:
"And David shepherded them with integrity of heart; with skillful hands he led them" (Psalm 78:72).

"The integrity of the upright guides them, but the unfaithful are destroyed by their duplicity" (Proverbs 11:3).

PERSONALITY PROFILE

Washington's family was descended from King John of England. Augustine and Mary Ball Washington had six children, of which George was the oldest. Washington's father died when he was only 12 years old and his mother was left to care for the six children.

Washington was home educated until he was 16 years old and his early education was along classical lines and included surveying. Washington received his surveyor's license in 1749 from William and Mary College. His first military responsibility was during the French-Indian-English war in 1755, where he distinguished himself as General Braddock's aide-de-camp. Washington was then sent as a delegate from Virginia to the First Continental Congress. He was named Commander in Chief of the Virginia Militia in 1755 and in June that same year he was unanimously chosen as Commander-in-Chief of the Colonial Army.

George and Martha Washington were well matched. They became a congenial couple and deeply cared for one another. Martha had given birth four times in her first marriage, but never in her second one to George. It could be that Martha was no longer able to give birth to children. Washington was a good father to Martha's children, who accompanied her to her new home and who became his responsibility. The country began to refer to the Presidents wife as "Lady Washington." Martha was a remarkable person; both modest and affectionate. When Washington left for his second inauguration in Philadelphia, it was the last time he saw her, since she was ill and suffering from breast cancer.

"James Flexner, George Washington's greatest biographer, called him the 'indispensable man' of the American founding. Without Washington, America would never have won our War of Independence. He played the central role in the Constitutional Convention and, as our first President, set the precedents that define what it means to be a constitutional executive: strong and energetic, aware of the limits of authority but guarding the prerogatives of office. Washington not only rejected offers to make him king, but was one of the first leaders in world history to relinquish power voluntarily. His peaceful transfer of the presidency to John Adams in 1797 inaugurated one of America's greatest democratic traditions."[1]

WASHINGTON'S CHARACTER AND INTEGRITY

For over 200 years mankind has lauded the character of George Washington.

Abigail Adams wrote a letter to her husband, John Adams, on July 6, 1775 and reflected on meeting Washington for the first time. "I was struck with General Washington…dignity with ease…the Gentleman and the Soldier look agreeably blended in him. Modesty marks every line in his face."[4] The purity of his private character was revealed by his public virtue.

"Washington wished to set an example, maintain a reputation, and proclaim a standard, worthy of us today. In all of this he had a spiritual sense of Providence, mentioned so often in his writings. This kept him humble and thankful. Among the maxims he would repeat to himself was, 'Labour to keep alive in your breast that Little spark of Celestial Fire called Conscience.'"

"How are we to react when the lofty standard first set by George Washington is sullied by a procession of some recent leaders who fall short of that standard? Do we plan to lower the standard with a shrug of our shoulders and a pronouncement that, 'everybody does it'? This is what the polls seem to advocate. However, the response should be that 'everybody shouldn't do it, especially our Presidents.' The first one kept the standard, despite flaws (like his temper) and shortcomings (like his military defeats)."[5]

"Washington was unanimously chosen to head the assembly that developed the Constitution, the foundation of American government. One of its provisions called for something known as a president, and immediately the delegates began whispering that there was only one man to consider for the position. Washington did not want the office, but he worked for over a year to ensure the Constitution's ratification, which was achieved in June of 1788." [6]

The country knew President Washington and loved him. During the winter at Valley Forge during the Revolutionary War, his army was demoralized. Washington had lost major battles and retreated to build log cabins for the soldiers. Desertion was rampant due to a lack of food, fatigue, and cold weather. Congress was no help. The British were buying food from the Americans and the American soldiers had no money to purchase food. Some recommended the American

"America has furnished to the world the character of washington, and if our American institutions had done nothing else, that alone would have entitled them to the respect of mankind."[2]
statesman Daniel webster

Upon the death of George Washington, Henry Lee described him with these memorable words, "First in war, first in peace, and first in the hearts of his countrymen, he was second to none in humble and enduring scenes of private life. Pious, just, humane, temperate, and sincere; uniform, dignified, and commanding; his example was as edifying to all around him as were the effects of that example lasting…Correct throughout, vice shuddered in his presence and virtue always felt his fostering hand. The purity of his private character gave effulgence to his public virtues… Such was the man for whom our nation mourns."[3]

NATIONAL PURPOSE

revolutionaries steal food, but Washington threatened to shoot anyone who did. He knew that if America would endure, it had to respect its citizens. This proved to be one of his most valuable assets in the coming years. Needless to say, the starving army was impressed with Washington's integrity.

"During Washington's presidency, his character would be tested often but it served him and the nation well. For example, he recognized that America's credit abroad, and its integrity at home, depended on honoring its war debt. Some Americans wanted to renege on payments we owed to patriots at home and the French abroad who had invested in our war for independence. Others, like James Madison, wanted to repay some, but not all, of the debt. Washington saw this as a character issue and helped persuade Congress to pass a revenue tariff to pay all our debts and establish our credit as a nation worthy of international respect."[7]

WASHINGTON'S ACCOMPLISHMENTS

Washington provided leadership for the American victory at Yorktown in October 1781. He was a master strategist in the Revolutionary War and also was called upon to formulate a Constitution. General Washington was elected President of the Constitutional Convention in 1787. He was unanimously elected President of the United States two times, in 1789 and in 1792. He overcame unbelievable hardships of building the Colonial army out of raw recruits. After serving two terms as President, he returned to Mt. Vernon to live the remaining two years of his life.

Washington's last words were on December 14, 1799. In his dying moments Washington spoke to his physician, "Doctor, I die hard, but I am not afraid to go." When Dr. Brown returned to the room Washington said, "I feel myself going, I thank you for your administration but I pray you to take no more trouble for me. I cannot last long."[9]

Upon the death of Washington, Chief Justice John Marshall spoke out of his deep affection and respect for the nations first President, "Our Washington is no more. The Hero, the Sage, and the Patriot of America—the man on whom in times of danger every eye was turned, and all hopes were placed lives now only in his own great actions, and in the hearts of an affectionate and afflicted people."[10]

"washington is the mightiest name on earth—long since mightiest in the cause of civil liberty; still mightiest in moral reformation. on that name no eulogy is expected. it cannot be. to add brightness to the sun, or glory to the name of washington, is alike impossible. let none attempt it. in solemn awe pronounce the name, and in its naked deathless splendor, leave it shining on."[8]

Abraham Lincoln

Washington held an awareness of the great pillars of the country. Said Washington, "Of all the dispositions and habits which lead to political prosperity, religion and morality are indispensable supports. In vain would that man claim the tribute of patriotism who should labor to subvert the great pillars of human happiness, these firmest props of the duties of man and citizens. The mere politician, equal with the pious man, ought to respect and to cherish them. Let it simply be asked, where is the security for property, for reputation, for life, if the sense of religious obligation deserts the oaths, which are the instruments of investigation in the Courts of Justice? And let us with caution indulge the suppositions that morality can be maintained without Religion. Reason and experience both forbid us to expect that national morality can prevail exclusion of religious principle." [11]

CONFIDENCE IN GOD'S WORD AND LOVE OF RIGHTEOUSNESS

In a letter to the General Assembly of Presbyterian Churches on May 1789, Washington summed up the religious religious responsibilities for their country;

"While I reiterate the professions of my dependence upon Heaven as the source of all public and private blessings; I will observe that the general prevalence of piety, philanthropy, honesty, industry, and oeconomy seems, in the ordinary course of human affairs, particularly necessary for advancing and conforming the happiness of our country. While all men within our territories are protected in worshipping the Deity according to the dictates of their consciences; it is rationally to be expected from them in return, that they will be emulous of evincing the sanctity of their professions by the innocence of their lives and the beneficence of their actions; for no man, who is profligate in his morals, or a bad member of the civil community, can possibly be a true Christian, or a credit to his own religious society." [13]

We know from Washington's pastor that prayer and fasting were part of his life. Washington's diary records that he prayed that God "would most graciously be pleased to dispose us all, to do Justice, to love mercy, and to demean ourselves with that Charity, humility, and pacific temper of mind which were the Characteristicks of the Divine Author of our blessed religion." [14]

"This gentleman does not belong to the so-called world of society, for he respects God's Word, believes in the atonement through Jesus Christ, and bears himself in humility and

"First in war, first in peace, first in the hearts of his countrymen." [12]

Major General Henry Lee, referring to George Washington

gentleness. Therefore the Lord God has singularly, yea, marvelously, preserved him from harm in the midst of countless perils, ambuscades, fatigues, etc., and has hitherto graciously held him in His hand as a chosen vessel." [15]

"A Christian in faith and Practice, he [Washington] was habitually devout." [16] Washington was a man of prayer and spent time every day in prayer. His prayers to God were recorded in his diaries. He was a man after God's heart and prayed "let my heart, therefore, gracious God, be so affected with the glory and majesty of Thine honor that I may not do mine own works, but wait on Thee and discharge those weighty duties which Thou requirest of me." [17]

A HEART CLEANSED FROM SIN

Washington asked for cleansing from sin saying, "Direct my thoughts, words and wash away my sins in the immaculate blood of the Lamb and purge my heart in Thy Holy Spirit…daily frame me more and more into the likeness of Thy Son Jesus Christ." [18] His contrite spirit is seen as he revealed his sins before God, "Oh most glorious God, I acknowledge and confess my faults, in the weak and imperfect performance of the duties of this day. I have called on Thee for pardon and forgiveness, but so coldly and carelessly that my prayers are becoming my sin and stand in need of pardon. But, oh God, who are rich in mercy and plenteous in redemption, mark not, I beseech Thee, what I have done amiss; remember that I am but dust, and remit my transgressions, negligences and ignorances, and cover them all with the absolute obedience of Thy dear Son, and those sacrifices of which I have offered may be accepted by Thee, in and for the sacrifice of Jesus Christ offered upon the cross for me." [19]

On Washington's tomb is engraved the verse John 11:25— "I am the resurrection and the Life, says the Lord, He that believes in Me, though He were dead, yet shall live, and whosoever lives and believes in Me shall never die" (John 11:25). Also on the Monument are the words, "Praise be to God. Suffer the little children to come unto me and forbid them not, for such is the Kingdom of God" (Luke 18:16), "Train up a child in way he should go and when he is old, he will not depart from it" (Proverbs 22:6), and "In God We Trust."

THE CONVICTIONS AND INTEGRITY OF GEORGE WASHINGTON

Many found Washington a leader who provided an example of integrity for generations and gave confidence to the hearts of other leaders and countrymen. Jefferson said that "He [Washington] was, in every sense of the words, a wise, good, and a great man…The whole of his character was in its mass perfect…And it may be truly said, that never did nature and fortune combine more perfectly to make a man great…Washington errs as other men do, but errs with integrity…his name will triumph over time and will in future ages assure its just station among the most celebrated worthiest of the world."[21]

"His mind was great and powerful…as far as he saw, no judgment was ever sounder. It was slow in operation, being little aided by invention or imagination, but sure in conclusion."[22]

In his first Inaugural address, President Washington spoke of America's dependence upon God, "It would be peculiarly improper to omit in this first official act, my fervent supplications to that Almighty Being who rules over the universe—who presides in the council of nations—and whose providential aids can supply every human defect, that his benediction may consecrate to the liberties and happiness of the people of the United States, a government utilized by themselves for these essential purposes."[23]

Abraham Lincoln wrote of him, "Washington is the mightiest name on earth—long since mightiest in the cause of civil liberty; still mightiest in moral reformation. On that name no eulogy is expected. It cannot be. To add brightness to the sun, or glory to the name of Washington, is alike impossible. Let none attempt it. In solemn awe pronounce the name, and in its naked deathless splendor, leave it shining on."[25]

WHAT PEOPLE SAID ABOUT WASHINGTON

"On the whole, his life affords the brightest model for imitation, not only to warriors and statesmen, but to private citizens; for his character was a constellation of all the talents and virtues which dignify or adorn human nature."[26]

"His private character, as well as his public one, will bear the strictest scrutiny. He … carried the spirit of piety with him, both in his private life and public administration." David Ramsay, military surgeon [24]

NATIONAL PURPOSE

"If virtues can secure happiness in another world, he is happy."
General Alexander Hamilton[27]

In his final farewell address, Washington reminded Americans on the importance of virtue for the lasting happiness of the nation.

"Observe good faith and justice towards all Nations; cultivate peace and harmony with all. Religion and Morality enjoin this conduct; and can it be, that good policy does not equally enjoin it? It will be worthy of a free, enlightened, and, at no distant period, a great Nation, to give to mankind the magnanimous and too novel example of a people always guided by an exalted justice and benevolence. Who can doubt, that, in the course of time and things, the fruits of such a plan would richly repay any temporary advantages, which might be lost by a steady adherence to it ? Can it be, that Providence has not connected the permanent felicity of a Nation with its Virtue? The experiment, at least, is recommended by every sentiment which ennobles human nature. Alas! is it rendered impossible by its vices?" [28]

WASHINGTON'S INTEGRITY

George Washington said, "Few men have virtue to withstand the highest bidder. I hope I shall always possess firmness and virtue enough to maintain what I consider the most enviable of all titles, the character of an honest man." [29]

THE WILLINGNESS OF SOLDIERS TO FOLLOW HIM

An aide to the Washington said, "The General hopes and trusts, that every officer and man, will endeavor so to live, and act, as becomes a Christian soldier defending the dearest rights and liberties of the country." [30]

Washington exhorted the nation to depend upon God, "The time is now near at hand which must probably determine, whether Americans are to be, freeman or slaves; whether they are to have any property they can call their own…. The fate of unborn millions will now depend, under God, on the course and conduct of this army…. Let us therefore rely on the goodness of the cause and the aid of the Supreme Being, in whose hands victory is, to animate and encourage us to great and noble actions." [32]

"A hero in a republic, he excites another sort of respect which seems to spring from the sole idea that safety of each individual is attached to his person…. The goodness and benevolence which characterize him are evidence in all that surrounds him, but the confidence that he calls forth never occasions improper familiarity."[33]

AN AWARENESS FOR GOD AND AMERICA'S PLACE UPON THE NATIONS

As President, Washington admonished the nation to honor God's intervention and sustenance in the affairs of the country. He said, "It having pleased the Almighty Ruler of the universe to defend the cause of the United American States, and finally to raise up a powerful friend among the princes of the earth, to establish our liberty and independence upon a lasting foundation, it becomes us to set apart a day for gratefully acknowledging the divine goodness, and celebrating the important event, which we owe to His divine interposition."[34]

"I now make it my earnest prayer, that God would have you, and the State over which you preside, in his holy protection, that he would incline the hearts of the Citizens to cultivate a spirit of subordination and obedience to Government, to entertain a brotherly affection and love for one another, for their fellow Citizens of the United States at large, and particularly for their brethren who have served in the Field, and finally, that he would most graciously be pleased to dispose us all, to do Justice, to love mercy, and to demean ourselves with that Charity, humility and pacific temper of mind, which were the Characteristicks of the Divine Author of our blessed Religion, and without a humble imitation of whose example in these things, we can never hope to be a happy Nation."[36]

George Washington's 1789 Thanksgiving Proclamation

Whereas it is the duty of all nations to acknowledge the providence of Almighty God, to obey His will, to be grateful for His benefits, and humbly to implore His protection and favor; and Whereas both Houses of Congress have, by their joint committee, requested me to recommend to the people of the United States a day of public thanksgiving and prayer, to be observed by acknowledging with grateful hearts the many and signal favors of Almighty God, especially by affording them an opportunity peaceably to establish a form of government for their safety and happiness:

Now, therefore, I do recommend and assign Thursday, the 26th day of November next, to be devoted by the people of these States to the service of that great and glorious Being

"Washington always rose before the sun came up and remained in his library until called for breakfast." [35]

Nelly Curtis, Washington's daughter

who is the beneficent author of all the good that was, that is, or that will be; that we may then all unite in rendering unto Him our sincere and humble thanks for His kind care and protection of the people of this country previous to their becoming a nation; for the signal and manifold mercies and the favorable interpositions of His providence in the course and conclusion of the late war; for the great degree of tranquility, union, and plenty which we have since enjoyed; for the peaceable and rational manner in which we have been enable to establish constitutions of government for our safety and happiness, and particularly the national one now lately instituted for the civil and religious liberty with which we are blessed, and the means we have of acquiring and diffusing useful knowledge; and, in general, for all the great and various favors which He has been pleased to confer upon us.

And also that we may then unite in most humbly offering our prayers and supplications to the great Lord and Ruler of Nations and beseech Him to pardon our national and other transgressions; to enable us all, whether in public or private stations, to perform our several and relative duties properly and punctually; to render our National Government a blessing to all the people by constantly being a Government of wise, just, and constitutional laws, discreetly and faithfully executed and obeyed; to protect and guide all sovereigns and nations (especially such as have show kindness to us), and to bless them with good governments, peace, and concord; to promote the knowledge and practice of true religion and virtue, and the increase of science among them and us; and, generally to grant unto all mankind such a degree of temporal prosperity as He alone knows to be best.

Given under my hand, at the city of New York, the 3rd day of October, A.D. 1789.

G. Washington[37]

MODERN-DAY EXAMPLE OF INTEGRITY
JOHN MACKENZIE

After finishing school, my wife, Ruthie, and I felt God was calling us to leave Seattle and move to upstate New York to work with kids. We started something called "Schenectady Teen Development." We were blessed to have John Mackenzie as the Chairman of our Board of Directors. John was one of the top lawyers for General Electric in Schenectady and cared a lot for the street kids there.

John had been involved with "Faith at Work" where being honest with yourself and others were hallmarks of their fellowship. He knew the meaning with subtleties of communication and hidden agendas and wanted everything to be "up front." He wasn't impressed with "numbers" but individuals and changed lives. He had a heart for the kids on the street and was willing to put his time and resources into reaching out to them.

I had never had a working relationship with someone of this stature before, so it was a learning experience. One of the things I learned was related to communicating with our supporters. Any kind of communiqué that wasn't clear or may have exaggerated what we were doing caught the attention of John. He would ask questions like "is that exactly what you want to say" or "are you sure of your facts?" John was a hands-on guy and wanted to know how I was doing spiritually. Not always comfortable to have around, but someone who knew about the importance of being above board in every situation. Everyone needs a person like John Mackenzie in his or her life. He was a man rooted in what was the truth and walked in the "fear and reverence of God." Even in his 80's, the Mackenzies have been involved in outreaches to the former Soviet Union, Africa, and South America. John Mackenzie is a man of integrity and a man of character.

Washington knew that the foundations of morality were in religion. "And let us with caution include the suppositions that morality can be maintained without religion. Reason and experience both forbid us to expect that national morality can prevail exclusion of religious principle. It is substantially true, that virtue or morality is a necessary spring of popular government." [38]

REVIEW

Q. How will the character trait of integrity make a difference in your life?

Q. List the ten characteristics of "integrity" from Psalm 15.

Q. Why was sound judgment critical during the Revolutionary War?

Q. Discuss the sense of "presence" Washington embodied in his persona and why this was critical to his success.

Q. According to those who knew him, Washington did not call attention to himself by bragging about his remarkable deeds. What does this tell us about him?

Q. When Washington referred to the "blessed author of our religion," who was he talking about and what were the implications of this statement?

Q. What was Washington's greatest wish for himself?

Q. How does one err with integrity?

Q. Discuss the statement made by Daniel Webster regarding the impact of Washington on the world.

Q. In writing to the military, Washington used the terms "as becomes a Christian soldier." How do you think a "Christian soldier" would conduct himself?

Q. Why do you think Washington wanted his soldiers to fear God and turn from all evil?

Q. How would those under Washington know he was concerned for their safety?

Q. Major Henry Lee's description of Washington said he was "first in the hearts of his countrymen." What do you think that meant?

Q. Washington believed that virtue sprang from religion and without these governments of the people, we cannot exist. Does this belief hold true today?

Q. How are the great pillars of human happiness being perverted today?

Q. Why do you think religious principles are being discarded today in favor of secular values?

Q. What virtues did Washington ask God to give to Americans?

Q. How did God preserve Washington many times from death?

Q. What does it mean to be habitually devout?

Q. Discuss some of Washington's requests to God for himself.

Character for Life

GOD'S PROMISE:

"And David shepherded them with integrity of heart; with skillful hands he led them" (Psalm 78:72).

GOD'S GOAL:

For Christians to live lives of integrity.

YOUR COMMITMENT:

To live life in such a way as to never be ashamed.

YOUR DAILY RESPONSE:

1. Realize that each day is an opportunity.

2. Live a life without regrets by living morally.

3. Understand that people are always watching what you do, as is the Lord.

4. Strive to live a pure life and be a witness to everyone in all you do.

FAILURE WILL MEAN:

Your witness is no longer credible because your actions don't match your talk.

BACKGROUND:

The word "integrity" means "complete or blamelessness," which, in a limited sense, humans can possess, although we are flawed by sin. By arming the believer with the power of the Holy Spirit, God completely equips him for a righteous walk. Integrity also means to "make straight." This means to change the crooked paths of life people take and turn them into the "paths of righteousness."

Jesus expressed integrity by not teaching ordinary integrity, but supernormal integrity, a likeness to our Father in Heaven. "'Teacher,' they said, 'we know you are a man of integrity and that you teach the way of God in accordance with the truth. You aren't swayed by men, because you pay no attention to who they are'" (Matthew 22:16b).

Jesus was a true shepherd and gave His life for the sheep. Jesus shepherded them with integrity of heart and was the manifestation of true integrity. "Then we your people, the sheep of your pasture, will praise you forever; from generation to generation we will recount your praise" (Psalm 79:13).

LIVING A LIFE OF INTEGRITY MEANS . . .

■ Showing moral uprightness in everything (Psalm 7:10).

■ Giving unselfish service to everyone (2 Corinthians 4:2).

■ Remaining loyal to your commitments (Proverbs 20:6-7).

■ Honest behavior and personal chastity (2 Corinthians 7:1).

■ Being guided by God and walking securely at all times (Proverbs 10:9).

■ The blessing of God in your life now and in the future (Psalm 11:7, 15, 84:11).

Chapter Twenty-Five: Learn more about Washington

Go to an Internet search engine.

Type in *George Washington's Character.*

Find topics 1-9 below and open up the websites.

1. A Guardian-George Washington
2. White House Studies: George Washington's character and slavery
3. George Washington and the legacy of character
4. The Character of George Washington by David Abshire
5. It's Still George Washington's birthday (Not President's Day)
6. Farewell Address 1796
7. WorldNetDaily: The Unique Character of George Washington
8. George Washington's Unimpeachable Character
9. The Religion of George Washington

Notes & Observations

chapter 26

Jealousy for God's Honor — charles finney

PURPOSE: Caring More About God's Reputation Than Your Own

character trait:
Jealousy for God's Honor

SUBJECT:
CHARLES FINNEY
(1792-1875)

PURPOSE:
Caring More About God's Reputation Than Your Own

FAMOUS QUOTE:
"It seemed as if I met the Lord Jesus Christ face to face…. I fell down at His feet and poured out my soul to Him…the Holy Spirit descended upon me in a manner that seemed to go through me, body and soul…. No words can ever express the wonderful love that was shed abroad in my heart."

SCRIPTURE DOCUMENTATION:
"Do not worship any other god, for the LORD, whose name is Jealous, is a jealous God" (Exodus 34:14).

"Do you not know that your body is a temple of the Holy Spirit, who is in you, whom you have received from God? You are not your own; you were bought at a price. Therefore honor God with your body" (1 Corinthians 6:19-20).

PERSONALITY PROFILE

Charles Grandison Finney was an American revivalist and theologian whose cause was the "Kingdom of God." Finney was born in Warren, Connecticut on August 29, 1792 to Sylvester and Rebecca Finney. His family immigrated to the West and settled in the town of Oneida County, N.Y. He taught school for two years and prepared to enter Yale College.

In 1814, his family moved to New Jersey where he began working through the Yale College Curriculum. He studied law and was admitted to the bar in 1818. In 1821 he experienced a dramatic conversion and left Law to preach the Christian gospel. He conducted revivals for ten years and eventually became a Congregationalist. In 1835 he began Oberlin Collegiate Institute, but he continued his New York ministry.

After the "Second Great Awakening" and the influence of English Deism and French infidelity, America needed another spiritual awakening. V. Raymond Edmond, former president of Wheaton College, said,

> I have read and reread with burning of heart the Autobiography and Revival Lectures by Finney, and have come to the persuasion that to a large extent we do not see revival because we do not know its pattern nor the mighty moving of God's spirit, as did Finney. Finney's 50 years of revival ministry brought the dynamic of the gospel to a very needy America. [Finney was] the most widely known and successful American revivalist. Just as the Erie channel was built for American commerce and enterprise, so was Finney's life a channel for the river of God to bring saving grace, morality, integrity, sobriety, and godliness to American life.[1]

Charles Finney was a man God used mightily during the 2nd Great Awakening. Some say over 500,000 people became Christians during his ministry. During one year alone, 150,000 people gave their lives to Christ. Finney, along with Jonathan Edwards, believed that "conversion" was a change in the ultimate purpose in life. Virtues were developed through a change in an individual's "affections."

Over time, Finney became known more as a social reformer than a theologian. His theology was defective in that Finney did not understand the meaning of "propitiation" in the atonement of Christ. (Propitiation is the removal of God's punishment for sin through the perfect sacrifice of our Lord Jesus Christ.) In my youth, I met many wonderful people who loved Finney, but like I, failed to understand that this teaching left people uncertain about their relationship with the Redeemer of those who trust Him.

For nine years Finney experienced revival, and it must have taken its toll on his body. The loss of his health required him to leave the full time revival ministry and pastor a church in New York City. He would ultimately spend six months a year there and six months in Oberlin, Ohio where he lived for 38 more years. The parents of Charles Finney were not "professors of religion." When Finney married, however, he involved his family in his revival ministry. Both Finney's first and second wife died. Finney married again later in life and was survived by his third wife.

fINNEY'S CONVERSION AND LIfE AS A PASTOR

Charles Finney tells about his conversion in his biography saying, "It seemed as if I met the Lord Jesus Christ face to face…I fell down at His feet and poured out my soul to Him…the Holy Spirit descended upon me in a manner that seemed to go through me, body and soul…. No words can ever express the wonderful love that was shed abroad in my heart."[2] Few Christians have ever had the passion for God seen in the life of Charles Finney.

Charles Finney received Presbyterian ordination in 1824 and became a pastor in New York in 1832. He approached the Scriptures as a trial lawyer and sought to understand the doctrines of the faith in a fresh way. In the 1820's America had moved away from the "dependence upon God" earlier generations had experienced. It was the "good feelings era" and the sense of God's holiness and another "great awakening" was desperately needed. Finney wrote on revival and rejected the doctrines of passive salvation available only to the elect. Many, especially in New England, had rejected the understanding of Christ's death for a select group of people. In Western New York, Finney's teaching brought about a powerful impact toward social reform–emancipation of the slaves as well as temperance, foreign missions, and women's rights.

fINNEY AND HIS ACADEMIC ACHIEVEMENTS

A student described a class under Finney with the following words, "Finney opened his class with the usual devotional period, but soon the great deep of his heart was broken up, and he poured out a mighty stream of supplication for the class, for his former co-laborers, for the ministry, for the church

FURTHER SCRIPTURE DOCUMENTATION:

"Let us rejoice and be glad and give him glory! For the wedding of the Lamb has come, and his bride has made herself ready. Fine linen, bright and clean, was given her to wear." (Fine linen stands for the righteousness of the saints) (Revelation 19:7-8).

fame is what
you have taken,
character is
what you give;
when to this
truth you
awaken, then
you begin to
live."[4]

Bayard Taylor

NATIONAL PURPOSE ▶

bought with Jesus' blood. Sometimes he seemed to be leading us: again he seemed to be alone with God…we remained on our knees a whole hour, and then rose and went silently to our rooms."[3]

A HUMBLE PRAYER ANSWERED

As president of Oberlin College in Ohio, Finney was also the pastor of the community church. During the summer of 1853, Oberlin had a terrible drought and the results were no feed for the cattle, crops withering, wells that were dried up, and a dry earth. On Sunday morning with the situation desperate Finney offered the following prayer, "O Lord! Send us rain. We pray for rain. Our harvests perish. There is not a drop for the thirsting birds. The ground is parched. The choking cattle lift their voices toward a brassy heaving and lowing, cry 'Lord give us water.' We do not presume to dictate to Thee what is best for us, yet Thou does invite us to come to Thee as children to a father and tell Thee all our wants. We want rain! Unless Thou givest us rain our cattle must die…. O Lord, send us rain! And send it now! For Jesus sake Amen!"[5]

A person in the congregation reflected on this prayer, saying, "Shortly after this the wind rattled the shutters of the old church…darkness came on the air and joy aroused our anxious hearts as great raindrops pattered on the sun-scorched shingles of the monumental old church. The congregation could not sing for weeping."[6]

THE INFLUENCE OF CHARLES FINNEY

The man who has placed after Wesley, the most indelible stamp upon Pentecostalism, was a man born a year after Wesley's death—Charles Finney. All the early Pentecostals could trace their spiritual ancestry to Charles Finney, who was one of the first important figures to emphasize the baptism in the Holy Spirit as a subsequent experience to salvation on Christian conversion. He was the grandfather of Pentecostalism.

Finney shifted the basis of theology from mystery to moral demands and reduced the question of religious faith to a simple exercise of the will. Finney helped form the "Benevolent Empire." This was an effort of societies to aid in solving social problems in the country. These included American Board of

Commissioners for Foreign Missions, American Bible Society, the American Sunday School Union, The American Tract Society, The American Home Mission Society, and the American Temperance Society. The combined budget of all these ministries was close to the federal budget of the United States.

The minister who succeeded Finney as pastor, said of the great evangelist, "A more genial, tender, sympathetic, childlike character I have never met. He always sent me away a wiser man and with a deeper longing to win men to Christ."[7]

Upon the death of Finney, President Fairchild of Oberlin College said, "Your destiny [the students and faculty] will be in a measure shaped by what he was and what he did…from that burning and shining in light, in which for so long a season we were permitted to rejoice, a thousand other lights have been kindled, and thus the darkness of the world shall be more and more enlightened."[8]

Charles P. Bush spoke of the impact of Finney's ministry in upstate New York, "The whole community was stirred; Religion was the topic of conversation in the house, in the shop, in the office and on the street…the Sabbath was honored, the sanctuaries were thronged with happy worshippers…there was a wonderful falling off of criminals. The courts had little to do, and the jail was nearly empty for years afterward."[9] Out of this revival, over 1,500 revivals broke out, Finney gave his whole soul to God.

GOD REQUIRES JUSTICE FOR ALL

Many who were converted under Finney's ministry became ardent abolitionists. In 1835 Finney became professor of theology at Oberlin in Ohio and served as president from 1851-66 and was active in evangelism. Under Finney, Oberlin became a focus for the "underground railroad" and graduated the first black women from college in the U.S. as well as integrated student bodies. The stand Finney took on slavery cut him off from many people. When Lincoln took office as president, he feared the beloved president was not as opposed to slavery as he should be. He was thankful when the President risked the future of the nation to unite the nation under true justice for all.

RIGHTEOUSNESS EXALTS A NATION

Finney believed that the mission of Christians is not just the saving of souls but the transformation of society. Finney

"With what burning, glowing zeal, did he assail the sectarianism which cares for sect more than for Christ, the conventionalism whose 'awful respectability' hampers ministers and churches by a false fastidiousness, and dares not break through the bonds of custom, and adopt a new measure, even to save a soul! With what scathing rebuke he exposes the idle neglect that leaves generations to die without the Gospel, though for each disciple to win one soul each year to Christ, would be to convert the world within a lifetime of a single generation! His preaching was spiritual in power as well as tone…. If any one secret of Mr. Finney's power be emphatic, it is this: he gave his whole soul to God."[10]

A.T. Pierson

understood God's relationship to man in terms of "Moral Government." Regeneration was described as a moral transformation.

To Charles Finney, "the principles of divine government were as intelligible as the Science of Law of Blackstone, as the system of nature was to Isaac Newton, or as the Laws of the Mind were to John Locke. He promised his hearers that God governs human affairs according to laws that can be known by any person possessed of common sense." [11]

"PRINCIPLES OF DIVINE GOVERNMENT"

Finney appealed directly to the reason and conscience of individuals. He devoted himself to the teaching of the "moral government of God over human life telling his hearers that God's ways are really understandable. God governs through rational, consistent and fully revealed laws." [12] Definition: "Sin is voluntary disobedience to the law." [13] Finney sought to help people repent of their excuses as to why they would not honor God. People hid behind their "inability" to turn from sin and Finney would have no part of that.

KEYS TO REVIVAL WHICH MUST BE OBEYED

Finney spoke of the need for the "spirit of prayer." "Unless I had the experience of prayer I could do nothing. If even for a day or an hour I lost the spirit of grace and supplication, I found myself unable to preach with power and efficiency, or to win souls by Personal conversation...I found myself so much exercised and so born down with the weight of immortal souls, that I was constrained to pray without ceasing. He [God] had made a promise to answer prayer and I could not and would not be denied." [14]

In Albany, New York, "prevailing prayer" resulted in a mighty spirit of overwhelming conviction...sudden and powerful conversions...great love and abounding joy of the converts. A love for righteousness in terms of one's ultimate choice...to live for self or God preceded God's spiritual blessings. Finney recalled that "he bellowed out the unutterable gushings of my heart" when he was baptized in the Holy Spirit. Finney believed the Holy Spirit guides our prayer and the Spirit excites desires too great to be uttered except by groans...making the soul too full to utter its feelings by words so that the person can only groan them out to God who understands the languages of the heart. Finney's life became a life of prayer.

In his Lectures on Revivals of Religion, Finney defined a revival. He believed "it was not a miracle in the sense of a physical change brought on solely by God, but a change of mind which, through influences by the Holy Spirit, is ultimately a matter of the individuals free will." [15] (His view may have influenced R.A. Torrey and Dwight L. Moody.) His definition of "Being filled with the Holy Spirit" is related both to "power for service and sanctification as well as involves a deepening of the prayer life which results in deeper union with the Lord Jesus." [16]

Finney believed that God will answer our prayers when we are persevering, offered from the right motives, offered by the intercession of the Holy Spirit, offered with agony of desire (the travail of the soul) offered in the name of Jesus Christ, offered after you have renounced all your sins, and prayed in faith. We must be constantly being washed through His Divine being.

Finney taught from Hosea that people were to "break up our fallow ground...for it is time to seek the Lord." [17] Since the mind is compared in the Bible to ground, the word of God needs to be sown into it. This meant preparing one's mind to bring forth fruit unto God. The result would be the softening of the heart. Finney focused on the need for the nation to repent and on man's ability to repent.

Finney categorized sin into "sins of omission" ("ingratitude, lack of love for God, neglect of the Bible, neglect of prayer, neglect of the means of grace, how we performed our responsibilities, lack of love for the souls of our fellowman, lack of love for those without Christ in other countries, neglect of our social duties, neglect of watchfulness over our own life, neglect of care for our fellow believers, neglect of self-denial") and "sins of commission." (Worldly mindedness, pride, envy, critical spirit, slander, levity, lying, cheating, hypocrisy, robbing God, bad temper, hindering others from being useful.)

GRIEF FOR GOD'S CHARACTER AND NEW UNDERSTANDING

Finney's grief over sin and how it affected the heart of God brought millions to a new understanding of God's character. "At one time he [Finney] beheld the glory of God about him and a bright ineffable light shone into his soul. He saw all nature worshipping God...except man, and he broke into a flood of tears that mankind did not praise God." [19]

"The whole community was stirred; Religion was the topic of conversation in the house, in the shop, in the office and on the street...the Sabbath was honored, the sanctuaries were thronged with happy worshippers...there was a wonderful falling off of criminals. The courts had little to do, and the jail was nearly empty for years afterward." [18]

Charles P. Bush

"During the winter, the Lord gave my own soul a very thorough overhauling and a 'fresh baptism' of His Spirit. My mind was greatly drawn out in prayer…My mind was exercised on the question of personal holiness. I gave myself to a great deal of prayer. I rose at four o'clock in the morning and engaged in prayer. I frequently prayed till…eight o'clock. Holiness to the Lord seemed to be inscribed on all the exercises of my mind…I often found myself smiling as it were in the face of God and saying that I did not want anything. I was happy for God."[20]

Finney believed that God is honored when we respect His Word (and do the things that please Him,) honor one another above ourselves, show proper respect to everyone (other believers, those in authority over us, those with whom we come in contact) honor our parents (listening, respecting and obeying are all implicit in honoring our parents) honoring the Lord with our finances, and honoring the Lord's Day.

MODERN-DAY EXAMPLE OF BEING JEALOUS FOR GOD'S HONOR
BROTHER ANDREW

Perhaps you are one of the hundreds of thousands of people who read the book "God's Smuggler" about Brother Andrew. In the late 60's and 70's Brother Andrew inspired thousands to begin to care for people "behind the Iron Curtain." He was tireless in his efforts and traveled constantly, alerting Christians to do everything in their power to get Bibles to those in great need. He said, "If we don't take the gospel to the former Soviet Union, they will bring Communism to the West and America." He told about the amazing way that God "blinded the eyes of the guards" and helped people make critical contacts with Christians in Russia who would distribute the precious Scriptures. What was at stake was the fact that Jesus would have the reward of his sacrifice. Brother Andrew spoke to the hearts of people and helped them focus on what was really important. He did it with simplicity and zeal reminding American Christians how much God had blessed our country and how we must pray. Pray we did and Andrew mobilized thousands to pray for the former Soviet Union. The God of heaven and earth brought down the wall separating the East and West and in 1989 we marveled to see the Berlin wall come down. A battle had been won.

Other ministries moved into Russia and Brother Andrew knew he must move on to China to bring our attention to the need for Bibles. The Muslim world was next for "Open Doors." Everyone must know about the Savior. Brother Andrew's jealousy for God's honor was the dominant concern of his life. If you haven't read the book "God's Smuggler," you are in for a treat!

REVIEW

Q. Finney was convinced that slavery was bringing God's judgment on the country and grieved God's heart. What was the Scriptural basis for abolition?

Q. "Willing the highest good" was a definition of righteousness. What is your definition of righteousness?

Q. Do you feel that people are capable of turning from sin? Explain.

Q. Why do you think Finney had such an amazing impact on America?

Q. Finney's heart was broken that man did not worship God. What does this tell us about his walk with God?

Q. On a personal level, what areas of sin in your life is God dealing with?

Q. How can I know if my heart is hardened before God?

Q. What are some of the consequences of a hardened heart?

Q. What does it mean to be filled with the Holy Spirit?

Q. What is your definition of "the Spirit of prayer"?

Q. What does the phrase "holiness to the Lord" mean to you?

Character for Life

GOD'S PROMISE:

"Do not worship any other god, for the LORD, whose name is Jealous, is a jealous God" (Exodus 34:14).

GOD'S GOAL:

For all people to worship only Him as God.

YOUR COMMITMENT:

To put off things in this life that "replace" God.

YOUR DAILY RESPONSE:

1. Getting rid of things that interfere with worshiping God and honoring Him.

2. Taking time each day to spend with God in prayer and His Word.

3. Making sure material items aren't ruling your life.

4. Being humble enough to realize when things are interfering with your spiritual life and asking God for His forgiveness.

FAILURE WILL MEAN:

Putting God on a back burner in your life.

BACKGROUND:

Jealousy has the sense of intense love when applied to God. Jealousy communicates the fierce intensity of God's commitment to His people, even when they turn from Him. Jealousy is a word closely associated with zeal. Godly jealousy, then, can be a strong desire for what is best for people because they belong to God.

The problem comes when God's people turn from Him. There is only one other thing to turn to..... the Kingdom of Darkness whose prince is set upon the destruction of men and women through devious means. As we have seen, this breaks God's heart.

"Do not worship any other god, for the LORD, whose name is Jealous, is a jealous God" (Exodus 34:14).

"They made me jealous by what is no god and angered me with their worthless idols. I will make them envious by those who are not a people; I will make them angry by a nation that has no understanding" (Deuteronomy 32:21).

"Then my wrath against you will subside and my jealous anger will turn away from you; I will be calm and no longer angry" (Ezekiel 16:42).

LIVING A LIFE JEALOUS FOR GOD'S HONOR MEANS . . .

■ Putting God first in everything.

■ Having no "idols" in your life.

■ Choosing God as the most important relationship!

■ Honoring God by praying and reading His Word.

■ Realizing that God is a jealous God because He is the only God!

■ Trusting God with all aspects of your life.

chapter 27

Joy—charles wesley

PURPOSE: Discovering the Blessing of Intimacy With God

character trait:
Joy

SUBJECT:
CHARLES WESLEY
(1707-1788)

PURPOSE:
Discovering the Blessing of
Intimacy With God

FAMOUS QUOTE:
"There is a sweet joy in knowing
that God knows all and notwithstanding loves us still."

**SCRIPTURE
DOCUMENTATION:**
"You love righteousness and hate
wickedness; therefore God, your
God, has set you above your companions by anointing you with the
oil of joy" (Psalm 45:7).

"Now this is eternal life: that they
may know you, the only true God,
and Jesus Christ, whom you have
sent" (John 17:3).

"Dear friends, do not be surprised
at the painful trial you are suffering, as though something strange
were happening to you. But rejoice
that you participate in the sufferings of Christ, so that you may be
overjoyed when his glory is
revealed" (1 Peter 4:12-13).

"Let the word of Christ dwell in
you richly as you teach and
admonish one another with all
wisdom as you sing psalms, hymns
and spiritual songs with gratitude
in your hearts to God"
(Colossians 3:16).

PERSONALITY PROFILE

Charles and John Wesley came from a
Christian family of 19 children, with
John Wesley being the 15th and Charles
the 18th. His mother Susanna was the
25th child in her own family and the last
child of a well-known Puritan preacher.

Both Charles and John were academi-
cally "gifted" and studied at Oxford to
prepare for the ministry in the Anglican
Church. With his brother John, and George Whitefield, Wesley
organized the "Holy Club," teaching members the disciplines of
the Christian life. The purpose of the club was frequent and careful reading of the Scriptures, attending to the sick, dying, poor,
and illiterate, conducting prayer meetings, and visiting prisons. In
his early life Wesley was deeply influenced by the "Moravians"
and their leader Count Zinzendorf, as well as Moravian Peter
Bohler.

Wesley was converted to Christ May 21, 1738. God gave him
Psalm 40:3 that very same day, "He put a new song in my
mouth, a hymn of praise to our God. Many will see and fear and
put their trust in the LORD."[1] The next day Wesley received his
first hymn from the Lord, "And Can It Be!" Since he was one of
three leaders and organizers of the "Holy Club," some thought
of him as the first "Methodist." Joseph Williams described the
music sung saying, "Never did I hear such praying or such
singing. Their singing was not only the most harmonious and
delightful I have ever heard but they sang 'lustily and with a
good course.'… If there be such a thing as heavenly music upon
earth I heard it there."[2]

"Charles was not one to seek publicity," his brother John said of
him. "If ever there was a human being who disliked power,
avoided prominence, and shrank from praise, it was Charles
Wesley."[3] Since he shunned the "limelight," God was able to use
him in a remarkable way.

JUSTIFICATION BEFORE GOD

Peter Bohler, a Moravian brother, was used by God to bring Charles Wesley into a relationship with Jesus Christ. When he visited Charles, who was sick and in the hospital, he inquired of his hopes for salvation. Charles was trusting in his "best endeavors" for the hope of eternal life. Bohler could only shake his head with disappointment. Again Bohler came to visit him and pointed out his danger, since he was "unjustified before God." The growing conviction came to Wesley that it was "through faith alone" that he could stand before God. Wesley writes his thoughts, "Who would believe that our church had been founded on this important article of justification by faith alone? I am astonished I should ever think of this a new doctrine, (as He had done). From this time I endeavored to ground as many of our friends, as came to see me, in this fundamental truth—salvation by faith alone; not an idle, dead faith, but a faith which works by love, and is incessantly productive of all good works and holiness."[4] The loss of Wesley's health brought him into a new intimacy with God and led to his spiritual birth.

While recovering in the home of Moravians, Wesley was deeply affected by their love and kindness to him. In his journal he wrote, "I now found myself at peace with God, and rejoiced in hope of loving Christ, I saw that by faith I stood, by the continual support of faith...I went to bed still sensible of my own weakness...yet confident of Christ's protection."[5] The next day Wesley's strength came back to him.

"After his experience (with the Moravians) Charles Wesley seemed as if this release was all that was needed to make him a channel for immense spiritual forces."[6] He [Wesley] prayed, "In me a quenchless thirst inspire, a longing infinite desire; and fill my craving heart. Less than thyself do not give; in might Thyself within me live; come all Thou hast and art."[7]

Wesley knew the reality of inner joy. He writes, "There is a sweet joy in knowing that God knows all and notwithstanding loves us still."[8]

Thomas Clayton Wolfe said, "There are some people who have the quality of richness and joy in them and they communicate it to everything they touch."[9] How true this was of Charles Wesley. Wesley's hymns were always full of praise to God. He wished that his hymns would be a means of expressing "joy" to Jesus and teaching Scriptural truth.

SONGS LOVED AROUND THE WORLD

The songs of Charles Wesley have been sung for over two centuries and are loved throughout the world. Wesley wrote 6,500 hymns during his lifetime (about three hymns a week), nine thousand poems, 27,000 stanzas, and 180,000 lines. Some of his famous hymns include: "O For a Thousand Tongues to Sing," "Jesus, Lover of My Soul," and "Hark, the Herald Angels Sing."

Wesley believed hymns were a means of teaching theology. Wesley ministered with his brother in open fields, prisons, and to coal miners. He sought out the underclass who were desperate and downtrodden. It's hard to imagine the sight of thousands of coal miners, their faces mixed with ashes and tears, hearing for the first time the songs God gave to Wesley, while having their hearts transformed.

In 1741, at Kingswood, Charles Wesley witnessed the power of the Holy Spirit and recorded: "It is finished." "As soon as I named my text, 'It is finished,' the love of Christ crucified so constrained me that I burst into tears and felt strong sympathy with Him in His sufferings. In like manner the whole congregation looked on Him whom they had pierced and mourned," [11] said Wesley.

Wesley spent a lifetime being disciplined by the Lord. His parents, as well as the nine years he spent at Oxford studying the classics, created the foundation of his being. Wesley also faced tragedy when, of his eight children, five died in infancy.

When he lay dying during the month of March, 1788, worn out from a life of service for his Lord, Wesley dictated a few lines to his beloved wife, Sally.

In age and feebleness extreme,
Who shall a helpless worm redeem?
Jesus, my only hope, Thou art,
Strength of my failing flesh and heart,
O, could I catch a smile from Thee,
And drop into eternity.

THE GIFT OF MUSIC

Wesley was a vessel God used to lift people from despair to a sense of God's presence in their lives. Zephaniah writes of God pictured as taking great delight over His children: "He will quiet you with his love, he will rejoice over you with singing"

(Zephaniah 3:1b). Jesus Himself was comfortable singing hymns with His disciples. Music began in the Bible and was inspired by the Holy Spirit through hymn-writers like Charles Wesley. The joy of heaven would come to earth. Wesley writes:

Hear Him, ye deaf;
His praise, ye dumb,
Your loosened tongues employ;
Ye blind behold your Savior come; and leap, ye lame, for joy.

Wesley also wrote:

He left His Father's throne above,
So free, so infinite His grace;
Emptied Himself of all but love, and bled for Adam's
  helpless race;
Tis mercy all, immense and free; for O my God, it found out me.
Amazing love, how can it be
That Thou my God, should die for me.

Some Wesley favorites are: "Joy to the World," "Jesus, the Joy of Heaven," "Christ the Lord Is Risen Today," and "Love Divine All Love Excelling."

Since Jesus was "the joy of heaven," the hymns of Charles Wesley came out of his relationship and experience of the joy of the Lord.

Christ the Lord is risen today, Alleluia!
Sons of men and angels say, Alleluia!
Raise your joys and triumphs high, Alleluia!
Sing, ye heavens, and earth reply, Alleluia!

THE "INWARD WITNESS" OF THE HOLY SPIRIT

On his deathbed, Charles Wesley's father instructed him, "Be steady. The Christian faith will surely revive in this kingdom. You shall see it; though I shall not."[13] Samuel Wesley then laid his hands on son John and spoke the prophetic words to him, "The inward witness, son, the inward witness, this is the proof, the strongest proof of Christianity."[14] John Wesley said about the experience, "I felt my heart strangely warmed. I felt I did trust in Christ, Christ alone, for salvation; and an assurance was given me that he had taken away my sins...and saved me from the law of sin and death."[15]

"To enjoy the things we (should) and to hate the things we ought has the greatest bearing on excellence of character."[12]

Aristotle

Rejoice the Lord is King;
Your Lord and King adore!
Rejoice, give thanks, and sing,
And triumph evermore;
Lift up your heart, lift up your voice!
Rejoice, again I say, rejoice!

Charles Wesley knew that singing could be a spiritual experience. Millions have discovered how true this really is. Wesley wrote in his journal:

By degrees the Spirit of God chased away the darkness of
    my unbelief.
My gracious Master and my God,
Assist me to proclaim,
To spread through all the earth abroad,
The honors of Thy name.

Jesus was filled with joy! We can no longer think of God as a miserable monarch, a frustrated parent, or an angry policeman on the prowl. Central to the understanding of the gospel today is understanding what God is really like. We should understand that God is the most joyous Being in the universe. Through his music, Charles Wesley brought the joy of Jesus to the Christians of his day.

MODERN-DAY EXAMPLE OF JOY
DAVID WILKERSON

Many years ago as an inner city youth worker in Schenectady, New York, I found myself filled with discouragement over the progress we were making. It was during the Vietnam era and it seemed that an entire generation of young people had lost their way and were abandoning themselves to drugs, sex, and demonic activity. We invited David Wilkerson, who was working in New York City and at Teen Challenge, to come and speak to the young people at Union College. The next day we were together for lunch and I shared with him my discouragement. The only counsel he gave me that I can remember was the promise that "the joy of the Lord would be my strength." I have often recalled this godly wisdom and know how very true it is. David knew from personal experience that discouragement is part of the life of a youth worker and joy is the antidote.

"If you will but live up to your privileges, you can rejoice with unspeakable joy." "I found myself convinced...I saw that by faith I stood."[17]

SINGING THE FAITH

Charles Wesley was involved in small groups and Methodists became known for singing their faith. This began to renew the Anglican Church in the 18th century. During his lifetime Wesley produced about 60 hymn books. He was not only a poet, but a theologian for the Methodist movement. The music was unlike anything heard in England.

MODERN-DAY EXAMPLE OF JOY
CHARLIE JONES

I had never met anyone like Charlie Jones before. He is an unforgettable character and as a young man I wanted to be just like him. Of course it wasn't long before I realized he was an original. No one would ever be like him. He was someone you never forget. He would challenge us youth workers by saying, "Do you think about what you want to think about and like to think about, or what you need to think about and ought to think about? Maybe your problem is that you are not thinking."

He would get right up in your face and the crowd would roar with laughter. He was irrepressible and you could not help but love him. I invited him to come to speak at our supporters' dinner one time. He drove from Harrisburg, PA to Schenectady, N.Y. We gave him a whopping honorarium of $75.00! He was thrilled. He loved to help those who loved kids.

Several years later I produced the "700 Club." Now Charlie could fly down to Virginia Beach. The program went great but there was no restaurant open at 10:00 at night, so we had bananas for dinner. He was ever joyful and grateful. Another time we had him at our house and we both went to get Kentucky Fried chicken to bring home. He announced, "Chicken was coming!" a half block away. He was simply overjoyed at life, marveling that God had saved him.

Joy was the key to the life of Charlie "Tremendous" Jones. He felt lucky to be alive and walking with Jesus was the greatest thrill imaginable. I would call him on the phone from time to time to ask him how he was, his answer, "If things get any better I don't think I could stand it." Joy and Charlie "Tremendous" Jones go together! Everything was tremendous! A tremendous wife...a tremendous son...a tremendous job. I asked him why his response was always "tremendous" and he said, "It's because I have such a limited vocabulary." What a man! He's the real McCoy...and his secret is "the joy of the Lord."

To many, hymn singing was a means of expressing joy as well as teaching the truths of the Bible. The hymns of Wesley brought thousands to experience the joy of Jesus in their lives.

SOCIAL INFLUENCE THROUGH THE REVIVALS

Out of a new concern for the suffering and poor, the Bible Society, Religious Tract Society, Missionary movements, abolition of slave trading, prison reforms, and Sunday Schools began to shape the character of England. This was, in part, how the "Second Great Awaking" began.

NATIONAL PURPOSE ▶

Philosopher and theologian Francis Schaffer maintained that without the Wesleys, "England would have had its own form of the French Revolution."[18] Generations of followers of Jesus Christ have experienced the presence and reality of God as a result of the hymns sung to God by Charles Wesley. Wesley's influence has deeply affected the Holiness, Revivalist, Pentecostal, and Charismatic groups into the 21st century. Charles Wesley may be the greatest hymn writer in the history of Christianity.

REVIEW

Q. Discuss the prayers that Charles Wesley offered to God for himself.

Q. Is there anything like a "holy club" in your community, and if not, could it be that God would use you to begin one?

Q. In many marriages, suffering drives people apart, but with Charles and Sally Wesley, it drew them together. What made the difference?

Q. Share one time in your life when you experienced incredible joy that you knew came from God.

Q. Why is joy important to have in our lives?

Q. What do you think is the secret to true and lasting joy?

Q. Prior to the incarnation of Jesus Christ as He was still in heaven, He looked forward with joy to redeeming those He had created who would respond to Him. It was this joy that sustained Him during His sufferings. What do you think is the greatest motivation for living a holy life?

Q. What did Jesus mean when He said, "that your joy might be complete" (John 15:11)?

Q. Wesley coupled joy with evangelicalism as the hymn reminds us that we should ask God "to assist us to proclaim, to spread through all the earth abroad, the honors of thy name." What should be our greatest motivation in life?

Q. Can the joy of Jesus be with us even during our final days on earth? Give examples.

Character for Life

GOD'S PROMISE:

"You love righteousness and hate wickedness; therefore God, your God, has set you above your companions by anointing you with the oil of joy" (Psalm 45:7).

GOD'S GOAL:

For Christians to be filled with joy.

YOUR COMMITMENT:

To keep the joy of Jesus the number one focus in your life.

YOUR DAILY RESPONSE:

1. Looking up when you feel down.

2. Remembering that God is in control.

3. Asking God daily to fill you with His joy.

4. Understanding the difference between true joy and human happiness.

FAILURE WILL MEAN:

Being unhappy and unfulfilled in everything you do.

BACKGROUND:

How did Jesus illustrate true joy? The Scripture says, "Let us fix our eyes on Jesus, the author and perfecter of our faith, who for the joy set before him endured the cross, scorning its shame, and sat down at the right hand of the throne of God" (Hebrews 12:2). One of the most outstanding features in the life of Jesus' personality was His sense of joy! Jesus prayed for His followers that, "your joy might be complete" (John 15:11).

J. Sidlow Baxter speaks of an encounter where Jesus transformed weeping into singing. The word had come from the house of Jarius, the synagogue ruler, that his daughter had died. "Don't bother the teacher any more," the servant told Jarius. When Jesus arrived he reminded people saying, "Don't be afraid; just believe, and she will be healed." Others in the crowd would bring words of discouragement, misdirection, and hurtfulness but Jesus overruled all these negatives with the words "Just believe." Jesus always turns our "sorrows into joys." Check out his encounters with people in need and rejoice!

"The joy of Jesus was the absolute self-surrender of Himself to the will of His Father; the joy of doing exactly what the Father sent Him to do. A person is only joyful when he fulfills God's creation of him or her and that is a joy that can never be quenched. The joy that Jesus gives is the result of our disposition being at one with his disposition." [19]

God anointed Jesus with immeasurable joy. "You [Jesus] have loved righteousness and hated wickedness; therefore God, your God, has set you above your companions by anointing you with the oil of joy" (Hebrews 1:9).

Jesus was joyful when He saw his disciples being fulfilled in their ministry. "At that time Jesus, full of joy through the Holy Spirit, said, "I praise you, Father, Lord of heaven and earth, because you have hidden these things from the wise and learned, and revealed them to little children. Yes, Father, for this was your good pleasure" (Luke 10:21).

"I have told you this so that my joy may be in you and that your joy may be complete" (John 15:11).

"The LORD your God is with you, he is mighty to save. He will take great delight in you, he will quiet you with his love, he will rejoice over you with singing" (Zephaniah 3:17).

LIVING A LIFE OF JOY MEANS . . .

- Having a genuine smile that is contagious.

- Allowing God to lift your spirits when you feel down.

- Finding good in everything.

- Praying for joy and reading joyous passages of Scripture daily.

- Trusting God to bring all things together for good.

- Having a peace in your heart that only comes from knowing Jesus.

Chapter Twenty-Seven: Learn more about Wesley

Go to an Internet search engine.
Type in *Charles Wesley's Joy*.
Find topics 1-5 below and open up the websites.
1. Charles Wesley's Revival Music
2. Charles Wesley (1707-88)
3. Faith Hall of Fame
4. The Theology of Christmas Carols
5. The Christian Bookshop

chapter 28

Justice—sojourner truth

PURPOSE: Discovering the Divine Viewpoint

character trait:
Justice

SUBJECT:
SOJOURNER TRUTH
(1797-1883)

PURPOSE:
Discovering the Divine Viewpoint

FAMOUS QUOTE:
"I cannot read a book, but I can read the people."

SCRIPTURE DOCUMENTATION:

"He has showed you, O man, what is good. And what does the LORD require of you? To act justly and to love mercy and to walk humbly with your God" (Micah 6:8).

"Do not pervert justice; do not show partiality to the poor or favoritism to the great, but judge your neighbor fairly" (Leviticus 19:15).

Nell Painter (Sojourner Truth's biographer) has "revealed her personal, religious, and historical realities that for a century have lain at the mysterious heart of the story of this fiercely enigmatic, African-American woman, an ex-slave who could neither read nor write and who, to be known, relied solely on her spoken words, her character, and the force of her personality."[1]

Sojourner Truth was born into slavery as Isabella Baumfree in upstate New York. A friend said, "She was tall, thin and angular with a deep voice, and I remember her always with a turban."[2] Truth was concerned because, "There is a great stir about colored men getting their rights, but not a word about the colored women."[3] Truth was convinced, "If colored men get their rights, and not colored women theirs; you will see the colored men will be masters over the women, and it will be just as bad as it was before."[4]

She believed that while white women needed the vote, black women needed it even more. "When we get our rights...we shall not have to come to you for money, for then we shall have more than enough in our own pockets; and maybe you will ask us for money."[5]

Painter believed that "her [Truth's] memory fell into the hands of successors to abolitionists and women suffragists, politically minded reformers whose religions or lack thereof were far from the beliefs she held most of her life."[6] In recent years, however, many people have recognized the faith of Truth. "Linked inextricably to feminists and insurgent blacks, her persona lost the religion of her free women's life. In future generations my hope would be that everyone interested in Christian social reforms would understand the deepest motivations of this remarkable person,"[7] said Painter.

AIN'T I A WOMAN?

Truth was a remarkable person who was led by God to speak before vastly different audiences. In Truth's day, "women's rights" to a black woman meant recognizing the basic dignity she had as a person made in the image of God. Her views were rooted in the Bible. Truth had lost her freedom and her human rights. "I could work as much, and eat as much as a man when I could get it—and bear the lash as well! And ain't I a woman? I have borne children and seen most of them sold into slavery, and when I cried out with a mother's grief, none but Jesus heard me. And ain't I a woman?" [8]

Said Nell Painter, "Whatever did not fit the tight mold of the black women—such as Truth's Pentecostalism or the gentility of her appearance in her photographs…fell out of the making of a symbol." [9]

Truth was tall and stately and spoke with a powerful voice. Her detractors rumored she was really a man. She chose to respond to the charge at a convention in New York City. Truth raised herself to her full six-foot height and said, "Look at me! Look at my arm." She bared her right arm and flexed her powerful muscles. "I have plowed, I have planted and I have gathered into barns. And no man could head me. And ain't I a woman?" [10]

Sojourner Truth was one of the first people in the country to link the oppression of black slaves with the oppression of women. She was freed when New York State emancipated slaves in 1828. Inspired by her faith in Jesus Christ, she was transformed from a domestic servant named Isabella into an itinerant Pentecostal preacher who believed in the leading of the Holy Spirit. She became a national symbol for strong black women and, in reality, for all strong women.

NATIONAL PURPOSE

On what qualifies a person to vote, she said, "What a narrow idea of reading qualification is for a voter! I know and do what is right better than many big men who read. And what's this property qualification! Just as bad, as if men and women themselves, who made money, were not of more value than the thing they had made. If I were a delegate to the Constitutional Convention I could make suffrage as clear as daylight." [11]

Truth spoke before Congress and two presidents. Eventually she advocated a "Negro State" in the West. Over a hundred years before Rosa Parks, Truth refused to face the indignities of Jim Crow segregation on streetcars in the Washington D.C. system and had a role in changing the attitudes of how streetcar drivers treated "Negroes."

A Quaker couple cared for and educated Truth. She finally had a bed to sleep in. The lives of these devoted Christians had a profound impact on Truth the remainder of her life.

Eventually Truth lost track of her parents and her 12 brothers and sisters. Her slave owner sold them. Truth had five children, but through the help of her Quaker family, was able to get only one of her sons back from slavery.

IMPRESSIONS OF TRUTH

William S. McFeely described Truth as "a fiery Pentecostal evangelist; dressed in honored memory, she is the emblematic strong black women and a tireless reformer." [13]

Said Wendell Philips about Truth, "Venerable for age, distinguished for insight into human nature, remarkable for independence and courageous self-assertion, devoted to the welfare of her race, she has been for the last forty years an object of respect and admiration to social reformers everywhere." [14]

Historically, real social reform begins when people turn to God. Truth knew this and had experienced deliverance from the bitterness and hatred of white people. As a result, people just revered her. According to Katherine Moulton of Battle Creek, Michigan, "When Sojourner Truth was coming to call, that was a big deal. She was a well-known personage in the community." [15] Dorothy Pennington said, "She had a wonderful way of relating to young people. She was the kind of person who could establish a rapport with lots of different kinds of people. She had a spiritual base that all her social causes emanated from." [16]

Truth loved the Word of God, she loved the Savior, and as a black slave woman, she knew she was made in the "image of God." Her last words were, "Be a follower of Jesus."

TRUTH'S TESTIMONY

Sojourner Truth told her story to Harriet Beecher Stowe, a famous author who was able to preserve it for future generations. Here is how Truth encountered the living God:

> I lived there (in the South) for two or three years and then the slaves in New York were all set free and old massa came to our home to make a visit and he asked me if I didn't want to

go back and see the folks on the old place. And I told him I did. So he said, if I'd just get into the wagon with him, he'd carry me over. Well, just as I was going to get out of the wagon, I MET God! And says I….O God, I didn't know you were so great! And I turned right around and come in this house and set down in my room, for it was God all around me. I could feel it burning, burning, burning all around me, and going through me; and I saw I was so wicked, it seemed as if it would burn me up. And I said…O somebody, somebody, stand between God and me! For it burns me!

Then honey, when I said so, I felt as it were something like an umbrella that came between me and the light, and I felt it was SOMEBODY, somebody that stood between me and God; and it felt cool, like a shade; and says I, Who's this that stands between me and God? Is it old Cato? (He was a pious old preacher) Is it old Sally?…And then honey, for a while it was like sun shinning! In a pail of water, when it moves up and down, for I begun to feel it was somebody that loved me; and I tried to know him. And I said, I know you! I know you! I know you! And then I said ….I don't know you…I don't know you…something spoke in me and says I…this is Jesus! And I spoke out with all my might…THIS IS JESUS! Glory be to God!

And then the whole world grew bright, and the trees they waved and waved in glory and every little bit of stone on the ground shone like glass; and I shouted and said; praise, praise, praise to the Lord! And I began to feel such a love in my soul as I never felt before…love to all creatures. And then all of a sudden, it stopped and I said. There's the white folks that have abused you and beat you and abused your people…think of them! But then there came another rush of love through my soul, and I cried out loud…Lord, Lord, I can even love the white folks. Honey, I just walked round and round in a dream. Jesus loved me! I know it, I felt it. Jesus was my Jesus. Jesus would love me always.[17]

As Sojourner told this story in the home of Harriet Beecher Stowe, with well-known, educated people surrounding her, a professor asked, "What makes you so sure there is a heaven?" Her response, "Well, cause I got such a 'hanker for it' in here."[19]

Her chief delight was to talk of glory and to sings songs of heaven. In the middle of this distinguished group Sojourner began to praise God. She sang in a "strange, cracked voice, but evidently with all her soul and might. Whether this was a

"man is unjust, but god is just; and finally justice triumphs."[18]

henry wadsworth longfellow

known hymn or a prophetic song coming to her at the moment is not known."

She sang:

There is a holy city, a world of light above, above the stairs and regions, built by the God of love…

An everlasting Temple, and saints arrayed in white, serving their great Redeemer and dwell with him light.

The meanest child of glory outshines the radiant sun; but who can speak the splendor of Jesus on his throne?

Is this the man of sorrows who stood at Pilate's bar, condemned by haughty Herod and by his men of war?

He seems a mighty conqueror who spoiled the powers below, and ransomed many captives from ever lasting woe.

The hosts of saints around him, proclaim, proclaim his work of grace, the patriarchs and prophets, and all the godly race,

Who speak of fiery trials and tortures on their way; they came from tribulation to everlasting day.

And what shall be my journey, a how long I'll stay below, or what shall be my trials, are not for me to know.

In every day of trouble I'll raise my thoughts on high, I'll think of that bright temple and crowns above the sky. [20]

SLAVERY'S IMPACT ON TRUTH

"In the spring of 1849, Sojourner made a visit to her eldest daughter, Diana, who has ever suffered from ill health, and remained with Mr. Dumont, Sojourners human master. She found him still living, though advanced in age and reduced in property and greatly enlightened on the subject of slavery." [22] He told her that slavery was "the wickedest thing in the world and the greatest curse the earth had ever felt." [23] Sojourner thanked the Lord with fervor, that she had lived to hear her master say such blessed things! She recalled the lectures he used to give his slaves on speaking the truth and being honest, and laughing, she says, "He taught us not to lie and steal, when he was telling all the time himself and did not know it! Oh! How sweet to my mind was this confession! A slave holding master turning into a brother! Poor old man, may the Lord bless him, and all slaveholders partake of his spirit!" [24]

TRUTH'S TAKE ON MEN

On one occasion at a rally, Sojourner went into the tent and began singing in her most fervent manner, with all the strength of her most powerful voice, the hymn on the resurrection of Christ. "It was early in the morning…just at the break of day...when he rose...when he rose, when he rose."[25]

The women in the audience began to cheer wildly. She pointed to another minister. "He talks about this thing in his head. What's that they call it? 'Intellect,' whispered a woman nearby. That's it honey. What's intellect got to do with women's rights or black folks' rights? If my cup won't hold but a pint and yours holds a quart, wouldn't you be mean not to let me have my little half-measure full?"[27]

"That little man in black there! He says women can't have as much rights as men. 'Cause Christ wasn't a woman.'" She stood with outstretched arms and eyes of fire. "Where did your Christ come from? From God and a woman! Man had nothing to do with him!"[28] The entire church now roared with deafening applause.

TRUTH'S CALLING

Truth was a woman who feared only God. Her calling was to make the people of the earth Christians. She saw how slavery had numbed her people to their rights and saw them as people who had been sinned against. She wore a banner that read: "Proclaim liberty throughout the land unto all the inhabitants thereof." This verse, of course, was from the Bible.

Truth said of herself, "I cannot read a book, but I can read the people."[29] She was one of the most remarkable people in American history.

TRUTH'S INFLUENCE AFTER THE CIVIL WAR

During the Civil War, Truth was involved in getting contributions of food and clothing for black regiments in the War. After the war she advocated a "Negro State" in Missouri. Her passions were mostly devoted to the temperance and women's rights movements. She saw that the "disfranchised of the earth had a common cause."[30] Shortly after the Civil War she was given the authority from the government to stop people who tried to steal slaves and bring them back to some kind of unofficial slavery. Sojourner and her abolitionists taught the former slaves about their rights and how to get assistance from the government.

EDUCATION FOR BLACK AMERICANS AFTER THE CIVIL WAR

Truth was known as the "angel of emancipation" and sought the establishment of industrial schools where former

"Justice is the virtue that gives to each his due."[26]

st. Augustine

slaves could be taught to become useful citizens. She longed that her people become an honor to the country which had so cruelly wronged them. She presented Congress with the following petition:

> Whereas, from the faithful and earthest representatives of Sojourner Truth we believe that the freed colored people in and about Washington, dependent upon government for support, would be greatly benefited and might become useful citizens by being placed in a position to support themselves: We, the undersigned, therefore earnestly request your honorable body to set apart for them a portion of the public land in the West, and erect buildings for the aged and infirmed, and otherwise legislate so as to secure the desired results.[32]

TRUTH'S ENCOUNTER WITH LINCOLN

Although in Sojourner's estimation Abraham Lincoln was the 'foremost man of all this world,' no idle curiosity prompted her to ask for this interview. She sought the authority of the President to enable her to do her part in bringing the message of freedom and liberty to the nation.

She wrote,

> It was about 8 o'clock a.m., when I called on the president. Upon entering his reception room we found about a dozen persons waiting, among them two colored women. I had quite a pleasant time waiting until he was disengaged, and enjoyed his conversation with others; he showed as much kindness and consideration to the colored persons as to the whites—if there was any difference, more. One case was that of a colored woman who was sick and likely to be turned out of her house on account of her inability to pay her rent. The president listened to her with much attention, and spoke to her with kindness and tenderness. He said he had given so much he could give no more but told her where to go and get the money, and asked Mrs. C—to assist her, which she did.
>
> The president was seated at his desk. Mrs. C. said to him, "This is Sojourner Truth, who has come all the way from Michigan to see you." He then arose, gave me his hand, made a bow, and said, "I am pleased to see you."
>
> I said to him, "Mr. President, when you first took your seat I feared you would be torn to pieces, for I likened you unto Daniel, who was thrown into the lion's den; and if the

lions did not tear you into pieces, I knew that it would be God that had saved you; and I said if he spared me I would see you before the four years expired, and he has done so, and now I am here to see you myself."

He then congratulated me on having been spared. Then I said, "I appreciate you, for you are the best president who has ever taken the seat." He replied: "I expect you have reference to my having emancipated the slaves in my proclamation. But," said he, mentioning the names of several of his predecessors (and among them emphatically Washington) "they were all just as good, and would have done just as I have done if the time had come." I then said, "I thank God that you were the instrument selected by him and the people to do it. I told him that I had never heard of him before he was talked of for president." Lincoln replied, "I had heard of you many times before that."[33]

Truth reflected, "I must say, and I am proud to say, that I never was treated by anyone with more kindness and cordiality than were shown to me by that great and good man, Abraham Lincoln, by the grace of God president of the United States for four years more. He took my little book, and with the same hand that signed the death-warrant of slavery, he wrote as follows; For Aunty Sojourn Truth, Oct. 29, 1864. A. Lincoln."[35]

Truth writes that, "He then showed me the Bible presented to him by the colored people of Baltimore." I said; "This is beautiful indeed; the colored people have given this to the head of the government, and the government once sanctioned laws that would not permit its people to learn enough to enable them to read this book. And for what? Let them answer who can."

"As I was taking my leave, he arose and took my hand, and said he would be pleased to have me call again. I felt that I was in the presence of a friend, and I now thank God from the bottom of my heart that I always have advocated his cause, and have done it openly and boldly. I shall feel still more in duty bound to do so in time to come. May God assist me."[36]

Some social reformers in the past have ignored the most important passions of Truth. They can't understand her deep love for Jesus, her forgiving heart, and passion about the Savior. Truth's life was characterized by fearlessness. She met all kinds of harassment as she marched to bring the cause of justice to the conscience of America. As ruffians were shaking the tent in which she was to speak she had a little talk with herself; "Shall I

"she [Truth] had a wonderful way of relating to young people. she was the kind of person who could establish a rapport with lots of different kinds of people. she had a spiritual base that all her social causes emanated from."[34]

Dorothy pennington

run away and hide from the Devil? Me, a servant of the living God. Have I not faith enough to go out and quell that mob, when I know it is written 'One shall chase a thousand, and two put ten thousand to flight?' I know there are not a thousand here; and I know I am a servant of the Living God. I'll go to the rescue, and the Lord shall go with and protect me." [37]

TRUTH (AT AGE 90) BEFORE CONGRESS REGARDING THE PLIGHT OF WOMEN

Sojourner spoke to the Congress and the following article was published in the Sunday paper during the administration of Grant. "It was our good fortune to be in the marble room of the senate chamber, a few days ago, when that old land-mark of the past—the representative of the forever-gone-age-Sojourner Truth, made her appearance. It was an hour not soon to be forgotten; for it is not often, even in this magnanimous age of progress, that we see reverend senators...extend the hand of

MODERN-DAY EXAMPLE OF JUSTICE MOTHER TERESA

In 1977 I had the opportunity of meeting and interviewing Mother Teresa of Calcutta. I had a film crew from Montana with me and we inadvertently found her "Sisters of Charity" and learned about her ministry. As I walked through the entrance she was seated at a small desk and I blurted out... "Why you are Mother Teresa!" "Why, yes I am," she said. We felt it was kind of a "divine encounter." I had scores of questions to ask, but first we were granted the opportunity of meeting patients and the sisters who were caring for those sick and dying with grace and tender love.

Her convictions were that everyone should die with great dignity and surrounded by love. These were "the poorest of the poor" having been taken off the streets of Calcutta and often left to die. Justice and love and the command of Jesus required action and compassion. She reminded me that when we care for the poor we are caring for Jesus. We do everything in His name out of love for Him. India is learning about God's command "to act justly and to love mercy and to walk humbly with your God" (Micah 6:8).

Mother Teresa's life touched the world. For one April afternoon it touched mine. We were overjoyed that God had given us the opportunity of seeing His justice and mercy through what the "Sisters of Charity" were doing.

welcome, praise, and (offer) substantial blessings, to a poor Negro woman, whose poor old form bending under the burden of nearly 90 years, tells but too plainly that her marvelously strange life is drawing to a close. But it was as refreshing as it was strange to see her who had served in the shackles of slavery in the great State of New York for nearly a quarter of a century before a majority of these senators were born."[38]

Sojourner exclaimed, "Truly, the spirit of progress is abroad in the land, and the leaven of love is working in the hearts of the people, pointing with unerring certainty to the not far distant future, when the ties of affection shall cement all nations, kindreds and tongues into one common brotherhood."[39]

REVIEW

Q. Upon her encounter with God, Sojourner Truth, as many other great saints, felt God's fire. Why do you think God chose to reveal His power to her?

Q. Since Truth could not read, it may be that God had to reveal Himself and Jesus as the Mediator between God and man. What was the effect of this revelation?

Q. Others, such as Paul and John, who were to endure terrible suffering for the sake of the gospel, were given revelations of what was going on in heaven. Do you think the revelations Truth saw affected her for the rest of her life? Explain.

Q. Truth had no doubt prayed for many years for the master who had abused her. She finds him a changed man and they share the same hatred of slavery. What was her response to this news?

Q. Discuss how Jesus' death upholds the law of God and exercises mercy toward us.

Q. What do you think accounted for Truth's boldness before people?

Q. What do her encounters with hostile people tell us about her character?

Q. What did President Lincoln and Sojourner Truth have in common?

Q. What were her impressions of President Lincoln?

Q. After their meeting, Truth was to live another 19 years, while Lincoln only lived another year. Why do you think she wanted his blessing on her life?

Character for Life

GOD'S PROMISE:

"He has showed you, O man, what is good. And what does the LORD require of you? To act justly and to love mercy and to walk humbly with your God" (Micah 6:8).

GOD'S GOAL:

For Christians to see justice given to all.

YOUR COMMITMENT:

To be a just person who treats all people with respect.

YOUR DAILY RESPONSE:

1. Get rid of prejudice in your life.

2. Realize that God's people are people from every nation and nationality.

3. Be willing to do your part to see that justice is done.

4. Honor everyone in everything you do.

FAILURE WILL MEAN:

Allowing people to be treated unfairly and not doing anything to stop it.

BACKGROUND:

Paul's point is that God, as moral governor of the universe, is morally bound to condemn the guilty. The death of Christ has at last demonstrated that there is a basis on which God as judge could validly leave sins unpunished. Jesus' self-sacrifice provides a basis on which God can be just and offer salvation to people today. Because of the cross, God can remain true to His own moral commitment to what is right, and still freely forgive sinners.

The New Testament emphasis is more on righteousness than justice, since justice often means only external behavior (or conformity to a standard or norm). Jesus focuses attention on righteousness, the inner person, from which character springs. God shows us that His solution is not to be found in life regulated by law (although in a sinful world, laws are important) but rather, it is found through God's action in Christ to change human character.

The Scriptures predict that God will teach us justice through His servant. Jesus illustrated justice in His life and ministry. The western world gets much of its concept of justice based on life and teachings of our Lord Jesus Christ.

"Here is my Servant whom I have chosen, the one I love, in whom I delight; I will put my Spirit on him, and he will proclaim justice to the nations" (Matthew 12:18).

Justice was withheld from Jesus. After a mock trial and false witnesses, He was hung on a cross. "You handed him (Jesus) over to be killed, and you disowned him before Pilate, though he had decided to let him go. You disowned the Holy and Righteous One, and asked that a murderer by released to you" (Acts 3:13b-14).

"In his humiliation he was deprived of justice. Who can speak of his descendants? For his life was taken from the earth" (Acts 8:33).

Jesus came to expose injustice and teach righteousness. "Woe to you, teachers of the law and Pharisees, you hypocrites! You give a tenth of your spices—mint, dill and cummin. But you have neglected the more important matters of the law—justice, mercy and faithfulness. You should have practiced the latter, without neglecting the former" (Matthew 23:23).

Jesus will ultimately judge the world. "Then the King will say to those on his right, 'Come, you who are blessed by my Father; take your inheritance, the kingdom prepared for you since the creation of the world. For I was hungry and you gave me something to eat, I was thirsty and you gave me something to drink, I was a stranger and you invited me in, I needed clothes and you clothed me, I was sick and you looked after me, I was in prison and you came to visit me'" (Matthew 25:34-36).

"Moreover, the Father judges no one, but has entrusted all judgment to the Son, that all may honor the Son just as they honor the Father" (John 5:22-23a).

"For He [God] has set a day when he will judge the world with justice by the man he has appointed. He has given proof of this to all men by raising him from the dead" (Acts 17:31).

LIVING A LIFE FULL OF JUSTICE MEANS . . .

■ Showing impartiality.

■ Not taking advantage of others.

■ Respecting the fatherless, the widows, and the alien in your midst.

■ Not perverting justice.

■ Being swift to do righteousness.

■ Caring for the weak and destitute.

■ Receiving instruction in wise dealing.

■ Correcting oppression.

■ Not being greedy for bribes.

■ Not defrauding laborers of their wages.

Chapter Twenty Eight: Learn more about Truth

Go to an Internet search engine.

Type in *Sojourner Truth's Justice.*

Find topics 1-6 below and open up the websites.

1. Sojourner Memorial Project
2. Sojourner Truth
3. Sojourner Truth Narrative - Condition of the Destitute Colored
4. Sojourner Truth..... "but not her loss of faith in God's justice"
5. This Far by Faith. Sojourner Truth PBS
6. The Narrative of Sojourner Truth

chapter 29

Kindness—

george washington carver

PURPOSE: Treating Others as God Treats Us

character trait:
Kindness

SUBJECT:
GEORGE WASHINGTON
CARVER
(1864-1943)

PURPOSE:
Treating Others as God Treats Us

FAMOUS QUOTE:
"It is not the style of clothes one wears, neither the kind of automobile one drives, nor the amount of money one has in the bank, that counts. These mean nothing. It is simply service that measures success."

SCRIPTURE DOCUMENTATION:
"In love a throne will be established; in faithfulness a man will sit on it—one from the house of David—one who in judging seeks justice and speeds the cause of righteousness" (Isaiah 16:5).

"Be kind and compassionate to one another, forgiving each other, just as Christ God forgave you" (Ephesians 4:32).

PERSONALITY PROFILE

No human ever had a more humble start in life. George Washington Carver never knew his mother or father, nor even the year he first saw the light of day. He was a Negro, born a slave early in the bloody civil war that ended legal slavery. He came into the world sickly, and it seemed certain that he would die as an infant.

He could easily have grown up embittered over life since "people of color" were treated little better than field oxen, and sometimes worse. His long life turned out just the opposite. There is little evidence of his anger toward the world and he was a beacon of hope during the stormy years following the terrible war, which divided the states.

Through his simple life Carver provided the impetus to begin the slow turn around of agriculture in the South, especially for Black people. The spent and sterile acres were provided with a new crop with which to sow them. He brightened the homes of impoverished men and women throughout the old Confederacy, and he gave to their children a measure of hope.

Carver was born in 1864, near Diamond Grove, Missouri, on the farm of Moses Carver. It was near the end of the civil war and shortly after his birth his mother was kidnapped by Confederate night-raiders and taken from him. She was gone forever. His father was a slave from a nearby farm who died in a logging accident. Moses Carver and his wife cared for the boys who would bear his name and gave them a start in life.

THE GREAT PRESENCE

Said George Washington Carver, "As a very small boy exploring the almost virgin woods of the old Carver place, I had the impression someone had just been there ahead of me. Things were so orderly, so clean, so harmoniously beautiful. A few years later in this same woods I was to understand the meaning of this boyish impression. I was practically overwhelmed with the sense of some 'Great Presence.' Not only had someone been there. Someone was there...years later when I read in the Scriptures, 'In Him we live and move and have our being.' I knew what the writer meant. Never since have I been without this consciousness of the Creator speaking to me...The out of doors has been to me more and more a great cathedral in which God could be continuously spoken to and heard from...Man, who needed a purpose, a mission, to keep him alive, had one. He could be...God's co-worker."[2]

Carver had a life-long conviction that God did not make anything useless. It was up to man to discover the purposes. He saw "nature as more or less a broadcasting system for God."[3] Perhaps he was reminded of the verse, "The heavens declare the glory of God; the skies proclaim the work of his hands" (Psalm 19:1).

CARVER'S SPIRITUAL LIFE

When Carver was ten years old he made a commitment of his life to the Savior. He saw "nature" as expressing the kindness of God. As a child, George fell in love with "nature" and his early education was on the farm. He learned to care for sick plants and had his own "secret garden." At the age of 12 he began his formal education studying at Minneapolis High School in Kansas.

His commitment led to membership in the Presbyterian Church in Minneapolis where he grew spiritually. As a teenager he was convinced that "God is going to reveal to us things He never revealed before if we put our hands in His."[4] He chose not to take books into his laboratory but relied on hearing God's voice to teach him. He apparently was the only black student in Minneapolis and was generally accepted by the community. He eventually moved to Fort Scott and was adopted by the Watkins family.

Carver spent most of his adult life searching for solutions to the poverty among landless black farmers by developing new uses for soil-replenishing crops such as peanuts and sweet potatoes.

"character is a by-product; it is produced in the great manufacture of daily duty."[1]
woodrow wilson

Early in his life Carver experienced a lot of rejection but none was more difficult than being turned down for college. He had applied to Highland College in Kansas and was thrilled when he was accepted. When the admissions people discovered he was a "Negro" he was told he was not welcome. This cut him to the core but he was finally accepted at Simpson College in Iowa when he was 30 years old. He was the first black student accepted into the school. At Simpson College, he survived as a result of the good will of the president of the school who provided a shack for him and he ate the leftovers from the school cafeteria.

Eventually Carver transferred to Iowa State University where he received a Bachelor of Science and Master's degree in bacterial botany and agriculture. The big questions of life became real to him. Why did God place me here on earth? What is my purpose for living? What can I do to serve my fellow man, especially the people of color? Apparently, these were times of great soul searching for Carver.

With his Master's degree in hand, he had what few black people had, a college education, and wanted to give back what he had received. In 1897 Booker T. Washington invited him to join the faculty at Tuskegee Institute in Alabama. He served there until his death in 1943. In 1928 he received an honorary doctorate from Simpson College.

NATIONAL PURPOSE ▶

One of the great blessings coming to farmers was to learn about crop rotation. The soil had worn out due to continual usage over the years and Carver told farmers that by rotating crops they could put nutrients back into the soil for the next crop. Farmers' conferences proved to be the answer. Carver would send out news bulletins to the farmers of the south providing information on the latest techniques in farming. He helped the white community get over their racial prejudices. From sweet potatoes alone he created 118 products. He created entirely new markets for the products and significantly elevated the American dream for millions. Carver had brought a better life to those of his generation; few match his legacy.

Carver taught that the opposite of kindness was self-pity. Self-pity was harmful to people. Carver believed, "It is not the style of clothes one wears, neither the kind of automobile one drives, nor the amount of money one has in the bank, that counts. These mean nothing. It is simply service that measures success."[5]

Early in Carver's career as an agriculture chemist, he asked the Lord to show him the secrets of the universe. According to

Carver, God told him he could not handle that kind of knowledge. Eventually God agreed that he could handle the knowledge of a peanut, one of God's smallest creations. Carver would get up every morning at 4:00 am and pray to his Creator. It was during these early hours that God began to speak to him and many breakthroughs came into his life. It was his relationship with his heavenly Father who was also the Creator of the Universe that made the difference.

Carver's inventions for uses for soybeans, pecans, sweet potatoes, buttermilk, bleach, and axle grease are but of few of the scores of products we enjoy today because of him. Carver found over 300 products made from the peanut. Boundless curiosity moved his inquiries into areas of discovery not thought about before. God was ever part of his sense and sum of things, ever his motivating force. He saw himself as only God's helper in this work.

TRAINING FARMERS

Knowing what he knew about agriculture could only help people across the South if the information was distributed. Farmers needed to be trained. Few could read in those days so he started his traveling college. Farmers needed to see and touch. They needed demonstrations and the first step was to bring the farmers to the school each month. The second was to go to the farmers to spend the weekends with them. Along with supplies, Carver and his assistant would travel to reach the "poorest of the poor" farmers with the hope of changing their lives. He pressed the farmers to save five cents each day. At the end of a year they would have $15.65, which would pay for three acres of land and leave a reserve fund of 65 cents.

A HUMBLE MAN

Carver was born during the later days of the Civil War and died in the middle of the Second World War. He impacted the virtues of America in a remarkable way. In 1939 Carver was awarded the Roosevelt medal with the following citations: "To a scientist humbly seeking the guidance of God and a liberator to men of the white race as well as the black."[7]

His biographer, Lawrence Elliott, writes, "He slept in their cabins, usually on a cleared patch of floor, and ate at their tables, although he always contributed a sack of fresh vegetables, and often the meat. His ways were simple and his words direct, and they were soon at ease. They liked him for he listened to them…and absorbed some of his lessons."[8]

"I determined to spend my life proving to the world that it should learn to respect [Negroes] both for what they were and what they should be able to do."[6]
Carver

He never accepted money from a new discovery since he believed that his insights were gifts God had given him and he thought it might result in his forgetting his people. He had learned to identify with the poor.

On January 5, 1943, George Washington Carver died in bed. He was mourned by laborers and politicians, students and businessmen…by men and women of diverse races and creeds. His life had touched millions of people and he was greatly loved.

CARVER'S TEACHING

A student told him, "You have shown me the one race, the human race. Color of skin or form of hair mean nothing to me now, but length, and width, and breadth of soul and loving kindness mean everything."[9]

Carver taught that inspiration was "the voice of God." Science and religion would be combined to serve others. On his tombstone were the following words, "He could have added fortune to fame, but caring for neither, he found happiness and honor in being helpful to the world. Nothing is more beautiful than the loveliness of the woods before sunrise."[10]

Carver gave credit for his accomplishments to God. He would go outdoors and just listen and play with the plants just so he could listen to what God had to tell him; "God speaks to us through nature," was his motto.

In both word and deed George Washington Carver taught the world about kindness. He said, "This world is perishing for kindness."[11]

With a few exceptions, society had withheld kindness from Carver during much of his life. He knew that while the world needed farms and crops, the real problem was sensitizing people to the needs of all Americans. He did this through his actions. He taught that God's true storehouse can never be exhausted for we can learn to synthesize materials for every human need from the things that grow. He helped break down the walls in the country by teaching us that, "A man's color has nothing to do with the love he feels for his country."[12]

CARVER EXPERIENCED GOD'S KINDNESS

Nearly everything he read and heard told Carver "the Negro race was the lowest and most hopeless of God's creatures." Carver said, "I determined to spend my life proving to the world that it should learn to respect (Negroes) both for what they were and what they should be able to do." [13]

After the war and reconstruction in the South "Carver saw again the haunted eyes of the cotton-pickers, yearning only for enough to eat and a warm, dry place to sleep. Eighty-five percent of his people were desperately dependent on what they could get from the soil, and so far they had neither the skills nor the strength to do more than barely survive." [14]

Carver knew that God's promises must be claimed for suffering people. One of his favorite verses was, "I will lift up my eyes to unto the hills from whence cometh my help." [15]

The Creator gave all knowledge to men and that knowledge was intended to be used in the service of other men. Only God knows how many were blessed with the financial help of Carver. He would delight in putting money in envelopes to help the students with their tuition. No repayment was necessary. Many lives were turned around as students weren't dropping out of school for lack of finances.

Carver accepted the indignities of racial prejudice without responding with bitterness, and would later be remembered for little acts of kindness, like helping students with their courses. He helped millions redefine the word kindness in his words, actions, and life.

KINDNESS BRINGS ABOUT SELFLESSNESS

Carver believed, "How far you go in life depends on you being tender with the young, compassionate with the aged, sympathetic with the striving and tolerant of the weak and the strong. Because someday in life you will have been all of these." [17]

Carver desired most of all that his students know Jesus. He started a weekly Bible study and it quickly grew to 100 students. His love for the Bible was real and the daily time he spent in the Scriptures provided him understanding for the ways of life.

In his eight years at Tuskegee Institute, Carver declined a raise in salary. When he died in 1943 he was still earning the same $125 a month he was making when he came to the Institute over 40 years before. He felt himself to be in God's hands, the mortal instrument of a divine revelation. Later, Carver would say, "The great Creator gave us three kingdoms, the animal, the vegetable, and the mineral. Now he has added a fourth—the kingdom of synthetics." [18]

"You have shown me the one race, the human race. color of skin or form of hair mean nothing to me now, but length, and width, and breadth of soul and loving kindness mean everything." [16]

carver's student

Thomas Edison once offered Carver $175,000 a year to come and work with him. He turned it down to continue his research to help fellow Americans. Money meant nothing to Carver. He donated his life savings of $33,000 for the building of the Carver Scientist Foundation at Tuskegee.

"Every day that he lived he labored toward some tangible end that would make this earth a little richer, or healthier, or livelier, for all (mankind). And when he died all those who lived were suddenly poorer."[19]

GOD'S KINDNESS SEEN IN HIS CREATION

Eventually his reputation grew and national leaders sought out understanding from Carver. During his meetings with Congressmen who inquired of him from what books he discovered the information, his response was, "The Bible. It says that God has given us everything for our use. He has revealed to me some of the wonders of the fruit of the earth." He encouraged them to reference Genesis 1:29; "Behold, I have given you every herb that bears seed upon the face of the earth, and everything bearing seed." "To you it shall be meat. There is everything there to strengthen, nourish and keep the body alive and healthy."[20]

He asked his students, "How can any of us deny the reality around us that the most valuable things in life are God's handiwork expressed in nature? Why else would He have put the herbs and the healing ointments of the fields on this earth if He didn't mean for us to use them?"[21]

Carver's discoveries freed the south from the tyranny of "King Cotton." He restored the essence of life to millions of spent and sterile acres, then found a vigorous new crop with which to sow them. Those who could never bring themselves to break bread with him, or even to call him "Mister," prospered by his genius, and blessed it. Without ever addressing himself to the indignities heaped on black men in a white world, he did more than any single soul to bring on the day when both would live peaceably, equally, side by side.

CARVER TAUGHT CHARACTER WILL PRODUCE KINDNESS

Carver was concerned about the character of his students. He encouraged them to:

Be clean both inside and out.

Neither look up to the rich nor down to the poor.

Lose, if need be, without squealing.

Win without bragging.

Always be considerate of women, children, and old people.

Always be too brave to lie.

Always be too generous to cheat.

Always take your share of the world and let others have theirs.[22]

MODERN-DAY EXAMPLE OF KINDNESS
BROTHER BACH

It's difficult to reconstruct the thoughts you had about people you met as a child. We don't always remember what they said but we do remember certain things like "kindness." I remember a man who had been a missionary in South America for 27 years, and then returned to America to encourage others to be involved in missions. He was T.J. Bach. Apparently Brother Bach was not always the kind man we knew and loved. He grew up in Denmark and was an engineering student and apparently pretty full of himself.

One day he encountered a Christian on the street who handed a tract to him about Jesus. He tore it up and threw it on the ground in disgust. The Christian's eyes were filled with tears as they both separated. T.J. Bach was amazed that someone would weep at his response and so he went back to pick up the pieces of the tract and put it together. That night he got on his knees and asked the Lord Jesus to come into his life. He was a new person. He became a missionary to South America for 27 years and eventually the General Director of the "Evangelical Alliance Mission." As kids, one of the great experiences we had was a visit from "Brother Bach." He stayed with us in our small home and we felt honored, believe me.

When my mom shared her testimony at church she would most often wind up crying with joy. She felt embarrassed. She decided to share her concern with Brother Bach. He told her "don't feel bad about it sister…feel bad if there are no tears." His counsel was to "walk softly, speak tenderly and pray fervently."

Prior to his passing on to be with the Lord, I found myself seated beside him at a luncheon in his honor. I asked him if he had any advice for a young youth worker and what he would do differently. His response was, "If I had only loved Him [Jesus] more I could have served Him better." He said, "One day I'm going to be checking out and checking in." Heaven was just around the corner. He died at Swedish Covenant Hospital where my wife trained as a nurse. The nurses who cared for him marveled at his kindness toward all who entered his room.

REVIEW

Q. How did Carver find happiness in the world?

Q. Describe an incident when God spoke to you through His creation.

Q. Provide some reason why getting up early to commune with God is beneficial.

Q. Identification with the suffering of his people brought Carver the loyalty he richly deserved. Why was it important for suffering black people to know Carver's deep commitment to them?

Q. Why are virtuous heroes important to people?

Q. Carver linked kindness toward the young, the aged, and the weak and suffering, with success. Discuss this philosophy toward life.

Q. Carver said this world is "perishing for kindness." What did he mean?

Q. Can you think of times when people you barely knew treated you with great kindness?

Q. Which principle taught by Carver is most important to you today?

Q. Why do you think God gave Carver such incredible wisdom?

Character for Life

GOD'S PROMISE:

"In love a throne will be established; in faithfulness a man will sit on it—one from the house of David—one who in judging seeks justice and speeds the cause of righteousness" (Isaiah 16:5).

GOD'S GOAL:

For Christians to show kindness to everyone they meet.

YOUR COMMITMENT:

To be a kind person and do kind deeds.

YOUR DAILY RESPONSE:

1. Take time each day to notice other people.

2. Ask people about their day and inquire about their life with genuine care.

3. Pray that God will show you people to show kindness to.

4. Trust God to bless your life as you go about doing good to others.

FAILURE WILL MEAN:

A selfish and self-centered life.

BACKGROUND:

How do we see kindness in the life of Jesus? The willingness of Jesus Christ to offer Himself to help the spiritually destitute shows the extent of His kindness. The followers of Jesus were reminded of this quality in the life of Jesus. Having experienced the kindness of the Lord, Paul summarized how we should relate to one another with these words, "Be kind and compassionate to one another, forgiving each other, just as Christ God forgave you" (Ephesians 4:32). As we study the pages of the gospels and see the value God placed on people, we can imitate His kindness in our relationship with others. It is the kindness of God that leads us to repentance.

"Or do you show contempt for the riches of his kindness, tolerance and patience, not realizing that God's kindness leads you toward repentance?" (Romans 2:4).

"Consider therefore the kindness and sternness of God: sternness to those who fell, but kindness to you, provided that you continue in his kindness. Otherwise, you also will be cut off" (Romans 11:22).

"Now that you have tasted that the Lord is good" (1 Peter 2:3).

"And to godliness, brotherly kindness, and to brotherly kindness, love" (2 Peter 1:7).

LIVING A LIFE OF KINDNESS MEANS . . .

■ Putting others first.

■ Caring for children, the poor and ill, and the old.

■ Taking time to stop and notice ways you can help those around you.

■ Living as Jesus did.

■ Genuinely caring for people and being interested in them.

Chapter Twenty Nine: Learn more about Carver

Go to an Internet search engine.

Type in *George Washington Carver*.

Find topics 1-5 below and open up the websites.

1. Fall98 Visions: George Washington Carver's Iowa State
2. Vision-George Washington Carver
3. Character Building Stories-George Washington Carver
4. ISU Extension News Release
5. Southwest Daily Times-Opinion

chapter 30

Love—

count ludwig von zinzendorf

PURPOSE: Laying Down Your Life For Others

character trait:
Love

SUBJECT:
COUNT LUDWIG
VON ZINZENDORF
(1700-1760)

PURPOSE:
Laying Down Your Life For Others

FAMOUS QUOTE:
"I have but one compassion...tis He, tis only He."

SCRIPTURE DOCUMENTATION:
"The LORD appeared to us in the past, saying: 'I have loved you with an everlasting love; I have drawn you with loving-kindness. I will build you up again and you will be rebuilt'"
(Jeremiah 31:3-4a).

"Love is patient, love is kind. It does not envy, it does not boast, it is not proud. It is not rude, it is not self-seeking, it is not easily angered, it keeps no record of wrongs. Love does not delight in evil but rejoices with the truth. It always protects, always trusts, always hopes, always perseveres"
(1 Corinthians 13:4-7).

"And live a life of love, just as Christ loved us and gave himself up for us as a fragrant offering and sacrifice to God"
(Ephesians 5:2).

"May the Lord make your love increase and overflow for each other and for everyone else, just as ours does for you"
(1 Thessalonians 3:12).

PERSONALITY PROFILE

Zinzendorf and the Moravians can trace their origins back to fourteenth century John Hus, and even the early Apostles. As a schoolboy, Zinzendorf started the "Order of the Grain of the Mustard Seed." At the age of ten, his heart was filled with compassion to take the good news of Jesus throughout the world. Said Zinzendorf, "I have but one compassion...tis He, tis only He." Zinzendorf wrote more than 2,000 hymns and many of them describe the sufferings of Christ and expressions of personal devotion to Jesus.

Born May 26, 1700, Zinzendorf descended from a noble family in the Archduchy of Austria. He lost his mother as a child. His father was the Minister of State in Saxony, but died early in Zinzendorf's life. As a result, Zinzendorf's grandmother raised him.

Zinzendorf learned early on the secret of prevailing prayer. So active had he been in establishing circles for prayer that on leaving college at age 16, he handed his famous professor Franke a list of seven praying societies.

Zinzendorf was a poet, pastor, teacher, missionary, theologian, and church statesman. He prayed for fresh outpouring of God's Spirit and in 1727 the Moravians experienced their Pentecost. John Greenfield wonders, "Was there ever in the whole of church history such an astonishing prayer meeting as that which began in 1727, [and] went on one hundred years? It was known as the 'hourly intercession.' It means that by relays of brothers and sisters, prayer without ceasing was made to God for all the work and (needs) of the church."[1]

Zinzendorf started Christian communities throughout Europe and America that were characterized by "intercession for the nations" and were called the "Watch of the Lord." He began "Love Feasts" where the focus was on the "Lamb who laid down His life for us." This drew the hearts of people together and set them ablaze to reach the nations for Jesus. Zinzendorf supervised the instruction of missionary candidates in medicine, geography, and languages.

Count Ludwig Von Zinzendorf's biographer called him "the knight of Jesus Christ." Isaac Watts, the hymn writer, thought of him as "a person of uncommon zeal and piety, and of evangelistic spirit."[2] John Albertini described the love of Zinzendorf as "a lifelong pursuit of God." "It was love to Christ that glowed in the heart of the child, the same love that thrilled his middle-age; the same love that inspired his every endeavor."[3] Phillip Doddridge referred to him as "the blessed herald of the Redeemer."[4] Theologian Karl Barth said of him, "His all-absorbing interest was to implement the idea of a free connections (association) of churches, based on their common love of the Savior."[5]

NATURAL LAW AND VATTEL

There is much to be learned from the Moravians and their abandonment to the welfare of the nations to which God sent them. Hugo Groitus stated that the "Law of the Nations" is based on "the Golden Rule" of Jesus. "Self-interest" would not be the primary basis of foreign policy decisions, but more importantly, what is good for the country one seeks to serve.

One of the most influential writers on "Natural Law" was Emmerich de Vattel. A "Founder" of America who was much influenced by Vattel was Benjamin Franklin. In December 1775 Franklin expressed his gratitude for W.F. Duma's book on Vattel. Said Franklin, "I am much obliged by the kind present you have made us of your edition of Vattel. It came to us in good season, when the circumstances of a rising state make it necessary frequently to consult the Law of Nations. According, that copy which is kept, has been continually in the hands of members of our congress, now sitting."[6]

Vattel's approach to "Natural Law" was rooted in the teachings of Jesus on (agape) love. Vattel, however, demonstrated that the Christian way of "loving your neighbor as you love yourself" needed to apply to nations as well as individuals. Vattel maintained that nations should organize its citizens into societies with the purpose of developing "agape love" between them. Churches certainly try to do this, but nations?

Vattel took it a step further, saying nations should "love each other."[7] This was the principle our "Founders" embraced as they labored over the Constitution. This was the "American System."

Vattel wrote of three principle objectives of good government: to provide for the necessities of the nation; to procure the true happiness of the nation; and for a nation to fortify

There would be no virtue except through Him...no other happiness but to be near Him, to think of Him and do His pleasure, no other self denial but to be deprived of Him and His blessings, no other calamity but to displease Him, no other life but in Him. The Moravians found nothing for moaning or pity at "the cross," but only the source of an intense joy and gratitude, which made them always ready to testify for Jesus.

"That we are born and die here, let us not love this world; let us ever, through love of God, pass on hence, let us by charity dwell among the heights, by that charity wherewith we love God. Let us during this our earthly pilgrimage be ever occupied with the thought that we shall not always be here, and by leading good lives, we shall be preparing a place whence we shall never pass on. Thou hast made us for Thyself, and the heart of man is restless until it finds its rest in Thee." [8]

St. Augustine

itself against external attacks. Vattel went on to say that true happiness comes from the love of a virtue that is inspired by piety (the love of God and one's country). Piety and religion are key to a healthy nation.

When Vattel spoke of seeking the "happiness of the nation," he was not thinking about self-indulgent actions and attitudes but the basic necessities of a people. Vattel pointed out that, "people may be unhappy in the midst of all earthly enjoyments, and in the possession of the greatest riches."[9]

Said Vattel, "The desire of happiness is the powerful spring that puts man in motion: felicity (happiness)...ought to be the grand object of the public will."[10] It is the duty of those who form or represent this public will (the rulers of the nation) to labor for the happiness of the people, to watch continually over it, and to promote it to the utmost of their power.

There is no question that Emmerich de Vattel was the favorite writer in America on the "Law of the Nations." Vattel's material was even used in college textbooks. In court proceedings from 1789 to 1820, Vattel was cited more than Grotius and Puffendorf; his influence grew. Those citing Vattel in legal cases and government documents were: Benjamin Franklin, John Adams, James Wilson, Alexander Hamilton, James Madison, John Jay, and John Marshall. John Marshall, during his thirty-four years as Chief Justice of the U.S. Supreme Court, quoted Vattel by far the most among all authors on the "Law of the Nations."

Vattel's principles included those of a "just war." Vattel expressed that governments should not be changed for "light and transient reasons, but only after a long chain of abuses to the fundamental rights of the people, with repeated requests for redress of grievance, which were refused."[11] A modern-day example of this might be seen in Iraq. Abuses of the rights of the people of Iraq required civilized nations who believed in the "Law of the Nations" to form a coalition to overthrow its tyrant president.

If nations care only of their "self-interest" or "strategic relationships," they would not likely be moved with compassion to help millions of people suffering under a tyrant. This was part of the "Law of the Nations" and "The Golden Rule." According to Vattel, a government can be changed if they fail to meet the unalienable rights of people—life, liberty, and the pursuit of happiness.

It fell to Jefferson to write the draft of The Declaration of Independence. Although Jefferson was a strong proponent of the philosophy of John Locke, who believed that mankind had a right to "life, liberty and property," the inclusion of the phrase "life, liberty, and the pursuit of happiness" reflected the philosophy and impact of Vattel. Vattel believed that happiness was one of the three unalienable rights of mankind.

A MORAVIAN COMMUNITY

In describing the Moravians, John Wesley writes, "With a church whose conversation is in heaven…as they have all one Lord and one faith, so they are all partakers of one Spirit, the Spirit of meekness and love, which uniformly and continually animates all their conversations."[13]

The Moravians sang continually, they especially enjoyed the Warrior songs, which brought deliverance to the communities and kept their pulse beating for missions.

A Moravian minister spoke of the Moravians commitment to Jesus as "the Lamb of God. It is impossible to utter any divine truth, or to speak anything, which one might call complete without mentioning the Lamb, our Savior. This must be the anointing, and the salt, the principle ingredient of every matter, of every sigh of every writing, of every sermon, yea of every thought."[14]

The last words of Zinzendorf's father were, "My dear son, they ask me to bless you, but you are more blessed than I am; although even now I feel as if I were already standing before the throne of Jesus."[15]

Robert Ellis Thompson said, "No sacrifice is more acceptable to God than zeal for souls. All true zeal for God is a zeal for love, mercy, and goodness."[16]

ZINZENDORf'S LOVE fOR JESUS

In telling the story of Zinzendorf and the Moravians, one is confronted with such a love for the Savior that it feels there is nothing comparable in the world today. Of course this may not be true, but the abandonment to the Lord Jesus and the love for His presence the Moravians displayed must have been especially dear to the heart of God.

Zinzendorf's goal was "to seek souls, souls in order that Jesus may receive those who love Him and His Kingdom may be inhabited. That is my work."[17] His passion was his lifelong pursuit and he was preoccupied with the person of Jesus.

To "love Jesus and His blessed presence" was his goal. There was no other happiness than happiness in Jesus. He preached "the religion of the heart" and the Moravians sought to bring

"The true measure of loving God is to love Him without measure."[12]

st. Bernard of clairvaux

The Marshall Plan
The world of suffering people looks to us for leadership. Their thoughts, however, are not concentrated alone on this problem. They have more immediate and terribly pressing concerns where the mouthful of food will come from, where they will find shelter tonight, and where they will find warmth. Along with the great problem of maintaining the peace, we must solve the problem of the pittance of food, of clothing and coal and homes. Neither of these problems can be solved alone.

– George C. Marshall
November 1945

"If thou didst know the whole Bible by heart, and the sayings of all the philosophers, what would all that profit thee without the love of God, and without His grace? Vanity of vanities; all is vanity except to love God and serve Him alone." [19]

Thomas à Kempis

Christians together in a common practical discipleship, which they believed was worth more than a "sea of knowledge." The joy of the Lord experienced by the community influenced travelers from all over the world.

Zinzendorf believed that since Christ had atoned for the sins of man, man no longer was forced into eternal penitence but instead was free to love and adore God. To attain salvation was not merely to believe in God and Christ, one had to learn to love Him.

"To Zinzendorf salvation was not a process of guilt, pain, sin and distress, but a joyful apprehension of a loving Father, persistently, yet gently leading his child into a new life of happy companionship with himself." [18]

Zinzendorf taught the Moravians that they must seek nothing for themselves, no seat of honor, no report of fame, like the cab-horses in London, the Count said, Moravians must wear blinkers and be blind to every danger and to every snare

HOW DOES GOD'S LOVE DIFFER FROM MAN'S IDEA OF LOVE?

There are various Greek words for the word "love." Two words used are "eros" and "agape." Both eros and phileo are limited in the sense that they do not include justice, liberty, and compassion for all. Phileo and eros can become exclusive.

EROS	AGAPE	PHILEO
Sexual and acquisitive	Sacrificial giving	To like, to be fond of
Seeks to gain its life	Seeks to lose its life for others	To care about
Egocentric love	Unselfish love	Desire the best
The desire to posses is at the heart of "eros"	Find its greatest joy in giving	Love for neighbor, stranger
Depends on the beauty, worth, and quality of the object and loves it	Not drawn by the beauty of the object	Covenant faithfulness
Selective and exclusive	Loves and creates value in the object	Loving behavior
Depends on performance, beauty or gifting of individual. When person loses his/her gift, ability or ability to perform, eros is lost.	Universal	Friendship
	Seeks the welfare of all	
	Seeks justice for all	
	Seeks liberty for all	
	Compassion	
	God's love in Christ	

and conceit. A Moravian must be content to suffer, to die, and be forgotten.

Zinzendorf taught believers, "Nothing ought to be so valuable to them as the consciousness, that (Jesus) was always near them…that they could tell Him everything, and that He Himself could look into their hearts. They ought to regard and listen to Him above all things and believe, to a certainty, that He alone was their best, and dearest, and most faithful friend. He [Jesus] ought to be their first thought, when they awake in the morning, they ought to spend the whole day in His presence, bring all their complaints before Him, expect all assistance from Him, conclude their laborers with Him, and in His company retire to rest." [20]

ZINZENDORF'S LOVE FOR OTHER CHRISTIANS

The Moravians believed that "fellowship" (koinonea) was the third Sacrament of the Church, since it breaks down all barriers of creed and constitution, of taste, outlook, class, and race—since the Lamb (Jesus) is at the center of the fellowship. They would meet at least three times a day, beginning early in the morning. On the Lord's Day they would meet all day long and would end the day with singing and marching around the grounds of the community.

The community of believers must have an oneness of purpose. The themes of many of the songs were exhortations to seek heart-felt unity, "Christian hearts, in love united, seek alone in Jesus rest; Has He not your love excited? Then let love inspire each breast. Members—on our Head depending, Lights—reflecting Him, our Sun, Brethren—His commands attending. We in Him, our Lord, are one." [21]

ZINZENDORF'S LOVE FOR THOSE IN DISTANT LANDS

The simple motive of the brethren for sending missionaries to distant nations was and is an ardent desire to promote the salvation of their fellow men, by making known to them the gospel of our Savior Jesus Christ. It grieved them to hear of so many thousands and millions of the human race sitting in darkness and groaning beneath the yoke of sin and the tyranny of Satan; and remembering the glorious promises given in the Word of God, that the heathen also should be the reward of the sufferings and death of Jesus; and considering His commandment to His followers, to go into all the world and preach the gospel to every creature, they were filled with

St. Francis of Assisi was devoted to Jesus Christ. With that devotion came a commitment to a life of preaching, service and voluntary poverty. Many are familiar with his book *The Imitation of Christ,* revealing his devotional life. He started a brotherhood called the "Franciscans," which commited themselves to learning and serving. In 1205, he performed charities among the lepers and began working on the restoration of dilapidated churches. In 1208, one day during Mass, he heard God's call telling him to go out into the world and, according to the text of Matthew 10:5–14, to possess nothing, but to do good everywhere. Francis began preaching. He gathered around him 12 disciples who became the original brothers of his order. St. Francis loved God's Creation and expressed his adoration of God through his "Canticle of the Sun," a poem of praise for God and His Creation. His devotion to Christ has inspired hospitals and acts of mercy through "Catholic Charities" serving the needy around the world.

confident hopes that if they went forth in obedience unto, and believing in His word, their labor would not be in vain. The Moravians had learned that the secret of loving the souls of men was found in loving the Savior of men.

On October 8, 1732, a Dutch ship left the Copenhagen harbor bound for the West Indies. On board were the two first Moravian missionaries, John Leonard Dober, a potter, and David Nitschman, a carpenter. Both were skilled speakers and ready to sell themselves into slavery to reach the slaves of the West Indies.

As the ship slipped away, they lifted up a cry that would one day become the rallying call for all Moravian missionaries. "May the Lamb that was slain receive the reward of His sufferings."[22] The Moravians' passion for souls was surpassed only by their passion for the Lamb of God, Jesus Christ.

JESUS EXPRESSED HIS LOVE FOR:

◆ For his disciples—"Having loved his own who were in the world, he now showed them the full extent of his love" (John 13:1b).

◆ For those who did not believe in Him— "Jesus looked at him and loved him. 'One thing you lack. Go, sell everything you have and give to the poor, and you will have treasure in heaven. Then come, follow me'" (Mark 10:21).

◆ For His enemies who crucified Him—"Jesus said, 'Father, forgive them for they do not know what they are doing'" (Luke 23:34).

◆ For His Father in Heaven—"But the world must learn that I love the Father and that I do exactly what my Father has commanded me" (John 14:31a).

◆ For all those who come to Him—"Whoever has my commands and obeys them, he is the one who loves me. He who loves me will be loved by my Father, and I too will love him and show myself to him" (John 14:21).

◆ For the Church—"And live a life of love, just as Christ loved us and gave himself up for us as a fragrant offering and sacrifice to God" (Ephesians 5:2). "Husbands, love your wives, just as Christ loved the church and gave himself for her" (Ephesians 5:25).

◆ For you and me—"So that Christ may dwelt in your hearts through faith. And I pray that you, being rooted and established in love, may have power, together with all the saints, to grasp how wide and long and high and deep is the love of Christ, and to know this love that surpasses knowledge—that you may be filled to the measure of all the fullness of God" (Ephesians 3:17-19).

"Our Lamb has conquered, let us follow Him."[23] David Smithers writes, "The Moravians recognized themselves in debt to the world as the trustees of the gospel. They were taught to embrace a lifestyle of self-denial, sacrifice and prompt obedience. They followed the call of the Lamb to go anywhere and with an emphasis upon the worst and hardest places as having the first claim. No soldiers of the cross have ever been bolder as pioneers, more patient or persistent in difficulties, more heroic in suffering, or more entirely devoted to Christ and the souls of men than the Moravian Brotherhood."[24]

The final instructions from Zinzendorf to the missionaries were to "live humbly among the lost, never lording it over them; preach the crucified Christ immediately and watch for individuals seeking after truth."[25]

THE MORAVIAN REVIVAL

The Moravian revival swept through the world, affecting people in all classes of society, from the poorest to the richest and the highest of the ranks of society. Nations such as America, England, India, Scotland, Africa, Western Europe, and many other lands were ultimately set ablaze from the fire bands of this revival. The hearts of well-known leaders were set afire by the blaze God started in the Moravians.

If Zinzendorf was alive and in America today, he would likely say, "The greatest challenge Christians face in life is to be abandoned to Jesus throughout our lives. His agenda is to be our agenda, His passions are to be our passions, His longings are to become our longings."[26]

For those of us who live in America, we are confronted with many needs throughout the day. To have a "first love" for Jesus is much like when a person first gets married and is overwhelmed that another person could love him or her so much. Following Jesus is simply loving Him with all our hearts. When we see things coming between Jesus and us, we need the courage to confess the sin, ask for forgiveness, and allow Jesus to restore us to the intimacy we once enjoyed. First love for Jesus is what He is after and what we long for deep down inside.

MODERN-DAY EXAMPLE OF LOVE
BOB PIERCE

Bob Pierce was the founder of "Samaritan's Purse" and "World Vision." He was also one of the pioneers of "Youth for Christ." During the Korean War "Dr. Bob," as he was known, became involved in helping orphans. He started the Korean Orphan Choir and brought the fatherless children to America to introduce the orphans of Korea to Americans. No doubt all who heard these children with their cherubic voices had their hearts stirred.

Out of these efforts a ministry was born and "World Vision" became a household name for millions of Americans who had the joy of helping orphans on a monthly basis. During the 50's and 60's the ministry spread to other countries and has touched the lives of tens of thousands of children. Bob was a remarkable communicator and to hear him on the radio empty his heart of love and compassion for the children of the world was a moving experience. Many emotions were stirred and people partnered with Dr. Bob and his vision.

Dr. Bob's involvement in other countries cost him in terms of relationships with his family. He would readily admit he was not a success in his own home. He told me about his encounters with the Lord in the early 70's where God had done something wonderful in his life. He had experienced a new revelation of God. A deeper love flowed from his heart for others.

I picked Dr. Bob up at his hotel prior to his participation as a guest on the "700 Club." What a joy it was to hear him pray for God to be glorified. He touched the heart of God through his prayers.

In 1977, I was traveling to Calcutta, India with Loren Cunningham of Youth with a Mission (YWAM). Four of my heroes were in Calcutta (Mark Buntain, Mother Teresa, Bob Pierce and Loren Cunningham). We were about to leave Calcutta when I learned that Bob Pierce had just returned from delivering a helicopter to missionaries in New Guinea and was in Calcutta. It had been two years since I had seen him and I was anxious to meet him with the hope that Loren could interview him for a film project we were working on at the time.

I knew Dr. Bob was sick from leukemia but I didn't know how sick he was. After learning he was in a hotel I decided to visit him. He was pretty sick, but after I knocked I could hear his weak voice asking me to come in. After hearing about his trip I asked him if Loren could interview him and, weak as he was, he wanted to do the interview. What an interview it was! I saw how God empowers people when they obey Him.

He began to talk about God's love for India. He was alive, animated, and filled with love for the people of India. After the interview, he was exhausted and asked me to travel with him to a Chinese Church he had started in 1949.

When asked to speak, he had no strength and asked me to help him. He leaned hard on my shoulders as he used all his strength to get to the platform and challenge the Chinese Christians to get out of their comfort zone and tell the Indians about Jesus. Dr. Bob was a vessel of love to the Chinese. He had exhausted all his strength to exhort them.

After his message he simply collapsed in my arms and I pretty much carried him to his seat. I learned so much from Dr. Bob. Caring for people when you are weak, sick, and lonely is part of the package of following Jesus. As a young mission worker, I felt honored to have these moments with him.

REVIEW

Q. Are there groups of Christians today that remind you of the Moravians' passion for Christ?

Q. Why did the Moravians refer to Jesus as "the Lamb"?

Q. How did Zinzendorf describe salvation?

Q. Since their 100-year prayer meeting spanned several generations, how do you think the Moravians passed on their commitments to their children?

Q. If fellowship (koinonea) was considered a "sacrament," how would this change the way Christians relate to one another?

Q. The Moravians knew that "distractions" would eventually destroy their zeal for God. What are the main distractions people in your country face today?

Q. What are the implications for a Christian to consider himself or herself a stranger and a Pilgrim?

Q. What is the supreme goal of being a "Pilgrim"?

Q. What is the secret of loving people?

Q. What benefits would come to Christians if they "chose to wear blinders"?

Character for Life

GOD'S PROMISE:
"The LORD appeared to us in the past, saying: 'I have loved you with an everlasting love; I have drawn you with loving-kindness. I will build you up again and you will be rebuilt'" (Jeremiah 31:3-4a).

GOD'S GOAL:
For Christians to show Christ's love to everyone.

YOUR COMMITMENT:
To live a life filled with love.

YOUR DAILY RESPONSE:

1. To see others as Jesus sees them.

2. To draw on Jesus' everlasting love.

3. To live this life on earth with purpose but focus on eternal things.

4. To be willing to look past other people's faults in order that they may find salvation.

FAILURE WILL MEAN:

Living a life where hate and selfishness rule.

BACKGROUND:

Human love is calculating—never carried beyond itself, it is not of the true nature of love. The characteristic of love is that it is spontaneous. It bursts up in extraordinary ways; it is never premeditated. If you love someone, you are not blind to their defects but you see their promise and potential. God sees all our crudities and defects, but He also sees the ideal for us. He sees every man perfect in Christ. His love for me is the basis of my love for others.

In love, God is sensitive to our sufferings (Psalm 31:7). He answers our prayers (Psalm 66:20, 69:16) and remains slow to anger (Psalm 86:15, 103:8). In love God provides redemption (Psalm 130:7) and teaches us His ways (Psalm 119:64, 124). God remains committed to fulfill His purpose in us (Psalm 138:8).

Only in Christ do we grasp the fact that God's love encompasses all of humanity. Only in Christ do we realize the depth of the love that impelled Him to sacrifice Himself on our behalf. We need to remember that it was not for God's friends that the Son sacrificed Himself. It was for His enemies: "You see, at just the right time, when we were still powerless, Christ died for the ungodly" (Romans 5:6).

LIVING A LIFE FULL OF LOVE MEANS . . .

■ Putting others first.

■ Sharing Jesus' love with everyone.

■ Genuinely caring about others' needs and concerns.

■ Loving your neighbor as yourself.

■ Allowing God's love to shine through you.

■ Thinking less of yourself and more of other people.

■ Living a Christ-like life.

When my wife and I were married, the minister officiating read a prayer you might enjoy by Dr. Louis H. Evans, the Pastor of a Presbyterian Church in Washington D.C. This prayer left more of an impression on my wife and I than anything else in the service.

MARRIAGE PRAYER

"O God of love, Thou has established marriage for the welfare and happiness of mankind. Thine was the plan, and only with Thee can we work it out with joy. Bless this husband. Bless him as provider of nourishment and raiment, and sustain him in all the exactions and pressures of his battle for bread. May his strength be her protection, his character be her boast and her pride, and may he so live that she will find in him the haven for which the heart of woman truly longs.

"Bless this loving wife. Give her tenderness that will make her great, a deep sense of understanding, and great faith in Thee. Give her that inner beauty of soul that never fades, that eternal youth that is found in holding fast the things that never age.

"Teach them that marriage is not living merely for each other; it is two uniting and joining hands to serve Thee. Give them a great spiritual purpose in life. May they seek first the Kingdom of God and His righteousness, and the other things shall be added unto them.

"May they never take each other's love for granted, but always experience that breathless wonder that exclaims, 'Out of all this world, you have chosen me.'

"When life is done and the sun is setting may they be found then as now, hand in hand, still thanking God for each other. May they serve Thee happily, faithfully, together, until at last one shall lay the other into the arms of God.

"This we ask through Jesus Christ, great Lover of our souls."[27]

Chapter Thirty: Learn more about Zinzendorf

Go to an Internet search engine.
Type in *Ludwig Von Zinzendorf's Love*.
Find topics 1-6 below and open up the websites.
1. Zinzendorf's Theology
2. Moravians asked to settle on Zinzendorf's land
3. The Task: Archive
4. Pastor's Pages Academic works Zinzendorf the Father of Modern Missions
5. Moravian Women
6. Pietism and Small Groups

chapter 31

Patience— George Mason

PURPOSE: The High Cost of Discipleship

character trait:

Patience

SUBJECT:
GEORGE MASON
(1725-1792)

PURPOSE:
The High Cost of Discipleship

FAMOUS QUOTE:
"Our patience will achieve more than our force."

SCRIPTURE DOCUMENTATION:

"The Lord is not slow in keeping his promise, as some understand slowness. He is patient with you, not wanting anyone to perish, but everyone to come to repentance" (2 Peter 3:9).

"Be patient, then, brothers, until the Lord's coming. See how the farmer waits for the land to yield its valuable crop and how patient he is for the autumn and spring rains. You too, be patient and stand firm, because the Lord's coming is near" (James 5:7-8).

"You need to persevere so that when you have done the will of God, you will receive what he has promised" (Hebrews 10:36).

"Let us fix our eyes on Jesus, the author and perfecter of our faith, who for the joy set before him endured the cross, scorning its shame, and sat down at the right hand of the throne of God" (Hebrews 12:2).

PERSONALITY PROFILE

Mason lost his father at the age of ten and grew up under the guardianship of his mother, Ann. John Mercer, his uncle, helped prepare him for life by taking responsibility for his education.

Fortunately, young Mason had access to his uncle's wonderful library of 1,500 books, a third of which were on law. He became part of his uncle's family, which helped prepare him for a remarkable life.

George Mason was a planter, a Revolutionary statesman and Constitutionalist. He came from a family of Virginians who immigrated from England after the battle of Worcester. Prior to 1775, Mason was more of a consultant and never in the center of things. His health, the loss of his first wife, and his large family prevented him from getting more involved.

Mason is rightly revered as the principle author of the "Virginia Declaration of Rights." Few men have had more of an impact on America than George Mason. He became a mentor to other prominent Virginian revolutionaries as they sought to lay the foundations for a new government. "Mason gave us concrete expressions for those 'unalienable rights' that belong to every American citizen and that today are the bedrock of our democracy."[1]

Pierce, who provided sketches at the Convention said, "Mr. Mason is a man of remarkably strong powers, and possesses a clear and copious understanding. He is able and convincing in debate, steady and firm in his principles."[2]

George Mason was truly one of the most famous revolutionary statesmen from Virginia. He is known as the "Father of the Bill of Rights." His insistence on the necessity of the "Bill of Rights" brought about the first "Ten Amendments" of the Constitution, which he practically wrote.

MASON'S IMPACT ON VARIOUS PRESIDENTS

Twentieth-century President Harry Truman, while visiting Guniston Hall, (Mason's home) commented saying, "Too few Americans realize the vast debt we owe to George Mason. His immortal 'Declaration of Human Rights' in 1776 was one of the finest and loftiest creations ever to come from the mind of man."[3]

According to Thomas Jefferson, Mason was, "A man of the first order of wisdom among those who acted on the theatre of the revolution, of expansive mind, profound judgment, cogent in argument, learned in the lore of our former Constitution. The wisest man in his generation."[5] Jefferson continued, "I had many occasional and strenuous coadjutors in debate, and [Mason] was one most steadfast, able and zealous."[6]

James Madison leaned heavily on Mason to bring lasting solutions in laying the foundations for the future of the country. Madison wrote, "My first acquaintance with him [Mason] was in the convention of Virginia in 1776. I retained however a perfect impression that he was a leading champion for the Instruction (for independence) that he was the author of the Declaration (Virginia Declaration of Rights) and that he was the Master Builder of the (Virginia) Constitution and its main expositor and supporter throughout the discussion…none who differed from him on some points will deny that he sustained throughout the proceedings of the body the high character of a powerful reasoner, a profound statesman and a devoted republican."[7]

MASON'S ACCOMPLISHMENTS

In 1776, Mason's outstanding contribution as a constitutionalist came by framing the Declaration of Rights. This became the basis for the first ten amendments to the Constitution of the United States. He thought that the convention did not give adequate attention to the rights of its citizens. His objection was simply that "there is no Declaration of Rights."

Mason was mostly concerned, however, that there was not an immediate ban on slave trading, He feared that the federal government would destroy state laws and would become a monarchy or a tyrannical aristocracy and the nation would sink to a weak country.

In 1787, Mason was one of the five most frequent speakers at the Philadelphia Constitutional Convention. Mason believed

Mason was a pioneer proclaiming the "rights of man," including the free exercise of religion. Believed Mason, "All men are equally entitled to the free exercise of religion according to the dictates of conscience; and that it is the mutual duty of all to practice christian forbearance, love, and charity, towards each other."[4]

NATIONAL PURPOSE

in the rule of reason and in the centrality of the "natural rights of man." Mason was justice of the Fairfax County court between 1754 and 1779. He wrote an open letter opposing the "Stamp Act" and explained the position of the colonists. He was trustee of the city of Alexandria from 1754 until 1779. In 1789, the first Congress convened in New York and James Madison, then a Congressman, introduced a series of amendments to the Constitution that formed the Bill of Rights. This was no doubt the most important contribution Mason gave to the country. For over 200 years Mason's influence has shaped the thinking of nations. People throughout the world are insisting that all people, "are by nature equally free and independent, and have certain inherent (God given) rights."[9] This is the great legacy of George Mason.

MASON'S WIFE AND FAMILY

At the age of 25, Mason married Anne Eilbeck and they built a new home, called "Gunston Hall." Together they brought nine children into the world. Mason and his wife were married 23 years. Anne died in 1773, leaving Mason with a family of children to care for. Upon her death, he said, "In the beauty of her person and the sweetness of her disposition, she was equaled by few, and excelled by none of her sex. She was blessed with a clear and sound judgment, a gentle and benevolent heart and humble mind; with an even calm and cheerful temper in a very unusual degree. Affable to all but intimate with few, her modest virtues shunned the public eye. Superior to passions and envy, a stranger to altercations of every kind, and content with the blessings of private station, she placed all her happiness here, where it is to be found, in her own family."[10] He continued, "An easy and agreeable companion, a kind neighbor, a steadfast friend, a human mistress, a prudent and tender mother, a faithful, affectionate and most obliging wife, charitable to the poor and pious to her Maker, her virtue and religion were unmixed with hypocrisy or ostentation."[11]

On the loss of his daughter's little girl, Mason wrote, "I most sincerely console with you for the loss of your dear little girl, but it is our duty to but submit with all the resignation human nature is capable of to the Divine Providence which bestows upon us our blessings, and consequently has a right to take them away. A few years of experience will convince us that those things which at the time they happened we regarded as great misfortunes have provided our greatest blessings. Your dear baby has died innocent and blameless, and has been called away by an all wise and merciful Creator, most probably from a life of misery and misfortune, and most certainly to one of happiness and bliss."[12]

In a letter to his son he wrote, "Live a frugal lifestyle, and without parade or ostentation, avoid all unnecessary expense, attend to business and strict integrity to the interest of your correspondence and enter into no engagements which you have the almost certain means of performing."[13]

THE RIGHTS OF MAN

Mason wrote, "We all come as equals into this world, and equals shall we go out of it. All men are by nature born equally free and independent. To protect the weaker from the injuries and insults of the stronger were the reasons societies were formed; every society, all government, and every kind of civil compact is, or ought to be, calculated for the general good and safety of the community."[14]

Mason believed that "life, liberty and property were central human rights. And that a man's life should not be at the mercy of another."[15] Mason also believed in the "Natural (God Given) Rights of mankind." Mason had come to John Locke's viewpoint, "that a republic had to begin with the formal, legally binding commitment that individuals had inalienable rights that were superior to any government."[16]

In the Virginia Bill of Rights Mason wrote, "That all men are by nature equally free and independent, and have certain inherent rights, of which, when they enter into a state of society, they cannot by any compact deprive or divest their posterity; namely, the enjoyment of life and liberty, with the means of acquiring and possessing property, and pursuing and obtaining happiness and safety."[17]

Believed Mason, "Government, is, or ought to be an institution for the common benefit, protection, and security of the people, nation, or community."[19] Mason believed that life, liberty and property were central human rights.

Mason regarded virtue, or the willingness to subordinate private desires for the good of the community, as the most important element in laying the foundations for a country. "Pursuit of selfish interest in the public good, is not only mean and sordid, but extremely short-sighted and foolish." Freedom Mason wished for everyone but it must be the freedom that comes with wisdom."[20]

"God sometimes permits us to be perplexed so that we may learn patience and better recognize our dependence upon Him."[18]
Thomas à Kempis

NATIONAL PURPOSE

Mason believed, "That religion, or the duty which we owe to our Creator, and the manner of discharging it, can be directly only by reason and conviction, not by force or violence, and therefore, all men are equally entitled to the free exercise of religion according to the dictates of conscience; and that it is the mutual duty of all to practice Christian forbearance, and love toward each other." [21]

MASON'S PERSONAL REFLECTIONS

Order and patience characterized the remarkable life of Mason. He planned everything in great detail; the home he built for his family is one example. He had nine children and provided small fireplaces throughout the home to keep them warm in the winter time. He kept his own books and planted his crops. He had much to be thankful for and thankful he was. Mason's favorite verse was, "From everyone who has been given much, much will be demanded; and from the one who has been entrusted with much, much more will be asked," (Luke 12:48b). A prayer book was also a part of his life. Mason was a man of history. "He had charted his way so thoroughly through English constitutional history that every significant precedent was recorded in his mind as a guidepost for future reference." [23] He saw order in the world and was committed to the "Natural Law" view of reality.

He must have lived in his library and absorbed the wisdom of the ages. He was apparently not a man who sought office and did not need the acclaim of others. It came to him, however.

MASON STOOD ALONE

The pressure on Mason to sign on to the "Constitution" and the pressures from his friend George Washington to sign it must have been difficult to stand up against. Mason was unwilling to sign it since it did not sufficiently limit the government's power from infringing on the rights of citizens. He was willing to "stand alone" when most of the "signers" disagreed with him.

In March 1789, Mason summarized his position; "You know the friendship which has long existed (indeed from our early youth) between General Washington and myself. I believe there are few men in whom he placed greater confidence; but it is possible my opposition to the new government, both as a member of the national and of the Virginia Convention, may have altered the case. In this important trust, I am truly conscious of having acted from the purest motives of honesty, and love to my country, according to that measure of judgment which God has bestowed on me, and I would not forfeit the approbation of my own mind for the approbation of any man, or all the men upon the earth."[24]

This lack of a "bill of rights" eventually was brought to the attention of Jefferson, who was Ambassador to France. Jefferson, a close personal friend of Madison, wrote Madison from France that he liked the "Constitution" but was "alarmed by the omission of a bill of rights. "Were I in America I would advocate it (a bill of rights) warmly 'till nine states should have adopted it," he said.[25]

THE WISDOM OF HAVING PATIENCE

Mason's authoring of the "Bill of Rights" greatly strengthened the Constitution. Mason's willingness to stand alone paid off. Mason's response was, "I have received much satisfaction from the Amendments to the federal Constitution, which have been lately passed by the House of Representatives." Mason wrote, "I hope they will also pass the Senate. With two or three further Amendments...I could cheerfully put my hand and heart to the new Government."[27]

Mason's leadership was evidenced in the fact that he was a man of principle and patience. His decision not to sign the Constitution proved in the long run to have been well-founded. His most important reason, however, was that the Constitution did not resolve the issue of slavery and in his final speech at Richmond he insisted that slavery was diabolical and disgraceful to mankind.

RELIGIOUS FREEDOM FOR FUTURE GENERATIONS

Mason realized that to protect the liberty we have been given, there must be a willingness to lay down our private desires. Selfish desires would eventually undermine our republic. Daniel L. Dreisback said, "Mason was a deft, untiring strategist in the bitter contests to guarantee religious freedom and to end the legal favors enjoyed by the established church in Virginia."[28] Dreisback continued, "He was a towering figure in the struggle to craft a distinctively American doctrine of religious liberty and church state relations for both the Commonwealth and the nation."[29]

"Mr. Mason is a man of remarkably strong powers, and possesses a clear and copious understanding. He is able and convincing in debate, steady and firm in his principles."[26]
William Pierce

The slaves in America had waited patiently for over two hundred years for freedom and despite his efforts with the bill of rights, Mason did not know how to bring emancipation about.

The fact that slavery was not dealt with at the "beginnings" of the nation almost destroyed the republic in the next century. Mason maintained, "Our patience will achieve more than our force." [31] Mason exhibited great patience but in the end it proved to be necessary.

Mason desired to end slavery but did not know of a way to end slavery while ensuring economic prosperity to plantation owners who depended on slave labor. Mason wrote, "Slavery is daily contaminating the mind and morals of our People. We become callous to the dictates of humanity, and all the finer feelings of the soul. We [Americans] lose that idea of the dignity of man which the hand of Nature had implanted in us, for great and useful purposes." [32]

MODERN-DAY EXAMPLE OF PATIENCE
FRITZ KLEIN

Fritz Klein is one of my heroes. I first met Fritz and his wife, Linda, when we lived in Kailua-Kona, Hawaii. About 40 families had moved to Hawaii to help start a Christian university, which ultimately became the "University of the Nations." All of us had responsibilities and Fritz had his. He was responsible to care for the huge grounds on the campus. He cheerfully carried out these duties and helped turn the jungle we found to a beautiful location after a few years.

Fritz had a hero and he was Abraham Lincoln. In his spare time he would memorize the speeches of the 16th President. His heart was stirred with the words of Lincoln. He must have thought how Lincoln would have been saddened to know that his country had drifted from its original convictions upheld during the "Revolutionary Days." Each day all of us had special times of prayer for one another and the nations of the earth. Each Saturday evening our community had "Love Feasts" with a dinner and special music and activities. One night a tall man dressed just like Lincoln showed up. It was Fritz! With his 6'3" frame he looked so much like President Lincoln it was scary. Then, slowly, deliberately he took a place behind a podium and delivered one of Lincoln's stirring addresses. We were transfixed! A ministry was born!

For almost 25 years Fritz Klein has touched the hearts of people through presentations of Lincoln's speeches. He had heard from God about a ministry that would touch thousands. He provided the willingness...God provided grace and patience to wait until the ministry was launched.

Mason knew that the nation must undergo God's Divine retribution for embracing slavery and warned,

> They (the sins of slavery) bring the judgment of heaven on a Country. As nations can not be rewarded or punished in the next world they must be in this. By an inevitable chain of cause and effects. Providence punishes national sins, by national calamities. We are now to rank among the nations of the world; but whether our Independence shall prove a blessing or a curse must depend upon our own wisdom or folly, virtue or wickedness…justice and virtue are the vital principles of government. If I can only live to see the American Union firmly fixed, and free Governments well established in our western world, and can leave to my children but a crust of bread and liberty, I shall die satisfied.[33]

REVIEW

Q. Discuss the meaning of the verse Luke 12:48b, "From everyone who has been given much, much will be demanded; and from the one who has been entrusted with much, much more will be asked."

Q. Where do the rights "life, liberty, and private property" come from?

Q. Discuss the pressure Mason must have experienced when he resisted signing the Constitution.

Q. Discuss an experience where you were standing alone on a principle.

Q. Mason chose to "fear God rather than man" (Revelation 14:7, Proverbs 29:25). What does this tell you about him?

Q. Compare the view for seeking public office in the eighteenth century with the twenty-first century.

Q. Discuss Mason's belief that slavery was destroying the character of the country.

Q. Mason questioned whether independence would be a curse or a blessing. What do you think he meant by a "crust of bread and liberty" to leave to his children?

Q. How does a person develop patience in his life?

Q. Describe someone you know who demonstrated Christian patience though his or her actions or inaction.

Q. In what areas do you have a need for patience?

Q. Why is patience so difficult to develop?

Character for Life

GOD'S PROMISE:

"The Lord is not slow in keeping his promise, as some understand slowness. He is patient with you, not wanting anyone to perish, but everyone to come to repentance" (2 Peter 3:9).

GOD'S GOAL:

For Christians to live patient lives.

YOUR COMMITMENT:

To work daily at having patience with others and life's circumstances.

YOUR DAILY RESPONSE:

1. To be content with what you have been given.

2. To trust God with your future and be willing to wait for His blessings.

3. Pray daily for patience.

4. Wait upon the Lord when you feel your patience growing thin.

FAILURE WILL MEAN:

Being an impatient and agitated person.

BACKGROUND:

One of the things we learn in life as we walk with Jesus is patience. If God has given you a vision for your life and you have a passion to undertake that vision, realize that the vision will come but probably not in your timing. The Father is preparing you to handle the vision and assignment. As hard as it may seem, He is more interested in you than in your vision. It is not what you do for God but what you are to God that is important. Over your lifetime your assignments will change. Can we accept assignments where no one really knows what we are doing but Jesus? If we can, more assignments are on the way, however humble they may be. The goal is Jesus Himself, not praise or even the encouragement from others. We could ask for nothing more than to hear Him say, "Well done, good and faithful servant" (Matthew 25:21). Even with the incarnation of the Son of God "when the time had fully come" He came to earth and carried out His mission. It will be the same for us as well. Trust God with His timing. It's the only way to go!

Christ does not give us power to work up a patience of our own. His patience is manifested if we will let His life dwell in us. There is no patience equal to the patience of God. As we learn to rely on the Spirit of God He gives us the resourcefulness of Jesus.

Jesus showed patience in His life and ministry. Toward the purposes His Father had for Him, the Bible says, "But when the time had fully come, God sent his Son, born of a woman, born under the law, that we might receive the full rights of sons" (Galatians 4:4).

Toward those who crucified Him the Bible says, "He was oppressed and afflicted, yet he did not open his mouth; he was led like a lamb to the slaughter, and as a sheep before her shearers is silent, so he did not open his mouth" (Isaiah 53:7). "But Jesus remained silent and gave no answer" (Mark 14:61).

Jesus waited patiently for the time when God would exalt Him. "The right time for me has not yet come" (John 7:6a).

To His disciples Jesus spoke about salvation and witnessing, saying, "But seed on good soil stands for those with a noble and good heart, who hear the word, retain it, and by persevering produce a crop" (Luke 8:15).

Toward future disciples He counseled, "By standing firm you will gain life" (Luke 21:19). "We do not want you to become lazy, but to imitate those who through faith and patience inherit what has been promised" (Hebrews 6:12).

LIVING A LIFE OF PATIENCE MEANS . . .

- Your eyes will be set on the goal Jesus Christ has for you. This will mean self-denial and looking at things from God's perspective.

- You will deny yourself of what is potentially harmful for you since this prize is the thrill of bringing joy to the heart of Jesus.

- You will battle through the discouragement and not give up but do good to everyone.

- You will discipline your body, mind, and spirit to be used for God's glory.

- You will set your heart on the assignments God gives you and not lose faith or give up. If God has called you to a task, determine to complete it, even if you face opposition or discouragement. The rewards of work well done will be worth the effort.

Chapter Thirty-One: Learn more about Mason

Go to an Internet search engine.
Type in *George Mason's Character.*
Find topics 1-6 below and open up the websites.
1. George Mason's Master Draft of the Bill of Rights
2. George Mason
3. The True Meaning of Christmas
4. The Bill of Rights Institute
5. Discover George Mason
6. Gunston Hall Plantation-George Mason Thoughtful
Revolutionary

chapter 32
Respectfulness—
daniel webster
PURPOSE: Valuing the Service of Others

character trait:
Respectfulness

SUBJECT:
DANIEL WEBSTER
(1782-1852)

PURPOSE:
Valuing the Service of Others

FAMOUS QUOTE:
"The blood of our fathers, let it not have been shed in vain...if we cherish the virtues and the principles of our fathers, Heaven will assist us to carry on the work of human liberty and human happiness."

SCRIPTURE DOCUMENTATION:

"I will never break my covenant with you" (Judges 2:1b).

"Obey them (earthly masters/employers) not only to win their favor when their eye is on you, but like slaves of Christ, doing the will of God from your heart. Serve wholeheartedly, as if you were serving the Lord, not men, because you know that the Lord will reward everyone for whatever good he does, whether he is slave or free" (Ephesians 6:5-7).

"Make it your ambition to lead a quiet life, to mind your own business, and to work with you hands, just as we told you, so that your daily life may win the respect of outsiders and so that you will not be dependent on anybody" (1 Thessalonians 4:11-12).

PERSONALITY PROFILE

Daniel Webster, along with Patrick Henry, was one of the nation's most remarkable orators. Senator Lewis Cass spoke of his faith in his eulogy to Senator Webster, "He died in the faith of the Christian—humble, but hopeful, adding another to the long list of eminent men who have searched the Gospel of Jesus Christ, and have found it to be the Word and the will of God."[1]

Webster's biographer, Claude Moore Fuess wrote, "It is my hope that Daniel Webster will emerge, not as a legendary figure, but a human personage, with weaknesses and shortcomings, perhaps but also with something of the glorious magnetism, which thrilled those whom he met. No one can read his utterances and look long at his portraits without being in some degree overwhelmed by the power of the majesty of the man."[2]

Henry W. Hilliard said about Webster, "There was in him a blended dignity and power...it seemed as if the whole weight of government might rest securely upon his broad shoulders."[3]

Daniel Webster was born in Salisbury, New Hampshire in 1782. His mother apparently was a brilliant woman and, recognizing his extraordinary mind, home-schooled him. He entered Dartmouth College in 1797. In 1808 he married Grace Fletcher, the daughter of a pastor. Grace was a godly woman with a deep faith in God.

Said Frederic Austin, "No man not possessed of a mental equipment of the first order could have achieved equal results under the circumstances. Retentiveness of memory, quickness and depth of perception, comprehensiveness of view, sanity and fairness of judgment, orderliness of thought and aptness in expression—these are the qualities which combined to produce in Webster a mental forcefulness well-nigh unsurpassable."[4]

Webster was the great orator of the nineteenth century as Patrick Henry was of the eighteenth century. People referred to Webster as "god-like." Sadly, this adulation brought pride into his life. For Webster, respect and respectability were virtues he longed for. In time, however, he recognized his heart and humbled himself before God.

Webster began to practice law and was soon known for his eloquence at the bar in 1805. He moved to Boston and was elected to the U.S. House of Representatives from 1813-17. In 1822 he was elected to the House of Representatives from Boston.

WEBSTER'S PERSONAL LIFE

During the summer of 1827, Daniel Webster's wife, Grace, died. She had been afflicted with a tumor for some time. Grace had little hope that politics could provide the solutions to the country's needs. It was said of Grace that she was "united with sweetness of disposition, unaffected," and that "Grace had frank and winning manners, no one could approach her without wishing to know her, and no one could know her well without loving her."[5] The Webster's had five children Grace, Daniel, Julia, Edward, and Charles. Only Daniel survived his father, however.

On hearing from the physicians that his wife had little time to live, Webster responded, "I hope I may be able to meet the greatest of all earthly afflictions with firmness, but I need not say that I am at present quite overcome."[6] During this time, Webster was filled with hope and despair but eventually became resigned to the reality of his wife's soon departure from this world. Grace was a devoted wife but her love for Jesus far exceeded his convictions. Following the death of his first wife, he devoted himself to his children. His life went on a downward spiral and he was plagued with financial difficulties and ended up seeking help from his friends.

Perhaps out of financial desperation, he once again married. Unlike Grace, who was the daughter of a minister, Webster's second wife was a daughter born to wealth. She reveled in the importance of her husband's position and encouraged his ambition.

In 1833, Webster was re-elected to the Senate and in 1841 he became the United States Secretary of State for President Harrison. In 1845, he was once again re-elected to the Senate. The Webster-Ashburton treaty and his work as Secretary of State averted a third war with Great Britain and ushered in a new period of peace. In 1850, he became the Secretary of State under President Fillmore. He was the Unsuccessful Whig candidate for president in 1836. His portrait appears in six different places in the Capitol Building. In 1852, Webster died as a result of an accident while riding his horse.

In a letter to Peter Harvey, Webster revealed that the crush of government responsibilities and the weaknesses of his physical health may have been due to the fact that he sought to live with very little sleep. Webster writes, "Since March 7th, there has not been an hour in which I have not felt a crushing weight of anxiety and responsibility. I have gone to sleep at night, and wakened in the morning with the same feeling of eating care. And I have set down to no breakfast or dinner to which I have brought an unconcerned and easy mind. It is over. My part is acted, and I am satisfied. The rest I leave to stronger bodies and fresher minds. My annual cold is now heavy upon me, weakening my body, and depressing my spirits…. I have had little sleep, not four hours a night, on an average for six months."[7] Webster made it a habit of getting up to see the dawn of a new day and "rejoiced at sunrise." He made it a lifelong habit to never miss one.

WEBSTER'S RESPECT FOR GOD AND COUNTRY

Webster became a prophet to the nation and reminded it of its historic Christian virtues. By the 1830's and 40's, the country had gotten off the path the "Founders" had laid down for it. Webster was a prophet in the wilderness it seemed, reminding people that "our ancestors established their system of government on morality and religious sentiment. Moral habits cannot safely be trusted on any other foundation than religious principles, nor can government be secure which is not supported by moral habits…whatever makes men good Christians, makes them good citizens. Our fathers were brought here by their high veneration for the Christian religion. They journeyed by its light, and labored in its hope. They sought to incorporate its principles with the elements of their society, and to diffuse its influence through all their institutions. Liberty and Union, now and forever, one and inseparable."[9]

Webster wrote,

> And now, fellow-citizens, let us not retire from this occasion without a deep and solemn conviction of the duties which have developed upon us. This lovely land, this glorious liberty, these benign institutions, the dear purchase of our fathers, are ours, ours to enjoy, ours to preserve, ours to transmit. Generations past and generations to come hold us responsible for this sacred trust. Our fathers, from behind, admonish us, with their anxious paternal voices; posterity calls out to us, from the bosom of the future; the world turns hither it solicitous eyes; all, conjure us to act wisely, and faithfully, in the relation which we sustain.[10]

WEBSTER'S RESPECT FOR THE BIBLE

Webster respected the Bible as the Word of God and respected his parents who taught him God's principles. Said Webster, "My heart has always assured and reassured me that the Gospel of Jesus Christ must be a Divine Reality. The Sermon on the Mount can not be a merely human production. This belief enters the very depths of my conscience. The whole history of man proves it."[11]

As Webster reflected on his amazing life he said, "If there is anything in my thoughts or style to commend, the credit is due to my parents for instilling in me an early love of the Christians."[12]

Webster gave a historic speech memorializing the two "Founders" who had died the same day in the year of 1826. Webster had respect for God who is the "governor of the nations" and protects the country. The nation was reminded of this fact with the death of Adams and Jefferson. Both died on Independence Day, July 4, 1826, fifty years from the "birth of the country." "Adams and Jefferson are no more, and we are assembled, fellow-citizens, the aged, the middle-aged, and the young…on our 50th anniversary, the great day of national jubilee, in the very hour of public rejoicing, in the midst of echoing and re-echoing voices of thanksgiving, while their own names were on all tongues, they took their flight together to the world of the spirits."[13]

Webster believed, "God gives liberty to those who love it, and are always ready to guard and defend it. The altar of our freedom should be placed near the altar of our religion. Thus shall the same Almighty Power who protects his own worship, protects also our liberties."[14]

Webster saw "the utter inability of any human being to work out his own salvation without the constant aids of the spirit of grace."[15] He knew this truth was real because the Bible revealed it.

WEBSTER'S RESPECT FOR AMERICA'S "FOUNDERS"

Webster had great respect for the "Founders" of America who made great sacrifices for the country. Upon the death of Jefferson and Adams he said, "If we had the power, we could not wish to reverse the dispensation of the Divine Providence. The great objects of life were accomplished, the drama was

"It is my hope that Daniel Webster will emerge, not as a legendary figure, but a human personage, with weaknesses and shortcomings, perhaps but also with something of the glorious magnetism, which thrilled those whom he met. No one can read his utterances and look long at his portraits without being in some degree overwhelmed by the power of the majesty of the man."[16]

Webster's biographer,
Claude Moore Fuess

> "He (webster) died in the faith of the christian— humble, but hopeful, adding another to the long list of eminent men who have searched the gospel of jesus christ, and have found it to be the word and the will of god."[18]
>
> senator lewis cass

NATIONAL PURPOSE ►

ready to be closed. It has closed; our patriots have fallen; but so fallen, at such age, with such coincidence, on such a day, that we cannot rationally lament that the end has come, which we knew could not be long deferred. Both had been President, both had lived to great age, both were early patriots...it cannot but seem striking and extraordinary, that these two should live to see the 50th year from the date of that act that they should complete that year and that then, on the day which had fast linked for ever their own fame with their countries glory."

Continued Webster, "Now two men now live, fellow-citizen, perhaps it may be doubted whether any two men have ever lived in one age, who, more than those we now commemorate, have impressed on mankind their own opinions more deeply into the opinions of others, or given a more lasting direction to the current of human thought. Their work doth not perish with them."

Webster concluded, "We can never, indeed, pay the debt which is upon us; but by virtue, by morality, by religion, by the cultivation of every good principle and every good habit, we may hope to enjoy the blessing, through our day, and to leave it unimpaired to our children. Let us feel deeply how much of what we are and of what we possess we owe to this liberty...let us acknowledge the blessing, let us feel it deeply and powerfully, let us cherish a strong affection for it, and resolve to maintain and perpetuate it. The blood of our fathers, let is not have been shed in vain...if we cherish the virtues and the principles of our fathers, Heaven will assist us to carry on the work of human liberty and human happiness." [17]

Webster had respect for the heritage of America and its national purpose. He testified, "Unborn ages and visions of glory crowd upon my soul, the realization of which, however, is in the hands and good pleasure of Almighty God; but under his Divine blessing, it will be dependent on the character and virtues of ourselves and our posterity. If we and they shall live in the fear of God, and shall respect His commandments...we may have the highest hopes of the future of our country... If we abide by the principles taught in the Bible, our country will go on prospering and to prosper, but if we and our country reject religious instruction and authority, violate the rules of eternal justice, trifle with the injunctions of morality, and recklessly destroy the political constitution which holds us together, no man can tell how sudden a catastrophe may overwhelm us, that shall bury our glory in profound obscurity." [19]

MODERN-DAY EXAMPLE
OF RESPECTFULNESS
G.T. GUNHUS

G.T. Gunhus (retired) was the "Chief of Chaplains" for the United States Army. His father was a chaplain and he decided to join the Army himself as a chaplain. I consider G.T. a friend of mine. We have known each other since we were in the seventh grade.

"G.T." had a lot of influence on my life. He was a born leader. I was a follower. His opinion mattered to me and just about everyone else in our class. He decided to go to Hillcrest Academy for his senior year in high school and asked me to join him. Both of us left for Fergus Falls, Minnesota, and those were wonderful years of growth for both of us. Coach Phil Werdal took a special interest in us and modeled the Christian life for those of us interested in sports.

After high school I lost track of "G.T." as we went to different colleges. In seminary I learned he was pursuing his degree in Minnesota. "G.T." went to Vietnam, as a chaplain caring for the spiritual needs of American soldiers. I had seen him in action on our basketball and football team. He had what it took to win—pulling everyone together. He was and is "a class act" and enjoys the respect of his peers in the Pentagon.

While in Minsk, Belarus, I met an American officer who had worked under General Gunhus when they were both in the 7th Army in Germany. I had not seen "G.T." in years and asked him how the General was doing. He went on to tell me about this remarkable man I had known for so many years and the respect everyone had for him. I knew General Gunhus would be used by God in a remarkable way.

A few years ago my wife, Ruthie, and I were invited by G.T. and his wife, Ann, to come to Washington for his installation as the Army Chief of Chaplains. What an experience it was! Once there I heard Four-Star and Three-Star Generals speaking with deep respect for my childhood friend. The Army Men's Chorus sang the prayer of St. Francis of Assisi…we never felt so proud of our country.

After September 11, 2001, President Bush spoke to military personal at the Pentagon. Just behind the President was General Gunhus who delivered a stirring speech. I asked him one time, "How could this happen to a guy from Seattle, Washington and Hillcrest Academy?" His response, "God has a real sense of humor!" I think he was as amazed as anyone that this had happened to him.

General Gunhus serves his God and country well. I'm sure he could never have accomplished this without his remarkable wife, Ann. She is greatly loved and respected. Promotions come from God, however, and God knows what he is doing.

> "The discipline of desire is the (real) goal of character."[20]
>
> JOHN LOCKE

REVIEW

Q. How can Americans today pay the debt owed to those who founded America?

Q. According to Webster, what were the deepest desires of the "fathers" of our country?

Q. What did Webster believe could bring on a catastrophe to America?

Q. Discuss Webster's conviction that "the altar of freedom should be placed near the altar of our religion."

Q. Upon what do you think the future of America will be dependent?

Q. What might happen if Americans reject religious instruction and authority, and discount eternal justice and morality?

Q. What are the evidences of inner decay in America?

Q. What evidence do you have from your personal experience that the loss of respect for God, the Bible, human life, etc. has taken place?

Q. Most would agree that the loss of respect for traditional institutions took a nosedive in the '60s and '70s in America. If you were asked to develop a plan to turn America around, what would your plan involve?

Character for Life

GOD'S PROMISE:

"I will never break my covenant with you" (Judges 2:1b).

GOD'S GOAL:

For Christians to respect others and be worthy of respect themselves.

YOUR COMMITMENT:

To live a life that is respectful of others and in turn find others' respect.

YOUR DAILY RESPONSE:

1. Live a life of character.

2. Realize that when people aren't watching, God is.

3. Be willing to respect others and wait for the time when others will respect you.

4. Respect God most of all and honor Him daily.

FAILURE WILL MEAN:

Being a person that no one cares to respect.

BACKGROUND:

Respecting one another means honoring that which is honorable in God's sight and seeing as disgraceful that which He sees as disgraceful. Respect is admiration, consideration, deference, esteem, and honor. Everyone we meet is made in "the image of God" and is of incredible value to the Creator. Everyone has the potential to have a relationship with Jesus Christ. In God's Kingdom, there is no room for looking down at other people or "marginalizing" individuals. Each person God created was brought into the world with the purpose of bringing honor to God and serving his or her fellow man. We need to pray that we can see people as God sees them. He yearns for intimacy with each of us. "Help us, Lord Jesus, to see people as You do and be sensitive to their needs. Amen."

Respect also involves having respect for yourself as God's creation. This will mean leading a godly lifestyle and making choices that reflect God's character. It will involve an ethical approach to life. "Do you not know that your body is a temple of the Holy Spirit, who is in you, whom you have received from God? You are not your own; you were bought at a price. Therefore honor God with your body" (1 Corinthians 6:19-20).

Respecting God includes respecting the earth and the environment. "God blessed them and said to them, 'Be fruitful and increase in number; fill the earth and subdue it. Rule over the fish of the sea and the birds of the air and over every living creature that moves on the ground'" (Genesis 1:28).

We must also respect our family members. "'Honor your father and mother'—which is the first commandment with a promise—that it may go well with you and that you may enjoy long life on the earth" (Ephesians 6:2-3). "Fathers, do not exasperate your children; instead, bring them up in the training and instruction of the Lord" (Ephesians 6:4). "Husbands, love your wives, just as Christ loved the church and gave himself up for her" (Ephesians 5:25). "Children, obey your parents in the Lord, for this is right" (Ephesians 6:1).

Most importantly we must respect the Word of God. "I have hidden your word in my heart that I might not sin against you." "Rulers persecute me without cause, but my heart trembles at your word. I rejoice in your promise like one who finds great spoil" (Psalm 119:11, 161-162).

LIVING A LIFE OF RESPECTFULNESS MEANS . . .

- Treating others as you would like to be treated.
- Putting others before yourself.
- Seeing everyone through God's eyes.
- Living a life of character.
- Being willing to be thought less of so others can be lifted up.

Chapter Thirty-Two: Learn more about Webster

Go to an Internet search engine.
Type in *Daniel Webster's Respectfulness.*
Find topics 1-6 below and open up websites.
1. Daniel Webster-The Union Address
2. Daniel Webster-Wikipedia, the free encyclopedia
3. Daniel Webster: On Conscription (1814)
4. The Great Speeches and Orations of Daniel Webster
5. Daniel Webster
6. The Constitution and Union Speech by Daniel Webster

Go to an Internet search engine.
Type in *Daniel Webster's Life.*
Find topics 1-2 below and open up the websites.
1. Daniel Webster's scholarly life
2. Bibliography

chapter 33
Responsibility—
John Adams

PURPOSE: Embracing God's Reasonable Requirements

character trait:
Responsibility

SUBJECT:

JOHN ADAMS
(1735-1826–Died on July 4, 1826, exactly 50 years from Independence Day, 1776)

PURPOSE:

Embracing God's Reasonable Requirements

SCRIPTURE DOCUMENTATION:

"…Every mouth may be silenced and the whole world held accountable to God" (Romans 3:19b).

"Nothing in all creation is hidden from God's sight. Everything is uncovered and laid bare before the eyes of him to whom we must give account" (Hebrews 4:13).

"So then, each of us will give an account of himself to God" (Romans 14:12).

"The only foundation of a free constitution is pure virtue; and if this cannot be inspired into our people in a greater measure than they have it now, they may change their rulers and the forms of government, but they will not obtain a lasting liberty. They will only exchange tyrants and tyrannies"[1]

John Adams

PERSONALITY PROFILE

The life of John Adams was characterized not only by politics, the revolutionary war, and social unrest, but also by religious faith, virtues, and friendships. Adams' influence was eventually to touch nations. Through the efforts of Benjamin Rush's mediation, a lost friendship between Adams and Jefferson was restored. The personal thoughts of John and Abigal Adams were preserved for history through their writings. Adams confronted thorny issues and difficulties and was not about to give in to the pressures of others when he believed the course of action was clear.

In reflecting upon his life, Adams believed that his election to the presidency was not the most significant accomplishment, but that his part was in "the long struggle to independence." Adams' contribution to America is much more appreciated now than it has been in the past. Jefferson and Hamilton ousted Adams from the White House, but in recent years most of his decisions have been vindicated. Adams was borne along by an irresistible sense of duty. An intense Puritan morality fortified Adams' fierce integrity and channeled him into Revolutionary politics. Adams latest biographer, David McCullough, points out the changes that took place in this remarkable person. Adams' goals in life were influenced, among others, by the Roman philosopher Cicero. Cicero was the one who said, "The first way for a young man to set himself on the road toward glorious reputation is to win renown." In his early years Adams was overly concerned with his own reputation but later in his life he learned to trust God in this area and was not too concerned with how history would remember him.

Deep love and commitment characterized Adams' relationships with his wife and children. Recently, over a thousand letters of his correspondence with his wife were made available to the public. These letters provide us with a deeper understanding of his inner life and love. John met Abigail when she was only 15 and Adams was 25. Chronic illness plagued Abigail as a child so she developed a great love of learning. Abigail was a rather shy woman, but Adams eventually drew out her personality.

After their marriage, Adams was trying to establish his career in law and this required a lot of travel. Eventually, they settled in Boston. In 1783 Adams traveled with his son to Europe, a trip that almost cost him his life. His wife traveled to Europe alone to be with him. Their life together was a remarkable love story of a husband and wife who were separated from each other a great deal but not by choice. Over the years, he became less harsh and less independent. Abigal wrote about John, "Years subdue the ardor of passion but in lieu thereof a friendship and affection deep rooted subsists...and will survive whilst the vital flame exists."[2]

Adams' respect for women came, in part, from his wife. Abigal would have fit right into the twenty-first century. In one of hundreds of letters to her husband she wrote, "I desire you would remember the ladies, and be more generous and favorable to them than your ancestors. Do not put such unlimited power into the hands of the husbands. Remember all men would be tyrants if they could. If particular care and attention is not paid to the ladies we are determined to foment a rebellion, and will not hold ourselves bound by any laws in which we have no voice, or representation."[3] Powerful advice in any generation!

Adams considered going into the ministry but struggled with the prevailing view of New England Calvinism. Instead he turned to law. Adams was admitted to the bar in 1758 and became the leader in opposing the Stamp Act in 1765. Adams graduated from Harvard in 1755 and took up law, particularly civil law. Since he was a delegate to the Continental Congress, Adams was at the core of the people who advanced the cause of "Independence."

FURTHER SCRIPTURE DOCUMENTATION:

"In the presence of God and of Christ Jesus, who will judge the living and the dead, and in view of his appearing and his kingdom, I give you this charge: Preach the Word; be prepared in season and out of season; correct, rebuke and encourage—with great patience and careful instruction" (2 Timothy 4:1-2).

"Obey your leaders and submit to their authority. They keep watch over you as men who must give an account. Obey them so that their work will be a joy, not a burden, for that would be of no advantage to you" (Hebrews 13:17).

NATIONAL PURPOSE

The many accomplishments of Adams include: proposing that George Washington should command the new Continental Army; authoring the Massachusetts Constitution; being appointed "Chief Justice of the Superior Court of Massachusetts" in 1775; serving as foreign ambassador to Holland in 1782; and signing the peace treaty which ended the American Revolution in 1783.

Adams also served as foreign ambassador to Great Britain from 1785-88. He became the "Ambassador at Large" in Europe during the Revolutionary War. He served two terms as Vice President under Washington and followed him as the second President of the United States. The list of accomplishments continues, he also established the United States Navy and prevented America from getting into another war. Adams' decision to avoid war made it possible for the United States to eventually acquire the Louisiana Territory.

HOW PEOPLE PERCEIVED ADAMS

David McCullough, a Pulitzer Prize winning author, has recently provided us with a wealth of new information on the life of Adams and greatly enhanced our understanding of our second President. McCullough described Adams as "blunt and thin-skinned—and consequently not good at taking criticism—but also as a person of great intelligence, compassion, and even warmth."[7]

A friend of Adams said, "He was an honest lawyer as ever broke bread."[8] An observer at the Continental Convention said, "He was the pillar of the Constitution and its ablest advocate and defender against the multifarious (people of different kinds) assaults it encountered."[9]

Jefferson said of Adams, "[He was] the colossus (large and powerful) of independence."[10] George Washington stated, "Adams possessed personal integrity, devotion to principle, intellectual intensity and strong will."[11]

One of Adams' greatest admirers was Dr. Benjamin Rush who said, "Adams possessed more learning probably, both ancient and modern, than any man who subscribed to the Declaration of Independence. This illustrious patriot has not his superior, scarcely his equal for abilities and virtue in the whole of the Continent of America."[12]

ADAMS' SENSE OF RESPONSIBILITY TO GOD AND CHRISTIANITY

Adams believed that Christianity was the source of morality, of all acceptable ideas of virtue, justice, decency, and civil order. As a young man, Adams resolved to rise with the sun and to study the Scriptures on Thursday, Friday, Saturday, and Sunday mornings, and to study some Latin on the other three mornings. He failed sometimes, of course, but he had a burning desire to subdue his passions.

Adams believed that the foundation of the government was "virtue" not fear. It was the Puritan within him, with a deep pessimism about man and his Puritan stress on moral virtues that gave a distinctly conservative thought to Adams revolutionary thought. The "Founding Fathers" saw education and religion going hand in hand. That is why they wrote, in the Northwest Ordinance of 1787, "Religion, morality and knowledge, being necessary to good government and the happiness of mankind, schools and the means shall forever be encouraged."[13]

Adams' life-long goal was to discover the "divine science" of sound government for human happiness. He wrote, "The science of government is my duty to study, more than all other sciences; the art of legislation and administration and negotiation ought to take place of, indeed to exclude in a manner, all other arts."[14] Adams believed that "Justice is the greatest interest of man on earth," and that "Liberty exists in proportion to wholesome restraint."[15] Reflecting upon the Constitution, he believed that new Constitution was the "greatest single effort of national deliberations that the world has ever seen."[16]

Adams never stopped learning and his correspondence is filled with insights into righteous government. Almost two years before his death, he wrote to Thomas Jefferson; referencing Sidney's "origins of liberty." "I have lately undertaken to read Algernon Sidney on government…As often as I have read it, and fumbled it over, it now excites fresh admiration (i.e., wonder)."[17]

Sidney had written,

> The creature having nothing, and being nothing but what the creator makes him, must owe all to him, and nothing to anyone from whom he has received nothing. Man therefore must be naturally free, unless he be created by another power that we have yet heard of. The obedience due to parents arises from hence, in that they are the instruments of our generation; and we are instructed by the light of reason, that we ought to make great returns to those from whom under God we have received all. When they die we are their heirs, we enjoy the same rights, and devolve the same to our posterity. God only who confers this right upon us, can deprive us of it: and we can no way understand that he does so, unless he had so declared by express revelation, or had set some distinguishing marks of dominion and subjection upon men; and, as an ingenious person not long since said, caused some to be born with crowns upon their heads, and all others with saddles upon their backs. This liberty therefore must continue, till it be either forfeited or willingly resigned. The forfeiture is hardly comprehensible in a multitude that is not entered into any society; for as they are all equal, and equals can have no right over each other, no man can forfeit anything to one who can justly demand nothing, unless it may be by a personal injury, which is nothing to this case; because where there is not society, one man is not bound by the actions of another.[18]

Responsibility was "the price of greatness."[19] Winston Churchill

"I alone am responsible for the wrong I do. God holds me responsible if I refuse to let Him deliver me from sin. I am responsible to allow the Son of God to manifest Himself in me. When we come to Jesus, God does not take away our responsibilities, but gives us new responsibilities. If I refuse to embrace His will for my life, that too is sin."[20]

Chambers

"The phrase 'rejoice ever more' shall never be out of my heart, memory, or mouth again as long as I live, if I can help it."[22]

John Adams

"Parents can only give good advice or put their (children) on the right path but the forming of a person's character is in their own hands."[21]

ANN FRANK

RESPONDING TO GOD AND MANKIND

On man's perfectibility Adams writes, "I consider the perfectibility of man as used by modern philosophers to be mere words without a meaning, that is mere nonsense."[23] Adams believed himself to be a person of "immense load of errors, weaknesses, follies and sins to mourn over and repent of."[24]

"St. Paul had taught him to rejoice ever more and be content. This phrase 'rejoice ever more' shall never be out of my heart, memory or mouth again as long as I live, if I can help it. This is my perfectibility of man."[25]

Toward the end of his life Adams attempted to answer the essential questions of life from his granddaughter, "The longer I live, the more I read, the more patiently I think, and the more anxiously I inquire, the less I seem to know. Do justly, love mercy. Walk humbly. This is enough. Your affectionate grandfather."[26]

"America must forsake selfish vice and embrace trust in God," said Adams. "Let a general reformation of manners take place, let universal charity, public spirit, and private virtue be inculcated, encouraged and practiced. Unite in a preparation for a vigorous defense of your country, as if all depend on your own exertions. And when you have done all things, then rely upon the good Providence of Almighty God for success, in full confidence that without His blessings, all our efforts will fail."[27]

Virtue to Adams meant more than avoidance of sin. "It is concerned with the welfare of society above self-centered aims," he believed. "One great advantage of the Christian religion," Adams wrote, "is that it brings the great principle of the law of nature and nations—Love your neighbor as yourself, and do to others as you would that others should do to you."[28]

Adams was very much aware of the remarkable events taking place all around him.

I always consider the settlement of America with reverence and wonder, as the opening of a grand scene and design in providence, for the illumination of the ignorant and the emancipation of the slavish part of mankind all over the earth. Liberty cannot be preserved without a general knowledge among the people, who have a right...and a desire to know, but besides this, they have a right, an indisputable, unalienable, indefeasible, divine right to that most dreaded and envied kind of knowledge, I mean the character and conduct of their rulers.[29]

MODERN DAY EXAMPLE OF RESPONSIBILITY DWIGHT NELSON

Dwight Nelson recently left Bethany Covenant Church in Mt. Vernon, Washington, after 24 years of ministry. He didn't leave for a larger church, however, but a smaller fellowship in Libertyville, Illinois. Recently the congregation asked if they could have a special service to celebrate what God has done through Pastor Nelson and his wife, Cathy, for over two decades. It was one of the most moving services I have ever seen.

Let me describe Pastor Nelson. He's a tall lean man, about 6'6," with kind compassionate eyes, who reminds a person some of our 16th president, Abraham Lincoln. He speaks softly and is an amazing listener. He has a great sense of humor and really celebrates life. His wife is a remarkable person and both of these people seem to be unaffected and natural in every sense of the word. They love people and enjoy life.

Pastor Nelson took a small fellowship and stuck with it through the good and tough times. He was probably as amazed as anyone when the church grew as it did, not just in numbers but also as real disciples of Jesus. This wasn't because he was particularly "charismatic" although he loved to worship God with his hands outstretched. He was deliberate, writing out his messages, and was clear about what God was saying.

Pastor Nelson is not a naturally outgoing person but most often waited until he was spoken to. What set him apart was his willingness to put others first. He provided opportunities for others to grow in their new "giftings." He even allowed the Associate pastor to take the larger service while he took the traditional service. Pastor Nelson had a proper estimation of himself and exemplified the word "servant leadership." He was comfortable with children and seniors and the people at Bethany Covenant simply revered him.

Twenty-four years is a long time for any pastor to serve. As I reflect on Pastor Nelson, I am filled with gratitude to God for this man. He believed in people and that the "grace of Jesus Christ" was available to all believers to do whatever God called them to do. Pastor Nelson was responsible first to God and then to people. His commitment to the Word, praise, and prayer was his foundation for life. I don't know how we will get along without him. He was "responsible to the heavenly vision" God had given him.

What responsibilities for God's Kingdom has God put on your heart? It may be caring for an elderly person who needs encouragement or praying for a missionary. As you are faithful with the responsibilities God gives you, He will give you more opportunities. It's easy to get involved in projects when our emotions are stirred but just knowing of a need doesn't always mean you are the one to meet that need. Pray about the opportunity. Get God's peace and confirmation in your heart that this is an assignment you are to undertake. Then, when the difficulties come, and they will, you can recall that you are doing this because God has put it on your heart.

REVIEW

Q. Discuss Adams' admonition to make a defense for one's country.

Q. Discuss the Northwest Ordinance and its significance to America.

Q. How did Adams' ideas on the perfectibility of man change?

Q. What was Adams final advice to his granddaughter?

Q. Words like "Atlas," Pillar," and "Colossus" were used to describe Adams role in the founding of the country. Discuss how you think these men viewed Adams.

Q. Do you believe there is a "Divine Science of Government"?

Q. Discuss the fears of John Adams.

Q. What was a prerequisite for holding office in Adams' day?

Q. Where do you think Adams developed this sense of "responsibility" for the future of the United States of America?

Q. What responsibilities do you believe God has given you for the future of the country you live in?

Q. Toward the end of his life Adams knew experientially about "rejoicing evermore." How can this attitude enable us to take on responsibility we would otherwise not accept?

Character for Life

GOD'S PROMISE:

"...Every mouth may be silenced and the whole world held accountable to God" (Romans 3:19b).

"So then, each of us will give an account of himself to God" (Romans 14:12).

GOD'S GOAL:

For Christians to live responsibly.

YOUR COMMITMENT:

To take responsibility for all that God has entrusted you with.

YOUR DAILY RESPONSE:

1. To live life fully and never be ashamed of the things you do.

2. To be a role model for others.

3. To live for Jesus and be worthy of His name.

4. To follow through on your actions, even when it is difficult.

FAILURE WILL MEAN:

Shirking responsibility and not caring what others think of you.

BACKGROUND:

There are things God is responsible for and things we are responsible for. We cannot save ourselves or make ourselves holy. God must do that. God, however, will not give us good habits. Neither will He give us character or make us live good lives. We have to do all that ourselves. We have to work out the salvation that God works in us. (See Philippians 2:12-13.) Jesus Christ accepted the responsibility for our sin, and on the basis of His redemption on the cross, people find their way back to Him and understand how life is to be lived.

"So then, each of us will give an account of himself to God. Therefore let us stop passing judgment on one another. Instead, make up your mind not to put any stumbling block or obstacle in your brother's way" (Romans 14:12-13).

"If I had not come and spoken to them, they would not be guilty of sin. Now, however, they have no excuse for their sin" (John 15:22).

LIVING A LIFE OF RESPONSIBILITY MEANS . . .

■ Living up to the calling God has for you.

■ Being willing to take a stand for what is right.

■ Following the words of the Bible and living a life filled with prayer.

■ Understanding that God will fulfill His purpose in you in His time.

Chapter Thirty-Three: Learn more about Adams

Go to an Internet search engine.
Type in *John Adams' Character, Responsibility.*
Find topics 1-6 below and open up the websites.
1. John Adams
2. John Adams, "Yet, in estimating his character"....
3. John Adams, "here lies John Adams, who took upon himself the responsibility of peace"
4. McCullough John Adams Summary
5. The Yale review of books.
6. RC.edu

chapter 34
Self-Control—
ʀoger sherman

PURPOSE: Allowing the Holy Spirit to Control Your Responses

character trait:
Self-Control

SUBJECT:
ROGER SHERMAN
(1721-1793)

PURPOSE:
Allowing the Holy Spirit to Control Your Responses

FAMOUS QUOTE:
"[Sherman was] as honest as an angel and as firm in the cause of American Independence as Mount Atlas." John Adams

SCRIPTURE DOCUMENTATION:

"Set a guard over my mouth, O LORD; keep watch over the door of my lips" (Psalm 141:3).

"But the fruit of the Spirit is love, joy, peace, patience, kindness, goodness, faithfulness, gentleness, and self-control" (Galatians 5:22-23a).

"If anyone considers himself religious and yet does not keep a tight rein on his tongue, he deceives himself and his religion is worthless" (James 1:26).

"Rather, he must be must be hospitable, one who loves what is good, who is self-controlled, upright, holy and disciplined" (Titus 1:8).

PERSONALITY PROFILE

Roger Sherman was born in 1721, in Newton, Massachusetts. He was the son of a captain who settled in Watertown, Massachusetts. He received no formal education but was influenced and educated under Rev. Samuel Dunbar. Roger was 20 years old when his father died and he moved to New Milford, Connecticut, where his brother was living. He became a cobbler and carried his tools to work throughout the region. His popularity and willingness to serve opened the door for him to purchase properties.

Roger Sherman was married first to Elizabeth Hartwell, with whom he had seven children before her death in 1760; and then to Rebecca Prescott, with whom he had eight children. His second wife, Rebecca, survived him. He wanted a new start and left New Milford and resettled in New Haven. Later he met Rebecca Prescott from Salem. She was only 20 years old but the courtship began and led to marriage and an even larger family.

Rebecca's father and grandfather were graduates of Harvard College and from the information available, it seems she was a person of great character with a warm personality. Each of Sherman's five daughters admired their father and married men of similar character as he, with integrity, public spirit, earnest religious faith, sound judgment, and large mental capacity.

He was elected to the upper house, a position he held for 19 years. Along with two others, Sherman was sent from New Haven to the "Continental Congress" and served from 1774 to 1781 and from 1783 to 1784. He also served as mayor of New Haven from 1784-93. He favored an executive dominated by the legislature. He also was on the Congressional Committee with Jefferson, Adams, Livingston, and Franklin that drafted the Declaration of Independence.

He was the only person to sign the Constitution, the Articles of Association of 1774, the Declaration of Independence, and the Articles of Confederation. Sherman also served on the Supreme Court of Connecticut. During the Constitutional Convention he delivered 138 speeches. Sherman served as a member of the U.S. House of Representatives where he helped frame the "Bill of Rights." He drew up a series of amendments designed to strengthen the Confederation, the chief of which provided that Congress should have the power to regulate commerce, levy imports, establish a supreme court and make laws binding on the people.

His correspondence with theologians revealed his insights into the kind of self-control and submission which would glorify God.

In 1776 Sherman began fighting for a sound system of credit and voted for Hamilton's measure for the assumption of state debts. He was responsible for "The Great Compromise" which broke the "deadlock" between the large and small states giving representation in the House of Representatives to the larger states on the basis of population while providing equality to all states in the Senate. He looked not only at the present but also looked to future generations.

FURTHER SCRIPTURE DOCUMENTATION:

"Everyone who competes in the games goes into strict training. They do it to get a crown that will not last; but we do it to get a crown that will last forever. Therefore I do not run like a man running aimlessly; I do not fight like a man beating the air. No, I beat my body and make it my slave so that after I have preached to others, I myself will not be disqualified for the prize" (1 Corinthians 9:25-27).

Sherman began to take an active part in town and church affairs. After purchasing a store, he began writing papers on injustice and a series of almanacs between 1750 and 1761 based on astronomical calculations and quotes from poets. He published the annual almanacs and became a household name. He became the justice of the peace and was elected to the legislature. This led him to move to New Haven where he imported merchandise, as well as books for Yale students.

SHERMAN'S BELIEFS AND IMPRESSIONS

Jonathan Edwards said that Roger Sherman was "profoundly versed in theology and he held firmly the doctrines of the Reformation."[1]

Roger Boardman, his biographer, said that Sherman was, "Of grave and massive understanding, [he was] a man who looked at the most difficult questions and untied their tangled knots without having his vision dimmed or his head made dizzy. He appears to have known the science of government and the relations of society from childhood—he needed no teaching because he saw the moral, ethical and political truths in all their relations, better than they could be interpreted to him by others."[2]

Said Jeremiah Wadsworth, "At the end of the Revolution, he [Sherman] was perhaps the most influential figure in Congress."[3] John C. Calhoun said, "He [Sherman] was one of

> *"The most precious of all possessions, is power over ourselves; power to withstand trial, to bear suffering, to front danger; power over pleasure and pain; power to follow our convictions, however resisted by menace and scorn, the power of calm reliance in scenes of darkness and storms. He that hath not a mastery over his inclinations; he that knows not how to resists the importunity of present pleasure or pain, for the sake of what reason tells him is fit to be done, [lacks] the true principle of virtue and industry, and is in danger of never being good for anything."*[6]
>
> *John Locke*

three men to whom we are indebted for a federal government instead of a national government."[4]

His biographer, Boardman said, "He [Sherman] ever adored the profession of Christianity which he made in youth; and was distinguished through life for public usefulness, died in the prospect of a blessed immortality. No man in Connecticut ever enjoyed the confidence of the people of the state more entirely, or for a longer period, than Roger Sherman."[5]

Looking at the character of Roger Sherman, one is struck with his practical wisdom. Sherman understood people and this was due in large part to his faith in Christ. He knew how to speak to the hearts of people and could perceive their motivations. Sherman was known for his common sense and this was evident in the many discussions he participated in as the "Founders" convened in Philadelphia. He was well acquainted with the "virtues and vices" of the representatives from the colonies. Sherman was also known for his integrity. He had no personal motives and sought to operate out of principle without allowing his emotions to get in the way. As a result of these virtues, Sherman had a significant influence on his fellow patriots.

One delegate, Fisher Ames, observed, "If I am absent during the discussion of a subject, and consequently don't know on which side to vote, I always look at Roger Sherman, for I am sure if I vote with him I shall vote right."[7]

SHERMAN DEMONSTRATED SELF-CONTROL IN HIS SPEECH

Jefferson spoke of Sherman as, "A man who never said a foolish thing in his life. One of the sound and strongest pillars in the Revolution."[8] John Adams said Sherman was, "As honest as an angel and as firm in the cause of American Independence as Mount Atlas."[9]

His pastor said of Sherman, "His abilities were remarkable, not brilliant, but solid, penetrating and capable of deep and long investigation. In such investigation was greatly assisted by his patient and unremitting application and perseverance."[10]

"Sherman was noted and esteemed for his calmness of nature and common sense in him rose almost to genius. Sherman had that dignity which arises from doing everything perfectly right. He was an extraordinary man—a venerable uncorrupted patriot,"[11] noted historian Forrest Morgan.

"In the whole course of his public life, Roger Sherman never failed to leave in those with whom (he spoke) an impression of deep sagacity, (profound knowledge, good judgment, understanding) and stern integrity, and he bequeathed, as a public man, to those who should come after him, the character of a great, and what is much more rare, of an honest politician."[12]

Governor Baldwin commented on Sherman, "His example will never die out of American memory, because it appeals to every man in every walk of life, and shows how character, perseverance, industry, joined to common sense, under our system of government, put within the reach of their possessor opportunity for doing public service and winning public esteem."[13]

THE DISCIPLINES SHERMAN DEVELOPED

His pastor, who introduced him to the love of reading, shaped Sherman's good habits. He read widely in theology, history, mathematics, and politics. He was very cautious in

PRACTICING SELF-CONTROL

In this Scripture "self-control" follows knowledge, suggesting that what we learn, we must put into practice. A few of the benefits of self-control are:

◆ Control over what we say.
"Set a guard over my mouth, O LORD; keep watch over the door of my lips" (Psalm 141:3).

◆ Control over what we do.
"Better a patient man than a warrior, a man who controls his temper than one who takes a city" (Proverbs 16:32).

◆ Control over our spirit.
"Like a city whose walls are broken down is a man who lacks self-control" (Proverbs 25:28).

◆ Control over our bodies.
"We all stumble in many ways. If anyone is never at fault in what he says, he is a perfect man, able to keep his whole body in check" (James 3:2).

"His example will never die out of American memory, because it appeals to every man in every walk of life, and shows how character, perseverance, industry, joined to common sense, under our system of government, put within the reach of their possessor opportunity for doing public service and winning public esteem."[14]

Governor Baldwin

making his decisions, exploring all the facts first. The discipline of taking the Sabbath seriously was a commitment Sherman made early in life.

"The Sabbath began at sunset...they went their way, with the children in quiet procession following, to a cheerless meeting house where a rigid Calvinistic theology was held up to the contemplation of adult and child alike for the greater part of the day." [15]

SHERMAN'S DESIRES FOR HIS FAMILY

Sherman desired his children to have the same familiarity with the Bible that he himself possessed. At the opening of each session of Congress he would buy a new Bible, use it daily in his private devotions throughout the session, and, at the close, on his return to New Haven, present it to one of his children." [17]

Sherman's "self-control" was coupled with "selflessness." He was pure in his motives. Rufus Griswold observed, "His [Sherman's] contemporaries fully recognized his ability, honesty, adroitness in legislative councils, but they were fond of recording his personal awkwardness and a certain rusticity of manner. His record attests industry, integrity, devotion to public duty, even moral grandeur. He is no orator, and yet not a speaker in the convention is more effective; the basis of his power is found, first, in the thorough conviction of his integrity; his countrymen are satisfied that he is a good man, a real patriot, with no little or sinister or personal ends in view." [18]

Boardman writes, "With no false pride or ambition to gratify, no favorites to flutter around him—fearless, modest, delicate in his mode of doing, he was able immediately to bring his best intellectual resources into the field of debate." [19]

MODERN-DAY EXAMPLE OF SELF-CONTROL
AL AKIMOFF

Al Akimoff heads up "Slavic Ministries" in Salem, Oregon. I first met Al in 1967 when we were together on a missions outreach to the Caribbean. We spent the summer in Jamaica and the Cayman Islands. In those days the Cayman Islands were not the place you went to for a vacation. There were about 27 different kinds of mosquitoes on the island, but our time was thoroughly enjoyable.

Al's family is from the Ukraine and they loved God supremely. The Akimoff's fled the Ukraine during Stalin's purge and the family walked out of Russia to China where Al was born. It's an amazing story of God's protection of a small community who fled for their lives.

Al grew up aware of his God's remarkable protection of his family and knew first hand the reality of Jesus in his life. Al has provided leadership for "Slavic Ministries" for over 20 years and I had the privilege of working with him for a year, which helped prepare us for our years in Russia.

Al is a remarkable individual and a quiet leader. One of his most outstanding qualities is his sense of "self-control." God has used this virtue to protect him when he traveled "behind the iron curtain" and shaped the way he led people. When others would say "Let's go for it now!" Al would say, "Let's pray and see what God is saying to us." As the leader of "Slavic Ministries," he knew man's wisdom was not enough. The "mind of God" was needed.

After the "Berlin wall" came down, thousands of Christians flocked to Russia and returned before they had overcome "jetlag." Al wrote an article saying, "Don't rush to Russia." It was counsel some needed to hear. His approach was always to pray and plan and get God's direction before announcing what you were going to do. We needed this kind of leadership in our group and Al provided it for us. His counsel was always prefaced with careful thought.

Al Akimoff seems to rejoice at whatever God is doing. It really doesn't matter to him who does it, as long as Jesus is glorified. It has been a joy to see how Al and his wife, Carolyn, have grown over the years. They know what it means to trust God and to practice "self-control." What great models they are to those who know them.

REVIEW

Q. What does Jefferson's assessment of Sherman tell you about Sherman?

Q. How do you think Sherman developed his analytical ability?

Q. What are some of the disciplines you are developing to prepare you for the future?

Q. What were the consequences of Sherman's life?

Q. Personal awkwardness or not being an orator did not handicap Sherman. How do you think he managed to overcome these weaknesses in his life?

Q. What are the root problems preventing "self-control" in our lives?

Q. What kind of damage can a lack of "self-control" bring into my life?

Q. What do I need to do to develop "self-control" in my life?

Character for Life

GOD'S PROMISE:

"Set a guard over my mouth, O LORD; keep watch over the door of my lips" (Psalm 141:3).

"But the fruit of the Spirit is love, joy, peace, patience, kindness, goodness, faithfulness, gentleness, and self-control" (Galatians 5:22-23a).

GOD'S GOAL:

For Christians to be self-controlled.

YOUR COMMITMENT:

To demonstrate self-control in all aspects of life.

YOUR DAILY RESPONSE:

1. Guard the tongue.

2. Pray for God's guidance at all times.

3. Think before speaking.

4. Take time for mediation on God's Word.

FAILURE WILL MEAN:

Being uncontrolled and difficult to be around.

BACKGROUND:

In 1 Corinthians 9:25, the Bible refers to athletes who practice self-control to gain a prize. It's the same with disciples of Jesus. The lack of self-control has disqualified many from being useful in their service to God and man. Our wills must be brought under the control of the Holy Spirit. Our lives are typically either "out of control" or "under the control" of the Holy Spirit. "And to knowledge, self-control; and to self-control, perseverance; and to perseverance, godliness" (2 Peter 1:6).

The following verses show how self-control was evident in the life of Jesus. "When they hurled their insults at him, he did not retaliate; when he suffered, he made no threats. Instead, he entrusted himself to him who judges justly" (1 Peter 2:23).

"He was oppressed and afflicted, yet he did not open his mouth; he was led like a lamb to the slaughter, and as a sheep before her shearers is silent, so he did not open his mouth. By oppression and judgment he was taken away. And who can speak of his descendants? For he was cut off from the land of the living; for the transgression of my people he was stricken" (Isaiah 53:7-8).

When Roman soldiers arrested Jesus, His disciple Peter drew his sword and cut off the ear of the high priest's servant. The response of Jesus is an amazing example of self-control. He told Peter to put his sword back and told him "for all who draw the sword will die by the sword" (Matthew 26:52).

Jesus knew His Father in Heaven could deliver Him but He would have had to abandon His mission to save us if He was not able to overcome the weakness of His body.

LIVING A LIFE OF SELF-CONTROL MEANS . . .

■ Praying first, acting second

■ Trusting God to help you control yourself in difficult situations

■ Living life with an inner peace

■ Understanding your own weaknesses

■ Being willing to step back and analyze situations

Chapter Thirty Four: Learn more about Sherman

Go to an Internet search engine.
Type in *Roger Sherman's Character.*
Find topics 1-2 below and open up the websites.
1. Colonial Hall: Biography of Roger Sherman
2. Correspondence of Thomas Jefferson/U

Go to an Internet search engine.
Type in *Roger Sherman's Life.*
Find topics 1-4 below and open up the websites.
1. Colonial Hall: Biography of Roger Sherman
2. Roger Sherman "The career of Roger Sherman"....
3. Roger Sherman "In July of 1793"....
4. Roger Sherman "Connecticut's Roger Sherman was the only American"....

chapter 35

Selflessness—John Jay

PURPOSE: Putting the Needs of Others Before Your Own

character trait:

Selflessness

SUBJECT:

JOHN JAY
(1745-1829)

PURPOSE:

Putting the Needs of Others
Before Your Own

FAMOUS QUOTE:

"They have the book."
(Jay's response when asked if he
had final words for his children.)

**SCRIPTURE
DOCUMENTATION:**

"It is enough for the student to be
like his teacher, and the servant
like his master" (Matthew 10:25a).

"The greatest among you will be
your servant. For whoever exalts
himself will be humbled, and whoever humbles himself will be
exalted" (Matthew
23:11-12).

"Whatever you do, work at it with
all your heart, as working for the
Lord, not for men, since you know
that you will receive an inheritance
from the Lord as a reward. It is the
Lord Christ you are serving"
(Colossians 3:23-24).

"God is not unjust; he will not
forget your work and the love you
have shown him as you have
helped his people and continue to
help them" (Hebrews 6:10).

PERSONALITY PROFILE

John Jay was born in 1745. His ancestors were Calvinist Protestants who fled
from France because of religious persecution. When Jay was a small boy, a
smallpox epidemic swept through New
York City. Jay's brother and sister were
blinded by it. Jay was the second to last
of seven children. He was born with a
speech impediment, yet overcame it.

Jay's mother taught him the basics of English and Latin. His
pastor taught him languages. Jay had prepared himself well for
the roles he would ultimately play in the founding of the
American Republic. His father wrote, "He [Jay] takes to learning
exceedingly well." Jay learned the French language as a child
(this became tremendously helpful later in his life since it was a
tool he could use in his diplomatic missions to France).

At the age of 14, Jay enrolled in King's College. Prior to enroll-
ment into college, he had to translate the first ten chapters of St.
John's Gospel from Greek to Latin. Jay developed a beautiful
writing style at King's College and became fascinated with
domestic and international law during his final years in school.

As an adult, Jay took on the responsibilities of his parents and
helped provide their physical security. Jay graduated from
Columbia and was admitted to the bar in 1766. He left law after
seven years of private practice to work in government services.
Jay became an attorney, public official, diplomat, and jurist. Jay
married Sarah Livingston and they enjoyed a wonderful relationship together. During much of his life, Jay experienced frequent
bouts of ill health due to his traveling in America and overseas.

Among his many accomplishments was serving as a member of
the Continental Congress from 1774-76 and from 1778-79 and
being appointed Chief Justice of the State of New York. He
resigned December 1778 to become "the President of the
Continental Congress" (1778-79). He signed the final peace
treaty with Great Britain in 1783. Jay went on to become the
First Chief Justice of the U.S. Supreme Court.

JAY'S ACCOMPLISHMENTS

John Jay was one of the key "Founders" of the American Republic. He, along with Franklin, Jefferson, Livingston, and Sherman, drafted the "Constitution." "Jay," Jefferson said, "owned the finest pen in the country."

Jay was a very able man but not a genius. His leadership and integrity were his invaluable contribution to American public life. He brought consistent intellectual vigor and moral tone into every office which he held. He was second to none of the 'Founders' in the fineness of his principles, uncompromising moral rectitude, and uprightness of private faith.

Jay proposed the section of the Constitution guaranteeing complete religious toleration without discrimination or preference. (This was the broadest emancipation of the principles of religious liberty that had as yet been granted by any state in the modern world.)

Jay was elected governor of New York in 1795. In his second term as governor, he sought to support a bill in Congress that would abolish slavery. It failed, but in 1799 he was able to see emancipation enacted in New York State. During his two terms of service as governor, he reformed the prison system, limited the death penalty, abolished flogging, built facilities for the prison system, and introduced humane treatment of prisoners.

JAY'S FAITH THROUGH LOSS

Jay's deep faith and trust in God and His character was never more real than during the passing of his wife and daughter.

In May of 1802, Mrs. Jay began to fail rapidly, and on the 28th, with her husband and children at her bedside, she died. In that tragic hour Jay remained calm. When he saw that death had claimed her he at once led his children into the adjoining room, took the family Bible and turned to 1 Corinthians 15. He looked forward to the reunion in heaven.

Upon the death of his daughter he said, "The removal of my excellent daughter from the house of her earthly, to the house of her Heavenly Father, leaves me nothing to regret or lament on her account. I hope we shall be favored with grace to derive consolations from the reflection that her departure was ordered by infinite wisdom and goodness, and that this temporary separation will terminate in a perpetual reunion."[2]

"I had rather starve and rot and keep the privilege of speaking the truth as I see it, than of holding all the offices that capital has to give from the presidency downward."[1]

Henry Brooks Adams

JAY'S CONTRIBUTION EVEN IN DEATH

In his last will and testament, John Jay wrote, "Unto Him who is the author and giver of all that is good, I render sincere and humble thanks for His merciful and unmerited blessings, and especially for our redemption and salvation by His beloved Son." As he was nearing the end of his life of serving the country, Jay was asked if he had any final words for his children, to which he responded: "They have the book." [3] Upon his death in 1829, Jay willed part of his money to be passed out among the widows and orphans in his town.

IMPRESSIONS OF JAY

President Adams said of Jay, "He is a man of wit, well-informed, a good speaker and an eloquent writer." [5] Jay's son described him as "a rare but interesting picture of the Christian patriot and statesman." [6] Said Pellew, "He [Jay] was remarkable for his strong reasoning power and comprehensive views, indefatigable application and uncommon firmness of mind." [7]

JAY NEVER SOUGHT PERSONAL RECOGNITION

While he was in Europe Jay was elected Governor of New York without knowing it. He had not even been asked if he wished to serve. Jay never once solicited an office but the offices came to him.

Jay's judgments were sound and inspiring and were written in a language the common person would be able to grasp. He did much to establish the Supreme Court as the honorable institution it is today. While Jay was the Secretary of Foreign Affairs, President Washington asked Jay to choose an office in the new government where he believed he could serve the country effectively. He chose the judiciary branch and his circuit included New York and New England. While still Chief Justice, Jay was chosen to be part of a special envoy to England. This was a difficult decision for Jay since the attitude toward England was hostile at that time. The invitations came to him for service.

Jay wrote, "[America must] forsake selfish vice and trust in God. Let a general reformation of manners take place—let universal charity, public spirit, and private virtue be inculcated, encouraged and practiced. Unite in a preparation for a vigorous defense of your country, as if all depended on your own exertions. And when you have done all things, then rely upon the good Providence of Almighty God for success, in full confidence that without his blessings, all our efforts will inevitably fail."[8]

JAY SELFLESSLY TOOK UNPOPULAR POSITIONS

"I have adhered to certain fixed principles and faithfully obeyed their dictates without regarding the consequences of such conduct to my friends or myself,"[9] said Jay. Jay wrote a letter to the people of Great Britain detailing the grievances of the people in the colonies. He was part of a select counsel to draft a Constitution for the United States and served as President of the "Continental Congress" and a member of the First and Second Congresses. He supported the insertion of a clause forbidding the continuance of slavery, an institution he held in deep abhorrence.

Jay became the first Chief Justice of the Supreme Court of the United States. Along with John Adams and Benjamin Franklin, he negotiated the peace treaty to end the War with England. Subsequently, he became the Secretary of Foreign Affairs. He authored "the Jay Treaty," which prevented the United States from getting involved in the war between France and England. While in Europe, Congress had appointed him Secretary of Foreign Affairs, a post he held from 1784-89. His experience in dealing with European powers convinced him of the need for a strong central government.

Jay's writings included his views on the Sabbath as a civil and divine institution. He was a leader in the temperance movement, Sunday schools, and missionary and educational thrusts that were taking place in the country.

JAY'S PASSION TO SHARE HIS FAITH

Convinced of the need to spread the Word of God to distant lands, Jay was first elected Vice President of the American Bible Society (1816-21) and in 1821 he became that organization's President. As Governor of New York (1795-1801) he was recognized for his honesty, his refusal to appoint or dismiss officials because of political affiliations, and his devotion to duty.

Jay was persuaded that, "Of all the dispositions and habits which lead to political prosperity, religion and morality are

"God uses for His glory those people and things which are most perfectly broken...those who are broken in wealth, broken in self-will, broken in their ambitions, broken in their beautiful ideas, broken in worldly reputation, broken in their affections, broken of times in health, those who are despised and seem utterly forlorn and helpless, these are the ones the Holy Spirit is seizing upon and using for God's glory."[10]

George Watson

indispensable supports. In vain would that man claim the tribute of patriotism, who should labor to subvert these great pillars of human happiness. The mere politician should respect and cherish them." [11]

NATIONAL PURPOSE ▶

Jay was a Christian and a brilliant man with extraordinary gifts. He saw the events of his country through the eyes of faith. He said, "We do not fight for a few acres of land, but for freedom—for the freedom of the millions yet unborn." [12]

On the subject of slavery Jay said, "We have the highest reason to believe that the Almighty will not suffer slavery and the gospel to go hand in hand. It cannot, it will not be." Jay believed, "Every member of the State ought to read and study the Constitution of his country. By knowing their rights, they will sooner perceived them when they are violated and be the better prepared to defend and assert them." [13]

After a life of service to his country that required him to be away from his family for so many years, Jay was worn out. After his wife died, Jay was able to reflect on his remarkable journey through life. He wrote, "Providence has given to our people the choice of their rulers, and it is the duty…of our Christian nation to select and prefer Christians for their rulers." [14] Jay combined with Hamilton and Madison wrote the Federalist papers which explained the principles of the Constitution. This was one of his greatest accomplishments.

If you are looking for examples of "selflessness," look to William Booth, the founder of the Salvation Army, and the thousands of Christians who have embraced the Army as their calling in life. General Booth could easily be thought of as one of our 37 heroes. Consider the impact of this mission in America and over 100 countries in the world. The Salvation Army operates as does most armies, but their motivation is to respond to Christ's words in Luke 4:18 to "preach good news to the poor. He has sent me to proclaim freedom for the prisoners and recovery of sight for the blind, to release the oppressed, to proclaim the year of the Lord's favor." The Army operates hospitals, community centers, alcoholic and drug rehabilitation programs, emergency and disaster relief, social work centers, and recreational programs. The mission of the Salvation Army is to win the world for Jesus.

ON MARCH 20, 1779 JAY PRESENTED A RESOLUTION IN CONGRESS

Resolved, that it be recommended to the several States to appoint the First Thursday in May next to be a day of Fasting, Humiliation and Prayer to Almighty God, that He will be pleased to avert those impending Calamities which we have but too well deserved: That He will grant to us His Grace to repent of our Sins, and amend our lives according to His Holy Word: that He will continue that wonderful Protection which hath led us through the Paths of Danger and Distress: That He will be a Husband to the Widow and a Father to the Fatherless Children, who weep over the Barbarities of a savage enemy; That He will grant us Patience in Suffering, and Fortitude in Adversity: That He will inspire us with Humility, Moderation and Gratitude in prosperous Circumstances: That He will give Wisdom to our Council,

MODERN-DAY EXAMPLE
OF SELFLESSNESS
ANDY BEACH

I first called this character trait the "servant heart," but in reality, it is selflessness, so we'll describe it as someone who puts the interests of others before himself.

I first met Andy when I served as a pastor in West Stephentown, New York. Andy was in the eighth grade at the time and was learning to type. He wanted to help and he provided me with a service I really needed.

I described his parents under the section under hospitality and Andy learned that as well. Andy had a "lightness" in his spirit that was contagious. He always had a quick response and a ready smile. He enjoyed life and somehow found a way to live above the negativism of life. He saw things on the "bright side."

I knew Andy well, and we communicated on a regular basis. He joined me in Virginia when we worked for the "Christian Broadcasting Network." I think that was my favorite job. Andy worked with me to schedule people for the program, among other things. He was a court stenographer and taking dictation was easy for him. These were the pre-computer days, so of course, the value of his work was immense.

One thing I learned about Andy was that he never felt "put upon." He embraced each assignment with the kind of response you would like to hear, like "no problem" or "I'll take care of it."

Andy developed the gift of anticipating the needs of those he worked for. Every employer should be so blessed! He made me successful and when we left the "Christian Broadcasting Network" it required several people to replace us. It was all Andy. Believe me! When we moved to Kona, Hawaii, to help start the university, Andy eventually joined "Youth With a Mission" and served God in Asia, the Pacific, and in Europe. He became the "scheduler" for Loren Cunningham, the president of the mission.

Several years ago Andy and his wife, Wilma, decided God was leading them to leave "Youth With a Mission," but they didn't know just where they were to go. God opened the door for Andy to work with Senator John Ashcroft of Missouri. When the Senator became the Attorney General of the United States he asked Andy to become part of his team. Andy anticipated the needs of the former Attorney General, scheduled his activities, and traveled with him on trips.

While Andy Beach didn't go to college, he did choose to become a disciple of Jesus Christ. He laid aside his own desires and God opened up the world to him. Now his wife, Wilma, and his daughter Tiara are a tight-knit family who live to bring honor to the Lord Jesus.

I am blessed to have known Andy for over 30 years. What a guy!

Firmness to our Resolutions, and Victory to our Arms: That He will bless the Labors of the Husbandman, and pour forth Abundance, so that we may enjoy the Fruits for the earth in due season; that He will cause Union, Harmony, and mutual Confidence to prevail throughout these States: That He will bestow on our great Ally all those Blessings which may enable him to be gloriously instrumental in protecting the Rights of Mankind and promoting the Happiness of his Subjects: That He will bountifully continue his paternal Care to the Commander in Chief, and the Officers and Soldiers of the United States: That He will grant the Blessings of Peace to all contending Nations, Freedom to those who are in Bondage, and Comfort to the Afflicted: That He will diffuse Useful Knowledge, extend the Influence of True Religion, and give us that Peace of Mind which the World cannot give: That He will be our Shield in the Day of Battle, our Comforter in the Hour of Death, and our kind Parent and merciful Judge through Time and Through Eternity. [15]

REVIEW

Q. What were the handicaps Jay had to overcome?

Q. How did Jay feel about the death of his wife and daughter?

Q. What did Jay mean on his deathbed when he said, "They have the book," referring to his children?

Q. Jay was a "Christian patriot and statesman." Explain how being a Christian patriot would make a difference in how you served your country?

Q. Jay was elected as governor of New York without even being asked. What does that tell you about the people of New York in Jay's time?

Q. How do you think the "Founders" like Jay might have felt knowing that they had not solved the problem of slavery during the Continental Convention and that the country was drifting apart?

Q. When Jay said that we fight for the "freedom of the millions unborn," what does that tell you about his outlook on life?

Q. How did Jay warn Americans that God would not allow slavery and the gospel to co-exist? What do you think he meant by this?

Q. What were the great "pillars of human happiness"?

Q. How long did God postpone the "pending calamities" Jay warned the nation about in 1779?

Q. List several things that Jay prayed for. Which of these are appropriate for our nation today?

Q. How do you think Jay was able to see a reality of the future most of us never see?

Q. What keeps us from becoming "selfless"?

Character for Life

GOD'S PROMISE:

"It is enough for the student to be like his teacher, and the servant like his master" (Matthew 10:25a).

GOD'S GOAL:

For Christians to live selflessly.

YOUR COMMITMENT:

To put the good of others before your own good.

YOUR DAILY RESPONSE:

1. To be a servant for Jesus each day.

2. To set goals that serve others, even those who may be of the next generation.

3. To give freely of your time and talents.

4. To do your best always and trust God with the outcome.

FAILURE WILL MEAN:

Being a person of self-indulgence.

BACKGROUND:

Jesus showed true selflessness. "For even the Son of Man did not come to be served, but to serve, and to give his life a ransom for many" (Mark 10:45).

The following are promises God gives to those who serve Him out of gratitude: "And if anyone gives even a cup of cold water to one of these little ones because he is my disciple, I tell you the truth, he will certainly not lose his reward" (Matthew 10:42). "Then I heard a voice from heaven say, 'Write: Blessed are the dead who die in the Lord from now on.' 'Yes,' says the Spirit, 'they will rest from their labor, for their deeds will follow them'" (Revelation 14:13).

LIVING A LIFE OF SELFLESSNESS MEANS . . .

■ Become a sacrament in God's hands.

■ Losing consciousness of "self" and what you are doing for God.

■ Becoming a living sacrifice of devotion to Jesus.

■ Your service is out of appreciation for what God has done for you.

■ Your devotion to God will allow you to serve others whether or not you are appreciated. If we only serve humanity, we will end up heartbroken and discouraged.

■ God's glory will to be seen through our fingertips, eyes, hands, and feet.

■ You will fulfill your spiritual destiny

Chapter Thirty Five: Learn more about Jay

Go to an Internet search engine.
Type in *Chief Justice John Jay's Character, Selflessness*.
Find topics 1-4 below and open up the websites.
1. John Jay 1745-1829 American Jurist and Statesman
2. The Laws of Nature and Nature's God
3. Christian Leaders for a Christian Nation
4. American Heritage: Are we a Christian Nation?

chapter 36

Thankfulness—

william Bradford

PURPOSE: Medicine For a Healthy Heart

character trait:
Thankfulness

SUBJECT:
WILLIAM BRADFORD
(1590-1657)

PURPOSE:
Medicine For a Healthy Heart

FAMOUS QUOTE:
"Thus out of small beginnings greater things have been produced by His hand that made all things of nothing and gives being to all things that are; and, as one small candle may light a thousand, so the light here kindled hath shone unto many, yea in some sort to our whole nation; let the glorious name of Jehovah have all the praise."

SCRIPTURE DOCUMENTATION:
"It is a good to praise the LORD and make music to your name, O Most High, to proclaim your love in the morning and your faithfulness at night" (Psalm 92:1-2).

"Speak to one another with psalms, hymns and spiritual songs. Sing and make music in your heart to the Lord, always giving thanks to God the Father for everything, in the name of our Lord Jesus Christ" (Ephesians 5:19-20).

"For we are God's workmanship, created in Christ Jesus to do good works, which God prepared in advance for us to do" (Ephesians 2:10).

"But thanks be to God! He gives us the victory through our Lord Jesus Christ" (1 Corinthians 15:57).

PERSONALITY PROFILE

William Bradford was born in 1590 in Austerfield, England. Both of his parents died while he was a child, so his grandparents and uncles raised him. Bradford attained the ability to master several languages, including Dutch, French, and Latin, as well as Greek and Hebrew. Bradford married Dorothea May on December 9, 1613.

The fellowship to which Bradford belonged came under severe persecution and he was sentenced to prison for several months. In 1607, as a result of this persecution, the Pilgrims departed from their home country of England and moved to Holland for safety reasons. Four years after arriving in Amsterdam, the company moved to Leyden.

The goal of the fellowship in Holland was to become a New Testament Church. Bradford wrote,

> I know not but it may be spoke to the honor of God and without prejudice to any that such was the true piety, the humble zeal and fervent love of this people towards God and His ways, and the single heartedness and sincere affection one towards another, that they came as near the primitive pattern of the first churches as any other church of these latter times have done, according to their rank and quality.... And first, though many of them were poor, yet there was none so poor but if they were known to be of that congregation, the Dutch would trust them in any reasonable matter when they wanted money, because they had found by experience how carefully they were to keep their word, and saw them so painful and diligent in their callings.[1]

Bradford continued describing the mood prior to the departure of the Pilgrims, "And the time came when they must depart, they were accompanied with most of their brethren out of the city, unto a town sundry miles off called Delftshaven, where the ship lay ready to receive them. So they left that goodly and pleasant city which had been their resting place near twelve years, but they knew 'they were pilgrims,' and looked not much on those things, but lifted up their eyes to the heavens, their dearest country, and quieted their spirits."[2]

The Pilgrims left for the new world in 1620. The human loss was staggering! Bradford's wife drowned shortly before their arrival. Thirteen of the 18 wives who came to the New World died and more than half of the married men perished. At the end of that frigid season, only three married couples had not been separated by death.

Bradford was elected Governor of Plymouth Colony in 1621 and was re-elected every year until his death in 1657 (except for five years in which he declined the position). His journal, or history, is our New England Testament. It is the story of the Pilgrim "Fathers" in Old England, in Holland and in New England, told by one who was from the beginning. Bradford believed the Pilgrims were similar to Gideon's Army.

While Boston's Puritans were establishing a hierarchy, William Bradford was trying to build in politics, as in religion, an earthly replica of the freedom Christ had promised. He was a thinker and a man of action, a writer of considerable charm, a linguist, farmer, business man, magistrate, diplomat, and man of God. In Plymouth, a classless society in an age of rigid class distinctions was founded. Bradford went to the "new world" with the conviction that all men could be free.

LIFE IN EARLY AMERICA

As leader of the "Colonists," William Bradford and others frequently reached the point of starvation. They tried to share all things in common but it didn't work out very well. The community decided each family should plant for themselves. Eventually, each family received land to farm and this changed the attitude of the early settlers. So many children were without parents that they established the first orphanage in America. They were working out the will of God by themselves, amid incredible hardship. They chose to deny themselves because they were sure God had called them to undertake this mission.

The Pilgrim "Fathers" were really young men and were viewed by traditional Christians as radicals in religion and in politics. The Pilgrims saw the corruption in English society and believed God's judgment was upon England.

Bradford Smith, a biographer, provides reasons to conclude that Bradford was a powerful influence, "That he was Plymouth's greatest man there is no doubt. He was a person of excellent temper [disposition]…under the inexpressible hardships they suffered the first three or four years. He bore a part in them all himself and encouraged the people by his own example. He was a man of strong mind, sound judgment, and

FURTHER SCRIPTURE DOCUMENTATION:
"Therefore, since we are receiving a kingdom that cannot be shaken, let us be thankful, and so worship God acceptably with reverence and awe, for our 'God is a consuming fire'" (Hebrews 12:28-29).

Our Pilgrim Forefathers made a covenant with God and God still remembers that covenant. He will not overlook it. Nations which have entered into a covenant with God have been blessed in amazing ways. The children of the first generation of "Puritans," however, entered into "half-convenants" (in short, their hearts were not totally devoted to Christ). God renewed their "first love" and a "Great Awakening" brought our forefathers to their knees in repentance. We who remember "9/11" now know about national chastisement. "The Lord will bring a nation against you from far away, from the ends of the earth, like an eagle swooping down, a nation whose language you will not understand, a fierce-looking nation without respect for the old or pity for the young." (Deut. 28:49–50). Perhaps 9/11 was a shot across the bow. For those who have "ears to hear," God has been trying to get our attention.

NATIONAL PURPOSE ▶

a good memory. He had read much of history and philosophy, but theology was his favorite study. He was a person of great gravity and prudence, of sober principles."[4]

Bradford and the Pilgrims wanted to separate themselves from "the world." "They were steeped in the lore of the Old Testament. They saw themselves as a 'Spiritual Israel' and wanted to get away from the temptations and corruptions of the city and the alarms of war, to carry the word of God to a new world and by careful husbandry to make the land yield its increase—this was what America promised. For this they were Pilgrims, and this was what William Bradford meant when he gave them the name. Thus America and the Old Testament were joined before ever the Pilgrims set foot on Cape Cod."[5]

The "Mayflower Compact" reveals the purposes for the Pilgrims coming to the new world in the words of William Bradford:

> In the name of God, Amen. We whose names are under-written, by the loyal subjects of our dread sovereign Lord, King James, by the grace of God, of Great Britain, France, and Ireland king, defender of the faith.
>
> Having undertaking, for the glory of God, and advancement of the Christian faith, and honor of our king and country, a voyage to plant the first colonie in the Northern parts of Virginia, do by these present solemnly and mutually in the presence of God, and one another, covenant and combine ourselves together into a civil body politic, for our better ordering and preservation and furtherance of the ends aforesaid, and by virtue hereof to enact, constitute and frame such just and equal laws, ordinances, acts, constitutions, and offices, from time to time, as shall be through most good and convenient for the general good of the Colonie, unto which we promise all due submission and obedience. In witness whereof we have hereunder subscribed our names at Cape Cod, the 11th of November, in the year of the reign of our sovereign lord, King James, 1620.[6]

BRADFORD'S GRATITUDE FOR DELIVERANCE AND BLESSINGS

Said Bradford, "To all ye Pilgrims: Inasmuch as the great Father has given us this year an abundant harvest of Indian corn, wheat, peas, beans, squashes, and garden vegetable, and has made the forests to abound with game and the sea with fish and clams, and inasmuch as he has protected us from the ravages of the savages, has spared us from pestilence and disease, has granted us freedom to worship God according to the dictates of our own conscience; now, I, your magistrate, do proclaim that all ye Pilgrims, with your wives and your little ones, do gather at ye meeting house, on ye hill, between the hours of 9 and 12 in the day time, on Thursday, November 29, of the year of our Lord one thousand six hundred and twenty three, and the third year since ye Pilgrims landed on ye Pilgrim Rock, there to listen to ye pastor and render thanksgiving to ye Almighty God for all His blessings."[7]

HAPPINESS IN ANOTHER WORLD

On May 7, 1657, the night after which the God of heaven so filled Bradford's mind with ineffable consolations that he seemed little short of Paul, rapt up unto the unutterable entertainments of Paradise. The next morning he told his friends

> "God has two dwellings; one in heaven, and the other in a meek and thankful heart."[8]
>
> Izaak Walton

MODERN-DAY EXAMPLE OF THANKFULNESS
BILL LEONARD'S SPEECH ON THANKFULNESS

California Assemblyman Bill Leonard recounted the story of Sqanto: "A few years ago at Thanksgiving I wrote about the role that an Indian named Squanto played in our nation's Thanksgiving story. The Pilgrims of Plymouth Colony in 1621 decided to hold a harvest celebration to express their thanks to God for providing a means for them to survive the upcoming winter. Their own efforts to raise barley and peas had failed. The previous winter, half of the Pilgrims had died. There rest would have died, too, had it not been for an Indian named Squanto who helped them harvest a crop of corn."

Leonard recalls that the Governor of the Pilgrim Colony, William Bradford, called Squanto "a special instrument of God" not only for his help in harvesting the food, but for his efforts helping the Pilgrims remain peaceful with other Indians.

Said Leonard, "This Thanksgiving I am again reminded of the need we have to acknowledge the Squantos in our lives–those people who have been special instruments of God. I think first and foremost of my parents who not only provided the necessities of life, but also created in me a love of learning and service that has enabled me to do the job I do today. Of courses, there is also my wife whose support and constant reaffirming love boosts me up and enlightens me daily."

I hope that each of us will look for ways to express our gratitude to God each day. Gratitude and thankfulness are like medicine bringing health to our bodies and souls. It is a wonderful experience to be with people who are grateful.

that the good spirit of God had given him a pledge on his happiness in another world and the first fruits of his eternal glory; and on the day following May 9, 1657, he died.

BRADFORD'S THANKFULNESS IN SPITE OF SUFFERING

The prayer of Bradford that first Thanksgiving Day revealed a great deal about his walk with God. Bradford wrote, "Blessed be the God of Heaven who brought us over the furious ocean. For what could sustain us but the Spirit of God and His grace." [10] Bradford quoted Deuteronomy 26:7 which says, "Then we cried out to the LORD, the God of our fathers, and the LORD heard our voice and saw our misery, toil and oppression." [11]

Like Peter, the Pilgrims knew they overcame their adversity by the "promises of God." Bradford quoted from Psalm 106 and 107, "Give thanks to the Lord for He is good, for His kindness endures forever." The people who founded America patterned the nation of Israel and gave thanks in faithful remembrance of the Creator and the source of joy. In less than a year, 45 percent of the company had perished. Hundreds of Native Americans had died from severe weather and a plague. Ninety braves came to the feast, and all together 147 people gathered together. God was building a country where thanksgiving would always ascend to His throne.

Bradford's history is the history of simple folk, directly inspired by a religious ideal, working out that will of God by themselves, amid incredible hardship. They underwent privation because they were absolutely confident that they were obeying the direct behests of God Himself, and that through all miseries and anguish He was watching over them and testing their loyalty to Him.

Bradford wrote, "Thus out of small beginnings greater things have been produced by His hand that made all things of nothing and gives being to all things that are; and, as one small candle may light a thousand, so the light here kindled hath shone unto many, yea in some sort to our whole nation; let the glorious name of Jehovah have all the praise." [12]

REVIEW

Q. How did the Pilgrims coming to America view themselves?

Q. According to the Mayflower Compact, what were the Pilgrims' purposes in coming to America?

MODERN-DAY EXAMPLE
OF THANKFULNESS
SIGRID GUNDERSON

I have thought about what person over the course of my life had the most grateful spirit of any person I have ever known. I chose to write about my Grandma. She was an amazing person and profoundly affected my life and the lives of hundreds of people.

Around the turn of the century, Sigrid Lunden came to America from Norway and settled in Wilmer, Minnesota where she met my grandfather and soon became Mrs. Gunderson. After they were married they moved to Norway Valley in Alberta, Canada. (It's close to Frog Lake...no doubt you know where that is!) My grandparents had met Jesus and He had changed their lives. Sigrid Gunderson was a mother of twelve children (two died early in life) as well as the grandmother of 47 grandchildren.

At the age of ten, I remember staying with my grandparents and hearing Grandma praying her heart out into the night hours. Jesus was just a breath away from her. The words "Thank you, Jesus" ascended to heaven throughout the day and night hours. Her heart was filled with gratitude to the Savior.

Several of her grandchildren were in Christian work and when they returned from their missions she would take them to the bank where she had put $10 a month (from her meager income) into a special account.

When I was in Korea, I was asked to call a man by the name of Han Oh Kim. He traveled all night long and told me an amazing story. He was wandering the streets when a worker from "World Vision" brought him into an orphanage. Grandma Gunderson became his sponsor. He told me that she supported him each month from the time he was about ten until he completed university. He was now a teacher.

He wanted to know "How is my Mother Gunderson?" He told me, "All I am is because of my Mother Gunderson!" I remember thinking to myself...she not only has time for her 10 children and 47 grandchildren, but a helpless child in Korea.

Grandma Gunderson taught me about thankfulness and praise. Often she would say, "Donnie...God has not given us a spirit of fear, but of power and love and a sound mind." She knew exactly what my problem was and gave me the answer. She knew that thankfulness and praise eliminate fear and create faith in our hearts.

In 1962 I was working at the Seattle World Fair and wanted her to see the marvels I had seen. She agreed to go but when we arrived she said, "You go and enjoy the Fair and I will stay here." She stayed outside the gate all day long passing out tracts and telling people about the One who saved her life. She was impressed with God and not too impressed with technology.

Norway sent a real treasure to America in Sigrid Gunderson. She taught us about life and about the true riches coming from a thankful heart.

Q. Why do you think the reality of "the goodness of God" needed to be planted in the Pilgrims' hearts?

Q. Do you think God tests our loyalty to Him?

Q. If their goal was to become a New Testament Church, what did that church look like for the Pilgrims?

Q. Who, like "Squanto," is responsible for being a helper in your life?

Q. Has God shown you the person or people he wants you to care for?

Q. Make a list of the people who have helped you in a very special way and take time to thank them.

Q. What attitudes develop in the lives of people who don't have a grateful heart?

Character for Life

GOD'S PROMISE:

"It is good to praise the LORD and make music to your name, O Most High, to proclaim your love in the morning and your faithfulness at night" (Psalm 92:1-2).

GOD'S GOAL:

For Christians to demonstrate thankfulness in their lives.

YOUR COMMITMENT:

To praise God and always give thanks.

YOUR DAILY RESPONSE:

1. Focus on the positive, not the negative in life.

2. Be willing to praise God even in difficulties.

3. Be thankful in how God provides for you spiritually and you will find blessings all around you.

4. Have a thankful heart and share that thankfulness with others.

FAILURE WILL MEAN:

Having an ungrateful heart and a discontented life.

BACKGROUND:

Thanksgiving is to acknowledge fully. It is the expression of joy Godward. It is the fruit of the Spirit. Believers are encouraged to abound in it. Appreciation and gratitude indicate a demonstration of a grateful heart (Luke 17:16; Acts 24:3; Romans 16:4). In the New Testament, the swelling sense of gratitude and appreciation expressed in thanksgiving has three primary associations. Thanks is given at the Eucharist (communion service) for the broken body and blood of Jesus (Matthew 26; Mark 14; Luke 22; 1 Corinthians 11). Thanks is given for the blessings that have come to us through Christ (1 Corinthians 15:57; 2 Corinthians 2:14, 9:15). Thanks is given for those who come to know Christ (1 Corinthians 1:4; Ephesians 1:16;

Philippians 1:3; Colossians 1:3). Remembering all that Jesus has done for us and in us, it is appropriate to address every prayer with thanksgiving (Philippians 4:6).

Jesus expressed thanks to His Father. "At that time Jesus said, 'I praise you, Father, Lord of heaven and earth, because you have hidden these things from the wise and learned, and revealed them to little children. Yes, Father, for this was your good pleasure" (Matthew 11:25-26).

"Then he [Jesus] took the seven loaves and the fish, and when he had given thanks, he broke them and gave them to the disciples, and they in turn to the people" (Matthew 15:36).

"While they were eating, Jesus took bread, gave thanks and broke it, and gave it to his disciples, saying, 'Take and eat; this is my body'" (Matthew 26:26).

"So they took away the stone. Then Jesus looked up and said, 'Father, I thank you that you have heard me" (John 11:41).

Jesus also expressed thankfulness for His disciples. "God is not unjust; he will not forget your work and the love you have shown him as you have helped his people and continue to help them" (Hebrews 6:10).

LIVING A LIFE OF THANKFULNESS MEANS . . .

■ Looking up and praising God in all circumstances.

■ Praying without ceasing through good times and bad.

■ Knowing that there is always something to be thankful for.

■ Focusing on others situations, not only on yourself.

■ Trusting God to work all things out for His good.

■ Having a heart that bubbles over with joy because of what Jesus has done!

Chapter Thirty Six: Learn more about Bradford

Go to an Internet search engine.
Type in *William Bradford's Life.*
Find topics 1-6 below and open up the websites.
1. William Bradford. 1657
2. William Bradford Website
3. Historical Presentation in William Bradford's
4. The Economic History of the Puritan Settlement
5. William Bradford. Will of William Bradford....
6. William Bradford, 1590-1657 governor of Plymouth Colony

chapter 37

Zeal—James Madison

PURPOSE: Discovering How God Wants Us to Serve Him

character trait:
Zeal

SUBJECT:
JAMES MADISON
(1751-1836)

PURPOSE:
Discovering How God Wants Us to Serve Him

FAMOUS QUOTE:
"You give me credit to which I have no claim in calling me the writer of the Constitution of the United States. This was not the offspring of a single brain. It ought to be regarded as the work of many heads and many hands."

SCRIPTURE DOCUMENTATION:

"Of the increase of his government and peace there will be no end. He will reign on David's throne and over his kingdom, establishing and upholding it with justice and righteousness from that time on and forever. The zeal of the LORD Almighty will accomplish this" (Isaiah 9:7).

"Never be lacking in zeal, but keep your spiritual fervor, serving the Lord" (Romans 12:11).

"'My food,' said Jesus, 'is to do the will of him who sent me and to finish his work'" (John 4:34).

"Who gave himself for us to redeem us from all wickedness and to purify for himself a people that are his very own, eager to do what is good" (Titus 2:14).

PERSONALITY PROFILE

Both conservatives and liberals looked to James Madison to define the relationship between church and state. Pastors were imprisoned during Madison's early years, and this no doubt influenced his outlook on religious liberty. This was another seminal point for future generations of Americans. Madison's zeal (passion) for religious liberty was ignited as he witnessed the flogging of 45 Baptist ministers. Before getting caught up in the church/state issue, however, take time to review the life of James Madison.

James Madison was born in Port Conway, Virginia. His family was among the early settlers of Virginia dating back to the 1650s. The Madisons came from a Quaker heritage. His ancestors were not among the wealthy of the country but they seemed to be comfortable. Madison was the first of ten children and his mother and grandmother were his first teachers. At the age of 12, Madison came under the tutelage of Donald Robertson who was a pastor. He was taught Latin, Greek, mathematics, literature, and possibly Spanish.

When it was time for college, his father chose Princeton rather than William and Mary because Princeton would provide Madison with a solid Christian education. At that time, he was planning on being a minister. Madison graduated from Princeton (formerly New Jersey College) in two years. Amazingly, Princeton had nine graduates who were to be at the Continental Convention. He was fortunate to have studied under Dr. John Witherspoon, the President of Princeton, who was considered one of America's most outstanding scholars. Madison continued his friendship with Witherspoon until his death. After graduating, Madison continued at Princeton for a year and a half to complete graduate work and consider a career in the ministry.

Madison had lost his health during his student days and felt he was going to die, suffering from exhaustion. Ultimately, he recovered and decided on a career in public service. His preparation for what was ahead of him included genuine self-denial.

Madison waited until he was in his 40s before meeting his wife to be. Senator Aaron Burr introduced Madison to his future wife, Dorothea Payne Todd, "Dolley," in 1794. Marriage changed Madison's life and apparently Dolley was just what he needed. The Madisons had a spiritual relationship and both loved the Scriptures. Together they "lived Christianity." She also was born into a Quaker family. Dolley loved the Quaker's emphasis on a clear conscience and seeing things spiritually, and nothing would shake her belief in God even through their most difficult trials.

Early in his career Madison was a congressman, but soon became the Secretary of State under Jefferson. The Madisons were close to Jefferson, and Dolley was in effect a substitute "first lady." Madison became President in 1809 and Dolley blossomed in this new role. She was both charming and friendly. After his presidency in 1817, the Madisons moved from Washington to "Montpellier" to care for his aged mother. The Madisons were extraordinarily happy as a couple.

"What James Madison brought back to Virginia from his years of intensive study at Princeton were an aroused commitment to the cause of the Patriot party and a deep sympathy for the plight of religious dissenters. Presbyterian Princeton stood foursquare against the establishment of religion—that is, government support of a favored religion by taxation of persons regardless of their religious preferment. Princeton's stated goal was 'to share in the instruction of the youth, to cherish the spirit of liberty and free enquiry: and not only to permit, but even to encourage their right of private judgment, without presuming to dictate with an air of infallibility.'" [1]

THE FLOGGING OF PASTORS

In 1775, young attorney Patrick Henry rode on his mount into Culpepper, Virginia, and found a man, in the town square, tied to a whipping post, his back laid bare and bloody with the bones of his ribs showing. He been scourged with whips laced with metal. Henry recalled, "When they stopped beating him, I could see the bones of his rib cage. I turned to someone and asked what the man had done to deserve a beating such as this." [2] "The reply given him was that the man being scourged was a minister who refused to purchase a license from the local government. He was one of the twelve who were locked in jail because they refused to purchase a license." [3] He died three days later from another scourging. A license was a way the government could control the servants of God. The brutal attacks on Baptist ministers had a powerful impact on both Henry and James Madison.

PRESIDENT MADISON

On the surface, it is hard to see how Madison became the fourth President of the United States. He was not a particularly "charismatic" individual but respect came to him as a result of diligent service to his country. Servant leadership characterized his life and he won the admiration of politicians on his convictions.

He presented the "Virginia Plan" to the conventions calling for a supreme legislature, (executive and judiciary) and a national legislature of two houses; one elected by people and the other a body of nominees submitted by the state. Madison was the youngest participant at the Convention in Philadelphia.

NATIONAL PURPOSE ▶

Madison was known as the "Father of the Constitution." He spoke 161 times at the Constitutional Convention. He was a contributing author of 29 of the 85 Federalist's papers along with Alexander Hamilton and John Jay. He became a leading advocate of freedom of conscience. Madison helped create the "Bill of Rights" and forced it on Congress. He also played a large part in forming the Department of State, Treasury, and War.

VIEWS OF MADISON

Thomas Jefferson held Madison in great esteem. (Quite a compliment since Jefferson was widely traveled.) Jefferson went on to say, "The chief cause of his success…were his general soundness and moderation of his views in all public questions. He was candid, conscientious, just …and high-minded. I can say conscientiously that I do not know in the world a man of purer integrity, more dispassionate, (selfless) and devoted to genuine 'Republicanism,' nor in the whole scope of America and Europe [am I able to] point out an abler head. He (Madison) is the greatest man in the world!"[4]

The Georgia delegate to the Convention, William Pierce said of Madison, "He blends together the profound politician, with the scholar. He is a most agreeable, eloquent and convincing speaker. He always comes forward the best-informed man of any point in debate. Mr. Madison is about 36 years of age, gentleman of great modesty, with a remarkable sweet (disposition)."[5] Historians agree that Madison was a man whose correspondence was absent of any hostility toward individuals.

"Youth, what man's ages is like to be doth shown; we make our ends by our beginnings known."[6]

John Denton

"His inexhaustible faith…held that a well-founded commonwealth may, as our motto declares, be immortal, not only because the people, its constituency, never die, but because the principles of justice in which such a commonwealth originates never die out of the people's heart and mind."[7]

Many of Madison's contemporaries realized that his stature had grown in the eyes of the "Founders." Some referred to him as the architect of the Constitution. Madison's response indicated his true humility: "You give me credit to which I have no claim in calling me the writer of the Constitution of the United States. This was not the offspring of a single brain. It ought to be regarded as the work of many heads and many hands."[8]

In the spring of 1835, James Madison understood that his time was running out. He had no fear but wanted to protect his wife and make a good death. Waking early on the 28th of June, James and Dolly Madison discussed their religious convictions. James' mind was clear; he spoke with great calmness and self possession, his viewpoint, like Dolly's, the age old one which affords the grandeur and love of God. The Madisons believed that death was merely a change in consciousness—that was all it was.

MADISON'S ZEAL FOR HIS PRINCIPLES

Marvin Olasky, a journalism professor at the University of Texas, provided the following observations: "What Madison did not anticipate…is that 20th century Constitution-twisters would throw out the evidence of what the Founder had in mind and attempt to establish instead a naked public square. And, as millions of people have refused to relegate religious teaching to private life only, a culture war has begun."[9]

Madison's views have been interpreted to the extent that the church has been told it should run away and hide. This view is quite contrary to that offered by Madison, however. It is true that Madison did maintain, "Christianity does not need the support of the state because it is not only a religion of innate excellence but also a religion that enjoys the patronage of its Author."[10]

Madison wanted Christianity to flourish in its purity and believed in his heart that the state would bring corruption to the Christian religion. He believed that forcing the churches to incorporate was dangerous since the churches did not need permission from the state to operate.

The Constitution is embedded in an all-encompassing world view and, properly interpreted, can express the values of only one world view. The Constitution, properly interpreted, is not, and cannot be, an eclectic document reflecting more than one world view. A "pluralism" or "diversity" of world views cannot provide a solid, workable foundation for our Constitution

Religious/theological views and values are foundational to any world view. Therefore, religious/theological views are inseparably related to legal/constitutional/judicial values and actions. There is not, and cannot be, a complete "wall of separation" between religious/theological/philosophical values and legal/constitutional/political values.

The world view in which the Constitution is moored is the Judeo-Christian world view. Therefore, the ultimate foundation of the Constitution is Judeo-Christian religious/theological values and views, revolving around a theistic God. The ultimate foundation of the Constitution is not the Humanistic world view, demanding that a human agent or group of human agents (i.e., judicial elite) ravage the Constitution with Humanistic perspectives, purposes, and values. Indeed, our constitutional republic will increasingly malfunction and eventually collapse if severed from its Judeo-Christian foundation. [11]

Virginia C. Armstrong, Ph.D.
President, Blackstone Institute

"He [Madison]
is the greatest
man in the
world!" [12]

Thomas Jefferson

The "Founders" provided a framework for mutual respect between "the church and state" but in recent years advocates of a "secular state" have had people of faith on the run. Francis Schaeffer points out that "tyranny" is the inevitable result. [13]

MARTIN LUTHER'S INFLUENCE ON MADISON

Martin Luther provided America with the principle of "Liberty of Conscience." (God has ordained the two governments: the spiritual, which by the Holy Spirit under Christ makes Christians and pious people; and the secular, which restrains the unchristian and wicked so that they are obliged to keep the peace outwardly.) [14]

One of the most important events in Western history was when Martin Luther stood before the "Diet of Worms" and told the authorities that it is neither safe nor open for one to act against his or her conscience. That changed the world dramatically. A seed was planted for all sorts of protests, both religious and political, based upon the principle of "liberty of conscience."

"Liberty of conscience" is the principle that states that people must be permitted to believe the ideas which, based upon their own reason and analysis of the evidence, they are convinced to be true. Luther argued that "liberty of conscience" was one of Jesus Christ's principles. It would go on to become one of the most fundamental concepts of both Protestantism and the American nation.

Madison's biographer Ralph Ketcham said, "There is no principle in all of Madison's wide range of private opinion and long public career to which he held with greater vigor and tenacity than this one of religious liberty." [15] Madison had embraced the view of Roger Williams and William Penn on religious liberty and had been taught by John Witherspoon the principle of "freedom of conscience." Witherspoon said that we must "defend and secure the rights of conscience in the most equal and impartial manner." [16]

Frost believed that Madison was the greatest "dreamer of the Founders." The "Founders" knew that without virtue and character, the country would disintegrate into a moral collapse and tyranny would be the end result.

How would this "American dream" take place? Through education! I believe it has been adequately verified in this book

NATIONAL PURPOSE

that the "Founders" of America had a vision to educate each generation of young people about "godly character." Many of them were models of character and virtue. References to the "founder of our religion" clearly referred to Jesus Christ. One role of our government is facilitating the teaching of "America's godly heritage." The Jefferson model at the University of Virginia used teachers and denominations to teach young people the Scriptures from their denominational perspective.

A CHANGE IN FOCUS

Beginning in the 1830's however, European philosophies began to take hold in our universities and within 100 years the foundations were laid to rest. John Dewey led the charge to dismantle "America's godly heritage." When we compromise the ultimate truth of the Bible, chaos is the ultimate outcome. "When the foundations are being destroyed, what can the righteous do?" (Psalm 11:3). It's clear now that the "righteous" in America must take back what was given to them by those who laid down their lives for this country so we truly can be "One nation, under God."

JAMES MADISON'S "MEMORIAL AND REMONSTRANCE"

With all of his efforts to forge a doctrine of "religious liberty" for the American people, Madison could not have imagined the day when government funds would be used to promote pantheistic worldviews such as the "Nature" series shown on public television. It is ironic that although most of the "Founders" were Christians and shaped the country, today the Christian world view is not allowed in public schools. An intolerance now prevails and mocks the "Christian world view." The total lack of integrity in looking at Madison's real concerns for the spread of character and virtues for future generations to come may be explained as hostility toward the "God of our fathers."

In a bill supported by George Washington, Patrick Henry, and George Mason entitled "A Bill establishing a provision for Teachers of the Christian Religion," Madison provided 15 principles of consideration weighing against the bill. These are summarized. Madison opposed Virginia's Declaration of Rights with a clause on religious liberty, which said "all men should enjoy the fullest toleration in the exercise of religion, according to the dictates of conscience." While many of us would have supported the bill presented by "Washington, Henry, and Mason," we need to look at the concerns of Madison and be thankful for them.

MADISON'S UNDERSTANDING OF THE SEPARATION OF CHURCH AND STATE

Madison rejected the use of the word "toleration" in the Virginia Bill advocating Christian Education since "it suggested that the state gave man the right to exercise his faith." Madison believed, "the right of liberty was a unalienable right and that all men are entitled to the full and free exercise of religion." He also believed that "freedom of conscience is the centerpiece of all civil liberties."[18]

Madison argued that "religion must be exempt from the authority of the society at large, still less can it be subject to that of a legislative body."[19] (Madison feared encroachment.) Worried Madison, "The same authority which can establish Christianity, in exclusion of all other religions, may establish with the same ease any particular sect of Christians, in exclusion of all the sects."[20]

Madison wrote, "Every page of it [the Christian Religion] disavows a dependence on the powers of this world; it is a contradiction to fact: for it is known that this Religion both existed and flourished, not only without the support of human laws; but in spite of every opposition from them, and not only during the period of miraculous aid, but long after it had been left to its own evidence and the ordinary care of Providence."[21]

Madison points to the history of the Christian Church to make his argument against the church seeking authority from the state to operate. "During almost fifteen centuries has the legal establishment of Christianity been on trial? What have been its fruits? More or less in all places, pride and indolence in the clergy, ignorance and servility in the laity, in both, superstition, bigotry and persecution. Enquire of the teachers of Christianity, for the ages which it appeared in its greatest luster; (the first three centuries) those of every sect point to the ages prior to its incorporation with Civil policy."[22]

Marvin Olasky sums up his feelings with this point. "Don't mess with individual, community, or state expressions of religion! Madison's point on funding also was sensible: compare the sorry situations of European churches that are still government-funded with the vibrancy of American churches that preach the biblical religion and rely on motivated voluntary support. A 'civil religion' would ultimately marginalize the church."[23]

There would always be a certain "tension" between church and state that would require transparency and openness between them to avoid usurpation. In a letter to Pastor Jasper Adams, the president of the College of Charleston, Madison wrote, "I must admit moreover that it may not be easy, in every possible case, to trace the line of separation between the rights of religion and the Civil authority with such distinctness as to avoid collisions and doubts on unessential points. The tendency to a usurpation on one side or the other, or to a corrupting coalition or alliance between them, will be best guarded against by an entire abstinence the Government from interference in any way whatever beyond the necessity of preserving public order, and protecting each sect against trespasses on its legal rights to others."[24]

Madison maintained that religion was not merely a private matter but for "the happiness of a people, and the good order and preservation of civil government, essentially depending upon piety, religion and morality. These cannot be generally diffused through a community but by the institutions of the public worship of God."[25]

MADISON'S ZEAL FOR RIGHTEOUSNESS

As a young man Madison admonished his friend William Bradford, saying, "A watchful eye must be kept on ourselves lest while we are building ideal monuments of Renown and Bliss here we neglect to have our names enrolled in the Annals of Heaven."[26]

On the nature of man, Madison believed that there is a degree of depravity about mankind, which requires a certain degree of circumspection and distrust. "Man's innate depravity…must be checked by counteracting forces; self-interest of individuals necessitates that government should limit it for the sake of the whole. That set of government must be shaped so that one set of interests will keep other sets of interests from dominating."[27]

Madison wanted Christianity to flourish in its purity and believed in his heart that the state would bring corruption. He believed that forcing the churches to incorporate was dangerous since the churches did not need permission from the state to operate.

As President, Madison issued a proclamation of prayer for

the nation with the following words, "I do therefore issue this my proclamation, recommend to all who should be piously disposed to unite their hearts and voices in addressing at one and the same time their vows and adorations to the 'Great Parent and Sovereign of the Universe…then render Him thanks for the many blessings He has bestowed on the people of the United States.'" [28]

Madison commented on virtue, "If there no virtue among us? If there be not, we are in a wretched situation, no form of government, can render us secure. To suppose that any form of government will secure liberty or happiness without any virtue in the people is a chimerical idea." [29]

Over a period of several years the revisions to the First Legal Statement of Religious Liberty provided the following, saying, "That Religion, or the duty which we owe to our CREATOR, and the manner of discharging it, can be directed only by reason and conviction, not by force or violence and therefore, all men are equally entitled to the free exercise of religion, according to the dictates of conscience, and that it is the mutual duty of all to practice Christian forbearance, love, and charity, towards each other." [30]

Madison also signed a bill that economically aided the Bible Society in its goal of mass distribution of the Bible.

MODERN-DAY EXAMPLE OF ZEAL
LOREN CUNNINGHAM

All of us are blessed to know people in whom God reveals His character in wonderful ways. As a seminary student in the 1960s, I met a man God used to redirect my life. He was the founder of Youth with a Mission. Loren Cunningham knew God in the way I longed to know Him. Over a period of 13 years I had the opportunity of being with Loren on special occasions. He introduced me to his friends who were convinced that Christians needed to focus on the "character of God" if they were to learn to trust God in all circumstance. Loren's zeal for God's Kingdom touched the lives of hundreds of thousands of people throughout the world, and also touched my life.

Apart from my father, no man has impacted my life as Loren Cunningham. There are many words to describe Loren but I have chosen the word "zeal." I first met Loren when I was in seminary and a youth pastor in Rockford, Illinois. Loren has one of the most infectious smiles you will ever see and exudes warmth and love so people are naturally attracted to him. Loren's dream was to see young people from all denominational backgrounds taking the "good news" to every nation on earth. He called his group "Youth with a Mission." It ultimately became the second largest mission with over 16,000 full-time workers.

Loren's vision is mind-boggling. Loren decided a long time ago that if he was to ask young people to go to distant countries, he had to go there first. At last count he had traveled to all of the 222 nations on earth. What is it that motivates this man? I believe it is the love of Christ and the desire that "Jesus would have the reward of his sufferings." He knows that zeal without knowledge will self-destruct so, under his leadership, over 800 teaching centers have been established.

Loren's vision for "Youth With a Mission" was, in part, modeled after the "Moravians" and intercessory prayer for the nations was the foundation to the success of the mission. Loren is usually five to ten years ahead of most of us in discerning what God is doing throughout the world, so it's hard to keep up with him.

I have asked myself why Loren Cunningham has impacted so many lives. Two phrases come to mind. Loren's abandonment to God and his zeal for God's glory! God has put Loren and his wife, Darlene, through some amazing tests in their lives. Incidentally, they seem to always come through with a greater understanding and love for God. Jesus is very real to them and it's infectious. Allow me to tell you a few of my experiences with Loren.

Young people all want someone to believe in them. Christian young people want to know that with Jesus as Lord of their lives, nothing is impossible. Loren taught me to trust God for everything, including finances. He asked me to head up a team to go to the Cayman Islands and prior to my departure from Kingston, Jamaica, he gave me a ticket and $15. He mentioned that the team of 14 people would arrive in a week. I started praying and found myself sitting across from a Christian on the plane. I shared the vision with him of young people coming to the Cayman Islands and sharing their faith. By the time we reached the Cayman Islands, God had solved our housing situation problem as well as provided bikes for our team members. The churches even provided the food. I learned from that experience that God only needs my joyful obedience and he will prove Himself.

Seeking the "mind of God" and hearing his "promptings" was something very new to me as a young person. I had used "reason" and my own "natural inclinations" and Loren would say, "Did you seek God on this Don?" Gradually, I began to understand I didn't need to rely on my own wisdom…I could tap into the wisdom of the eternal God.

When my father died, God brought Loren into my life to help me receive God's healing from some painful experiences. He wanted young people to go to the world filled with the joy of the Lord and knowing the reality of Jesus in their lives. Healing of broken relationships was extraordinarily painful but from the time my friend Loren got on his knees with me in Bangkok, Thailand, where I was able to bring my great hurt to the cross…I began to experience God's healing.

"Zeal" is an intense desire, passion, and earnestness for people. For Loren, it was a zeal that Jesus would be glorified in my life. How blest we are when people care, really care about us, the way Jesus cares.

REVIEW

Q. How will the character trait of zeal make a difference in your life?

Q. Why would some people think that democracy ultimately leads to pantheism (worship of nature)?

Q. The floggings of pastors had a powerful effect on Madison. If you had seen your pastor flogged, how would it affect you?

Q. Madison confessed that the line of separation between church and state was blurred, even in his day. How do you see the influence of Christians reduced today?

Q. Do you believe that Madison's conviction on the "separation of church and state" is biblical?

Q. Provide an example of someone who is zealous for God and for God's work.

Q. Do you think that the separation of church and state has been beneficial or detrimental to America and Christianity?

Q. Do you agree with Madison, or others such as Joseph Story and Patrick Henry?

Q. What is the ACLU's (American Civil Liberties Union) view of "separation of church and state"?

Q. What other possible understanding could there be when it comes to "separation between church and state"?

Q. When governments take positions that are hostile to the Christian faith, what options do we have?

Q. Does signing a bill aiding the Bible Society seem like a contradiction of Madison's beliefs? Explain.

Q. Why do you think Madison used the term, "Great Parent and Sovereign of the Universe" in his proclamation?

Q.. Do you agree with Madison that Christianity does not need the support of the state?

Character for Life

GOD'S PROMISE:

"Of the increase of his government and peace there will be no end. He will reign on David's throne and over his kingdom, establishing and upholding it with justice and righteousness from that time on and forever. The zeal of the LORD Almighty will accomplish this" (Isaiah 9:7).

GOD'S GOAL:

For Christians to have zeal for doing God's work.

YOUR COMMITMENT:

To be zealous in spreading the gospel and in your Christian walk.

YOUR DAILY RESPONSE:

1. To be willing to take risks to do what is right.

2. To trust God to fulfill His will in your life.

3. To follow your convictions, even when difficult.

4. To be zealous but also careful to do the right thing always.

FAILURE WILL MEAN:

Being apathetic with regard to all things in life.

BACKGROUND:

Neither God nor humans are cold, computer-like beings. Persons have emotions as well as intellect and will, and often these emotions are strong. Zeal is one of the stronger emotions. It is good to remember that God desires, as He works in our lives, not to rob us of our emotions. Instead, He wants to capture and channel our capacity for intense commitment. He wants us to have a Godly jealousy or zeal for others, and to be zealous for everything that is good. We lose godly zeal when we begin to surrender morally and when we are not so diligent about the habits of our spiritual life.

Zeal was seen in the life of Jesus. This was said prophetically of Jesus: "My zeal wears me out, for my enemies ignore your words" (Psalm 119:139).

"In the temple courts he found men selling cattle, sheep and doves, and others sitting at tables exchanging money. So he made a whip out of cords; and drove all from the temple area, both sheep and cattle; he scattered the coins of the money changers and overturned their tables. To those who sold the doves he said, 'Get these out of here! How dare you turn my Father's house into a market!' His disciples remembered that it is written: 'Zeal for your house will consume me'" (John 2:14-17). In this account about Jesus, we see that zeal has the sense of intense love. It implies the fierce intensity of Jesus' commitment to His people and His Father's glory and honor.

The Apostle Paul warned, saying, "It is fine to be zealous, provided the purpose is good, and to be so always and not just when I am with you" (Galatians 4:18).

"'My food,' said Jesus, 'is to do the will of him who sent me and to finish his work'" (John 4:34).

LIVING A LIFE OF ZEAL MEANS . . .

■ Having great conviction for doing what is right.

■ Following God with all of one's heart.

■ Trusting God with the outcome.

■ Living each day for Jesus as if it is your last.

Chapter Thirty Seven: Learn more about Madison

Go to an Internet search engine.

Type in *James Madison's Character, Zeal.*

Find topics 1-7 below and open up the websites.

1. WowEssays.com
2. Two Views: James Madison's and Joseph Story (Relationship between Church and State)
3. Excerpts from Madison's detached memoranda (Church and State)
4. James Madison "substantially lacked a national character founded on"
5. James Madison "but the existing character"....
6. Church and State separation by Gene Garman
7. Welcome to the American Presidency (Biography on Madison)

HISTORIC MORAL VALUES FOR AMERICA

For the person of faith who holds a sacred view of the world, values are important because he or she discerns the Creator behind them. "Whatever you do, in word or in deed, do all to the glory of God" (Col.3:17). While "virtures" are rooted in the "Character of God," "values" should be thought of as "preferences" (apples and oranges). The word "values" is not applicable when it comes to "Christian character," however.

VALUES FOR AMERICA INCLUDE...

Relationships with our Creator based on:

- Historic Virtues or Character Traits
- Natural Moral Law
- Prayer
- The Ten Commandments
- The Beatitudes

Relationships with other nations based on:

- Liberty and Freedom
- The Golden Rule
- Democracy
- Preventing Evil and a Just War

Relationships with God's Creation based on:

- Intelligent Design
- Stewardship of God's Creation
- God's Design and Purposes for Human Beings
- The Redemption and Resurrection of Jesus Christ

"By renouncing the Bible, philosophers swing from their moorings upon all moral subjects. It (the Bible) is the only map to the human heart that ever has been published. All systems of religions, morals and government not founded upon it must perish."

Dr. Benjamin Rush

Relationships with God's community based on:

- The Ten Commandments
- Individual and Corporate Responsibility
- Justice for All
- Integrity
- Impartiality
- Compassion
- Care for the Elderly and Helpless
- Decency
- Kindness
- Manners

Relationships with our families based on:

- Honor for Parents
- Loyalty
- Strong Ties
- Abstinence Education

Relationships with people of faith based on:

- Church and State Working Together for Good of All
- Role of the Scriptures in American History
- Role of Godly people in American History
- America's Responsibility Among Nations

EVIDENCE IN HISTORY THAT SHAPED THE FOUNDERS THEISTIC WORLD VIEW

A study done by Lutz and Hyneman supports this case. They examined the references cited by our Founding Fathers from 1760 to 1805. Of 3,154 items cited by the Founding Fathers, 34% came from the Bible. Nine percent were from classical authors like Cicero, Plutarch, Livy, and Plato. Thus, 1,256 citations came from the Bible and the classics, making up 43% of the citations. Eighteen percent were from Whig writers, 11% derived from English common law, and 18% from so-called Enlightenment thinkers. Significantly, Montesquieu, the author of The Spirit of the Laws, was most frequently cited; three times as often as John Locke.

Aristotle

Christianity adapted Aristotle's doctrine by saying that all of creation was for God's purpose. The purpose in each thing was its drive to grow to achieve whatever God impelled it to be. This ran "natural" and "rational" together via God's role as omnipotent creator.

Aristotle stands in the Greek philosophical tradition that asserts that nature is understandable. This tradition, opposed to the idea that nature is under the control of capricious deities that are to be appeased rather than understood, is one of the roots of science.

Aristotle constructed his view of the Universe based on an intuitive feeling of holistic harmony. Central to this philosophy was the concept of teleology or final causation. He supposed that individual objects (e.g. a falling rock) and systems (e.g. the motion of the planets) subordinate their behavior to an overall plan or destiny. This was especially apparent in living systems where the component parts function in a cooperative way to achieve a final purpose or end product.

Aristotle argued that there must be an "unmoved mover," something that can initiate motion without itself being set in motion.

Marcus Cicero

In Book 1 of The Laws, Cicero describes the nature of man and defines the substance of law and justice. He says of man and of reason:

#22 The creature of foresight, wisdom, variety, keenness, memory, endowed with reason and judgment, which we call man, was created by the supreme God to enjoy a remarkable status. Of the types and species of living creatures he is the only one that participates in reason and reflection, whereas none of the other do. What is there, I will not say in man, but in the whole of heaven and earth, more divine than reason (a faculty which, when it has developed and become complete, is rightly called wisdom)?

#23 Since, then, there is nothing better than reason, and reason is present in both man and God, there is a primordial partnership in reason between man and God.

#24 ...whereas men derived the other elements in their make-up from their mortal nature—elements which are fragile and transitory—their mind was implanted in them by God.

St. Augustine

Of the liberty proper to man's nature, and the servitude introduced by sin, —a servitude in which the man whose will is wicked is the slave of his own lust, though he is free so far as regards other men.

This is prescribed by the order of nature: it is thus that God has created man. For "let them," He says, "have dominion over the fish of the sea, and over the fowl of the air, and over every creeping thing which creepeth on the earth." He did not intend that His rational creature, who was made in His image, should have dominion over anything but the irrational creation—not man over man, but man over the beasts.

Thomas Aquinas

Excerpted from Treatise on Law, by Thomas Aquinas

This doctrine fed easily into Christianity and its God-based ethical theory (and gave the church a measure of power over kings). God was the rational creator of the world. The laws of physics were God's laws, as were the moral laws. God is the embodiment of rational purpose in the Universe. All valid law is a manifestation of its workings and must be ultimately consistent. The moral law is a rational account of our place and purpose in the overall scheme of God's plan for the universe. Any legislation by secular states that violates that is not valid or binding law.

Aquinas sees the universe as governed by divine reason—the continuum again. Eternal law imprinted on each thing as its inclination to proper acts and ends. (For example, water seeks its own level.) In humans who are the only "rational" animals, the law is imprinted as principles and capacities to infer to action. What we call "natural law" (essentially real morality) is that part of eternal divine law that is accessible to our finite limited reason as principles or maxims.

Baron Charles-Louis de Secondat de Montesquieu

Charles Montesquieu, a 16th century political philosopher, writer, and jurist, wrote in his Spirit of Laws, "God is related to the universe, as Creator and Preserver; the laws by which He created all things are those by which He preserves them. He acts according to these rules because He knows them. He knows them because He made them; and He made them, because they are in relation to His wisdom and power..."

Laws, in their most general signification, are the necessary relations arising from the nature of things. In this sense all beings have their laws: the Deity His laws, the material world its laws, the intelligences superior to man their laws, the beasts their laws, man his laws.

God is related to the universe, as Creator and Preserver; the laws by which He created all things are those by which He preserves them. He acts according to these rules, because He knows them; He knows them, because He made them, and He made them, because they are in relation to His wisdom and power.

Since we observe the world, though formed by the motion of matter, and void of understanding, subsists through so long as succession of ages, its motions must certainly be directed by invariable laws, and could we imagine another world, it must also have constant rules or it would inevitably perish.

Thus the creation, which seems an arbitrary act, supposes laws as invariable as those of the fatality of the Atheists. It would be absurd to say that the Creator might govern the world without those rules, since without them it could not subsist.

These rules are a fixed and invariable relation. In bodies moved, the motion is received, increased, diminished, or lost, according to the relations of the quantity of matter and velocity; each diversity is uniformity, each change is constancy.

Hugo Grotius

Hugo Grotius states that the plan by which God, as ruler of the universe, governs all things, is a law in the true sense. Since it is not a plan conceived in time we call it the eternal law…Reasoning creatures follow God's plan in a more profound way, themselves sharing the planning…This distinctive sharing in the eternal law we call the natural law, the law we have in us by nature. For the light of natural reason by which we tell good from evil (the law that is in us by nature) is itself an imprint of God's light in us.

What is Divine Law is sufficiently apparent from the term itself; namely, that which has its origin from the Divine Will; by which character it is distinguished from Natural Law…To the human race, the Law has thrice been given by God; at the Creation, immediately after the Deluge, and at the coming of Christ. These three sets of Laws oblige all men, as soon as they acquire a sufficient knowledge of them.

Fredrick Leibniz

Leibniz's God is the Creator, who is able to transform the universe to higher levels of perfection, in a fashion which is reflected in man's transformation of human society. To illustrate how God transforms the universe, Leibniz used the example of an eternal book on the Elements of Geometry. Each new copy is made from the previous one, with new advances being added, in a lawful process of change. The nature of this lawful process of change from one copy to the next, is illustrated by the scientific discoveries made by Leibniz and his collaborators. The new copy of the Elements of Geometry is not reached by principles of formal logic, but through a scientific discovery which takes the form of a Platonic idea. "What is true of books, is also true of the different states of the world; every subsequent state is somehow copied from the preceding one (although according to certain laws of change)." Leibniz quoted Plato's Phaedo, to describe how the Creator orders the universe according to reason, and is continually acting to further the perfection of his creation.

For Leibniz, the highest right, and the source of true happiness, is piety, when man lives so that he seeks to perfect himself, in conformity with the perfection of the Creator.

Rene Descartes

In the 18th century, Rene Descartes and Jean Jacques Rousseau took "natural law" in a totally different direction. "Natural Law" became the basis for democratic and egalitarian principles. The damage was done however since "natural law" had laid the foundations for positivism, empiricism and materialism. "Positive Law," originating with man, ultimately won out. The Western World had changed. Man no longer needed God's laws. Descartes said, "I think, therefore I am." This was reason enough to explain his existence. Revelation knowledge was no longer needed. What happened in France in the 18th and 19th century, happened in America in the 20th century. Revelation knowledge had been eliminated.

William Blackstone

Sir William Blackstone, whose writings trained American's lawyers for its first century, capsulated such reasoning:

"For as God, when he created matter, and endured it with a principle of mobility, established certain rules for the...direction of that motion; so, when he created man, and endued him with freewill to conduct himself in all parts of life, he laid down certain immutable laws of human nature, whereby that freewill is in some degree regulated and restrained, and gave him also the faculty of reason to discover the purport of those laws."

"Man, as a physical being, is like other bodies governed by invariable laws. As an intelligent being, he incessantly transgressed the laws established by God, and changes those of his own instituting. He is left to his private direction, though a limited being, and subject, like all finite intelligences, to ignore and error: even his imperfect knowledge he loses; and as a sensible creature, he is hurried away by a thousand impetuous passions. Such a being might every instant forget his Creator. God has therefore reminded him of his duty by the laws of religion. Such a being is liable every moment to forget himself. Philosophy has provided against this by the laws of morality. Formed to live in society, he might forget his fellow-creatures; legislators have therefore by political and civil laws confined him to his duty."

Emmerich De Vattel

Chapter Two instructed us regarding two interpretations of "natural law." The natural law espoused by Leibniz and de Vattel provided our "founders" with a "Theistic World View" rooted in a Creator and Redeemer who had revealed Himself. God's Laws would be binding upon those He created. In their view, natural law originates with God. It is binding on all people, not just Christians. Natural Law can be traced to the Greeks who saw it as the foundation for moral principles which undergird all legal systems. In the 17th and 18th centuries, natural law became the basis for ethics.

Benjamin Franklin

"I am much obliged by the kind present you have made us of your edition of Vattel. It came to use in good season, when the circumstances of a rising state make it necessary frequently to consult the Law of Nations. Accordingly, that copy which I kept, has been continually in the hands of the members of our congress, now sitting."–Benjamin Franklin, letter to Charles W.F. Dumas, December 1775

"Here is my creed. I believe in one God, the Creator of the universe. That he governs it by His Providence. That He ought to be worshiped."

Benjamin Franklin (so well known he needs no introduction), said: "I believe in one God, the Creator of the Universe." March 9, 1790, in a letter to Ezra Stiles.

James Madison

James Madison, known as the father of the Constitution and its Bill of Rights was a solid Bible-believing Christian and creationist. His manuscripts include elaborate notes on the four Gospels and Acts in particular, specifically acknowledging the deity and bodily resurrection of Christ, and praising the example of the Berean Christians in studying the Scriptures.

We hold it for a fundamental and undeniable truth "that religion, or the duty which we owe our Creator, and the manner of discharging it, can be directed only by reason and conviction, not by force or violence." The religion, then, of every man must be left to the conviction and conscience of every man: and that it is the right of every man to exercise it as these may dictate.

James Madison, the fourth President, was known as the "Chief Architect of the Constitution," and the original author and promoter of the Bill of Rights. In the Constitutional Convention he spoke 161 times. Madison said: "It is the duty of every man to render to the Creator…homage," and defined "religion" thus: "Religion … the duty we owe our Creator."

Alexander Hamilton

Alexander Hamilton, signer of the Constitution and author of 51 of the Federalist Papers said, "Natural liberty is a gift of the beneficent Creator to the whole human race" and "(L)iberty is a gift of the beneficent Creator."

Thomas Jefferson

The Founders saw these as moral duties between individuals. Thomas Jefferson wrote:

"Man has been subjected by his Creator to the moral law, of which his feelings, or conscience as it is sometimes called, are the evidence with which his Creator has furnished him…The moral duties which exist between individual and individual in a state of nature, accompany them into a state of society. Their Maker not having released them from those duties on their forming themselves into a nation."

What Jefferson was content to leave implicit, however, was made more explicit by the other members of the committee. They changed the language to read that all men are "endowed by their Creator" with these rights. Later, the Continental Congress added phrases which further reflected a theistic perspective. For example, they added that they were "appealing to the Supreme Judge of the World for the rectitude of our intentions" and that they were placing "firm reliance on the protection of divine Providence."

In a letter to John Adams, Jefferson writes: "So irresistible are these evidences of an intelligent and powerful Agent that, of the infinite numbers of men who have existed thro' all time, they have believed, in the proportion of a million at least to Unit, in the hypothesis of an eternal pre-existence of a creator, rather than in that of a self-existent Universe. Surely this unanimous sentiment renders this more probable than that of the few in the other hypothesis. Some early Christians indeed have believed in the coeternal pre-existence of both the Creator and the world, without changing their relation of cause and effect."

Although the phrasing of the Declaration certainly follows the pattern of John Locke, Jefferson also gave credit to the writer Algernon Sidney, who in turn cites most prominently

Aristotle, Plato, Roman republican writers, and the Old Testament. A Christian view of government is based upon a balanced view of human nature. It recognizes both human dignity (we are created in God's image) and human depravity (we are sinful individuals). Because both grace and sin operate in government, we should neither be too optimistic nor too pessimistic. Instead, the framers constructed a government with a deep sense of biblical realism (Kirby Anderson).

Thomas Jefferson, third President of the U.S.A., chosen to write the Declaration of Independence, said: "I have little doubt that the whole country will soon be rallied to the unity of our Creator, and, I hope, to the pure doctrines of Jesus also." He, too, recognized that it was the God of the Bible who founded our country when he said in his inaugural address in 1805: "I shall need, too, the favor of that Being in whose hands we are, who led our forefathers, as Israel of old, from their native land and planted them in (this) country."

Edmund Burke

Edmund Burke, outstanding orator, author, and leader in Great Britain, defended the colonies in Parliament. "There is but one law for all, namely, that law which governs all law, the law of our Creator."

Patrick Henry

Patrick Henry, five-time Governor of Virginia, whose "Give me liberty or give me death" speech has made him immortal, said: "It cannot be emphasized too strongly nor too often that this great nation was founded, not by religionists, but by Christians; not on religions, but on the Gospel of Jesus Christ…" He defined religion, like many others of our Founders, thus: "That religion, or duty which we owe to our Creator, and the manner of discharging it…"

John Jay

John Jay, first Chief Justice of the U.S. Supreme Court said: "We (by the Bible) enable (people) to learn that man was originally created and placed in a state of happiness, but, becoming disobedient, was subjected to the degradation and evils which he and his posterity have since experienced. The Bible will also inform them that our gracious Creator has provided for us a Redeemer, in whom all the nations of the earth shall be blessed…" From an address as President of the American Bible Society, May 13, 1824.

George Mason

George Mason, the richest man in Virginia, American Revolutionary statesman, and member of the House of Burgesses, was the author of the Virginia Constitution and Virginia Bill of Rights. He said the first ten amendments to the Constitution "are practically his." He too stated that religion is "the Duty which we owe our Creator." "In his Last Will and Testament, (he) wrote: '. . . My soul, I resign into the hands of my Almighty Creator, whose tender mercies are over all His works.'"

John Adams

John Adams, sixth President of the United States (so well educated he was only a boy of 14 when made secretary to the ambassador to Russia), said: "I see Him (Jesus Christ) explicitly and repeatedly announced, not only as having existed before the worlds, but as the Creator of the worlds without beginning of days or end of years." Written from London, December 24, 1814.

George Washington

Said George Washington, "It is impossible to account for the creation of the universe, without the agency of a Supreme Being...It is impossible to govern the universe without the aid of a Supreme Being. It is impossible to reason without arriving at a Supreme Being."

In many ways the history of the founding and further history of our country in modern times does seem to parallel that of God's chosen nation of Israel in ancient times. One fascinating example of this is found in a very early Independence Day address by Dr. Elias Boudinot, President of the Continental Congress in 1783.

"No sooner had the great Creator of the heavens and the earth finished His almighty work, and pronounced all very good, but He set apart...one day in seven for the commemoration of His inimitable power in producing all things out of nothing... The deliverance of the children of Israel from a state of bondage to an unreasonable tyrant was perpetuated by the Paschal lamb, and enjoining it on their posterity as an annual festival forever... The resurrection of the Savior of mankind is commemorated by keeping the first day of the week...Let us then, my friends and fellow citizens, unite all our endeavors this day to remember, with reverential gratitude to our Supreme Benefactor, all the wonderful things He has done for us, in our miraculous deliverance from a second Egypt—another house of bondage."

Has the creator identified himself?

The Holy Scriptures make it very clear that the identity of the co-creator of the Universe is none other than the Son of God, Jesus Christ Himself. The Scriptures speak for themselves.

"In the beginning God created the heavens and the earth" (Genesis 1:1).

"Ask of me, and I will make the nations your inheritance, the ends of the earth your possession" (Psalm 2:8).

"By the word of the Lord were the heavens made, their starry host by the breath of his mouth" (Psalm 33:6).

"Who has gone up to heaven and come down? Who has gathered up the wind in the hollow of his hands? Who has wrapped up the waters in his cloak? Who has established all the ends of the earth? What is his name, and the name of his son? Tell me if you know!" (Proverbs 30:4).

"Remember your Creator in the days of your youth, before the days of trouble come and the years approach when you will say, 'I find no pleasure in them'" (Ecclesiastes 12:1).

"'To whom will you compare me? Or who is my equal?' says the Holy One. Lift your eyes and look to the heavens: Who created all these? He who brings out the starry host one by one, and calls them each by name" (Isaiah 40:25-26a).

"Do you not know? Have you not heard? The Lord is the everlasting God, the Creator of the ends of the earth. He will not grow tired or weary, and his understanding no one can fathom. He gives strength to the weary and increases the power of the weak. Even youths grow tired and weary, and young men stumble and fall; but those who hope in the Lord will renew their strength. They will soar on wings like eagles; they will run and not grow weary, they will walk and not be faint" (Isaiah 40:28-31).

"This is what the Lord says—your Redeemer, who formed you in the womb: 'I am the Lord, who has made all things, who alone stretched out the heavens, who spread out the earth by myself'" (Isaiah 44:24).

"It is I who made the earth and created mankind upon it. My own hands stretched out the heavens; I marshaled their starry hosts" (Isaiah 45:12).

"But you, Bethlehem Ephrathah, though you are small among the clans of Judah, out of you will come for me one who will be ruler over Israel, whose origins are from of old, from ancient times" (Micah 5:2).

"In the beginning was the Word, and the Word was with God, and the Word was God. He was with God in the beginning. Through him all things were made; without him nothing was made that has been made. In him was life, and that life was the light of men. The light shines in the darkness, but the darkness has not understood it" (John 1:1-5).

"'The God who made the world and everything in it is the Lord of heaven and earth and does not live in temples built by hands. And He is not served by human hands, as if He needed anything, because He himself gives all men life and breath and everything else. From one man He made every nation of men, that they should inhabit the whole earth; and He determined the times set for them and the exact places where they should live. God did this so that men would seek Him and perhaps reach out for Him and find Him, though He is not far from each one of us. 'For in Him we live and move and have our being.' As some of your own poets have said, 'We are His offspring'" (Acts 17:24-28).

"He is the image of the invisible God, the firstborn over all creation. For by Him all things were created: things in heaven and on earth, visible and invisible, whether thrones or powers or rulers or authorities; all things were created by Him and for Him. He is before all things, and in Him all things hold together. And He is the head of the body, the church; He is the beginning and the firstborn from among the dead, so that in everything He might have the supremacy" (Colossians 1:15-18).

"In the past God spoke to our forefathers through the prophets at many times and in various ways, but in these last days he has spoke to us by his Son, whom he appointed heir of all things, and through whom he made the universe" (Hebrews 1:1-2).

"But about the Son he says, 'Your throne, O God will last forever and ever, and righteousness will be the scepter of your kingdom. You have loved righteousness and hated wickedness; therefore God, your God, has set you above your companions by anointing you with the oil of joy.' He also says, 'In the beginning, O Lord, you laid the foundations of the earth, and the heavens are the work of your hands'" (Hebrews 1:8-10).

"By faith we understand that the universe was formed at God's command, so that what is seen, was not made out of what was visible" (Hebrews 11:3).

For a summary of "Interpretations of History," please go to the following website: http://www.truthinhistory.org/interpretations.htm

State Motto's

Alabama	Audemus jura nostra defendere (We dare defend our rights)
Alaska	North to the Future
Arizona	Ditat Deus (God enriches)
Arkansas	Regnat populus (The people rule)
California	Eureka (I have found it)
Colorado	Nil sine Numine (Nothing without Providence)
Connecticut	Qui transtulit sustinet (He who transplanted still sustains)
Delaware	Liberty and independence
Florida	In God we trust (1868)
Georgia	Wisdom, justice, and moderation
Hawaii	Ua Mau Ke Ea O Ka Aina I Ka Pono (The life of the land is perpetuated in righteousness)
Idaho	Esto perpetua (It is forever)
Illinois	State sovereignty, national union

Indiana	The Crossroads of America
Iowa	Our liberties we prize and our rights we will maintain
Kansas	Ad astra per aspera (To the stars through difficulties)
Kentucky	United we stand, divided we fall
Louisiana	Union, justice, and confidence
Maine	Dirigo (I lead)
Maryland	Fatti maschii, parole femine (Manly deeds, womanly words)
Massachusetts	Ense petit placidam sub libertate quietem (By the sword we seek peace, but peace only under liberty)
Michigan	Si quaeris peninsulam amoenam circumspice (If you seek a pleasant peninsula, look around you)
Minnesota	L'Étoile du Nord (The North Star)
Mississippi	Virtute et armis (By valor and arms)
Missouri	Salus populi suprema lex esto (The welfare of the people shall be the supreme law)
Montana	Oro y plata (Gold and silver)
Nebraska	Equality before the law
Nevada	All for Our Country
New Hampshire	Live free or die
New Jersey	Liberty and prosperity
New Mexico	Crescit eundo (It grows as it goes)
New York	Excelsior (Ever upward)
North Carolina	Esse quam videri (To be rather than to seem)
North Dakota	Liberty and union, now and forever: one and inseparable
Ohio	With God all things are possible
Oklahoma	Labor omnia vincit (Labor conquers all things)
Oregon	Alis volat Propriis (She flies with her own wings) (1987)
Pennsylvania	Virtue, liberty, and independence
Rhode Island	Hope
South Carolina	Animis opibusque parati (Prepared in mind and resources) and Dum spiro spero (While I breathe, I hope)
South Dakota	Under God the people rule
Tennessee	Agriculture and Commerce (1987)
Texas	Friendship
Utah	Industry
Vermont	Vermont, Freedom and Unity
Virginia	Sic semper tyrannis (Thus always to tyrants)
Washington	Al-Ki (Indian word meaning "by and by")
West Virginia	Montani semper liberi (Mountaineers are always free)
Wisconsin	Forward
Wyoming	Equal rights (1955)

▶ bibliography

Badget, Richard G., Kistler, Charles E., *The Nation Under God* (Boston, MA: The Gorhman Press, 1924).

Bartlett, John, *Bartlett's Familiar Quotations* (Boston, MA: Little, Brown and Company, 1855).

Barton, David, *Original Intent* (Washington, D.C.: Eagle Publishing, 1966).

Barton, David, *The Myth of Separation* (Aledo, TX: WallBuilder Press, 1991).

Baxter, J. Sidlow, *Awake My Heart* (Grand Rapids, MI: Kregel Publications, 1960, 1964).

Bemis, Samuel Flagg, *John Quincy Adams and the Foundations of American Foreign Policy* (Westport, CN: Greenwood Press, 1997).

Benson, Allan L., *Daniel Webster* (New York, N.Y.: Cosmopolitan Book Corporation, 1929).

Binger, Carl, *Revolutionary Doctor* (New York, N.Y.: W. W. Norton and Company, 1966).

Bradford, M. E., *Founding Fathers* (Lawrence, KS: University Press of Kansas, 1981).

Bobbs, *The Correspondence of John Adams and Thomas Jefferson* (Indianapolis, IN: Merrill Publishers, 1925).

Bunch, Lonnie G., III, *The American Presidency* (Washington, D.C.: Smithsonian Institution Press, 2001).

Butterfield, L.H., *Diary and Autobiography of John Adams* (Cambridge, MA: Belknapp Press of Harvard Press, 1856).

Campbell, Norene Dickson, *Patrick Henry: Patriot and Statesman* (Old Greenwich, Conn.: Devin-Adair Co. Publisher, 1968).

Chambers, Oswald, *My Utmost for His Highest* (Nashville, TN: Thomas Nelson Publishers, 1995).

Dawson, Steve C., *God's Providence in American History* (Rancho Cordova, CA: Steve C. Dawson, 1988).

DeMar, Gary, *A Model of Christian Charity* (Atlanta, GA: American Vision, 1993).

Donovan, Frank, *John Adams Papers* (New York, N.Y.: Mead and Company, 1975).

Dunne, Gerald T., *Justice Joseph Story and the Rise of the Supreme Court* (New York, NY: Simon and Schuster, 1971).

Edwards, Ethel, Hardwick, James T., *Carver of Tuskegee* (St. Louis, MO: University of Missouri Press, 1971).

Eidsmore, John, *Christianity and the Constitution* (Grand Rapids, MI: Baker Books, 1987).

Elliott, Lawrence, *George Washington Carver, The Man Who Overcame* (Englewoods Cliffs, N.J.: Prentice-Hall, Inc., 1966).

Federer, William, *America's God and Country* (New York, N.Y: Face Publishing House, 1966).

Ferling, John, *John Adams, A Life* (Knoxville, TN: University of Tennessee Press, 1992).

Flexner, James Thomas, *George Washington and the New Nation* (Boston, MA: Little, Brown and Company, 1969).

Foster, Marshall, *The American Covenant* (Thousand Oaks, CA: The Mayflower Institute, 1992).

Frankline, Burt, Henry, William Wirt, *Patrick Henry—A Life* (New York, NY: Correspondence and Speeches, 1968).

Geisler, Norman L., Thomas Aquinas, *An Evangelical Appraisal* (Grand Rapids, MI: Baker Books, 1991).

Harrison, E., Myers, *Fanny J. Crosby* (Chicago, IL: Moody Press, 1945).

Houston, James M., Blaise Pascal, *The Mind on Fire* (Minneapolis, MN: Bethany House Publishers, 1997).

Jones, Stanley E., *A Song of Assents* (Nashville, TN, New York, N.Y.: Abington Press, 1968).

Knoph, Alfred A., Nagel, Paul C., John Quincy Adams, *A Public Life, A Private Life* (New York, NY: Random House Publishers, 1997).

Manuel, David, Marshall, Peter, *From Sea to Shining Sea* (Old Tappan, N.J.: Fleming H. Revel Co., 1986).

Manuel, David, Marshall, Peter, *The Light and the Glory* (Old Tappan, N.J.: Fleming H. Revell Co., 1977).

Manuel, Frank E., *The Religion of Isaac Newton* (London, England: Oxford University Press, 1974).

McCullough, David, *John Adams* (New York, N.Y.: Simon and Schuster, 2001).

McGill, John Barker, *Pascal in England during the Age of Reason* (London, England: McGill-Queen's University Press, 1975).

Millard, Catherine, *The Rewriting of American History* (Camp Hill, PA: Horizon House Publishers, 1991).

Miller, John C., Alexander Hamilton, *Portrait in Paradox* (New York, N.Y.: Harper and Brothers, 1959).

Morgan, Edmund S., *The Puritan Dilemma, The Story of John Winthrop* (Sydney, Australia: Harper Collins Publisher, 1958).

Morris, Richard B., *Seven Who Shaped Our Destiny* (New York, NY: Harper and Row, 1973).

Newmyer, Kent R., *Supreme Court Justice Joseph Story, Statesman of the Old Republic* (Chapel Hill, N.C., London, England: University of North Carolina Press, 1986).

Northrop, D.D., Stephen Abbott, *A Cloud of Witnesses* (Portland, OR: American Heritage Ministries, 1987).

Northrop, Stephen Abbott, *Treatise of the Religion of the Quakers* (Portland, OR: American Heritage Ministries, 1987).

Packer, J.I., *The Starting Puritan* (Carol Stream, IL: Creation House Publishers).

Painter, Nell Irvin, *Sojourner Truth, A Life, A Symbol* (New York, N.Y., London, England: Norton and Company, 1966)

Pollock, John, *George Whitefield and the Great Awakening* (Garden City, N.Y.: Doubleday and Co., 1972).

Rollins, Richard M., *The Long Journey of Noah Webster* (Philadelphia, PA: University of Pennsylvania Press, 1980).

Russell, Francis, John Adams, *An American Dynasty* (New York, N.Y.: American Heritage Publishing Co., 1976).

Rutland, Robert, James Madison, *The Founding Father* (New York, NY: McMillan Publishing, 1995).

Rutland, Robert A., Ed, *The Papers of George Mason* (Chapel Hill, NC: North Carolina Press, 1970).

Shepherd, Jack, *John Adams Chronicles* (Boston, MA: Little Brown and Co., 1975).

Sider, Erma, *Celebration of Hospitality* (Springfield, MO: Evangel Publishing House, 1998).

Tuveson, Ernest Lee, *Redeemer Nation* (Chicago, IL: University of Chicago Press, 1974).

Webster, Daniel, *The Works of Daniel Webster* (Boston, MA: Little, Brown and Company, 1853).

Wildman, Edwin, *The Founders of America* (Freeport, NY: Books for Library Press, 1924).

Willison, George F., *Patrick Henry and His World* (Garden City, NY: Doubleday and Company, Inc., 1969).

Woodward, William W., *The Works of the Rev. John Witherspoon* (Newark, DE: University of Delaware Press, 1802).

index

footnotes

NOTES

After months of research in libraries in the Midwest and Northwest, the resources I found there did not enable me to accomplish the task I sought—to adequately describe the "heroes" depicted in this book and the "character" of those chosen to describe God's character. I had only one alternative, to turn to Internet sources. I discovered that many outstanding Christians had provided resources I needed to write this book. The sources provided below are from both books and the Internet. It is my hope that you will find the wealth of information provided a true treasure.

CHARACTER FOR LIFE MANUAL

1. Norman Geisler and Ralph McKenzi, *Roman Catholic and Evangelical Agreements and Differences* (Grand Rapids, MI: Baker Books, 1995), p. 459.
2. Dinesh D'Souza, *What's So Great about America?* (Washington D.C.: Regnery Publishers), [April 24, 2002] p. 86.
3. Ibid., p. 187.
4. www.myutmost.org/08/0809.html
5. www.myutmost.org/08/0829.html
6. www.jawbreak.org/9_11_Encouragement_Sholund.htm
7. www.mydevotion.com/ss/verses-00feb.asp-
8. Probe Ministries, 1900 Firman Dr., Suite 100, Richardson, TX 75081
9. Ibid.
10. Ibid.
11. Ibid.
12. Ibid.
13. Ibid.
14. Ibid.
15. Ibid.
16. Ibid.
17. Ibid.
18. Ibid.
19. Ibid.
20. www.2.univ-reunion.fr/~duban/Ressources_civ._US/Glossaries/glossary_2.html
21. www.directionjournal.org/article/?46
22. www.crossroad.to/text/articles/sexed9-98.html
23. www.crossroad.to/articles2/Aldous.htm
24. www.christian-bible.com/Dialogue/Interfaith/globalethic.htm
25. www.crossroad.to/text/articles/ChurchYouth.html
26. Ibid.
27. Ibid.
28. www.brainyquote.com/quotes/quotes/o/oswaldcham120295.html
29. www.enterprisingwomen.com/business_biblical.htm

CHAPTER 1

1. www.op.org/domcentral/study/aumann/st/st10.htm
2. www.sageplace.com/parenting-work.htm
3. J. Budziszewski, Departments of Government and Philosophy, University of Texas at Austin. author of *Written on the Heart: The Case for Natural Law*, IVP. Information found on the Internet—http://www.designinference.com/inteldes.htm
4. www.catholic-forum.com/saints/saintt03.htm
5. Ibid.
6. www.newgenevacenter.org/biography/kant2.htm
7. www.catholic-forum.com/saints/stt03bw.htm
8. www.engineeringnews.co.za/eng/views/columnist/onlife/?show=57160
9. www.avoidingevil.com/blog/archives/000198.htm-
10. www.faithnet.org.uk/a2%20Subjects/Ethics/natural_law.htm
11. www.jrcm.faithweb.com/religion/ihomosexuality2.hhml-
12. www.heritage.org/Research/Africa/BG1692.cfm-
13. www.abundantlife.org/onlinebooks/resunshakable.chapte2.htm
14. www.Loveisgreat.com/ABOUT_Love/Truisms.htm
15. www.worldofquotes.com/author/E.-Stanley-Jones/1/
16. www.hermes-presscom/perrennial - tradition/ptch11.htm

17. www.natreformassn.org/statesman/04/clnatlaw.html
18. www.archives.gov/national_archives_experience/charters/declaration/transcript/html
19. www.propertyrightsresearch.org/law_of_the_land.htm
20. www.gospelcom.net/rbc/questons/answers/ethics/sex/purpose.xml/-
21. www.esjpc.com/-

CHAPTER 2
1. www.ucq.org./booklets/GE/consequencesofideas.htm
2. www.scienceworld.wolfram.com/biography/newton.html
3. www.historicist.com/Newton/Newtonword.htm
4. www.josh.org/download/pdf/arguments_for_Gods_existence.pdf
5. www.asa3.org/ASA/PSCF/1987/PSCF6-87Herrmann.html -
6. www.homepage.eircom.net/~odyssey/ Quotes/Life/Mind/Knowledge.html
7. www.orange-street-church.org/text/yeare.htm -
8. www.geocities.com/Athens/Crete/4516/
9. www.quakerhillbooks.org/cgi-bin/ qhb.cgi/category_products?category_id=29
10. www.tagnet.org/hop/serm0001.htm-
11. www.christiianansers.net/q-eden/edn-c014.html
12. www.historicist.com/newton/title.htm
13. www.historicist.com/newton/title.htm
14. www.abc.mpib-berlin.mpg.de/users/ptodd/publications/99abc1/99abc1.doc
15. www.wikquote.org/wiki/newton
16. www.media.mit.edu/~pickard/newton.htm
17. www.twilightbridge.com/iconsl/issacnewton.htm
18. www.web.media.mit.edu?~picard/newton.html
19. Ibid.
20. Ibid.
21. www.sparknotes.com/bibliography/newton/section6.html
22. www.scienceworld.wolfram.com/biography/newton.html
23. www.fordham.edu/halsall/mod/newton-optics.html
24. www.Rmfe.org/respost.html
25. www.pbs.org/wgbh/evolution/darwin/diary/1882.html -
26. www.media.mit.edu/~pickard/newton.html
27. www.historicist.com/newton/treatise.htm
28. www.historicist.com/newton/treatise.htm
29. Ibid.
30. Ibid.

CHAPTER 3
1. www.oregonstate.edu.instruct/phl302philosophies/grotius.html
2. www.allsaints.ch/Chaplain/History.html -
3. www.home.att.net/~jrhsc/wilson.html
4. Ibid.
5. www.primitivebaptist.org/writers/hassell/history/chapter17.asp?print=1
6. Ibid.
7. www.wallbuilders.com/resources/search/detail.php?resourceID=4l
8. www.catholic-forum.com/saints/stt03bw.htm
9. www.law.emorys.edu/eilr/volumes/spring96/betterman.html
10. www.natreformassn.org/statesman/99/natlawgodslaw.htm
11. www.gospelcom.net/chi/dailyf/2001/08daily-08-28-2001.shtml
12. Ibid.
13. www.thespeechsite.com/quotes/abigail/adams-g.htm
14. www.wildstreet.com/finance/league+nation+wilson.html

CHAPTER 4
1. www.titus2woman.com/momstuff/fanny.html
2. www.sermoncentraolcom/sermon.asp?sermonID=56691-contributorID=105
3. www.wholesomewords.org/biography3.html
4. www.nyfrt.org.htm
5. www.titus2women.com/momstuff/fanney.html
6. www.byfaithonly.com/fanneycrosby.html
7. www.answers.google.com/answers/threadview?ID=31432
8. www.theremnant.com/crosby.html
9. www.desiringgod.org/library/biographies/90brainerd.html
10. www.disabilitymuseam.org/lib/docs/1653.htm?page=print
11. www.believersweb.org/view.cfm?ID=83

CHAPTER 5

1. www.wholesomewords.org/missions/biobrainerd2.html
2. www.revival-library.org/catalogues/world1/edwards-brainerd/06/htm
3. www.wholesomewords.org/missions/biobrainerd7.html
4. www.wholesomewords.org/missions/biobrainerd2.html
5. www.matthew548.com/T-Brain.html
6. www.wholesomewords.org/missions/biobrainerd2.html
7. www.wholesomewords.org/missions/biobrainerd2.html
8. www.revival-library.org/catalogues/world1/brainerd-journals/01.htm
9. www.desiringgod.org/library/biographies/90brainerd.html
10. www.wholesomewords.org/missions/biobrainerd2.html
11. www.wholesomewords.org/missions/biobrainerd2.html
12. www.wholesomewords.org/missions/biobrainerd6.html
13. www.wholesomewords.org/mission/biobrainerd2.htm
14. Ibid.
15. www.eternallifeministries.org/brainerd.htm
16. www.raptureready.com/resource/hills/hdm3_11.html
17. www.wholesomewords.org/missions/biobrainerd2.html
18. www.wholesomewords.org/missions/biobrainerd.html
19. www.desiringgod.org/library/biographies/90brainerd.html
20. www.pillaroffire.co.uk/sermons/d_wolfram/david_brainerd_-_missionary.html
21. www.wholesomewords.org/missions/biobran.html
22. www.wholesomewords.org/missions/biobrainerd2.html

CHAPTER 6

1. www.christianitytoday.com/tc/9r3/9r3015.html
2. www.firstthings.com/ftissues
3. www.leaderu.com/orgs/probe/docs/pascal.html
4. www.leaderu.com/apologetics/pascalmethodology.html
5. www.leaderu.com/orgs/probe/docs/pascal/html
6. www.westmont.edu/~work/articles/witness.html
7. Ibid.
8. www.leaderru.com/orgs/probe/docs/pascal/html
9. Ibid.
10. Ibid.
11. Ibid.
12. www.probe.org/docs/pascal.html
13. Ibid.
14. www.bible.org/illus.asp?topic_id=1347
15. www.brainyquote.com/quotes/quotes/b/blaisepasc137317.html
16. www.keanuvision.com/archives/000808.html
17. www.leaderu.com/orgs/probe/docs/pascal.html
18. Ibid.
19. Ibid.
20. www.christianity.co.nz/moralit2.htm
21. www.geocities.com/berserkrl/twilight3.htm

CHAPTER 7

1. www.colonialhall.com/adamss/adamsElizabethC.php
2. www.geocities.com/bramlett2000/achp8.html
3. www.chef-missouri.com/Articles/WF_1.htm
4. www.nochurchianity.com/Insight.html
5. www.whitehouse.gov/kids/dreamteam.samueladams.html
6. www.cooperativeindividualism.org/Jefferson
7. www.choicesforliving.com/spirit/part4/america8.htm
8. www.educatetheusa.com/addamss.htm
9. www.masshist.org/digitaladams/aea/cfm/doc.cfm"ID=D11
10. www.archiver.rootsweb.com/th/read/blacksheep/1999-07/0931130832
11. www.face.net/articles/learningeart.tm
12. www.masshist.org/digital/adas/aea/cfm/doc.cfm?ID=011
13. www.conservativeforum.org/quotelist.asp
14. www.barefootsworld.net/libertyindanger.html
15. Ibid.
16. www.history.hanover.edu/texts/adamss.html
17. www.etext.lib.virginia.edu/etcbin/foley-browse?id=liberty
18. Ibid.

CHAPTER 8

1. www.catholiceducation.org/articles/history/us/ah0015.html
2. Dictionary of American Bibliography, (New York, N.Y.: Charles Scribner and Sons, 1959).
3. www.duel2004.weehawkenhistory.org/reenactscript.pdf
4. www.claremontorg/writings/crb/winter/20031guel20.html
5. Ibid.
6. Ibid.
7. www.members.tripod.com/~american_
8. www.ourcivilisation.com/smartboard/shop/burkee/extracts/chap20.htm
9. www.almac/hamphau.htm
10. www.bartleby.com/268/8/24.html
11. Letters to Mrs. Hamilton from Judge James Kent
12. www.lehmaninstitute.org/education/essays-4.html
13. www.digitalhistory.uh.edu/learning_history/burr/bur_runuptoduel.cfm

CHAPTER 9

1. www.edwardsgenerations.net/familyrecords/1John/l.l.l.3.htm
2. www.gospelcom.net/bpf/guide19.html
3. www.cbn.com/spirituallife/biblestudyandtheology/discipleship/a_greatawakening_stirs_the_colonies.asp
4. www.puritansermons.com/bio/bioedwar.htm
5. www.dylee.keel.com.ship-edu/ubf/leaders/edwards.htm
6. Ibid.
7. www.pro-american.com/Good_Thoughts/good_thoughts.html
8. www.biblebb.com/files/edwards/charity1.htm
9. www.biblebb.com/files/edwards/charity1.htm
10. www.puritansermons.com/bio/bioedwar.htm
11. www.banner.org.uk/tb/edwards2.html
12. www.biblicaltheology.com/classics/Jonathan%20Edwards/edwards93.html
13. www.jonathanedwards.com/text/Personal/resolut.htm
14. Ibid.
15. www.jonathanedwards.com/text/piper.htm
16. www.desiringgod.org/library/topics/edwards/edwards_enjoying_god.html
17. www.chosunjournal.com/edwards.html
18. www.reformedorg/books/edwards/redemption/redem_pt3_si.html
19. www.studiesintheword.org/peace_to_come.htm
20. www.chosunjournal.com/edwards.html

CHAPTER 10

1. www.uua.org/uuhs/duub/articles/johnquincyadams.html
2. www.commentarymagazine.com/summaries/v11612P63-1.htm
3. www.pbs.org/newshour/character/quotes.
4. www.foreruner.com/forerunner/x0205_john_quincy.html
5. www.strike-the-root.com/4/weiner/weiner1.html
6. www.rzministries.com/history/x0074_john_Quincy_Adams.html
7. www.renewameric.us/columns/creech/041025
8. www.nyfrt.org/jqadams.htm
9. www.uua.org/uuhs/juub/articles/johnquincyadams.html
10. www.americanide.org/handouts/02080201.htm
11. www.restonweb.com/community/restontalk/messages010525/5507/html
12. www.americanhistory.about.com/cs/johnquincyadams/a/quotejqadams.htm
13. www.geocities.com/~newgeneration/dining.htm
14. www.forefuner.com/forerunner/?X0205_John_Quincy_Adams.html
15. www.thisnation.ocm/library/jqadams1821.html
16. www.rebelswithavision.com/johnqadams.com
17. www.assumption.edu/ahc/Kansas/abolition/abolition.html
18. www.nas.com/res/opriesti/p56.htm
19. www.cooperativeindividualism.org/miller_johnquincyadams.html
20. www.forerunner.com/forefuner/X0205_john_Quincy_adams.html
21. www.innercity.org/columbiaheights/newspaper/holt_article.html
22. www.lkwdpl.org/wihohio/figures.htm-
23. www.umkc.edu/imc/adams

CHAPTER 11

1. www.bible.org/illus.asp?topic_id=1241
2. www.constitutionparty.com/news.php?aid=42
3. www.thomasmc.com/1122.htm

4. www.nationalcenter.org/lincoln'sfarewell.html
5. Ibid.
6. www.nationalcenter.org/wcto82304.html
7. www.historywise.com/KoTrain/ Courses/AL/AL_The_First_Lady.htm -
8. www.qts.edu/alums/sp2003.shtml
9. www.piney.com/hsexp.html
10. www.jmm.aaa.net.au/articles/4651.htm
11. www.inspire21.com/site/stories/God_trust.html
12. www.nationalcenter.org/wct082304.html
13. www.digitallibrary.mcgill.ca/lincoln/exhibit/text/theman.html
14. www.geocities.com/regkeith/linkholidaysthanks2.htm
15. www.showcase.netins.net/web/creative/ lincoln/speeches/philadel.htm -
16. www.forerunner.com/forefunner/x0542
17. www.bartleby.com/73/1069.html
18. www.dianedew.com/lincoln.htm
19. www.lincoln.org.al/quotes.htm
20. www.drinkthis.typepad.com/
21. Ibid.
22. www.nationalcenter.orghousedivided.html
23. www.claremont.org/writings/precepts/
24. www.ashbrook.org/publicat/oped/eastman/01/adarand.html
25. Ibid.
26. Ibid.
27. www.freedomwriter.com/quotes.htm
28. www.quotedb.com/quotes/368/
29.www.freedomwriter.com/quotes.htm
30. Ibid.
31. www.hebrewbible.com/LINC.HTM
32. Ibid.
33. www.quotedb.co/quotes/3272
34. www.LINCOLNS_birthday.123holiday.net/lincoln_quotes.html
35. www.mr.Lincoln.com/Churchprograms
36. www.foreruner.com/forerunner.html
37. www.showcase.netins/net/web/creative/lincoln/speeches/quoteweek.htm
38. www.ablelincoln.com/walbert_malice_toward_none.html
39. www.adherents.com/misc/lincoln.html
40. www.peerhansen.com/casualties_of_faith.htm
41. www.healthy-elements.com/lincoln.html

CHAPTER 12

1. www.newadvent.org/fathers/1311.htm
2. www.touchstonemag.com/ frpat/2004_01_11_frpatarchive.html - 30k
3. www.bible.com/bible/Bquotes.html - 15k
4. www.snyders.ws/alan/quotes/henry.htm
5. www.famousamericans.net/patrickhenry/
6. www.doctorsenator.com/PatrickHenry.html
7. www.brainyquote.com/quotes/quotes/j/johannwolf162815.html
8. www.authorama.com/american-spirit-in-literature-9.html
9. www.graceandlaw.com/artman/publish/printer_128.php
10. www.home.earthlink.net/~truth/sec2-1Truth.html
11. www.doctorsenator.com/PatrickHenry.html
12. www.1.love-quotes.com/45869.htm
13. www.redhill.org/calendar.html
14. www.libertyonline.hypermall.com/henry-liberty.html
15.www.youthspecialties.com/articles/topics/culture/truth.php
16. www.livingwaters.com/witnessingtool/lastwords.shtml
17. www.bible.com/bible/Bquotes.html

CHAPTER 13

1. www.personal.pitnet.net/primarysources/pennletter.html
2. Ibid.
3. www.providenceforum.org/resources/qui25.php
4. www.christianmystics.com/traditionalquakers/penn.shtml
5. www.wisdomquotes.com/ccat_character.html
6. www.dhpress.org/quakerpages.ghoa/penn1694.htm
7. www.dhpress.org/quakerpages/qhoa/pennl.htm

8. Ibid.

9. www.quakernet.org/Discipline%201974/quakermovement.htm

10. www.quaker.net.org/sermons2004-2005/sermons_120504.htm

11. www.ghpress.org/quakerpages/ghoa/penn1.htm

12. www.members.aol.com/vtpa/agc001.html

13. www.qhpress.org/quakerpages/gwhp/pp340.htm

14. www.ghpress.org/quakerpage/ghoa/penn.htm

15. www.ucc.org/ucnews/apr03/grace.htm

CHAPTER 14

1. www.colonialhall.com/witherspoon/witherspoon.php

2. www.reformed.org/documents/Knox/Knox_toMaryKnox_to_Mary.html

3. www.restoringamerica.org/archive/larson/republic_vs_democracy.html

4. www.netgeist.com/success.htm

5. www.heritage.org/Press/Commentary/ed060303.a.cfm

6. www.new-life.net/parent07.htm

7. www.constitutional.net/006.html

8. www.snyders.ws/alan/quotes/witherspoon.htm

9. www.geocities.com/bramlett2000/achp8.html

10. www.colonialhall.com/witherspoon/witherspoon5php

11. www.classicauthors.net/Burke/ConciliationAmerica

12. www.electricscotland.com/history/other/witherspoon.htm

13. www.oll.libertyfund.org/Texts/LFBooks/Sandoz0385/HTMLs/0018_Pt03_Part2.html

14. Ibid.

15. www.thelandofthefree.net/quotationchristian.html

16. www.snyders.ws/alan/quotes/witherspoon.htm

17. www.members.aol.com/endthewall/Educ_Bible.htm

18. www.witherspoonsociety.org/about_us/john_witherspoon.htm

19. www.wallbuilders.com/resources/search/detail.php?ResourceID=24-49k

20. www.diarysearchcom/bibliography/1784ad.htm

CHAPTER 15

1. www.electriceggplant.com/davidmccullough/adams_excerpt.htm

2. www.godstruthfortoday.org/elhananwinchester/winchester019.htm

3. www.diarysearchcom/bibliography/1784ad.htm

4. www.odur.let.rug.nl/~usa/P/tj3/writings/brf/jef208.htm-

5. www.ewtn.com/library/humanity/FR87205.TXT

6. www.buchan.org/pray-quotes.html

7. www.godstruthfortoday.org/elhananwinchester/winchester019.html

8. www.colonialhall.com/rush/rush.php

9. www.naacd.com/issues_founding_fathers.htm

10. www.geocities.com/peterroberts.geo/Relig-Politics/BRush.html

11. www.ewtn.com/library/humanity/FR87205.TXT

12. Ibid.

13. www.eadshome.com/quotesofthefounders.com

14. www.homeschoolrepublican.tripod.com/msgfromchairman.html

15. www.humantruth.org/formcar.htm

16. www.geocities.com/peterroberts.geo/relig-politcs/brush.html

17. www.truthorfiction.com/rumors/r/religious-depections.htm

18. www.errantskeptics.org/foundingfathers.htm

19. www.colonialhall.com/rush/rush.php-

20. www.christianamerica.com/foundingfathers/bcn_rush.htm

21. www.godstruthfortoday.org/ElhananWinchester/Winchester019.html

22. www.christianamerica.com/foundingfathers/ben_rush.htm-

23. www.americandecency.org/bulletin/btnaugust04.pdf

24. www.echozoe.blogdns.com/index.php?p=798 - 32k

CHAPTER 16

1. www.donika.com/philosphy.htm

2. www.ourworld.compuserve.com/homepages/ccfhub/wilberf.htm

3. www.acct.tamu.edu/smith/ethics/BP_wilberforce.htm

4. www.calvarychapelcom/redbarn/wesley/.htm

5. www.spu.edu/depts/csfd/dayofcommonlearning.asp

6. www.dspace.dial.pipex.com/town/terrace/adw03/c-eight/people/wilberf.htm

7. www.desiringgod/library/biographies/02/wilberforce.html

8. www.calvarychapel.com/redbarn/wesley.htm

9. Ibid.

CHAPTER 17

1. www.kocmicki.com/234/cityhill.htm
2. www.bombobeach.com/communications/spirit%20of$0awareness$20.information/noticies.html
3. www.winthropsociety.org/doc_charity.php
4. www.natreformassn.org/statesman/99/colfound.html
5. Ibid.
6. Ibid.
7. www.mason.gmu/~drwillia/winthrop.html
8. www.quoteeb.com/quotes/1228
9. www.kosmicki.com/234/cityhill.htm
10. www.historytools.org/sources/winthrop-city_on_hill.pdf
11. www.wowessays.com/dbase/afi/arm324.shtml
12. www.xroads.virginia.edu/~DRBR/cotton1.html
13. www.fullbookscom/the-beginnings-of-newengland3.html
14. www.dylee.keel.econ.ship.edu/ubf/winthrop.htm
15. www.brainyquotes.com/quotes/quotes/g/gilber/kd104748.html
16. www.apuritanmind.com/stewardship/rykenlelandpuritansandmoney.htm
17. www.puritans.net/curriculum/john%20winthrop.pdf
18. www.harvardsquare/library.org/chistory/section7.htm
19. www.acton.org/publicat/randl/liberal.php?id=495-
20. www.hisotry.umd.edu/faculty/berlin/doc1.htm
21. www.winthropsociety.org/doc_charity.php

CHAPTER 18

1. www.204.157.64.200/focus/f-news/1099311/posts
2. www.txdirectnet/~tgarner/dwight1.htm
3. www.aspire.now.com/thought.htm
4. www.ifca.org/voice/99mar-apr/goerge.htm
5. www.rickwalton.com/lincoln/linc387.htm
6. www.members.tripod.com/~candst/tnppage/qwebstrn.htm
7. www.outpost-of-freedom.com/verbno-.htm
8. www.homeschooltoday.com/articles/articles/legacy_of_noah_webster.php-
9. www.changinglives.org/academy/html
10. www.quotedb.com/quotes/2129
11. www.earlyamerica.com/review/2003_summer_fall/american_dictionary.htm
12. Ibid.
13. Ibid.
14. www.frontlineorg.za/articles/books_of_books.htm
15. www.livinglifefully.com/character.html
16. www.people.cs.uchicago.edu/~dhehoi/cmse10100/music/History/Websterpatriot.pdf
17. Ibid.
18. www.daily.encouragement.net/customart/cardtemplates/faithful.doc
19. Ibid.
20. www.dianedew.com/relipoli.htm
21. www.av1611.com/kjbp/kjv_dictionary/love/html
22. www.people.cs.uchicago.edu/~dhehoi/cmse10100/music/History/Websterpatriot.pdf
23. www.rickwalton.com/lincoln/line387.htm
24. www.shalomjerusalem.com/heritage/heritage15.html
25. www.nyfrf.org/noahweb.htm
26. www.westwood2k.com/CF.shtml
27. www.members.tripod.com/~candst/tnppage/flawq.htm
28. www.rbc.org/utmost/ - 9k - May 17, 2005
29. www.abundantlife.org/onlinebooks/resunshakablechapter2.htm

CHAPTER 19

1. www.lawbuffalo.edu/Faculty_and_staff/submenu%5Cprofiles%5Ckonefsky_alfred_cv.pdf
2. www.constitution.org/js/js_344.htm
3. www.members.aol.com/testoath/10hel_us.htm
4. www.natreformassn.org/drdosc.html
5. www.members.tripod.com/~candst/joestor2.htm
6. www.saidwhat.co.uk/topic/characterphp
7. www.members.tripod.com/~canst/joestor3.htm
8. www.wvu.edu/~lawfac/jelkins/lp-2001/story.html
9. www.amistad.mysticseaport.org/discovery/people/bio-storyjoseph.html
10. www.bartleby.com/73/63.html
11. www.quotelady.com/subjects/goodness.html

12. www.karmel.at/ics/john/dichos.htm
13. www.members.tripod.com/~candst/case09.htm
14. www.eadhome.com/josephstory.htm
15. www.errantspeptics.org/foundingfathers.htm
16. Ibid.
17. www.bible.org.asp?page_id=55/
18. www.members.tripod.com/~candst/joestor2.htm
19. www.eadshome.com/QuotesoftheFounders.htm
20. www.members.tripod.com/~candst/tnppage/misq4.htm
21. www.tripod.com/~candst/case03.htm
22. www.retakingamerica.com/great_america_bench.html
23. www.eadshome.com/QuotesoftheFounders.htm
24. www.members.tripod.com/~candst/case03.htm
25. www.three-peaks.net/annette/Godly.htm
26. www.ecclesia.org/truth/rulings.html

CHAPTER 20
1. www.ravelhill.org/whitefield.htm
2. www.dylee.keel.econ.ship.edu/UBF/leaders/whitefild.htm
3. www.ranulrich.com/rfuged/fam
4. www.dylee.keelenon.ship.edu/ubf/leaders.whitfild.html
5. Ibid.
6. www.believers.web.org/view.cfm?ID=920
7. www.ravenhill.org/whitefield.htm
8. www.biblelife.coil/article.php?ID=99
9. www.godrules.net/library/wsermonswsermons53.htm
10. www.ravenhill.org.whitefield.htm
11. Ibid.
12. www.geocities.com/blueslowmotion/causal.html
13. www.godrules.net/library/wsermons.53.htm
14. Ibid.
15. www.ccel.org/w/wesley/sermons/htm/v.liii.htm
16. www.gospel.com.net/chipastwords/chi030.shtm.1
17. www.christiancomunitychurch.us/teacher9.html

CHAPTER 21
1. www.godstruthfortoday.org/ethanwinchester/winchester019.htm
2. www.revival-library.org/catalogues/world/ryle/01.htm
3. www.members.cov.net/stegcra/meditation2/html
4. www.ccel.org/w/wesley/journal/htm/vi.i.v.htm
5. www.praiseofglory.com/heartswarmed.htm
6. www.aacrc.org/bulletins_announcements/sp%20disc$20booklet.pdf
7. www.worldofgreatquotes.com/tpics/christianity/47/
8. www.tellout.com/mystical3.htm
9. Ibid.
10. www.nccumu.org/missions/cuba_ministries.htm
11. www.gbgm-umc.org/umw/wesley/walk.stm
12. Ibid.
13. www.geocities.com/donaldm.joy/walkon.doc
14. Ibid.
15. www.godrules.net/library/wesley/274wesley_h12.htm

CHAPTER 22
1. www.batteryb.com/crimean-war/biographies/nightengale.html
2. www.casacanada.com/quota.html-
3. www.geocities.com/hvf_win/chaot04.htm
4. www.spartacus.schoolnet.co.uk/EUdunant.htm
5. www.gutenberg.org.dirs/1/2/0/8/12081-h/12081-h.htm
6. www.worldwideschool.org/library/books/hst/biography/eminentvictorians/chap10.html
7. www.bartleby.com/189/204/html
8. www.bartleby.com/189/204.html
9. www.distinguishedwomen.com/biographies/nightingale_florence.html
10. Ibid.
11. www.users.rcn.com/borneo/nightingale/nutting.htm
12. www.distinguishedwomen.com/biographies/nighting.html
13. www.wellcome.ac.uk/doc_WTX023084.html

14. www.embassy.org.nz/encycl/n3encyc.htm
15. www.digital.library.upenn.edu/women/nightingale/nursing/nursing.html
16. www.livinglifefully.com/character.html
17. www.elvis.rowan.edu/~kilroy/JEK/05/18.html
18. Ibid.

CHAPTER 23

1. www.utu/sa.edu/law/classes/rice/constitutional/story/00_vol1_intro.html
2. www.motivatingquotes.com/character.htm
3. www.utulsa.edu./law/classes/rice/constitutional/story/00_onevol/_intro.html
4. www.multied.com/documents.govson.html
5. www.press_pubs.uchicago.edu./founders.documents/a3_2_1s50.html
6. www.brainyqyote.com/quotes/authors/w/william_penn.html
7. www.wordsmith.org/words/stump_speech.html
8. www.washingtonpost.com/wp-srv/style/longterm/books/chapt1/johnmarshall.htm
9. www.uba.org/jmfinfo.htm
10. www.wmedu/oieahc/wmq/jul01/marshallju/2100l.pdf
11. www.cygneis.com/anastap/o/collections/rpcc\/roc.7.htm
12. www.innsofcourt.org/inns/marshallinn/
13. Ibid.
14. www.archives.gophercentral.com/indix.php!op!news!id!825
15. www.brainyquote.com/quotes/quotes/w/williampen163853.html
16. www.geocities.com/Athens/Oracle/7445/letter.htm
17. www.feelingemotional2.tripod.com/id27.html
18 www.answers.com/topic/john-marshall
19. www.dcba.org/brief/sepissue/1997/art10997.htm
20. www.errantskeptics.org/foundingfathers.htm
21. www.innsofcourt.org/inns/marshallinn/
22. www.richmondthenandnow.com/Newspaper-Articles/Jefferson-Marshall.html
23. www.washingtonpost.com/wp-srv/style/longterm/books/chapter1/johnmarshall.htm
24. www.blackmask.com/books22c/jmatc.htm
25. www.historicaltextarchive.com/books.php?op=viewbook&bookid=36&cid=2
26. Ibid.
27. Allen B. McGruder American Statesman Series.
28. Ibid.
29. www.members.tripod.com/~candst/tnppage/jasper.htm
30. www.alliance4lifemin.org/amchristii.html
31. www.historicaltextarchive.com/books.php?op=viewbook&bookid=36&cid=8 - 49k
32. www.washingtonpost.com/wp-srv/style/ longterm/books/chap1/johnmarshall.htm
33. Ibid.

CHAPTER 24

1. www.johndee.org/charlotte/pdf/Chapter21.pdf -
2. www.wesley.nnu_wesley/chrisitan_library/vo/15/part%vi.htm
3. www.bartelby.org/100/pages/page812.html
4. www.bartleby.com/100/604.12html
5. www.gigibeads.net/prayerbeads/saints/hooker/html
6. www.lawandliberty.org/chu_sta2.htm
7. Ibid.
8. www.bartleby.com/100/126.html
9. www.wesley.nnu_wesley/christian_library/vo/15/part%vi.htm
10. www.religion-online.org/showchapter.asp?title+
11. www.gigibeads.net/prayerbeads/saints/hooker.html
12. www.trinity.utoronto.ca/library/theology/partone.html
13. www.nd.edu/~dharley/hist/ideasgrace-hooker-natlaw.pdf
14. wwwtrinitybeth.org/hooker/primer.html
15. www.users.iglide.net/rjsanders/theo/hk1.htm
16. www.trinitysem.edu/journal/jwmrevu2.html
17. www.opensourcetheology/.net/node/332

CHAPTER 25

1. www.heritage.org/Research/PoliticalPhilosophy/EM719.cfm
2. www.house.gov/petri/gw002.htm
3. www.gwpapers.virginia.edu/project/exhibit/mourning/response.html
4. www.house.gov/petri/gw002.htm
5. www.thepresidency.org/pubs/dmaCharacterofGWessay.htm

6. www.americanpresident.org/history/GeorgeWashington/biography/LifeBeforePresidency.common.shtml
7. www.mackinac.org/article.asp?ID=1652
8. www.aabibliography.com/lincoln_temperance.htm
9. www.famousamericans.net/georgewashington/
10. www.house.gov/petri/gw002.htm
11. www.heart-cry.com/america.html
12. www.answers.com/topic/the-first-of-long-island-corporation
13. www.pbs.org/georgewashington/collection/other_1789may.html
14. www.truthorfiction.com/rumors/w/washmonument.htm
15. www.restoringourheritage.com/ourbeliefs.htm
16. www.members.aol.com/jasonte/faith.htm
17. www.eadshome.com/WashingtonPrayer.htm
18. www.hyperhistory.net/apwh/bios/b4washingtong.htm
19. www.touchet1611.org/GeorgeWashington.html
20. www.worldnetdaily.com/news/article.asp?ARTICLE_ID=37212
21. www.cr.nps.gov/history/online_books/hh/26/hh26a.htm
22. www.worldofquotes.com/topic/US-Presidents/1/
23. www.eagleforum.org/educate/washington/advice.html
24. www.worldnetdaily.com/news/article.asp?ARTICLE_ID=37212
25. www.aabibliography.com/lincoln_temperance.htm
26. www.earlyamerica.com/lives/gwlife/chapt13/indexb.html
27. www.worldnetdaily.com/news/article.asp?ARTICLE_ID=37212
28. www.law.ou.edu/hist/washbye.html
29. www.victoriastation.us/Wisdom%20Washington.htm
30. www.wallbuilders.com/resources/search/detail.php?ResourceID=78
31. www.chnm.gmu.edu/courses/henriques/hist615/softersidedw.htm
32. www.oldandsold.com/articles22/george-washington-42.shtml
33. www.house.gov/petri/gw002.htm
34. www.moralconcerns.org/past/America.htm
35. www.whateveristrue.com/heritage/washington.htm
36. www.upsaid.com/Prydain/archives.php?min=1088491794&max=1089011066
37. www.earlyamerica.com/earlyamerica/firsts/thanksgiving/original.html
38. www.yale.edu/lawweb/avalon/washing.htm

CHAPTER 26

1. www.eccucc.org/the_caller_files/0505Caller.pdf
2. www.amazon.com/exec/obidos/ISBN=0871230615/
3. www.oberlin.edu/alummag/oamcurrent/oam_fall98/finney.html-
4. www.eccucc.org/the_caller_files/0505Caller.pdf
5. www.christiansteps.com/daily/revival.html   Rain
6. Ibid.
7. www.stopsinning.info/old/finney_bio/finney_bio_8.html
8. www.gospeltruth.net/lawsonbio.htm
9. Ibid.
10. www.gospeltruth.net/Reminiscenses/pierson.htm
11. www.oldlandmarks.com/revivalf.htm
12. www.gospeltruth.net/1851Sys_Theo/st15.htm
13. www.claremont.org/writings/crb/summer2004/mcwilliams.html
14. www.whatsaiththescripture.now/Voice/Oberlin_1855/OE1855.On.Prayer.Text.html
15. www.memory.loc.gov/learn/lessons/gw/time.html
16. www.aldersgaterenewal.org/background/guidelines.html
17. www.worthynews.com/fineyground.html
18. www.gospeltruth.net/Reminiscenses/reminindex.htm
19. www.truthinheart.com/EarlyOberlinCD/CD/Finney/OE/431220_gods_glory.htm
20. www.whatsaiththescripture.com/Voice/Finneys.Autobiography.4.html

CHAPTER 27

1. www.citivision.org.sg/aboutus.htm
2. www.christian-bookshop.co.uk/free/biogs/cwesley.htm
3. www.igracemusic.com/igracemusic/hymnbook/authors/charles_wesley.html
4. www.gbgm-umc.org/umhistory/wesley/hymns/umh385.stm
5. www.biographies.texasfasola.org.charleswesley.html
6. www.christian-bookshop.co.uk/free/biogs/cwesley.htm
7. www.goodnewsmag.org/library/articles/kirk-jf93.htm
8. www.christian-bookshop.co.uk/free/biogs/cwesley.htm
9. www.bookrags.com/biography/W.html

10. www.gospel.com.net/rbc/utmost/devo/08-31.shtml
11. www.christian-bookshop.co.uk/free/biogs/cwesley.htm
12. www.quotes.tubegator.com/aristotle.php
13. www.home.sc.it.com/imarc/history6.html
14. www.christian-bookshop.co.uk/free/biogs/cwesley.html
15. www.countzinzendorf.org/years/1.html
16. www.mark-shea.com/secret_f.html
17. www.logosresourcespages.org/laugh.html
18. www.peopleforlife.org/francis.html.
19. www.myutmost.org/08/0831.html

CHAPTER 28

1. www.archive.ala.org/booklist/v93/14.html
2. www.foxacre.com/samples/orphsamp.pdf
3. www.afroamhistory.about.com/library/blsojourner_truth_1867speech.htm
4. www.ku.edu/kansas/crossingboundaries/page6b1.html
5. www.afroamhistory.about.com/library/blsojourner_truth_1867speech.htm
6. www.docsouth.unc.edu/neh/truth75/truth75.html
7. www.africana.com/research/encarta/tt_930.asp
8. www.gos.sbc.edu/t/truth.html
9. www.spirithistory.com/sojurn.html
10. Ibid.
11. www.womenshistory.about.com/od/sojournertruth/index.htm
12. www.inspirationpeak.com/library/ihaveadream.html
13. www.ku.edu/kansas/crossingboundaries/page8cont.html
14. Ibid.
15. www.africawithin.com/bios/sojourner_narrative.htm
16. www.leaderu.com/everystudent/black/truth/truth2.html
17. www.factmonster.com/t/hist/mlkanth1/1.html
18. Ibid.
19. Ibid.
20. www.brainfly.net/html/books/ambrose1.htm
21. www.afroamhistory.about.com/library/bltruth_last_interiew.htm
22. Ibid.
23. Ibid.
24. www.webdelsol.com/Del_Sol_Review/ep1-marb.htm
25. www.newadvent.org/cathen/07292c.htm
26. www.uuokc.org/Sermons/2004/06_06.htm
27. www.kyphilom.com/www/truth.html
28. www.timeforkids.com/TFK/class/sn/article/0.17585.203495.00.html
29. www.womanshistory.about.com/library/bio/bltruth.htm
30. www.ku.edu/kansas/crossingboundaries/page8cont.html
31. www.afroamhistory.about.com/library/bltruth_destitute.htm
32. www.ku.edu/kansas/crossingboundaries/page6b3.html
33. www.africawithin.com/bios/sojourner_narrative.htm
34. Ibid
35. Ibid
36. www.africawithin.com/bios/sojourner/narrative.htm
37. Ibid.
38. www.afroamhistory.about.com/library/bltruth_part_second.htm
39. www.afroamhistory.about.com/library/bltruth_part_second.htm

CHAPTER 29

1. www.quotations.about.com/od/stillmorefamouspeople/a/WoodrowWilson1.htm
2. www.t3.preservice.org/TO211921/default.html
3. www.minneapolisks.org/morecarver.asp
4. www.minneapolisks.org/morecarver.asp
5. www.nagna.org/hallfame.htm
6. www.freecongress.org/commentaries/2003/030219PW.asp
7. www.jcsm.org/Devos/Devoc344.htm
8. www.seedsofunfolding.org/issues/xvi/losu_2_c.htm
9. www.trailblazerbooks.com/books/Forty-acre/Forty-bio.htm
10. www.ukblackout.com/cullture/gw_carver.htm
11. www.trailblazerbooks.com/books/Forty-acre-Forty-bio.thm.
12. www.inspirationline.com/Quotes/inspirational-quotes-tolerance-diversity.htm
13. www.wowessays.com/dbase/aa/as4/dlil32.shtml

14. www/newrenbooks.com/about/messages3.html-
15. www.dmuuc.org/minister/John/Help/html
16. www.seedsofunfolding.org/issues/xvi/losu_2_c.htm
17. www.quotationspage.com/quote/26308.html
18. www.dreamhawk.com/George.HTM
19. www.backwoodshome.com/articles/silveira31.html
20. www.san.beck.org/Rising2.html
21. Ibid.
22. www.thecarveracademy.com/public/carver:nsf/generalcontent/SWBV-

CHAPTER 30

1. www.momentin.com/revstudy/chap03philadelphia.html-
2. www.gospelcom.net/chi/DAILYF/2001/06/daily-06-17-2001.shtml
3. www.halanda.nitc.ac.in/resources/english/etext-project/history/moravian/book-3chapter15.html
4. www.zindendorf.com/hutton2.htm
5. Ibid.
6. www.east_west_dialogue.tripod.com/vattel/id3.html
7. www.constitution.org/vattel/vattel_cmt.htm
8. www.newadvent.org/fathers/1701032.htm
9. www.east_west_dialogue.tripod.com/vattel/idl.html
10. Ibid.
11. www.east_west_dialogue.tripod.com/vattel/id3.html
12. www.latin-mass.org/on_loving_god.htm
13. www.btz.It/English/Giedrius/works/mypastorallhero.htm
14. www.geocities.com/Athens/Parthenon/6528/fund55.htm
15. www.countzinzendorf.org/birth/1/html
16. www.famousamericans.net/robertellisthompson/
17. www.btz.It/English/Giedrius.works/mypastoralhero.htm
18. Ibid.
19. www.age-of-the-sage.org/interefaith_studies.html
20. www.countzinzendorf.org/years/2.html
21. www.watchword.org/smithers/ww22a.html-
22. Ibid.
23. www.gloryofhiscross.org/revive12.HTML
24. Ibid.
25. www.myutmost.org/06/0613.html
26. Ibid.
27. www.wrvm.org/marriage_prayer.htm-

CHAPTER 31

1. www.gunstonhall.org/georgemason/quotes.html-
2. www.fas-history.rutgers.edu/~clemens/constitution.html-
3. www.gmu.edu/pubs/pres97/speech.html-
4. www.gunstonhall.org/georgemason/quotes.html-
5. Ibid.
7. Ibid.
8. Ibid.
9. www.weeks-g.dircon.co.uk/quotes_p.htm-
10. www.gunstonhall.org/georgemason/warren_essay.html
11. www.gunstonhall.org/georgemason/eulogy.html
12. www.christianheritagemins.org/articles/George_Mason.htm
13. www.chnm.gmn/courses/henriques/hist615/ymhb.htm-
14. Ibid.
15. www.gunston.org/georgemason/quotes.html
16. www.mises.org/fullstory.aspx?Id=458-32k
17. www.smithsonianmag.com/smithsonian/issues00/may00/mason.html-
18. www.batr.org/autonomy/111804.html-
19. www.practicegodspresence.com/brotherlawrence/practice_text04.html
20. www.ddleague-usa.net/vbor.htm-
21. www.gmm.edu/departments/law/faculty/papers/docs/03-41.pdf
22. www.theholidayzone.com/fourth/julyquotes.html
23. www.desiringgod.org/library/biographies/01newton.html
24. Ibid.
25. www.gunstonhall.org/georgemason/quotes.html-
26. Ibid.
27. www.usconstitution.net/constframe.html

28. www.odur.let.rug.nl/~usa/B/gmason/gmas05.htm
29. www.gunsonhall.ore/georgemason/dreisback-essay.html
30. www.gunstonhall.org/georgemason/dreisback-essay.html-
31. www.quotedb.com/quotes/1206-
32. www.quotationspae.com/quote/2242.html-
33. www.gunstonhall.org/memorialgarden/carving.html-

CHAPTER 32
1. www.adena.com/adena/usa/rv/rv099.htm
2. www.state.nh.us/nhsl/nhbooks/people.html
3. www.globusz.com/ebooks/Jefferson/00000017.htm
4. www.bioguide.congress.gov/scripts/bibdisplay.pl?index=W000238
5. www.hoodmuseum.dartmouth.edu/exhibitions/previous/hats/gracefletcher.html
6. www.search.eb.com/elections/micro/633/92.html
7. www.danielwebster.org/-
8. www.bible-history.com/quotes/henry_h_haley.1.html-
9. www.coralridge.com/impact/2002_Nov_Pg5.htm-
10. www.dartmouth.edu/~dwebster/speeches/adams-jefferson.html-
11. www.bartleby.com/66/48/63448.html
12. www.bible-history.com/quotes/henry_h_haley_1.html
13. www.globusz.com/ebooks/Jefferson/ooooooo17.htm-
14. www.wildershow.com/fourthquotes.htm-
15. www.theologue.info/synergism_martin.htm-
16. www.state.nh.us/nhsl/nhbooks/people.html-
17. www.forerunner.com/forerunner/X0291_Need_for_Printed_wor.html
18. www.franklaighter.tripod.com/cgi-bin/histprof/misc/danielwebster.html
19. www.borntomotivate.com/Desire.html
20. www.wheilaomalley.com/archives/000124.html

CHAPTER 33
1. www.earstohear.net/Heritage/quotes.html - 33k
2. www.pointpresbyterian.org/archives/000031.html
3. www.thelizlibrary.org/suffrage/abigail.htm
4. www.heritage.org/research/features/almanac/pdf/adams.pdf
5. www.olasky.com/Archives/liberty/11.pdf
6. www.4america.com/default.asp
7. www.aolsvc.bookreporter.aol.com/reviews/0743223136-excerpt.asp-
8. www.colonialhall.com/adamsj/adamsj4.asp-
9. www.sptimes.com/News/070101/Comumns/John_Adams_A_portrai.shtml-
10. www.61.1911encyclopedia.org/0H/OHIO.htm-
11. www.zaadz.com/quotes/topics/agriculture/
12. www.quotedb.com/categories/liberty
13. www.members.aol.com/EndTheWall/NWOrd.htm
14. www.constitution.org/as/foreward.htm
15. www.constitution.org/as/dcg_333.htm
16. www.motivatingquotes.com/greatness.htm
17. www.oll.libertyfund.org/Intros/Sidney.php
18. www.constitution.org/as/dcg_333.htm
19. www.walkupsway.com/quotesresponsibility.htm
20. www.crossroad.to/HisWord/notes/oswald/cross.htm
21. www.rcs.k12.va.us/csjh/quotations97.98.htm
22. www.nebraskahumanities.org/Magazine2002.htm-
23. www.squizfloats.com/log20040430.html-
24. www.iotconline.com/index.php?id=22-
25. www.personal.pitnet.net/primarysources/adamsdiary.html-
26. www.brainyquote.com/quotes/authors/j/john_adams.html
27. www.americanreformation.org/policy/GunControl/bearingarms.htm-
28. www.freepages.genealogy.rootsweb.com/~jdevlin/bios/litchfield_ct_bios.htm
29. www.army.mil/cmh-pg/books/RevWar/ss/sherman.htm-

CHAPTER 34
1. www.members.aol.com/EndTheWall/Sherman.htm
2. www.rockvillemama.com/nmbios1.htm
3. www.army.mil/cmh-pg/books/RevWar/ss/sherman.htm
4. www.freepages.genealogy.rootsweb.com/~jdevlin/bios/litchfield_ct_bios.htm
5. www.ctssar.org/patriots/roger_sherman.htm

6. Ibid.

7. www.alliancealert.org/2005/commandments/federerinformation.pdf

8. www.colonialhall.com/sherman/sherman.asp

9. www.fas-history.rutgers.edu/~clemens/constitution.html-

10. www.constitutionalfacts.com/fbody2.shtml-

11. www.geocities.com/Heartland/7006/caveat.html-

12. Ibid.

13. www.colonialhall.com/sherman/sherman.php-

14. www.reclaimamerica.org/Pages/News/newspage.asp?story=1858-

15. www.army.mil/cmh-pg/books/RevWar/ss/sherman.htm-

16. Ibid.

17. www.freepages.gnealogy.rootsweb.com/~jdevlin/bios/litchfield_ct_bios.htm-

18. www.groups.msn.com/Traditions/lifein1700s.msnw?action=get_message&mview=0&1D_Message=9541&LastMod...

19. www.freepages.genealogy.rootsweb.com/~jdevlin/bios/litchfield_ct_bios.htm

CHAPTER 35

1. www.llywelyn.net/docs/quotes/h_adams.html

2. www.bioguide.congress.gov/scripts/guidedisplay.pl?index=J000065-

3. www.nationmaster.com/encyclopedia/John-Jay

4. www.brainyquote.com/quotes/authors/j/jacqueline_bisset.html

5.www.members.aol.com/viperash50/psalm33/psalm33.html-

6. Ibid.

7. www.fortuncity.com/victorian/milton/864/federalist1.htm-

8. www.supremecourthistory.org/04_library/subs_volumes/04_c15_k.html-

9. www.members.surfeu.fi/wpk/arcive/lame/deeper.htm-

10. www.lissack.com/greatideas/giws/Wc7f3dada55b39.htm-

11. www.earstohear.net/warnings.html

12. www.familyrightsassociation.com/news/rchive/2004/may/am17.html-

13. www.gospelweb.net/country.htm-

14. www.talkaboutgovernment.com/group/alt.politics.prayer/messages/1html-

15. www.twelvetribes.com/pdf/greetingcards/2002-thanksgiving.pdf-

16. www.vcu.edu/engweb/eng571/bradford.htm-

CHAPTER 36

1. www.ccg.org/english/s/p264.html

2. www.vcu.edu/engweb/eng571/bradford.htm

3. Ibid.

4. www.angelfire.com/ny4/djw/williambradford.html-

5. www.americanindians.com/Thanksgiving.htm-

6. www.mayflowersteps.co.uk/mayflower/compact.html-

7. www.stmatthews.prairienet.org/sermons/021128.html

8. www.quotationspage.com/quote/29639.html

9. www.pilgrims.net/plymouth/history/-

10. www.republicansabroad-spain.org/newsevents/Articles/Thanks.html-

11. www.gospel.net/chi/GLIMPSEF/Glimpses/glmps020.shtml-

12. www.jamesmadisonbookaward.org/madison.html-

CHAPTER 37

1. www.frontiernet.net/~docwolfe/pathen.html-

2. www.iahushua.com/T-L-J/henry.html-

3. www.digitalhistory.uh.edu/databse/article_display.cfm?HHID=229-

4. www.jmu.edu/maidson/gpos225-madison2/creativeburst.htm-

5. www.geocities.com/peterroberts.geo/Relig-Polics/JMadison.html-

6. www.biblequiz.freeservers.com/Pgs/Tmb/Appxs/appxa.html-

7. www.suite101.com/article.cfm/presidents_and_first_ladies/105332

8. www.olasky.com/American/1997/A709%2-cjircj%state%202.pdf

9. www.dentongeneology.org/johnl759.htm-

10. www.ashbrook.org/books/banning.html-

11. www.eagleforum.org/court_watch/ alerts/2003/may03/Manifesto.shtml

12. www.the-highway.com/articleOct01.html-

13. www.mars.wnec.edu/~grempel/courses/wc2/lectures/luther.html-

14. www.ubcaustin.org/history_faith/session08.htm-

15. www.wais.stanford.edu/Religion/religion_churchandstate12402.html-

16. www.jmu.edu/madison/gpos225-madison2/cretiveburst.htm-

17. www.un.org/Overview/rights.html-

18. www.usinfo.state.gov/products/pubs/rightsof/roots.htm-

19. www.lonang.com/exlibris/misc/remonstrance.htm-
20. www.churchandstate.us/church-state/mad-hen2.htm-
21. www.longang.com/exlibris/misc/remonstrance.htm-
22. www.un.edu/centers/christld/moralld/vln3.htm-
23. www.members.tripod.com/~candst/chaptest.htm-
24. www.nhinet.org/ccs/docs/ma-1780.htm-
25. www.eadshome.com/QuotesoftheFounders.htm-
26. www.afa.net/journal/february/religousb.asp-
27. www.members.aol.cmo/EndTheWall/maidson2.htm-
28. www.nochurchianity.com/Insight.html-
29. www.gunstonhall.org/georgemason/dreisbach-essay.html-
30. www.gunstonhall.org/georgemason/dreisbach-essay.html